Designing for Print Production: Essential Concepts

Designing for Print Production: Essential Concepts

John C. Luttropp, M.F.A.

Department of Art and Design
College of the Arts
Montclair State University

Martin L. Greenwald, Ed.D

Department of Art and Design
College of the Arts
Montclair State University

DELMAR
CENGAGE Learning™

Australia • Brazil • Japan • Korea • Mexico • Singapore • Spain • United Kingdom • United States

**Designing for Print Production:
Essential Concepts**

John C. Luttropp and Martin L. Greenwald

Vice President, Career and Professional
Editorial: Dave Garza

Director of Learning Solutions: Sandy Clark

Acquisitions Editor: James Gish

Managing Editor: Larry Main

Product Manager: Nicole Calisi

Editorial Assistant: Sarah Timm

Vice President, Career and Professional
Marketing: Jennifer McAvey

Marketing Director: Debbie Yarnell

Marketing Coordinator: Jonathan Sheehan

Production Director: Wendy Troeger

Production Manager: Stacy Masucci

Senior Content Project Manager:
Kathryn B. Kucharek

Art Director: Joy Kocsis

Technology Project Manager:
Christopher Catalina

Production Technology Analyst:
Thomas Stover

For product information and technology assistance, contact us at
Professional & Career Group Customer Support, 1-800-648-7450

For permission to use material from this text or product,
submit all requests online at **cengage.com/permissions.**
Further permissions questions can be e-mailed to
permissionrequest@cengage.com

Library of Congress Control Number: 2008924151

ISBN-13: 978-1-4180-4227-1

ISBN-10: 1-4180-4227-7

Delmar
5 Maxwell Drive
Clifton Park, NY 12065-2919
USA

Cengage Learning products are represented in Canada by Nelson Education, Ltd.

For your lifelong learning solutions, visit **delmar.cengage.com**

Visit our corporate website at **cengage.com**

Notice to the Reader

Publisher does not warrant or guarantee any of the products described herein or perform any independent analysis in connection with any of the product information contained herein. Publisher does not assume, and expressly disclaims, any obligation to obtain and include information other than that provided to it by the manufacturer. The reader is expressly warned to consider and adopt all safety precautions that might be indicated by the activities described herein and to avoid all potential hazards. By following the instructions contained herein, the reader willingly assumes all risks in connection with such instructions. The publisher makes no representations or warranties of any kind, including but not limited to, the warranties of fitness for particular purpose or merchantability, nor are any such representations implied with respect to the material set forth herein, and the publisher takes no responsibility with respect to such material. The publisher shall not be liable for any special, consequential, or exemplary damages resulting, in whole or part, from the readers' use of, or reliance upon, this material.

Printed in Canada
1 2 3 4 5 6 7 12 11 10 09 08

CONTENTS

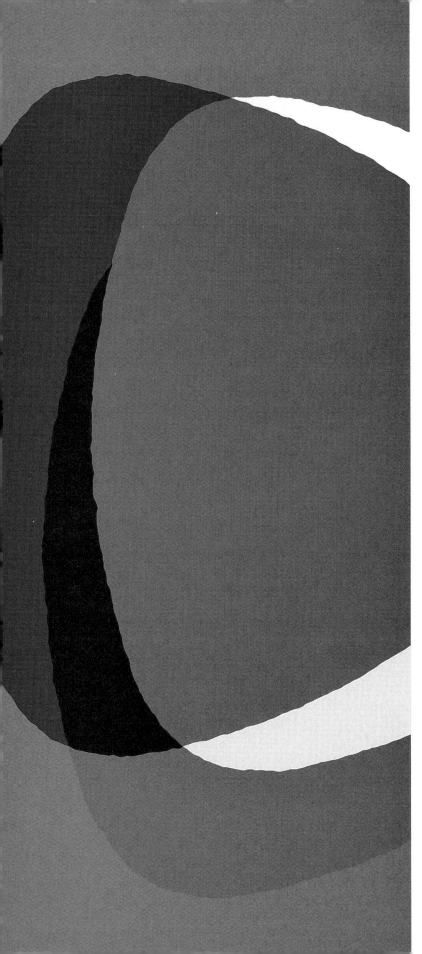

Preface

We recently had the opportunity to meet with a former student who graduated from our university's graphic arts technology program about 25 years ago. Since then he has been in charge of an in-plant production facility for a large publishing company. Several years ago his facility changed their production methods from traditional offset printing to high-speed digital presses; the offset presses and photographic plating related equipment were donated to local high school technology education programs, and high-speed scanners, electrostatic/digital printers, and perfect- and wire-binding machines have taken their place. As we discussed recent changes in the printing industry and the graphic arts, we wondered how much of what he learned as an undergraduate was still current. His answer was an astounding "almost nothing." Following up, we asked him what parts of his educational background were still relevant. His answer: "the basic concepts of design and production."

It should come as no surprise that teaching basic concepts, even in a world of rapidly changing technology, remains a relevant strategy for the long term. In fact, concepts are probably one of the few icons that transcend technological innovation. How effectively a brochure is designed and the quality of its reproduction are far more important than the process used to create the actual design piece or the method used to mass-produce it.

Few other disciplines within the arts have been so profoundly impacted by the introduction of the computer as have the graphic arts. The release of the Apple Macintosh computer in 1984 was the first in a series of changes within the printing and publishing industries that would become as important as the invention of moveable type in 1455.

Practically overnight, the jargon and lexicon of the closed society of commercial printers and typesetters were now used by office staff members composing weekly company newsletters using a new program called Pagemaker. Technical terms like *fonts* and *points* became common notations familiar to most people who used computers (although few people can tell you the mathematical measurement of a point). The gaps left by the disappearance of jobs and occupations of photoengravers, layout and stripping technicians, typesetters, and line and halftone photographers began to be filled by people who knew how to use computers, yet knew little or nothing about the printing and publishing industries.

Technological innovation highlights the obsolescence of devices and techniques that were once familiar objects in our lives. Digital cameras now rival the picture-taking quality of film-based cameras. Software programs and computer processing power now permit the creation of images that could be produced only by hand a few short years ago. Entire books are now designed on the computer screen, allowing electronic combination of text and images. Final books are output to high-speed image setters to produce either film or direct-to-plate media for printing presses. Based on the number of copies needed, a book's computer file can also be sent to a high-speed digital print engine for direct electrostatic on-demand printing. Before these digital technologies, hundreds of hours were spent creating pages by constructing mechanicals in preparation for photographing and subsequent plate making. Ten years from now, what new technologies will replace the digital printing techniques that are just coming online as we navigate through the new millennium?

In this changing technological landscape, obsolescence is no secret. Current students are keenly aware of the lesson learned by my former student; many specific skills learned today in graphic design and computer application courses (as well as many other college subject areas) are likely to become obsolete in the near future. Within this context, it is clear that future employment opportunities will go to individuals with knowledge and training in digital, rather than analog, technologies. This situation will continue to dictate employment within the industry. This text examines the status of digital technologies in the graphic design and production fields, focusing on the content, concepts, and instructional strategies that will be relevant long after our students have left the classroom.

Most students now enrolled in design and production coursework were not yet born when the IBM PC was introduced in 1981 (the first Apple Macintosh computer, ca. 1984, is displayed in the Smithsonian Institute as a museum piece). To place the digital world in historical perspective, Chapters 1 and 2 detail the development of the graphic arts technologies. We examine the relationships among the major technological breakthroughs and the development of the design principles that highlight the evolution of human communication.

Traditionally courses in design and production have been taught as two separate and distinct fields of study: one of the technologist, the other of the artist/designer. On the surface, it appears that computerization has significantly blurred this distinction. Production capabilities previously available only from large, specialized printing firms and service bureaus are increasingly in the hands of individuals using desktop computers. Design and production functions are increasingly performed by the same people—individuals trained to work on both sides of the design and production continuum.

The variety of computer options, display devices, printer variations, differing film and slide scanners, image and plate setters, and digital cameras can be daunting to even a seasoned professional. Material within this text will help students prioritize these choices, matching required inputs to the most advantageous output options.

Regardless of the number and variety of software applications, image generation on a computer is accomplished in one of two basic ways, referred to as either *bitmap* or *vector-based* graphics. The advantages, disadvantages, and basic techniques of each methodology are highlighted throughout. This text's approach to computer-based image generation is not program specific, concentrating instead on the techniques and approaches that yield consistent, reliable results across different computer operating platforms.

Scanning technology, with its reliance on charge-coupled devices (CCDs) and photomultiplier tubes (PMTs), is the foundation of most currently available digitizing techniques and is examined in detail. The requirements of computer files destined for film or direct-to-plate image setters differ from those of files that will be output directly to a digital printing press. The file formatting requirements for each of these production systems are examined in detail.

The creation of page layout programs, beginning with the introduction of Pagemaker in the middle 1980s, coupled with the Macintosh computer, revolutionized both the design and publishing industries. For the first time, the sophisticated tools necessary to create flyers, brochures, and printed materials of every description were available for use on relatively affordable and accessible desktop computers. Design and production methodology within a completely digital framework comes into focus when it is compared with traditional methodologies and techniques used to create the printed page. Our discussions not only highlight specific work and production areas, but analyze cost comparisons of digital and analog design, short- and long-run color printing, and printing techniques. Finishing processes, including binding techniques and other options, are addressed as well.

We examine the digital printing engine, the foundation on which most digital copiers and printing presses rely, and then look at state-of-the-art digital printing devices—from low- and medium-volume copiers to high-volume digital printing presses.

Designing for Print Production concludes with a glossary of digital print terms and appendixes highlighting professional organizations, Web sites, and suggested readings to keep students up to date on all developments within the industry.

We invite our readers to send us any comments or suggestions concerning this text. We can be reached at the following e-mail addresses:

luttroppj@mail.montclair.edu
greenwaldm@mail.montclair.edu

John Luttropp and Martin Greenwald

ACKNOWLEDGMENTS

In deciding to write this textbook, the first thing we thought of was how the text will benefit students of graphic design and printing technology. With that in mind, we would like to thank all of our students over the years who have shared in our growth as educators. Their questions, interest, and excitement about the field have been of great benefit to us. In a field that changes almost daily, our students give us insights that cannot come through research alone.

Our acquisitions editor at Delmar Cengage Learning, Jim Gish, kept this project going, and his help and advice are greatly appreciated. We would also like to thank Nicole Calisi, our production manager, who provided assistance whenever we needed it—which was often. Thanks also go to Larry Main and the production team at Cengage.

Cowriting a book is not always an easy process, and we would like to thank all of our family, friends, and colleagues who supported us and assisted us during the writing of this text. Special thanks go to our wives, Reesa Greenwald and Lynda Hong, who put up with us while we were sequestered in our offices over the past 2 years.

Final thanks go to all the people throughout the history of graphic design and graphic arts who made the events, theories, ideas, and innovations depicted in this text come to life.

Introduction to Design and Production: Chapter 1

Chapter Objectives

Present an overview of the design, printing, and publishing industries.

Understand the major processes of printing.

Know how to print and output files from the computer.

Examine the relationship of computers to the graphic arts.

INTRODUCTION

Chapter 1 offers an overview of the design and publishing industries, highlighting employment opportunities and the role of the graphic designer within this wide commercial sector of the American economy. This overview continues with an introduction to the major printing and graphic reproduction processes, from early relief printing techniques to present-day high-speed waterless offset and digital presses and copiers.

THE GRAPHIC DESIGN INDUSTRY

Graphic designers practice the applied art of composing images and text to communicate a message. Graphic designers are often thought of as applied artists, skilled in a number of different fields: advertising, publication design, packaging design, identity (logo) design, typography, web design, and multimedia. Graphic designers are often illustrators and animators as well. Thus the label *graphic designer* is not an exclusive title but rather is limited only by the skills of the practitioner.

Graphic design became a distinct professional discipline around the end of the nineteenth century. Much of the development of graphic design in the early twentieth century was a reaction against the design and typography of the late nineteenth century. Graphic design continued to gain wide acceptance through the first half of the twentieth century, especially from the boost given it by the post–World War II consumer economy, which witnessed an ever-increasing need for advertising, packaging, and other consumer-oriented graphic design.

Although many modern graphic designers work almost entirely on computers, manual and traditional tools are also used in creating designs. Creative freedom and expression are now limited only by the talent of the designer, enabled by the computer and coupled with creative software like Adobe Photoshop, Adobe Illustrator, and Adobe InDesign, along with an almost unlimited availability of typeface designs.

As an industry, graphic design is a significant factor in the American economy. Industry revenues for both graphic design businesses and freelance consultants are over $11 billion. At present over 16,000 graphic design firms employ more than 60,000 people. Most of these firms are small, with fewer than four employees. Freelance graphic designers (about 75,000) outnumber those employed by design firms.

The design industry, like most other sectors of the economy, suffered a significant downturn entering the new millennium, which lasted for several years. That downturn has ended, and the industry appears poised to grow. For a more complete description, the reader is directed to a report recently published about the graphic design industry: *The U.S. Graphic Design Business 2004–2009* (Strategies for Management, Inc., Harrisville, RI, 2004).

THE PRINTING AND PUBLISHING INDUSTRIES

The printing and publishing industries are a major force in American business. (These industries are often referred to as the **graphic arts.**) People unfamiliar with the two areas often confuse the terms *graphic design* and *graphic arts* as having the same meaning, but they are two separate industries: Graphic design is the creative side, and graphic arts is the production side. Printing and publishing combined rank as one of the largest manufacturing industries in the United States, with over 40,000 individual printing plants employing around 750,000 people. Revenues from printing products and related services are estimated at about $150 billion. More than two out of every three print shops employ fewer than ten people. Offset lithography is the dominant sector of the industry, accounting for about 40 percent of total employment and about a third of all printing facilities. Digital printing, an area that receives much attention due to rapidly advancing technologies, accounts for about 5 percent of all printing activity. This figure will grow as increasing amounts of work within the industry move to short-run digital press output,

influenced by on-demand printing and just-in-time publishing to cut warehousing and production costs.

The publishing industry, while associated with the printing trades, is an economically distinct category. Separate market segments result in sales of over $20 billion within the publishing trades. These markets are composed of adult and juvenile hardback and paperback books, mail order and book club offerings, religious and professional editions, and mass-market paperback books. Educational sales of secondary, postsecondary, and college texts and standardized tests round out these categories. The growth rate within the publishing industry is healthy, averaging about 8 percent a year for the past 12 years.

For a complete breakdown of these industries and future trends within them, the reader is directed to the latest edition of *The Occupational Outlook Handbook*, published by the U.S. Department of Labor, Bureau of Labor Statistics (http://www.bls.gov/oco).

CLASSIFICATION OF PRINTING SYSTEMS

One way of classifying the print production industry is by the major categories of commercial printing technologies. These are letterpress, offset, gravure, screen process, flexography, and digital printing. We'll take a closer look at these different printing systems and their place within the overall print production landscape.

Relief Printing/Letterpress Printing

Relief printing, also referred to as **letterpress printing**, is the oldest printing technique. In this process an image is transferred from an inked surface that is raised, or in *relief* from, the nonprinting areas. The dual terminology is rooted in the fact that printing from type is usually referred to as letterpress printing, whereas

Figure 1–1.
Relief printing from
foundry type.

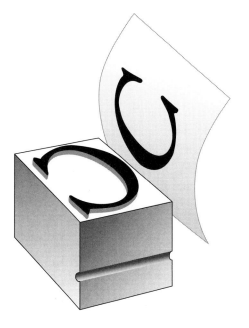

printing from wood blocks is known simply as relief printing (Figure 1–1).

The process of relief printing dates back more than 1500 years. The Chinese used wood blocks on which images were first carved in relief, then inked and pressed against a smooth surface to produce a print. Block printing was also used in Europe in the thirteenth century. All this changed in 1455, when **Johann Gutenberg** developed what many consider to be one of the greatest inventions in human history: perfecting the process of casting many individual pieces of

type from just one mold. This led to the first book in history to be produced mechanically: a two-volume version of the Latin Bible. The parts of a typical piece of cast type, also known as **foundry type,** are illustrated in Figure 1–2.

Prior to Gutenberg's mechanical printing system, scribes in European monasteries reproduced books—primarily bibles—by hand. **Scribes** were religious monks who devoted their lives to copying books by hand using quills and reeds as writing and illustrating instruments. Although the work produced by these scribes was very beautiful and contained highly decorated and illustrated pages, this type of work was extremely slow. It would take months, sometimes years, to reproduce one copy of a book. The work of the scribes is credited with saving many religious scriptures as well as numerous other ancient classic manuscripts. The Black Plague, which struck Europe in the mid-fourteenth century (about 1347–1350), killed about a third of Europe's population. These deaths also left a shortage of scribes to produce book manuscripts. Around the same period, the availability of paper as a commodity grew as a result of the rapid expansion of trading that took place in the late Middle Ages. Thus the stage was set for the arrival of Gutenberg's timely inventions.

Gutenberg's contributions were not limited to the process of multiple casting of individual letters of type. He also developed a printing press and printing inks to be used with his moveable type. But Gutenberg was not a particularly good businessman. After borrowing money from a lender named Johann Fust, Gutenberg was unable to repay the loan. Fust sued Gutenberg and was eventually awarded all of Gutenberg's printing shop assets. Fust then went into business with a man named Peter Schoffer, who eventually became his printing partner

Figure 1–2.
Type nomenclature.

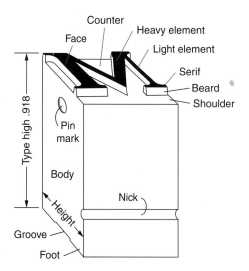

and son-in-law. The first publication of Fust and Schoffer was the *Psalter,* a book of prayers and illustrations from the Bible, published in August 1457. The *Psalter* was the first book printed with a publication date. Gutenberg died in 1468, relatively penniless and probably unaware of the magnitude of his contributions, which would enable great social changes to take place as a result of his genius.

After publication of the Bible in 1455, book production in Europe spread rapidly. Printers also became publishers. At this point there were no professional graphic designers. Instead printers would both compose the layout and print the manuscripts.

With the new availability of relatively cheap books, literacy in the European world increased rapidly. Once the written word could be mass-produced, the world began to move from the medieval era to the early modern period of history.

With industrial mechanization, printing presses became high-speed, automatically fed devices. By the beginning of the twentieth century, letterpress printing was king. Newspapers were printed on high-speed rotary letterpresses. Ottmar Mergenthaler, a German-born naturalized citizen of the United States, invented the **Linotype machine** in 1886. The Linotype allowed moveable type to be set at very high speed, using type matrices that were assembled automatically, line by line, as a machine operator sat at a keyboard console. This method of typesetting is sometimes referred to as **hot type composition** because each line of type was made by pouring molten lead into the type matrices set by the machine operator. Each line of cast type was then assembled by hand into full pages. The relief printing process is illustrated in Figure 1–3.

Letterpress printing continued to be the most widely used method for book and newspaper publishing until it was replaced by offset lithography in the 1960s. Currently hot type composition on a commercial level is virtually extinct, replaced by high-speed computer-driven typesetting equipment, referred to as **cold type composition** (because no hot metal is involved in the process). Letterpress printing now survives primarily as an art form and a hobby. Flexographic printing, also a relief printing process, is a highly successful commercial printing technology that will be discussed next.

Flexography

Flexography (flexo) is a modification of the relief printing process. Both flexographic and conventional letterpress printing plates are relief plates with raised images. Only the raised images come into contact with the ink rollers and the material to be printed, often referred to as the *substrate,* during the printing process.

Flexography is the main printing technology used for printing a variety of packaging materials, such as corrugated cardboard containers, folding cartons,

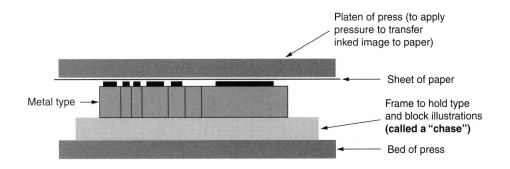

Figure 1–3.
The principle of image transfer in the relief printing process.

Figure 1–4.
The principle of
flexographic printing.

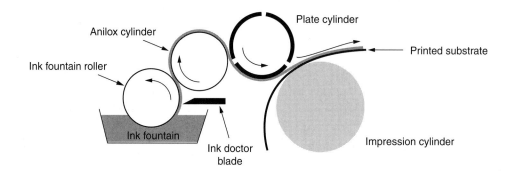

plastic bags, milk and beverage containers, newspapers, and food wrappers. Almost anything that can be fed through a web-fed printing press can be printed using the flexo process, including decorated toilet tissue, cellophane and polyethylene plastic films, and wallpaper.

The name *flexography* comes from its primary use in printing corrugated cardboard. Because the surface of this cardboard is uneven, the only way to transfer an image from plate to cardboard completely is to ensure that the printing plate remains flexible. Also, stray inked areas on the flexo plate must not print onto the high points on the cardboard. To guard against this, the flexo plates are prepared with sufficient relief between the image and nonimage areas, using both traditional photographic and digital

techniques. The principle of flexographic printing is illustrated in Figure 1–4.

Flexo presses are usually multiple-color presses, running four, five, six, or more individual color printheads. During printing, ink is metered from the ink fountain by use of a doctor blade as it is picked up onto an **anilox** inking roller. The anilox roller spreads ink to the plate cylinder. The anilox roller is an engraved steel cylindrical roller with a series of engraved channels, or cells, running across its surface. During press operation, ink collects in the depressions of these cells and transfers to the plate cylinder. Depending on the type of job being printed and the specific inks being used, the anilox rollers and plate cylinders are changed in pairs as necessary. A four-color flexo press configuration is shown in Figure 1–5.

Figure 1–5.
Configuration of a four-color flexographic press.

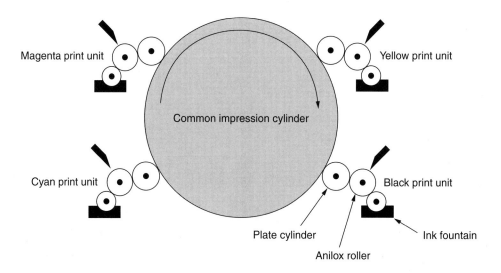

The term *anilox* comes from the historical use of aniline dyes to manufacture flexographic printing inks. Aniline-based inks were in widespread use until the 1950s, when the aniline dyes were suspected of being health hazards. Pigment-based inks replaced the aniline-dye inks in the early 1960s. Currently water-based inks predominate in flexo printing. Most flexography is done from web-fed rolls of paper or substrate rather than from individual sheets of paper, cardboard, or plastics.

Flexo plates are made from either flexible rubber or polymer-based materials. The plates, which can vary in size based on job requirements, are mounted onto the plate cylinder using a double-faced adhesive. If close registration is required during a four-color printing run, the plates might be backed up on the plate cylinder with thin brass plates or fastening straps to prevent them from moving. A major advantage of flexography over other processes like offset lithography is flexo's ability to print on a broad range of materials. Due to the relatively low pressures between the plate and impression cylinder in flexo, these plates can last for millions of impressions. Flexo inks are low-viscosity and dry quickly by evaporation of the ink solvents. The solvents are removed either by heat or by using ultraviolet (UV) curing inks. A small section of a rubber-based flexography plate is shown in Figure 1–6.

Screen Process Printing/Stencil Duplicating/Serigraphy

Screen process printing, also known as **stencil duplicating** and **serigraphy**, is a versatile printing process. The surface to be printed does not need to be under pressure as in a conventional printing press. Also, the surface of the item to be printed does not

Figure 1–6.
Flexographic rubber printing plates.

have to be flat. Screen printing is used for printing on a variety of materials, including textiles, wood, ceramics, metal, paper, glassware, and different types of plastics. Electronic circuit boards are also printed using screen process techniques to provide the electrical circuit paths created when the circuit boards are acid-etched after being printed. Screen printing is especially useful when images need to be wrapped around objects, such as on glassware and odd-shaped materials. When screen printing is sometimes referred to as *serigraphy,* the prints produced are called *serigraphs*. The term comes from the Latin word *seri,* which means silk, and the Greek word *graphein,* which means to write or to draw.

Although the industrial process of silk screen printing began in the early 1900s, it is based on the process of stencil printing, which has been used by Japanese artists for centuries. The first patent for printing with a mesh screen was issued to Samuel Simon in Manchester, England, in 1907. Shortly afterward a patent was issued in California to John Pilsworth for developing a multicolor process for screen printing. Screen printing continues to grow as both an artistic medium and an industrial printing technique. In screen printing, ink

Figure 1–7.
Screen process printing.

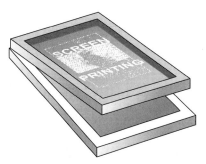

Step 1 - Prepare stencil

Step 2- Ink and print

Step 3 - Remove printed sheet

Step 4 - Final print

is forced through a stencil-covered fabric or wire mesh screen, which is mounted inside a wooden or metal frame. Ink is forced through the open areas of the fabric onto the paper, or printing substrate, which is positioned below the silk screen frame. This process is illustrated in Figure 1–7.

Five materials are currently used in screen printing: silk, organdy, nylon, polyester, and metal mesh. Silk, once the fabric of choice for this type of printing, has largely been replaced by synthetic materials. Nylon and polyester are both highly durable and are used for printing on a wide variety of flat and odd-shaped objects. Metal mesh screens made from stainless steel, copper, or brass are used for printing on plastic substrates.

The stencils used in screen printing can be prepared in a variety of ways. Paper stencils are hand-cut and easily applied, and are ideal for short press runs. Water- and lacquer-soluble

stencils are also hand-cut. Water and lacquer stencils are made from a gelatinous image coating layered over a plastic support base. The water or lacquer gelatin is cut away from the plastic base of the stencil. The plastic support base and remaining gelatinous layer are adhered to the underside of the screen, and the plastic support base is peeled away, leaving the stencil ready for printing.

Stencils can also be prepared photographically using a direct or indirect process. In the indirect process, a separate piece of photosensitive emulsion is photographically exposed and processed. During processing, the image areas wash away, and the stencil is adhered to the screen. The direct method uses a photosensitive material that is applied directly to the screen fabric. After exposure, the image areas are processed away, and the emulsion that remains is embedded into the screen fabric.

Commercial silk screen presses print slowly compared to their letterpress and offset counterparts. The illustration in Figure 1–8 highlights the operating principle of a flatbed screen process printing press.

Intaglio/Gravure/Engraving/Etching Print Processes

Intaglio printing is the process of printing an image from a recessed surface on a printing plate. **Engraving** and **gravure** are forms of intaglio printing. In the engraving process, an image is cut into the surface of the printing plate. This recessed, or sunken, image is filled with ink, and the surface of the plate is then wiped clean so that the only ink left on the plate is in the sunken image areas. During printing, pressure is applied, which presses the page firmly against the plate. This pressure lifts the ink out of the recessed image areas and onto the paper.

Gravure printing is a major commercial printing process, used for food packaging, wallpaper, wrapping paper, paneling and furniture laminates, greeting cards, magazines, and—oh yes—money. Almost all gravure presses are web-fed and are used for long-run applications. The color-printed supplements to many Sunday newspapers are often referred to as the *rotogravure sections* of the newspaper.

Gravure Cylinders

Images to be printed are prepared either manually or on a computer. There are, however, different methods for preparing a gravure cylinder for printing. A separate cylinder is required for each color or image to be printed. The gravure cylinder is made from either steel or aluminum, then copper-plated and polished to a predetermined diameter within an accuracy of a thousandth of an inch (.001″). After the image has been etched, the cylinder is electroplated with a thin layer of chrome to help protect it from wear and abrasion.

Gravure cylinders are prepared using photomechanical, electromechanical, or laser

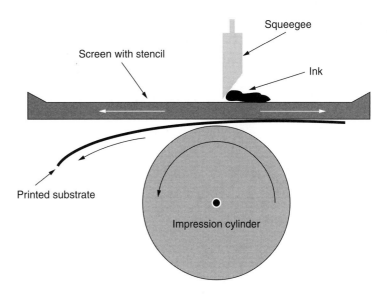

Figure 1–8.
Configuration of a flatbed screen printing press (typical).

cutting techniques. In the photomechanical method, the image is exposed onto a photosensitive mask, which is applied and developed on the cylinder. The image areas of the mask are very thin, and when placed in an acid bath, they quickly dissolve. The copper-plated gravure cylinder is then etched away in the image areas. After etching, the mask is removed, and the cylinder receives final chrome plating.

In the electromechanical process, the image is scanned into a computer. This image data file is then fed into a diamond stylus cutter head, which engraves the image into the cylinder. In the laser cutting process, the image is scanned and then cut into the cylinder using a narrow laser beam.

A series of grooves, or wells, remains in the surface of the gravure cylinder after it has been prepared. The colors, tonal range, and resolution characteristics of the final print are a function of the characteristics of the image wells, as shown in Figure 1–9.

Gravure Printing

A typical web-fed gravure press consists of the etched plate cylinder, a rubber-coated impression cylinder, a doctor blade, and

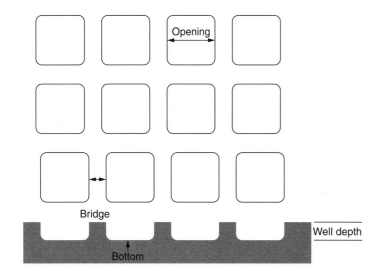

Figure 1–9.
Characteristics of gravure printing wells.

alloy blade against the cylinder are aligned and adjusted to prevent premature wear and erosion of the plate cylinder. Ink remaining in the gravure plate wells forms the image, which is transferred to the printing substrate (paper, plastic, or the like).

The impression roller is made from a tubular steel sleeve coated with a rubber compound. Pressure between the impression roller and the printing substrate is carefully adjusted for proper transfer of ink from the plate cylinder to the printing substrate and also to move the substrate web between the press printheads. A modification of conventional gravure is the offset gravure process, which adds a transfer roller to the standard roller configuration. The gravure cylinder prints first to the transfer roller and then from the transfer roller onto the substrate. Offset gravure is used for printing on materials with irregular surfaces, such as wood veneers.

To accomplish two-sided printing (also known as **perfect printing**), two different methods are used. In one system, the web is first printed on one side, rewound, and flipped over for printing on the other side of the web.

an ink fountain. The arrangement of these components is illustrated in Figure 1–10.

During press operation, the gravure cylinder rotates within the ink fountain, picking up ink on both its image and nonimage areas. To remove ink from the nonimage surface areas of the cylinder, a doctor blade shears, or scrapes, ink from the cylinder surface. The blade has an angular cut on its edge, enabling it to penetrate the surface of the ink coating in the ink fountain. The pressure and angle of the flexible steel

Figure 1–10.
Operation of a gravure printing press.

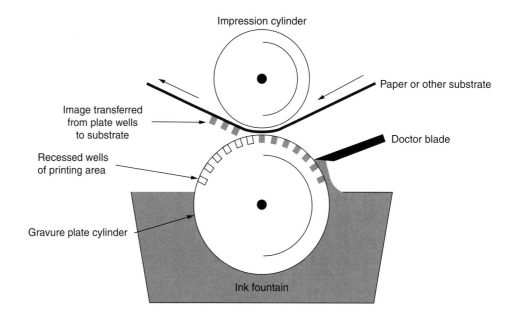

In a second method, the press incorporates a unit that flips the paper roll 180 degrees and then runs it through a second series of printheads to print the second side of the web.

Gravure Inks

Inks used in gravure printing are low-viscosity, which allows for easy pickup and transfer from the ink fountain to the recesses in the printing plate. Often drying units are incorporated between the press printheads to ensure that the ink is dry before the substrate reaches the next printhead, or printing station. Typically a recovery system is used to remove the volatile fumes from the ink-drying stations. These fumes are then collected and removed as hazardous **volatile organic compounds (VOCs)**.

Lithography/Planography/ Offset Printing

Often called **stone printing** or **planography**, **lithography** is technically classified as a chemical printing process. In a single-color lithographic process, an image is first drawn on polished limestone with a grease-based crayon or grease-based ink. Water is then applied over the surface of the stone. The porous stone accepts the water while the grease-based image repels it. While the stone is still wet, a grease-based ink is applied to the stone. The wet parts of the stone repel the ink, which adheres only to the image areas on the stone. After the image has been inked, it is transferred from the stone to paper under pressure. Because this printing process is based on the principle that grease- or oil-based materials and water repel one another, lithography is classified as a chemical-based printing technique. The term *planography* or *planographic printing* refers to the fact that both the image and nonimage areas of the lithographic stone are on the same flat geometric plane. This distinguishes lithography from relief printing and intaglio printing, both of which rely on either raised or recessed surfaces for printing an image.

Alois Senefelder, an Austrian actor and playwright, invented lithography, currently the most widely used printing process, in 1798. Senefelder was looking for an inexpensive way to publish a play he had written, and he began experimenting with grease-based inks on slabs of smooth, polished limestone. He continued working on his lithographic techniques until they were perfected, publishing the results of his work in 1818.

The lithographic process quickly gained widespread acceptance, especially as an artistic medium. Rather than requiring specialized engraving tools and advanced skills to produce intaglio and block prints, artists could easily draw with pens using grease-based inks. By the 1820s the production of multicolor lithographs was common.

Ira Rubel, a printer working in Nutley, New Jersey, discovered the process of **offset lithography**, in which an image is first printed onto an intermediate rubber-covered roller and then transferred onto paper. The lithographic presses at that time were direct image presses. Paper was placed over the inked lithographic stone, and a rubber-backed impression cylinder enabled the inked stone to transfer its image to the paper. Rubel noticed that when paper misfeeds occurred, the lithographic stone printed directly onto the rubber-backed impression cylinder. The next sheet of paper that was fed into the press then printed on both the front and back of the sheet. Comparing the two images, Rubel noticed that the image printed from the rubber blanket onto the back of the sheet of paper was sharper and clearer than the image printing directly from the stone. This image clarity was due to the ability of the soft rubber to more effectively transfer an image than the hard lithographic stone. This process of first printing, or *offsetting,* an

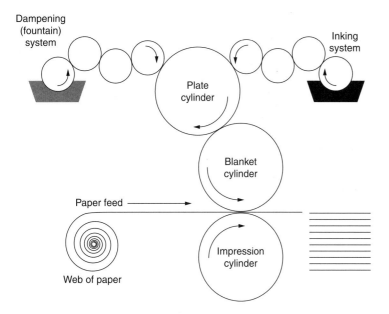

Figure 1–11.
Operating configuration of a web offset press (typical).

is attached to the plate cylinder. As the plate cylinder rotates, it first comes in contact with the dampening system rollers, which wet the surface of the printing plate. The water is accepted on the plate surface with the exception of the image areas, which are grease-based and therefore repel the water. Next the plate comes in contact with the ink rollers. The ink is repelled by the wet plate in all areas except the image areas. As the press continues to rotate, the plate prints an image onto the blanket cylinder. Paper feeding from a web roll passes between the blanket and impression cylinders, where the image is transferred from the blanket cylinder onto the paper. The impression cylinder provides a solid backing for the paper during the image transfer.

Unlike the direct lithographic process which uses lithographic stones on which the artist must draw an image in a reverse, mirror image to get a correct, right-reading print, offset plates are prepared with right-reading images. The offset plate images prints a mirror image on the blanket which, in turn, transfers a right-reading image onto the paper (Figure 1–12).

image from the plate to a rubber blanket and then printing onto a sheet of paper is known as *offset lithography*.

By the 1950s offset had become the dominant commercial printing process—a position that continues to hold today. The offset market is split between sheet-fed and web-fed presses, depending on the length of the press run. Generally, low to medium volume requirements (press runs below 25,000–40,000) are printed on sheet-fed presses. High-volume jobs are almost always printed on web-fed presses. You can see the operating principles of a single-color web offset press in Figure 1–11.

Note the direction of rotation of the cylinders in Figure 1–11. The lithographic plate

Dry Offset and Letterset Printing

In conventional offset printing, water is the medium used to prevent ink adhesion in the nonimage areas of the offset plate. A modification of the conventional offset process is known as **waterless offset**. In waterless offset, a principle known as *differential adhesion* is used to separate the

Figure 1–12.
Offsetting an image from plate to blanket to paper in offset printing.

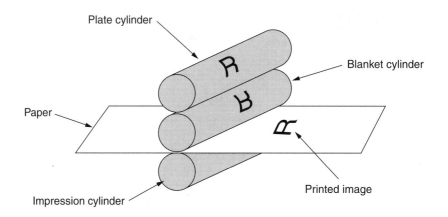

image and nonimage areas during printing. Differential adhesion is achieved by using a silicone surface on the printing plate. During plate preparation, the silicone surface of the plate is removed from the image areas of the plate, exposing the base metal of the plate. The image areas on the base material of the plate are now slightly recessed below the plate surface. These recesses form small pockets in which ink can be deposited. The silicone surface remaining on the nonimage areas of the plate resists ink. To achieve effective separation of ink from the image and nonimage plate areas, the viscosity of the ink is controlled by a combination cooling and heating system running through the ink roller cores. This temperature control keeps the ink viscosity constant. Note the configuration of a typical single-color waterless offset press in Figure 1–13.

A distinction needs to be made between waterless offset and what is sometimes referred to as either **dry offset** or **letterset** printing. The waterless offset system pictured in Figure 1–13 relies on differential adhesion of ink using specially prepared silicone-surfaced plates. Although the water has been replaced by silicone for separating ink from image and nonimage areas on the printing plate, the process is still a chemical printing process.

Dry offset, or *letterset*, printing uses relief plates that transfer an inked image to an intermediate, rubber blanket–covered cylinder. The offset image from this intermediate blanket cylinder is then printed onto the paper. Image transfer in this process is not direct from plate to substrate as in conventional relief printing. Dry offset printing has the advantage of softening the final printed image. Also, the rubber blanket cylinder can print slightly irregular surfaces, unlike conventional letterpress printing from type, blocks, or photoengravings.

PRINTING AND OUTPUTTING FROM COMPUTERS

This text distinguishes between the techniques of printing from computers and outputting from computers.

Printing from computers is direct, low-volume output to either a dedicated or networked printer. Direct printing uses small-format inkjet, bubble jet, ion deposition, and office-sized electrostatic (laser) printers and copiers. Also in this category is low-volume

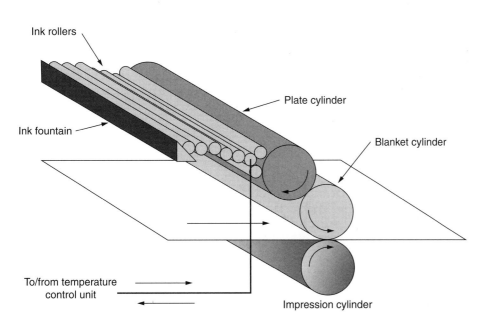

Ink rollers

Ink fountain

Plate cylinder

Blanket cylinder

To/from temperature control unit

Impression cylinder

Figure 1–13.
Waterless offset press configuration.

printing on wide-format inkjet printers producing indoor and outdoor signs, as well as fine art reproduction printing (sometimes referred to as a **giclee,** pronounced gee-clay).

In contrast, outputting from computers describes data files that are sent to digital plate makers, offset presses, and high-volume electrostatic-based printing devices. Computer output options will be discussed in greater detail in Chapters 9 and 10, and they are introduced as basic production concepts in the following information.

Printing from Computers

Printing from computers falls primarily within the small business and personal use applications. Such printers are usually inexpensive, quiet, and reliable, and many models are capable of producing photo-quality output. They can be categorized as inkjet, thermal wax, dye sublimation, solid ink, UV-capable, small- and wide-format printers, and electrostatic copiers and printers.

Inkjet Printers

Inkjet printers are a long-standing technology, dating back to 1951, when the Siemens Corporation patented the first inkjet printing device. There are three different types of inkjet printing technologies: piezoelectric drop-on-demand, bubble jet drop-on-demand, and continuous inkjet. Inkjet printing technology is dominant in two main marketing areas: desktop color printers and wide-format devices.

PIEZOELECTRIC DROP-ON-DEMAND

Piezoelectric drop-on-demand inkjet printers use a small piezoelectric (PE) crystal to control the flow of ink from a small nozzle onto the printing substrate. When an electric current is applied to a PE crystal, the crystal bends, forcing ink droplets out of the nozzle (Figure 1–14).

BUBBLE JET DROP-ON-DEMAND

A modification of the piezoelectric technology is the drop-on-demand **bubble jet** technology originally developed by Canon. Also referred to as *thermal inkjet printing,* the print cartridge contains a series of small heaters. When current passes through the heaters, an ink vapor bubble quickly forms and is ejected from the printhead onto the paper. Excess ink from the surface of the paper is sucked back from the paper when the ink bubble condenses. The principle of a bubble jet printhead is shown in Figure 1–15.

Figure 1–14.
A piezoelectric inkjet nozzle.

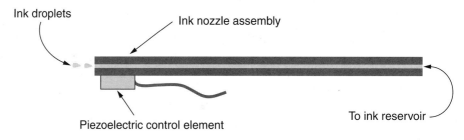

Figure 1–15.
A bubble jet ink nozzle.

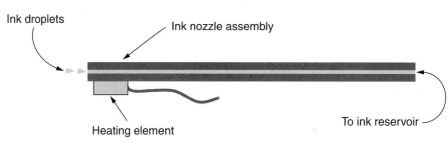

A typical bubble jet printer contains between 64 and 128 separate ink delivery nozzles. Due to system technology, the inks used in bubble jet printers must be water-based. Care must be exercised when handling these prints. Alcohol and water-based markers will smudge and blur bubble jet images. Bubble jet printheads are generally less expensive to produce than other inkjet system printheads, but the bubble jet printheads are fragile and relatively expensive to replace.

CONTINUOUS INKJET PRINTERS

Whereas piezoelectric and bubble jet systems print with individual ink droplets, **continuous inkjet printers** deliver a continuous stream of ink. A piezoelectric crystal produces a continuous stream of ink that forms individual droplets after the ink is ejected from the nozzle head. These droplets are then exposed to an electrostatic charging field. The charge on the electrostatic field varies, so each droplet can have a different electrostatic charge. Once charged, the ink droplets are either directed onto the printing substrate or deflected into a collection gutter, where they are recirculated and used again. During printing, most of the ink forced from the nozzle is recirculated; only a small portion is actually used for printing. Continuous inkjet printers use solvent-based inks that dry quickly, and they find a major market in marking and bar coding a variety of packaged materials.

Inkjet printers have a number of advantages over other low-volume printing methods. They are quiet and relatively inexpensive compared to some of the more expensive print technologies like wax thermal and dye sublimation systems. The output of current inkjet printers is virtually photographic quality. Although inkjet printers are generally less expensive than laser printers, they are more expensive to maintain when costs are calculated on a page-by-page basis.

WIDE-FORMAT INKJET PRINTERS

The term **wide-format printer** applies to printers designed to print on substrates that are more than 24 inches wide. Most wide-format printers use some form of inkjet or ultraviolet ink technology. The term *plotter* also refers to a wide-format printer—usually a wide-format contour cutting device, distinguishing it from its inkjet printer counterpart. Wide-format printers are ideally suited for printing a variety of large paper and vinyl signs, banners, point-of-purchase (POP) advertising, outdoor advertising posters, and the like.

Wide-format printers were adapted from small desktop printers. From the initial designs, the printheads and ink cartridges were manufactured as an integral unit, simplifying service and maintenance of the printer. If the printer uses a thermal rather than a piezoelectric design, the printhead will need to be changed frequently because constant application of heat during printing degrades the integrated electronics within the printhead. Although a piezoelectric printhead will last longer than its thermal counterpart, it is more expensive to replace. Note the placement of the four-color printheads along the track of a typical wide-format inkjet printer (Figure 1–16).

Figure 1–16.
Wide-format inkjet printheads travel along a precision-ground horizontal guide bar, ensuring accuracy of the resulting print.

Because wide-format printers are used to print signs and banners requiring large amounts of ink, most of these printers use bulk ink tanks rather than small cartridges for ink storage and delivery; however, the printheads on these systems are often integrated with small ink storage cartridges. These cartridges even out the storage and flow of ink to the print nozzles from the bulk tanks. Also, multiple sets of bulk storage tanks can be filled with different types of ink that are easily changed, depending on the job requirements. For example, when printing outdoor signs, ink tanks with waterproof outdoor inks can be easily installed in the printer (Figure 1–17).

Many wide-format printers are equipped to print with more than four-color ink systems. Printing with a six-color ink set enables the printer to achieve smoother transitions between colors as well as print a wider range of colors than is possible using a standard four-color printhead. Six-color printers are equipped with cyan, magenta, yellow, and black (**CMYK**) ink, as well as light cyan and light magenta. Printing with lighter cyan and magenta inks rather than the darker versions enables the printer to achieve greater resolution in highlight and midtone areas of the print. In addition to six-color ink sets, eight- and twelve-color printers are also used in signs, banners, and high-resolution art reproductions. Wide-format printers, and the additional services they let printers offer their customers, will help to ensure that this segment of the marketplace will continue to experience significant growth levels in the coming years.

UV Print Technology

Although **ultraviolet (UV) curing inks** have been used for printing for about thirty years, this technology has recently been gaining wider acceptance and popularity within the industry.

Regular printing inks contain solvents composed of **volatile organic compounds (VOCs)**, which are released into the air as the ink evaporates and dries. VOCs have been a major target in reducing air pollution because they are a key contributor to harmful pollutants such as ozone. In some conventional solvent-based printing inks, the solvents can make up from 50 to 70 percent of the ink, releasing large amounts of VOCs into the plant atmosphere. Because UV inks contain no volatile solvents, they are classified as a *zero-emission print medium*.

Like regular inks, UV inks contain resins and pigments. However, in place of the solvents in conventional inks, UV inks contain small carbon-based molecules called *monomers* and *oligomers* that can form long, stable chemical chains called *polymers*. To get this chemical process started, UV inks contain UV light–sensitive components called either *photo initiators* or *photocatalysts*. Therefore, UV-capable presses incorporate a UV curing unit to carry out this drying process. A basic curing unit incorporates a UV *irradiator*—a high-intensity, medium-pressure mercury vapor lamp housed within a heat-resistant mounting system. Sometimes

Figure 1–17.
Changeable bulk ink tanks on a wide-format printer.

a cooling system is designed into the curing unit to help remove the considerable heat generated. The process that takes place when UV inks cure is called *polymerization* and occurs very rapidly—often within seconds—after the UV ink is laid down on the printing substrate. As UV inks cure, almost the entire ink deposit is transformed into a solid polymer. This drying process contrasts to that of conventional inks, in which the solvents, often composing a majority of the ink deposit, evaporate during the drying process. Although UV inks are more expensive than their solvent-based counterparts, a gallon of UV ink goes a long way because it contains no solvents.

UV printing does have disadvantages. Many people find the smell of UV inks unpleasant, so additional ventilation is often installed in areas where UV devices are operating. Also, adequate shielding and eye protection must be ensured to prevent human exposure to UV light when people work with this form of printing.

Thermal Wax Printers

Thermal wax printers are used for generating high-quality presentation transparencies and for color proofing. The color proofing process creates test documents and images for customer approval before a job is sent to the printer.

Thermal wax printers use belt-driven CMYK ribbons printing on specially coated papers and transparency films for image production. These units' printheads contain heating elements, or contacts, that melt the colored wax from the ribbons onto the paper as it is fed through the printer. These printers print only one color at a time, so paper must be fed through a printer four separate times to produce a full-color print.

Thermal wax printers produce prints with stronger color hues and intensities than those from conventional inkjet printers, but they are more expensive to operate.

Dye Sublimation Printers

Dye sublimation printers can produce high-quality color prints for proofing and presentation applications. Often referred to as *dye-subs,* the relatively high cost of these prints is secondary to the precision and detail they are capable of producing, which are required for graphic arts and scientific presentations.

Dye-sub printers use media rolls that resemble colored cellophane transparent film. Embedded in this film are the CMYK dyes (cyan, magenta, yellow, and black) that are the basis of all multicolor printing technologies. The film passes over the heated printhead, causing the dyes to instantly vaporize or *sublimate* from a solid to a gas. The gaseous dyes then condense and embed in the print paper. The amount of the dye absorbed by the paper is controlled by the amount and duration of heat in the printhead. This process is shown in Figure 1–18.

As the dyes condense onto the paper, they tend to diffuse around the edges. This blurs the edges of the printed dots, giving the print a true continuous-tone appearance. This differs from the relatively hard dots produced by conventional inkjet printers. Also, as the

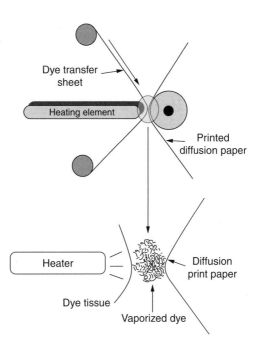

Figure 1–18.
Operating principle of dye sublimation printers.

dyes condense to form an image, they are embedded or *infused* into the paper, giving dye-sub prints great durability.

In addition to conventional dye-sub printers, several inkjet printers on the market can produce dye-sub prints. Rather than using ribbon technology as the source of the dyes, these printers use dye-sub inks in specially manufactured cartridges. The inks are heated to form a gas, triggering the ink sublimation process. These printers are less expensive than standard dye-sub printers and find their largest application in the consumer photographic print market.

SOLID INK PRINTERS

Solid ink printers are used primarily in the packaging and industrial design areas. Solid ink printers use sticks of colored wax–based inks that are melted and then sprayed through small stainless steel nozzles in a printhead. After printing, the paper or other printing substrate runs through a fusion roller that sets the ink and forces it into the substrate. Solid ink printers produce highly saturated color hues and can print on almost any surface. The resolution of solid ink printers falls between that of laser printers and inkjet technology. Conventional color laser printers offer resolutions of 600 dots per inch (dpi); solid ink printers can achieve 1,200 dpi; and inkjet printers top the list at close to 6,000 dpi.

Outputting from Computers

Outputting from a computer is used for high-volume production of an image. The options available when outputting from a computer are detailed in Figure 1–19.

Outputting Film and Plates

Although technological sophistication has greatly increased high-volume digital printing options, much industry printing is still accomplished using traditional techniques. The first two pathways highlighted in Figure 1–19, **computer-to-film (CTF)** and **computer-to-plate (CTP),** use digital technologies to prepare either conventional film or plates for offset printing.

The traditional image setter, a mainstay of the industry for more than 25 years, is capable of outputting either film or plate material. Increasingly, outputting film negatives for flats that are used to prepare offset plates is giving way to direct preparation of offset plates. Specially manufactured rolls of infrared (IR)-sensitive polyester plate material are imaged using the internal laser of the image setter. The polyester plates are then developed using a two-stage processing unit and are ready for printing. Also, dedicated plate production units using plate setters can produce aluminum and bimetallic plates for almost any commercial offset printing press. For a more in-depth discussion of CTF and CTP output, please see Chapter 9.

Outputting to Digital Print Devices

Recent trends in the commercial printing market have been directed at just-in-time printing and delivery. Printing only what is needed in the short term significantly reduces

Figure 1–19.
Options available when outputting images from a computer.

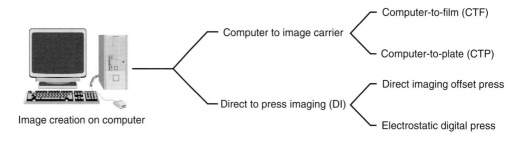

Image creation on computer — Computer to image carrier — Computer-to-film (CTF), Computer-to-plate (CTP); Direct to press imaging (DI) — Direct imaging offset press, Electrostatic digital press

warehousing costs. Therefore, changes in business strategy that necessitate alterations in printed media are more easily accomplished, with little or no inventory going to waste due to outdated content. Also, marketing strategies that target individual customers, incorporating personal interest content within a mass-marketing campaign, rely on the ability to print customized data on every sheet. In such **variable data printing,** marketing material can be prepared for all customers, with special interest information inserted and printed for each customer.

The two most common options for high-volume printing from a computer are outputting to a direct imaging offset press and outputting the data file to a high-speed electrostatic-based digital printing press.

DIGITAL OFFSET PRESSES

Offset presses that are capable of imaging plates directly on the press from computer data files are referred to as **direct imaging** or **DI** presses. DI presses are usually waterless in design. The silicone-surfaced plates are imaged directly on the plate cylinder of the press using IR heat lasers that burn away the silicone coating on the plate, exposing the base material of the plate as the grease-receptive image areas. The silicone that remains on the plate repels the ink. The waterless DI press in Figure 1–20 incorporates a sophisticated computerized front end for image input and manipulation, as well as monitoring all press systems during printing.

Digital Electrostatic Copiers and Presses

Without question, the greatest advances in printing and publishing have taken place in short-run, electrostatic-based printing presses. Advanced laser and toner technologies and sophisticated electronics have combined to produce a generation of digital printing presses that rival, and in many cases exceed, the time-proven results of conventional offset printing.

The digital press in Figure 1–21 is capable of printing up to 8,000 impressions per hour (IPH)—or 4,000 IPH with four-color output and a resolution of 230 lines per inch (LPI). The color range of the press can also be expanded by using a six-color print set, which increases the number of toner cartridges from four to six colors: cyan, magenta, yellow, black, violet, and orange.

Figure 1–20.
Digital imaging waterless offset press (courtesy Presstek, Inc.).

Figure 1–21.
Electrostatic toner-based
digital press (courtesy
Xerox, Inc.).

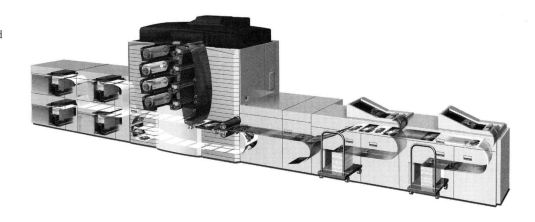

Based on electrostatic technology and advances from the early techniques used in designing and producing the familiar office copier, current machines are capable of two-sided (*perfect*) printing. Because each page in these presses is imaged separately, variable-data printing capability lets the commercial printer explore markets such as personalized direct mail, versioned manuals, personalized calendars, photo albums, greeting cards, and the like, as well as on-demand marketing brochures, flyers, and catalogs.

Many digital presses can also be integrated with a variety of inline finishing machines, such as booklet makers, automatic punches, and perfect binding equipment. Figure 1–22 highlights a complete small-scale publishing system that incorporates a computer workstation, high-speed digital press,

collating station, and booklet maker into one unit. This type of integrated technology is a new direction for small, medium-sized, and in-plant publishers, thanks to the rapid pace of technological advancements within digital output technologies. Chapter 9 offers more in-depth discussion of digital offset and DI system technology.

COMPUTERS AND THE GRAPHIC ARTS

Few industries are as dependent on computers for product creation and production as are design, publishing, and commercial printing. In the preface of this text we discussed how the computer has flattened what were formerly well-defined fields of study: those of the designer and the production technologies.

Until recently designers worked with and created images, either manually or on a

Figure 1–22.
Integrated small-scale
digital publishing
system (courtesy Canon
U.S.A., Inc.).

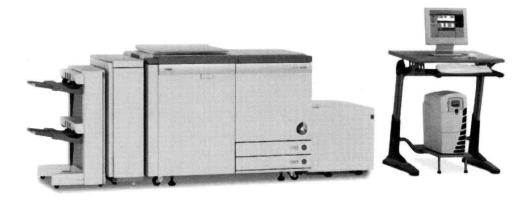

computer. After designs were completed, a printing firm or service bureau assumed the responsibility for finalizing file formats, proofing, and printing. However, the design and production cycle is evolving as sophisticated software and digital printing options allow all of these activities to be performed by the same people: individuals trained to work in both design and production.

The role of the computer has defined this changing landscape. After the release of the Apple Macintosh (Mac) in 1984, coupled with drawing, painting, and page composition programs like Aldus Pagemaker, the Mac assumed a dominant role within the industry. As software evolved, so did its interoperability. Currently all of the landmark software programs used within the industry now operate cross-platform (Macintosh and PC) almost seamlessly. While the Mac still enjoys a dominant role with designers, production software and printer front ends are predominantly PC-based. Current and future practitioners must know both systems. Increasingly, designers and production people will need to understand and communicate with each other. The computer, of course, helps all this happen.

SUMMARY

This chapter introduced the basic concepts of the print production industries. The place of these industries within our economic structure was established with reference to industry revenues, employment, and their forecast economic outlooks.

The design, publishing, and printing industries have been dominated by six major printing processes since the invention of moveable replica-cast type by Johann Gutenberg in 1455. These processes are relief printing, flexography,

screen process printing, intaglio or gravure printing, lithography, and the digital printing technologies. The underlying concepts of each of these systems were presented here, with more in-depth coverage of lithography and digital printing systems highlighted in Chapter 9. The chapter concluded with a discussion of the role of the computer in design and production. This discussion was framed by the idea that design and production activities will increasingly be performed by the same individuals trained to look both cross-platform and cross-discipline at how images are created and printed.

Review Questions

1 Explain the difference between the terms *graphic arts* and *graphic design*.

2 What are the major differences between bubble and continuous inkjet printers?

3 How do electrostatic copiers differ from digital printing presses?

4 How do the plates used in waterless offset presses differ from conventional, water-based offset printing plates?

5 Explain the differences in the images produced by a dye sublimation printer and by a conventional inkjet printer.

Suggested Student Activities

1 Identify the six major printing processes. For each of these processes, highlight the following concepts:

  a The time period of the development of the process.

  b The image transfer concept of the process.

  c The major applications of each process in the marketplace.

2 Distinguish between printing and outputting from a computer.

3 Describe the differences between traditional and waterless offset printing technologies. Which process can print a smaller dot, and why?

4 Explain one advantage and one disadvantage of ultraviolet (UV) printers over their conventional inkjet counterparts.

5 Illustrate the lithographic process by taking a prepared aluminum offset printing plate, manually wetting the plate, and then inking the plate with an ink brayer or roller. Print an image from the plate onto a sheet of paper by pressing the sheet on the surface of the plate.

Graphic Design and Printing Technology through the Ages: Chapter 2

Chapter Objectives

Develop an understanding of the historical context within which current design and publication technologies exist.

Highlight the relationship of design and human technological achievement.

Understand the impact of the invention of moveable type on the spread of literacy throughout the world.

Interpret the development of graphic design as a distinct profession and in its relationship with the graphic arts (publishing and print production).

Discuss notable achievements in both design and technology throughout the nineteenth and twentieth centuries.

INTRODUCTION: THE BEGINNINGS

Throughout history, the need to communicate has been at the core of humanity. Recent discoveries in northern Italy have found that the world's oldest known cave paintings and sculptures date back more than 36,000 years. From these earliest expressions of artistic ingenuity to the complex digital communication systems of today, the study of how we communicate with words and images strives to highlight the relationship between the art and the technology of human expression.

From their beginnings as hunter/gatherers, humans documented their activities through pictures and sculptures to help explain their world (Figure 2–1).

Most **Paleolithic art** created by early humans, dating to about 10,000 BC, took the form of crude drawings and paintings made on clay. These early paintings and sculptures exhibit great creativity and insight into different aspects of basic and advanced design principles. Both humans and animals are drawn with a high degree of accuracy. Artistic attention in these works was paid to the detail of limb movement as well as the balance of the illustration. Although there are many explanations of cave art, modern humans will probably never fully understand what role it played within early societies, other than the satisfaction gained from documenting and storytelling within these early communities.

Increasing numbers of sites containing early artwork are being discovered as sophisticated radar sensing devices and changing seawater levels continue to expose caves. The subject matter of most of these paintings consists of animals of the period, including wild cattle, bison, and goats, together with simple finger drawings and hand imprints. The paint used in these drawings was made by mixing blood, animal fat, or other natural juices with natural colorants such as metallic oxides, charcoal, and available minerals. The paint was applied onto the cave walls or ceilings with brushes made from animal hides or with sticks.

Cave paintings are sometimes referred to as *pictographs,* which means "writing with pictures." The art of cave painting continued through the Mesolithic period (Middle Stone Age), the Neolithic period (New Stone Age), and well into the Bronze and Iron Ages—a range of time covering approximately 10,000 BC to 4000 BC. The greatest

Figure 2–1.
Deer hunt, Paleolithic era, Spain (courtesy American Museum of Natural History, New York City).

concentrations of artwork have been found in France, Spain, Russia, South America, and Africa. North and South America also have caves containing painted rock faces and walls.

Examining humans' progression from these early hunter/gatherers, we find that with the onset of farming and agricultural systems, divisions of labor developed within society as farmers began raising and selling surplus food. Freed from the land, societies developed specialized production functions within different sectors of the economy. Barter systems grew more complex as money evolved into a medium of exchange for goods and services.

Within this expanding complexity of societies, artistic design and communication systems began to flourish. Gutenberg's printing press and replica typecasting set the stage for the spread of literacy throughout Western Europe. No longer were books restricted to the wealthy. The world found itself with a distinct shortage of scribes to copy and produce books as Europe and Asia emerged from the Black Death, a fourteenth-century plague that is believed to have killed approximately one-third of Europe's population. Gutenberg's inventions were quite timely. When Aldus Manutius founded the Aldine Press in Venice, Italy, in

the late 1490s, his attention was focused on saving early Greek literature by publishing as many of these classics as possible. Manutius also developed the **italic typeface,** which, as a condensed type form, enabled him to publish the first small-format pocketbooks. For the first time in history, classical works of literature and theology could be transported and shared among many people. The foundations were laid for all people to have access to books and to the power of their words and ideas. These early events formed the very beginning of modern mass communication systems.

As this chapter continues, we look at some events in the evolution of communication technology that lend historical perspective. To further enhance your studies of the history of visual communication, please refer to the suggested reading list in Appendix II.

HIEROGLYPHICS AND THE DEVELOPMENT OF THE ALPHABET

Pictures and symbols that represent ideas, objects, and symbols in a formalized writing system are known as **hieroglyphics.** The term *hieroglyphics* comes from the Greek *hieroglyphika grammata,* meaning "sacred carved letters." More far-reaching than the Greek definition, hieroglyphic texts addressed

Figure 2–2.
Letter and symbolic counterparts of hieroglyphic symbols.

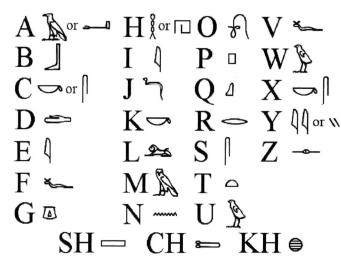

sophisticated ideas can be represented in this writing system, many ideographs are needed to communicate a message. For example, both the Chinese and Japanese writing systems, which still contain ideographs, require more than 10,000 symbols. Figure 2–2 illustrates some basic Egyptian hieroglyphic symbols, along with their letter and symbolic counterparts.

many more subjects than simply religion. Although many hieroglyphic texts have been deciphered, many remain a mystery due to insufficient information necessary for analysis. The major key to deciphering ancient Egyptian hieroglyphic texts came with the discovery of the **Rosetta Stone,** which contains a decree issued in 196 BC and written in three languages: Greek, Egyptian hieroglyphics, and Demotic (a cursive evolution of hieroglyphic text and symbols). French scholar Jean Champollion deciphered the stone in 1822. Keys from this stone have been used to understand many hieroglyphic texts. The Rosetta Stone is on permanent display at the British Museum in London, England.

Hieroglyphic texts evolved from simpler forms of pictorial art as various societies developed increasingly complex writing systems to keep up with their cultural development. Hieroglyphic texts use **ideograms;** that is, each sign or drawing represents some object or concept that is derived from the graphic. Many hieroglyphic texts are also phonetic and represent basic grammatical expressions. Although

The evolution of hieroglyphic texts eventually led to the invention of letters. Alphabetic writing began to appear in Egypt around 3000 BC. The Phoenicians are thought to have developed the first system of representing sound with written symbols: the basic **Phoenician alphabet.** The Phoenicians were trading widely throughout the Middle East around 1100 BC and were known to have imported papyrus for writing. It is likely that they adopted Egyptian alphabetic letters for their own alphabet.

By the fourth century BC the Greeks had adopted and modified the Phoenician alphabet system, adding vowels. The Greeks reversed the direction of some letters because the Phoenicians wrote from right to left and the Greeks wrote from left to right. The Greeks also changed the names of some letters. The Romans later adapted the Greek alphabet to their own language. The **Roman alphabet** was modified during the Middle Ages with the addition of three letters to become the 26-letter alphabet we use today. Figure 2–3 illustrates this evolution.

Figure 2–3.
Evolution of the modern alphabet.

PAPERMAKING, MOVEABLE TYPE, AND THE PRINTED WORD

The development of an efficient and inexpensive system of making paper and printing from moveable type began to converge during the fourteenth and fifteenth centuries AD. Although book production enabled the spread of literacy, paper was still a rare commodity. Not until the late eighteenth century, when mass-produced paper became available, did newspapers, books, and magazines become affordable to the majority of people.

When humans first began to communicate ideas with drawn images, any material could be used as a writing tablet. Cave and rock walls were replaced by clay and wooden tablets. Clay and wood in turn were eventually replaced with easier-to-work materials like **papyrus.** Most Egyptian hieroglyphic texts were printed on papyrus—a reed that grows on the banks of the Nile River, from which paperlike sheets were made by cutting the plant's stem into strips. These strips were overlapped, dried under pressure, and then adhered to one another. Papyrus remained in widespread use throughout Europe into the twelfth century. Parchment, made from tanned calfskins or goatskins, was also used extensively for writing until paper made from plant fibers replaced it.

The process of making paper is credited to a Chinese court official named Tsai Lun around 105 AD. The Chinese were able to keep the process of papermaking a secret for more than 500 years. Eventually knowledge of the process spread, and by the sixteenth century paper mills were established throughout much of Europe. Papermaking at this time was a manual process. Linen and wood were reduced to a pulpy mass by suspension in water. A wire mesh screen was then dipped into the pulp vat. When the screen was removed, it had a thin layer of pulp on its surface. As water drained through the screen, the linen and wood fibers bonded to form a sheet of paper, which could then be pressed and dried. This manual papermaking process was slow, restricting the amount of paper available for printing. A mechanized process would be needed to supply the increasing amounts of paper necessary to feed the printing presses of the day.

The mechanized process for making paper, still in use today, was developed in 1798 by Frenchman Nicolas Robert. Robert's papermaking machine uses an endless wire mesh screen that runs between two drive rollers. The screen vibrates as it moves, and a mixture of watery pulp from a vat called a *head box* is fed onto the moving screen. The vibration of the screen helps remove excess water from the pulp and allows the water to drain through the screen. The vibration also aligns the pulp fibers, creating what is called *paper grain*. The pulp fibers lock together as they move down the screen, forming an endless web of paper. The paper web is then sent through a series of rollers to establish uniform thickness and surface finish. The Fourdrinier brothers further refined the papermaking process by building the first commercially successful papermaking machine in England in 1804. The **Fourdrinier process** is illustrated in Figure 2–4.

Until a process for mass-producing the printed word was developed, information was accessible to the relatively few people who could afford hand-printed or scribed manuscripts. Both block-printed and scribed materials had severe limitations. Wooden blocks used for printing had to be carefully handcrafted, and each block represented only a single book page. The printing presses of the time were modified from wine presses and used heavy pressure against the blocks to print pages, which eventually flattened out the blocks, rendering them useless. As an alternative to block printing, scribed manuscripts were expensive because scribes

Figure 2–4.
Configuration of a
Fourdrinier paper
machine.

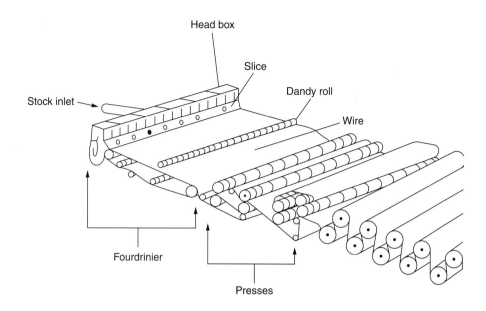

were in short supply and demanded high
wages for their craft.

Fifteenth-century Europe was poised for the
invention of **moveable type** and mechanized
printing. The process of papermaking had
developed to the point where it was now
cheaper and more readily available than either
parchment or papyrus. Relative affluence after
European recovery from the plague resulted in
an abundant supply of linen for papermaking.
At this point in history Johann Gutenberg
offered his landmark invention to the world.

As we discussed in Chapter 1, Gutenberg's
great contribution to civilization was his
development of a method to produce moveable,
easily replicated metal letters. Gutenberg's

early attempts at printing used wooden
letters that were held together in lines by
running a wire through a hole drilled at the
base of each piece of type. With the lines
of type held in place within a frame, pages
could be printed. However, the wooden type
quickly wore down, and Gutenberg began to
experiment with other materials for making
type. Drawing on his skills as a goldsmith,
Gutenberg introduced the process of replica-
casting individual pieces of type, in which
each alphabet letter was carved in relief to
form a master letter punch. This master
was used to punch the letter into a brass
matrix. Type was then cast one letter at a
time in the matrix. The mold was reusable,
so many identical letters of type
could be cast from the same
mold. (This process was an early
forerunner of the principle of
interchangeable parts.) The metal
used was an alloy of lead, tin, and
antimony, and it is still used today
to cast what little metal foundry
type is produced for special-
purpose printing applications. The
process of replica typecasting is
illustrated in Figure 2–5.

Figure 2–5.
The process of replica
typecasting.

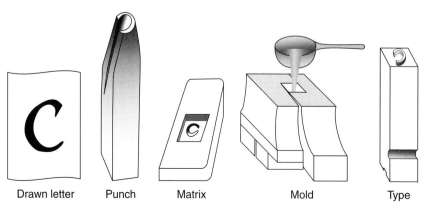

Drawn letter   Punch   Matrix   Mold   Type

Gutenberg adapted the wine presses of the day for use in printing pages of both type and illustrations. He also developed a printing ink that was formulated to adhere to the type metal alloy. Ink used to print from this new type had to be different from the inks used to make prints from wood blocks because the surface adhesion of metal is different from that of wood. The basic design of the Gutenberg printing press is illustrated in Figure 2–6.

The **Gutenberg Bible,** also known as the Forty-Two-Line Bible (based on the number of lines of text on each page), was published around 1455. This text, more than 1,300 pages long, was printed two pages at a time, by hand, on Gutenberg's first-generation printing press. Historians question whether this Bible was actually published by Gutenberg or by Johann Fust and Peter Schoffer. Fust and Schoffer took over Gutenberg's press and materials after Gutenberg defaulted on his repayment of their loans.

Despite his milestone technological achievement, Gutenberg abandoned printing in the 1460s and died in 1468, still heavily in debt. Yet Gutenberg's invention led to the spread of knowledge and literacy throughout Europe by enabling the distribution of inexpensively produced books.

First-generation type designers were busy throughout Europe following the development of moveable type and mechanized printing. One of the most famous type designers was a Venetian, Aldus Manutius, a printer who pioneered the production of inexpensive books that could be easily carried about—the first pocketbooks. Manutius set to work printing translations of the Greek classics and is responsible for the development of the italic typeface. This typeface was originally designed with graceful, slanting letters to mimic handwritten characters.

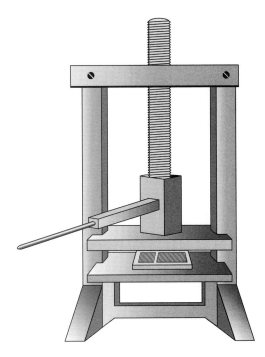

Figure 2–6.
Design of Gutenberg's relief printing press.

Another Venetian printer, Nicolas Jenson, began work around 1470. Jenson, an artist by profession, was responsible for perfecting the basic form and beauty of the Roman typeface. Roman typefaces are those used in most textbooks and other text-intensive applications. Jenson's letter style is still used today in the design and appearance of modern Roman typefaces.

Typecasting was an integrated activity in early print shops. A French printer and typographer, Claude Garamond, was the first person to elevate **type design** and typecasting as a separate undertaking. Garamond began work as a printer, but eventually he focused solely on the design and production of typefaces for other printers, creating the first type foundry. This development of the type foundry as a separate entity from the print shop freed printers from the chore of designing and casting their own type. Now printers could concentrate on printing and page composition.

William Caxton was a merchant and writer who, while visiting Belgium, was introduced to the art of printing. While in the city of Bruges, Caxton produced the first book printed in the English language. Caxton later returned to England, bringing his printing presses with him. Shortly after setting up shop in London, he produced the first dated book printed in England in 1477.

Through the end of the seventeenth century and into the eighteenth century, English printers were forced to rely on type imported from the Netherlands because there were no type foundries in England. Then, in the early eighteenth century, William Caslon, using his background as an engraver, set up the first type foundry in London. Caslon printed a type specimen sheet in 1734 that included typeface designs that still bear his name. His work began an industry that eliminated the British need for imported typefaces.

John Baskerville, a contemporary of Caslon, was a writing master who later became a type designer and printer. Baskerville's contributions to typeface and typographic design were impressive. His accomplishments also included the development of richly toned printing inks and glossy papers. As official printer to Cambridge University, Baskerville printed a Bible in 1763—a book that is considered one of the finest examples of eighteenth-century printing. Figure 2–7 illustrates several landmark type designs from this period that are still in wide use today.

Figure 2–7.
Letterforms of six different classic typefaces.

Caslon   Garamond

Caxton   Bodoni

𝕱𝖗𝖆𝖐𝖙𝖚𝖗   Baskerville

COPYRIGHT PROTECTION

In 1709 the British Parliament passed the **Statutes of Anne,** which extended **copyright protection** to all citizens. These laws established that the rights of property belong to the creator of that property. United States copyright laws are based on these statutes. The main purpose of copyright protection is to encourage the creation and dissemination of information while protecting the rights of the creator of a book, photograph, or product, such as the right to earn money from the creation.

The need for copyright protection was recognized shortly after the invention of the printing press. European governments, fearing that widespread printed information could undermine their authority, began to enter into individual copyright agreements with printers. In these early arrangements, governments would allow printers to publish and sell their materials only if they adhered to and followed government censorship rules.

It is essential that anyone working in graphic design and the associated technical industries be familiar with the basic concepts of copyright law. Current worldwide copyright laws allow the creator of intellectual property (books, films, photographs, and so forth) to control and distribute its creation, earn income from it, and prevent others from using it without permission. Copyright protection is a vital issue for those in the graphic design and communication technology areas because questions can arise about the property rights of materials whose origins are unknown.

As barriers between people and countries have evaporated with increasing computerization and globalization of economies and societies, issues of copyright protection have become increasingly complicated, necessitating frequent revisions and updating of copyright statutes. Although all professionals involved in design and publishing need to be familiar with copyright law, a good rule of thumb on these issues for the beginner is known as the *man-on-the-street rule*. This rule states that if someone with no graphic design or technical training feels that two images bear a striking resemblance to each other, it is reasonable to assume that a copyright infringement has probably taken place. In other words, if you didn't create an image yourself, you can assume that you are using another person's material. Unless you have permission to use the material, you are likely in violation of the law.

Figure 2–8.
Benjamin Franklin: printer, statesman, and inventor (courtesy Scott Gordley).

THE ESTABLISHMENT OF PRINTING IN NORTH AMERICA

The North American printing industry began in 1638. Stephen Daye, a locksmith from Cambridge, England, contracted with a New England minister, Jesse Glover. Glover, interested in promoting an understanding of the Bible in the British Colonies, felt the best way to do this was to set up a print shop to spread the word of the Bible. On the way back from England with Daye, Glover died before the shop was established. Glover's wife took over the responsibility of setting up the shop, and Stephen Daye fulfilled his contract. In 1640 Daye published *The Book of Psalmes*, the first book printed in British North America. Only eleven copies of this 300-page book (which took almost a year to complete) remain. After the death of Glover's widow (who eventually remarried a Harvard University president), the press was moved to Harvard. This marked the beginning of what is now the oldest continuously operated publishing press in the United States: the Harvard University Press.

Perhaps the most famous of all early American printers was Benjamin Franklin (Figure 2–8). Franklin wore many hats, including those of printer, political leader, statesman, inventor, and philosopher. One of thirteen children, Franklin began his career in his father's trade as a mechanic and candlemaker. However, he soon began to work as an apprentice for his brother James, who published the *New England Courant*. Franklin was a voracious reader as well as a prolific author. He began writing articles for the *Courant* satirizing everything from religion to authoritarianism. Franklin moved from his brother's employ to Philadelphia, where he established the *Pennsylvania Gazette*. He began printing *Poor Richard's Almanac* in 1732, expanding both his business and influence. Students of American history are familiar with Franklin's other accomplishments, including his careers as diplomat, abolitionist, and, of course, one of the designers of the Declaration of Independence and the Constitution of the United States.

In America printing press construction featured easily disassembled wood and metal components. These construction features were adaptable to westward expansion in America. Robert Hoe, working with his furniture manufacturer brothers-in-law, bought the patents to several press designs of the time, modified them, and began to build what was known as the **Washington press** in the 1830s. In 1847 Hoe designed the first

Figure 2–9.
Robert Hoe's ten-cylinder rotary press, circa 1850.

American version of a rotary cylinder press. The press featured in Figure 2–9 was a ten-cylinder press, containing thousands of finely machined components. The first Hoe press used type mounted directly onto the press cylinders.

Isaac and Seth Adams developed the first **steam-driven lithography press** in the 1860s. In their design, steam drove the moving parts on the press, on which lithographic stones were prepared for image transfer. This adaptation was much faster than the typical hand-powered printing presses of the time. Press technology continued to evolve rapidly with the widespread use of **stereotype plates** (rather than original type forms) on cylinder presses in the 1860s. Stereotype plates let printers run the same job on different printing presses at the same time. The plates were cast replicas from original type forms, fitted to run on presses with the same cylinder curvatures.

On March 4, 1880, the first printed halftone picture appeared in the *New York Daily Graphic*. The **halftone picture process** breaks a continuous-tone photograph into a series of dots, allowing images to be printed alongside type. Before this invention, engravers had to create line art illustrations based on photographs.

The Washington press became the standard machine for high-volume printing operations and remained viable into the 1930s, when higher-volume sheet- and web-fed printing presses became popular.

THE NINETEENTH CENTURY: PRESSES, CAMERAS, AND ARTISTIC DESIGN COME OF AGE

The nineteenth century brought significant changes in both artistic graphic design and the technologies associated with printing and publishing. From his early experiments with images drawn on limestone, Alois Senefelder had perfected his technique of direct lithography so that by the 1820s, full-color printing from multiple lithographic stones had become an established art form.

Along with American developments in building high-speed printing presses, paper began to be produced commercially based on the designs perfected by the Fourdrinier brothers in England in 1804. Paper had finally become an affordable commodity.

Developments in photography set the stage for photo-based reproduction processes that would eventually dominate the printing and publishing industries for more than 100 years. The introduction of the Kodak camera in 1888 forever changed how people communicate. **Photography** has played a key role in communication technology, both as an art form and as a foundation process in most printing and graphic reproduction processes.

Long before the introduction of the Kodak camera, artists and photographers were using a device called a **camera obscura,** which was basically a darkened room with a pinhole opening in one outside wall. Light from an object that was illuminated outside the room passed through this small pinhole opening and was projected upside down on the opposite wall. This process is illustrated in Figure 2–10.

Experimentation replaced the darkened room with a smaller, portable light-tight box. The opening in the wall was replaced by a simple focusing lens, which allowed the image to be projected right side up.

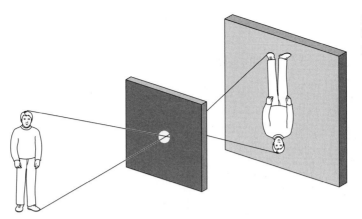

Figure 2–10.
Principle of a darkroom pinhole camera obscura.

When film was added to the back of a light-tight box to capture the projected image, the modern camera was born.

Frenchman Louis Daguerre developed the first commercial camera. In a process named after its inventor, called **daguerreotype,** a glass photographic plate coated with a light-sensitive chemical emulsion was placed inside the light-tight box. A long exposure was made, after which the plate was processed in a chemical bath to fix the image. Daguerreotype was a wet-plate process.

The relatively low sensitivity of the chemical emulsions required long exposure times to produce a photograph. Thus the stage was set for a technological development that would expedite the photographic process: a flexible film base using dry process chemistry housed within the framework of a portable light-tight box—the Kodak camera. Around 1880 George Eastman developed a machine that produced dry-coated gelatin-based photographic plates. This process was a great improvement over the relatively messy wet plate process, and the history of Kodak cameras began. The original Kodak camera came prepackaged from the factory with a 100-exposure roll of film. After the pictures were taken, the camera was sent back to the factory, where the film was processed with liquid chemicals, and the negatives were printed onto photosensitized paper using an enlarger. The camera was reloaded with a new roll of film and returned

to the customer, along with prints of the previous photos. Continuous improvements in film and camera technology, combined with electronic circuit miniaturization, eventually led to the fully automatic point-and-shoot, professional, and digital cameras with which we are familiar today.

HOT TYPE COMPOSITION

The ancestry of computerized imaging can be traced back to the development of the first **typewriter** by Christopher Sholes after the Civil War. The Sholes typewriter introduced the now familiar QWERTY keyboard layout. Several stories surround this QWERTY arrangement, a name derived from the top row of keys whose first six letters (Q–W–E–R–T–Y) are placed just below the numeric keys. One story relates how the keys were arranged in this way to enable a typewriter salesman to easily type the word *typewriter* using just the top row of keys. A more popular version is that Sholes arranged the keyboard to slow down fast typists who would otherwise jam the sluggish machine, which had metal type placed at the end of arms, called *typebars,* which were connected to the keyboard. When a key was pressed on the keyboard, the typebar would rise to make contact with an inked ribbon, transferring ink from the ribbon to a sheet of paper. If multiple keys were pressed at the same time, the typebars

Figure 2–11A.
Mergenthaler's Linotype machine (courtesy Smithsonian Institution, Washington, DC).

could easily jam together. Sholes's financial backer Amos Densmore, an educator and inventor, studied commonly used pairs of letters and placed the typebars and keys at safe distances from one another to avoid jamming. Proper placement, it seems, was able to overcome poor machining. The resulting patents and manufacturing rights for the typewriter were eventually sold to the Remington Arms Company. For many years this company manufactured the famous Remington typewriters.

Figure 2–11B.
Linotype matrices (courtesy Smithsonian Institution, Washington, DC).

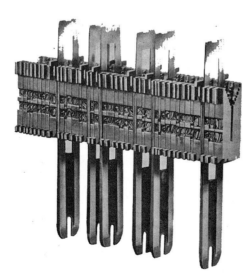

While the typewriter was beginning production, Herman Hollerith invented a **punch card tabulating machine** to help analyze the data for the 1890 United States Census. Hollerith's invention was based on principles developed for a punch card–driven loom invented in the early 1800s by a French silk weaver named Joseph Marie Jacquard. The punch cards controlled the actions of the loom and enabled it to weave intricate patterns automatically. Hollerith's modifications to punch card technology were based on a device that could read the presence or absence of holes in a punch card. This was accomplished by using spring-mounted nails that, when passed through a hole in the card, completed an electrical contact, which in turn triggered an electrical counter. Electrical data entry, sorting, and analysis were off to a successful beginning. Hollerith's tabulating company eventually became the International Business Machine Corporation (IBM), and punch card technology continued to be a data entry computer mainstay through the 1970s.

Although many patents were issued for mechanical typesetting devices during the latter nineteenth century, mechanized production of the printed word was clearly defined by the invention of the **Linotype machine** by Ottmar Mergenthaler. Mergenthaler, a German-born watchmaker, was a skilled constructor of patent models. Financed by a group of publishers, Mergenthaler's machine was installed in the *New York Tribune* building and began producing type on July 3, 1886. Mergenthaler's Linotype machine used molten metal to cast lines of type from brass molds. Separate lines of type could be quickly assembled into complete pages of text by a compositor. The Linotype machine, which set the typesetting standard for the next 60 years, is shown in Figure 2–11A. A line of Linotype matrices and spacing bands placed between the words to justify the line are illustrated in Figure 2–11B. Molten metal

Figure 2–12.
The first Christmas card, attributed to John Callcott Horsley, circa 1843.

was poured into the matrices to produce the finished cast lines of type.

One limitation of the Linotype machine was that it could set only standard point sizes of type; it was not capable of setting the larger type required for headings and display applications. To fill this gap, the **Ludlow machine** was developed by Washington Ludlow in 1913. The Ludlow machine allowed compositors to set individual lines of display type in a composing stick and, from the composing stick, cast the individual handset line of type into a lead slug, similar to the slug produced by the Linotype. Using these two machines, pages containing both text and display type could be quickly created and assembled.

During the next 70 years, both the Linotype and Ludlow machines encountered and successfully fought off competition from a variety of other manufacturers. However, by the late 1960s and early 1970s, the age of hot metal typesetting was over. First- and second-generation phototypesetters—machines made possible by the transistor and microelectronic circuitry—relegated hot metal typesetting to little more than an art form.

Graphic design as a distinct profession began to emerge in the nineteenth century.

As an indication of things to come, the first Christmas card was published in 1843 (Figure 2–12). Credit for this card is given to John Callcott Horsley, a well-known painter who designed the card at the request of Sir Henry Cole, an author, publisher, and founder of the Victoria and Albert Museum in London. Cole was also closely associated with the Great Exhibition of 1851. The Great Exhibition was conceived by the British royal family (Queen Victoria and her husband Prince Albert) to symbolize the industrial, military, and economic superiority of Great Britain. Millions of people journeyed to see over 13,000 exhibits on display at the Crystal Palace, a huge building constructed of iron and glass specifically for the exhibition. The Industrial Revolution had begun, and England, through its adoption of industry and technology, had become the greatest power of the time.

Whereas the Victorian reign had placed industrialization and mass production on a pedestal, a group of artists and social reformers led by William Morris sought to reestablish the roles of artists and craftsmen away from mass production. Morris and his group believed that mass production created inferior, poorly produced goods. In reaction to the 1851 Great Exhibition, Morris and his followers decried what they believed was a dehumanization of the workers who built the mass-produced exhibits. Morris was both an artist and a political activist. Within what he called the **Arts and Crafts movement,** he sought to instill both socialism and political activism among his followers in an effort to restore dignity to the worker, who he felt had been taken advantage of by the Victorian doctrine of progress through industrialization and mass production. He believed that each artisan within a profession should be able to accomplish all tasks and processes associated with that craft: Artists should grind their own pigments for paint, and architects should not hesitate to work alongside apprentice bricklayers.

In the United States, the Arts and Crafts movement took hold with the formation of the first American Workers Guild in 1885. The effects of this movement were far-reaching. The Manual Training High School in St. Louis, run by Calvin Woodward, gave birth to the Manual Training movement, which evolved into industrial arts and technology education as currently taught in secondary schools today. Eventually the political goals and wider vision of the Arts and Crafts movement lost momentum. In America capitalism—emphasizing promoting, marketing, and commercializing mass-produced goods—was highlighted in a speech by the famous architect Frank Lloyd Wright, who spoke about the machine and the possibilities it held for both art and industry. Although the Arts and Crafts movement as a distinct political and social entity has been gone since the 1930s, its influences, highlighting simplicity and honesty of materials in design and craftsmanship, are still alive.

About the same time the Arts and Crafts movement was gaining in popularity, a style of decoration and architecture known as

Art Nouveau (French for "new art") began to develop in the late nineteenth century. The Art Nouveau style is characterized by intricate patterns of curved lines and serpentine curves as shown in **Figure 2–13** in the color section of this text. Artists of the period working within this style include some famous painters, architects, and illustrators: the Spanish architect Antoni Gaudi, the American stained glass artist Louis Tiffany, the Scottish designer/architect Charles Rennie Mackintosh, and the French artist Toulouse Lautrec to name just a few. Although Art Nouveau began in the late nineteenth century, it is considered by many art critics and art historians to be the first new decorative and artistic style of the twentieth century. Art Nouveau, although tied to the Arts and Crafts movement in its attention to detail and craftsmanship, was also a reflection of life in the twentieth century—influenced and dominated by the machine and its possibilities for expression—and in part a result of the influence of Japanese block printing and early trade with Japan, a country that was closed to foreigners until the mid-1800s. The flattening of space and organic lines of the Japanese **Ukiyo-e** block prints are evident in most Art Nouveau graphics. The decorative ornamental ironwork of the period is an example of the intricate expression in materials made possible by new tools and techniques. Many architectural expressions of Art Nouveau, such as Hill House by Mackintosh and the entrances to the Paris Metro (underground rail system) by Hector Guimard, illustrate the artistic and design elegance of this period.

During this period French printers hired artists to design large street posters advertising everything from performances to products, and these early graphic designers are an important part of the history of visual communication. French poster artist Jules Chéret not only created over 1,000 posters during his lifetime but also has been credited with loosening the conservative structure of the Victorian era through his depictions of the "modern" free-spirited woman. He was awarded the French Legion of Honor in 1890 for his contributions to printing and advertising. Another Frenchman, Alphonse Mucha, whose posters are highly collectible today, helped define the Art Nouveau poster style through his use of flattened space and organic lines. Mucha's famous Job cigarette poster is shown in the color section as **Figure 2–14.**

THE TWENTIETH CENTURY: THE CONVERGENCE OF HIGH TECHNOLOGY AND GRAPHIC DESIGN

The twentieth century began with a great deal of suspicion between artists, designers, and the machine technologies that seemed to hover menacingly. This was still the era of the Arts and Crafts movement, whose ideals were in opposition to the beginnings of true mass production and industrialization.

The Art and Craft of the Machine

In 1901 the famous American architect Frank Lloyd Wright was invited to give a lecture at Hull House in Chicago. In this landmark presentation, Wright dismissed artists' distrust of machines and industrialization in favor of viewing machines as simplifiers, freeing the mind and body to create objects that would be affordable and available to every person. Suggesting a patient, scientific approach to the study of machines, he marveled at the ability of the printing press, for example, to shrink the world through the production and distribution of newspapers. Printing, he felt, was the greatest event in human history. Humanity, he said, was about to witness a convergence of art, design, and technology, resulting in a freedom of expression and technological sophistication that would forever change the direction of human history.

Shortly after the turn of the century, Ira Rubel, working in a small print shop in New Jersey, noticed that whenever his lithographic press had a misfeed, the press, rather than printing onto the sheet of paper, printed instead onto the rubber-covered impression cylinder. The next time a sheet of paper was fed into the press, it printed on both sides of the sheet: the direct lithographic print on the front of the sheet and the offset image printed from the rubber blanket on the back of the sheet. When examining both images, Rubel found that the image transferred from the rubber blanket was sharper than the direct image from the lithographic stone. Based on these observations, he built his first **offset printing press** around 1904 (Figure 2–15). Other presses of this type and design soon followed, and the offset printing industry was born. Offset printing remains the dominant worldwide printing process to this day.

The early part of the twentieth century was an era of turbulence and change. America was experiencing growing pains—opening national parks, building the Panama Canal, fighting corporate monopolies, and working its way through a world war and the Great

Figure 2–15.
Ira Rubel's offset printing press, on display at the Smithsonian Institution, Washington, DC (courtesy Smithsonian Institution, Washington, DC).

Depression. In Europe the 1900s through the 1930s witnessed World War I and its influence on culture, the opening of the Bauhaus School of Design in Germany, the Russian Revolution, and the rise of the Art Deco style. These events led to many changes in art, design, and architecture.

World War I: Futurism and Dada

The Great War, the War to End All Wars,—although known by different names at different times—World War I, fought in Europe between 1914 and 1918, was a time of great world upheaval. In warfare, new technologies, such as airplanes, tanks, and other motorized vehicles, together with new weapons, demonstrated the negative side of the new Industrial Age. In the chaos of the war, two movements that affected graphic design also came into being: Futurism and Dada.

Futurism actually began before the war in 1909, when the Italian poet Filippo Marinetti published his *Manifesto of Futurism*. His manifesto glorified the new: fast machinery, modern life, and enthusiasm for change—even through war. The futurists envisioned their roles as rabble-rousers and troublemakers, determined to bring down the old forms of art and culture through any means necessary. Futurist graphic works disregarded established design principles, exploding words on the page in ways not seen before, as illustrated in the color section of this text in a page layout by Filippo Marinetti (color section, **Figure 2–16**). Futurists attempted to express the meaning of words and sounds in their designs. While never making a large impact on mainstream design of their time, their work has been inspirational to many designers and artists since.

In opposition to Futurism, **Dada** was a reaction against the chaos of the war. It began in 1916 with the opening of Cabaret Voltaire in Zurich, Switzerland, by poet Hugo Ball. Many artists who had fled their home countries to live in neutral Switzerland were drawn to Zurich, the country's cultural center. Cabaret Voltaire became a refuge for these artists, who formed Dada as a way to express their dissatisfaction with the current state of the world. Dada rejected all known forms of art and sought to express the nonsensical through chance and randomness. Like the art of the Futurists, Dadaist graphic work rejected traditional ideas of formatting and layout. Kurt Schwitters, Hannah Hoch, and later Marcel Duchamp and John Heartfield are best remembered for their graphic and artistic expressions of the Dada movement. Dada was never a mainstream design style, but its influence had an impact on styles to follow, especially through John Heartfield's photo collage work, a technique still in use today (now created in Adobe Photoshop).

The Russian Revolution and Russian Constructivism

At the same time as World War I, a major upheaval of society occurred in Russia. The Russian Revolution was sparked by the imbalance between the rich ruling class and the poor working class. The Red Army, representing the working class, eventually overthrew the czarist rulers and was determined to start a new "society of the people." Artists and designers represented this new society in their works, many of which were based on new ideals of pure abstraction, use of new technologies, and principles of geometry. Artists such as El Lissitzy (color section, **Figure 2–17**), Alexander Rodchenko, and the Stenberg brothers (Georgy and Vladimir) used these principles, along with the new technologies of photography and film, to create dynamic compositions for posters, books, magazines, and even buildings and interiors. The founders of this movement labeled it *Konstruktivizm*, seeing their work as constructions rather than paintings, drawings, or designs. We now refer to the period as **Russian Constructivism.**

The Bauhaus

The **Bauhaus** (the literal translation means "architecture house") existed in three different cities and under three different directors in Germany: from 1919 to 1925 in Weimar under Walter Gropius; from 1925 to 1932 in Dessau under Hannes Meyer; and from 1930 to 1933 in Berlin under Ludwig Mies van der Rohe. Subsidized by the German government when it first opened, the Bauhaus was closed in 1933 by the Nazi regime, which opposed its philosophy of modern design.

The Bauhaus sought to combine the crafts, arts, and industrial art using the newest technology available. The school included workshops for producing household utensils, photography, typography, metal and wood sculpture, furniture and cabinet making, weaving, glass painting, and architecture. Bauhaus philosophy saw the building as the ultimate aim of all creative activity. The fine arts were an integral part of architecture to creatively bring out the character of a building as a unified structure, along with highlighting its component parts. An extension of the Arts and Crafts movement, its philosophical goal sought to combine architecture, sculpture, and painting within the framework of the artist as a craftsman, without the traditional class distinctions that existed between artists and craftsmen.

Incorporating developing theories of modern design by such movements as De Stijl (Dutch for "the style"), Russian Constructivism, and architectural influences of Frank Lloyd Wright and French architect LeCorbusier, the Bauhaus sought to create a modern design aesthetic. This was accomplished by stripping away superficial ornamentation from objects, letting the nature of the manufacturing processes define a simple elegance that was refined by the artist. The initial goal of the school was to have the students design everyday objects—such as fabrics, lighting, furniture, posters, and books—and connect with industry to produce the goods, which would then be sold to support the institution and spread its design philosophy. Although this was never fully realized, in part due to economic difficulties and problems in running such a complex business model, many developments initiated at the Bauhaus have been influential in the education of designers today.

Perhaps the most widely influential theory from the Bauhaus is that of learning the foundations of art and design during the beginning years of secondary education. Students at the Bauhaus began their first year with studies in color theory, drawing, and explorations of the nature of materials. From this they would choose a path that would refine their education along the lines of fine art or design, and then narrow those choices to specific areas of the arts. Most art and design schools still follow this model.

Many of the Bauhaus teachers left significant contributions: Josef Albers and Johannes Itten developed new theories of the use and nature of color; Herbert Bayer and Lazlo Moholy-Nagy explored new ways of working with type and photography; Walter Gropius and Mies van der Rohe helped to define modern architecture. The poster shown in the color section **(Figure 2–18)** is a prime example of the graphics work done at the Bauhaus. Other artists and designers working in the region also had an impact on defining the modern style of graphic design of the time, although they were not directly connected with the Bauhaus. These included Jan Tschichold in Germany, El Lissitzky in Russia, and Piet Zwart and Paul Schuitema in Holland.

Art Deco

The **Art Deco** movement got its name from the 1925 Paris Exposition des Arts Decoratifs (Paris Exposition of Decorative Art). This exhibition showcased French luxury items and design and sought to show the world that France was still an international center of style and design after World War I. Art Deco designs and artwork were characterized by the use of materials such as aluminum, stainless steel, wood and metal inlays, and lacquered finishes. Design featured the use of a zigzag, stepped form and sweeping curves, with a strong geometric basis. Egyptian art, fashionable in Europe after the discovery of King Tut's tomb in 1923, was an important influence on the development of the Art Deco style. Art Deco became a worldwide style that can still be seen today. The geometric sunburst, used as a design element in the auditorium of Radio City Music Hall and on the spire of the Chrysler Building in New York City, is in the Art Deco style. Art Deco had a dramatic impact on architecture: The Empire State Building, the Chrysler Building, and Rockefeller Center in New York, as well as the Golden Gate Bridge in San Francisco, are all examples of Art Deco architecture. Art historians sometimes refer to Art Deco as the beginning of Modernism in art and design. Figure 2–19 shows the Art Deco stainless steel crown of the Chrysler Building, designed by William Van Alen and completed in May of 1930. It is still considered by many fans to be the ultimate skyscraper design. Graphic works by A.M. Cassandre in France and E. McKnight Kauffer in England expressed the strong geometric abstraction of Art Deco.

Figure 2–19.
An Art Deco masterpiece: the Chrysler Building in New York City.

Modernism

The 1930s and 1940s witnessed groundbreaking research and development in many areas: television, color photography, and the forerunner of modern digital printing equipment—the photocopy process.

One-step photography, pioneered by Edwin Land, was developed by Land's Polaroid Corporation in 1947. Land began this work with polarized light and then applied this technology to automotive headlights, reduced-glare filters, glasses, and three-dimensional motion picture photography. The single-step **Polaroid camera** was introduced to the public in 1947. A color version of the camera became commercially available in 1963.

Around the same time that Land was experimenting with polarized light, another American inventor, Chester Carlson, was developing the foundations for what would eventually become electrostatic printing—later to be known as **Xerography** and today usually referred to as photocopying. Carlson sold the rights of his process to the Xerox Corporation in 1938.

The early signs of artistic Modernism also continued to grow during this time. In 1939 Raymond Lowey, a graphic and industrial designer, transformed two locomotives for the Pennsylvania Railroad into works of art by applying curved metal shrouds and striped lines. The S1 Turbine and GG1 locomotives stood out not only as technological achievements but also as artistic landmarks. When he wasn't designing locomotives, automobiles, or the interior of NASA's Skylab Space Station, his work as a graphic designer created the Exxon, Shell, and Lucky Strike logos, to name just a few.

Emigrants to the United States before, during, and after World War II helped bring the Modern style to America and spread their influence across the country in magazine and advertising design. Russian Alexi Brodovitch came to New York via Paris, where he had worked as a graphic designer. In the United States he had a strong impact on magazine design by combining young, experimental photographers' work with new and interesting typographic layouts. Walter Gropius, Mies van der Rohe, and Laszlo Moholy-Nagy, formerly of the Bauhaus in Germany, moved to the United States, where they took influential teaching posts on the East Coast and in the Midwest. Many other designers and artists also immigrated to the United States and lent their talents to the emerging design and advertising industry.

THE TRANSISTOR AND MICROELECTRONICS

The invention of the **transistor** stands as a milestone development of the twentieth century and, along with the development of printing from moveable type, is one of the greatest achievements in human history. The transistor set the stage for all future developments in electronic circuit miniaturization and the subsequent computerization of virtually all aspects of modern life.

The transistor was invented in 1948 by three Bell Laboratory physicists: Walter Brattain, John Bardeen, and William Shockley. The transistor is, in effect, an electronic valve. It can control large electrical current flow between two areas within a semiconductor crystal, using only a small amount of power. The transistor performs the same function as a vacuum tube, acting as either an amplifier or a switching mechanism; but it is only a fraction of the size of the tube, generates almost no heat, and is highly reliable. The operating features of the transistor ushered in the era of smaller electronic circuits, microelectronics, and eventually the integrated circuit, which is the basis for the heart of all computers: the microprocessor.

The transistor was invented shortly after the development of the first **ENIAC** computer. *ENIAC,* an acronym that stands for "electronic numerical integrator and computer," was developed at the Moore School of Engineering at the University of Pennsylvania. Construction started on ENIAC during World War II because the U.S. Navy needed to perform mathematical calculations for ballistic trajectory tables. Completed after the war, ENIAC was a marvel of modern electronic circuitry containing more than 17,000 vacuum tubes and able to perform 5,000 mathematical calculations per second, an astounding feat for the time. The ENIAC, a section of which is on permanent display at The Smithsonian, is pictured in Figure 2–20.

As an interesting note about ENIAC, the term *bugs,* referring to computer errors and software glitches, originated from the problems that occurred in ENIAC when insects got stuck between the contacts of the ENIAC switching terminals. In 1951 John Mauchly and John Eckert, the engineers responsible for building the ENIAC, who were then working for the Remington Rand Corporation, delivered the first UNIVAC

Figure 2–20.
ENIAC: Electronic
Numerical Integrator
and Computer, circa
World War II (courtesy
Smithsonian Institution,
Washington, DC).

(Universal Automatic Computer) to the United States Census Bureau.

THE BIRTH OF THE COMPUTER

The first computers were built using vacuum tubes; however, by the late 1950s transistors became the dominant electronic features of computer construction. The introduction of the integrated circuit by Robert Noyce, a physicist working for the Fairchild Semiconductor Corporation in 1959, both reduced the size and increased the efficiency of computers. The integrated circuit paved the way for the microprocessor by combining thousands of individual electronic circuit components on one small chip. When the central **microprocessor** chip was introduced by the Intel Corporation in 1971, the stage was set for the development of powerful personal and business computers. The central microprocessor replaces many integrated circuits, enabling further size reductions and corresponding increases in system and circuit efficiency.

The first personal computer to gain public acceptance was the Altair 8800.

The Altair, based on an Intel microprocessor, was offered to computer and electronic hobbyists as a do-it-yourself kit. Other companies, such as Apple and Kaypro, then entered the home computer market, producing machines like the Apple II series. The infant personal computer market received its biggest boost, however, with the introduction of the IBM personal computer (PC) in 1981. An almost unbelievable explosion of advances in digital technology has taken place since that time. In fact, a viable market has developed for antique computers. First- and second-generation machines such as the Apple I series and original IBM PCs have become valuable commodities in a market that defines fifteen-year old technology as *antiques*.

The introduction of the Apple Macintosh computer in 1984 was especially noteworthy. The Macintosh showed through its **graphical user interface** (GUI) that icon-based intuitive computing is an elegant alternative to arcane command strings that strain both memory and patience. The effectiveness of the GUI was further demonstrated several years later when Microsoft introduced its Windows operating system. With the introduction of the Power PC by Apple Computer and other advanced microprocessors, as well as the continued evolution of the Apple and Windows operating environments, the GUI remains an integral part of personal and business computing.

DESIGN LEGITIMIZES MATERIALISM AND THE CONSUMER SOCIETY

In both Britain and America, consumer optimism grew quickly during the years following World War II. The youth culture and pop music phenomena of the 1950s and 1960s were accompanied by a movement that was aimed at broadening artistic taste into the more popular and less academic orientations of the fine arts. The era of **pop art** coincided with these movements, giving rise to American artists like Robert Rauschenberg, Roy Lichtenstein, and Andy Warhol. Art was suddenly a fashionable endeavor, reflecting the new consumer culture. The period is immortalized in images like Andy Warhol's painting of Campbell's soup cans. An image of this series of paintings can be found in the color section in **Figure 2–21.**

The core of pop art is exploring everyday images that are an integral part of our consumer culture, including consumer product packages, celebrity photographs, and comic books, to name a few. The painting by Roy Lichtenstein shown in **Figure 2–22** in the color section, for example, is based on an anonymous newspaper ad.

MODERN AMERICAN GRAPHIC DESIGN

Modern graphic design in America was centered in New York, bringing together influences of European (especially German and Swiss) design and new advertising and photography. The **international style** of Swiss grid-based design had a profound impact on corporate design in America, where its organized structure and strong use of the grid was beneficial in designing multiple catalogs and corporate literature. The artistic approaches of New York designers Alvin Lustig, Bradbury Thompson, Cipe Pineless, and Paul Rand helped to define this design period.

Perhaps no other American designer defines the art and spirit of modern graphic design as well as Paul Rand, who was born in Brooklyn in 1914. Rand's work is often described in four phases. He began his career as a cover and media designer at *Esquire* and *Apparel Arts* magazines from 1935 through 1941. During his second career as an advertising designer at the William Weintraub agency in New York, he pioneered the close integration of graphic and copy design, working with well-known copywriter William Bernbach.

Rand's third career phase began in 1954, when, working as a freelance corporate identity design consultant, he created the famous logos for IBM, Cummins Engine, Westinghouse, and United Parcel Service.

Rand's design philosophy is a foundation of today's graphic design field: Good design will always add to the value of a product, and it reflects the business it represents. A good logo design, for example, need not have anything to do with the business it symbolizes. Rather, the design is an icon of the business or product that it stands for.

Rand's fourth career was as a teacher, lecturing at Cooper Union and Pratt Institute in New York City, and as a professor of graphic design at Yale University. His four books are *Thoughts on Design,* published in 1947; *Paul Rand: A Designer's Art,* released in 1985; *Design, Form, and Chaos,* published in 1993; and *From Lascaux to Brooklyn,* published in 1996. Rand's writing defines the foundations of today's graphic designer.

THE TWENTIETH CENTURY IN PERSPECTIVE

When we view technological developments in the communication arts from our current vantage point, we might wonder why things seemed to move so slowly during the first half of the twentieth century and so quickly since then. For example, the process of offset printing, developed around 1904, today remains similar in its most fundamental aspects to when it was first developed. **Digital printing presses,** however, which didn't exist even in 1990, can now electronically print directly from a computer front end, bypassing all the intermediate steps involved in traditional typesetting, camera work, stripping, plate making, and preparation time needed for a printing press. Environmentally friendly digital printing presses rely on no chemicals other than toners—no inks, solvents, or messes—thus reducing or eliminating much of the hazardous waste disposal traditionally associated with the pressroom. What separates the development of technology and the subsequent achievements of the two halves of the twentieth century is the invention of the transistor.

However disconnected the rates of development between the first and second halves of the twentieth century might seem, keep in mind that events usually occur in a natural progression, each building on another. Also, many devices and technological adaptations appear years before any practical applications are available for them. For example, the transistor was developed several years before it was used as a component in computers.

It was during the last thirty years of the twentieth century that tools, techniques, and design came together, refining graphic design as a distinct applied art form and creating the graphic designer whom we know today. Graphic designers working in the United States, such as Herb Lubalin, Milton Glaser, Lou Dorfsman, Saul Bass, Massimo Vignelli, and Paula Scher all contributed to the ever-changing profession of graphic design during the last quarter of the twentieth century. From the 1950s through the 1980s graphic design was traditionally a hands-on craft, relying heavily on photographic technologies to produce copy ready for printing. Text could be prepared in a number of ways. Preprinted type, referred to as *transfer type,* consisted of pressure-sensitive letters that were rubbed and transferred onto a sheet of paper. Other methods of text preparation included justifying typewriters and composition machines referred to as *strike-on text composers*. Photographic typesetting machines also prepared both body text and headlines. The photo strip printer in Figure 2–23 used a photographic negative strip to expose text headlines onto a strip of photographic paper. After developing, the paper strip headline was pasted onto a mechanical with the rest of the text and images for final photographing in a graphic arts process camera.

Before the development of digital output capabilities, continuous-tone black-and-white and color copy had to be photographed by a graphic arts process camera to produce the halftone negatives that would be used for

Figure 2–23.
Photo strip printer. Devices like the strip printer were used before the availability of digital typesetting equipment.

black-and-white and color printing. Once completed, the various elements of the project, including line and halftone negatives, artwork (whether generated on a computer or hand-drawn), and text came together during final image assembly. This final layout, with all of the copy set in place, was called a **mechanical**. The mechanical was photographed, stripped into a flat, and exposed onto a plate for printing. Preparation of a mechanical, once the mainstay of the designer's craft, has been replaced by outputting to film or plates or imaging directly on a digital printing press.

During the 1990s scanner technology became more sophisticated, dropping desktop scanner prices to the point at which an average consumer could purchase a machine for $200 that only 5 years earlier would have cost $50,000. The possibilities of digital photography, first introduced to a wide consumer base with Apple's QuickTake camera in 1994, enabled for the first time the digital combination of text and images using a desktop computer.

As the sophistication of digital imaging techniques increased, so did file size. Multigigabyte disk storage, along with erasable CDs and DVD formats, was introduced around 1995 and provided the capacity to work with and manipulate the large files generated by image editing and output programs. With the introduction of the Apple G4 computer in 1999, the century closed on a note of remarkable achievement with the integration of design, technology, and digital capabilities that altered or eliminated 100 years of traditional crafts, skills, and design techniques.

The Macintosh computer opened up new possibilities for graphic designers. While initially seen by many traditional designers as an inferior work method, by the mid-1990s it had been proven as a new way to create work. Early adopters of the Mac included California-based designers April

Greiman, whose early Macintosh-created poster is shown as **Figure 2–24** in the color section, and Rudy Vanderlans. Vanderlans's wife, Zuzana Licko, created some of the first consumer typefaces for the Macintosh (Figure 2–25); and their type company, Émigré, still creates and sells typefaces today. Although the work of these early adopters was experimental in relation to other, traditionally produced graphic design work of the time, their experiments showed the possibilities of computer-aided design. By the end of the twentieth century, computers and design software had advanced so that all design studios were using computers for design and production. Today it is a given that designs are composed and produced on computers. Even hand-created work, such as illustrations, is now either created on a computer or scanned in for final placement in a design.

During the twentieth century, the profession of graphic design was firmly established around the world and grew in many different ways. Many people from both graphic design and graphic arts—many of whom will never be mentioned in history books—helped shape the rich history of these interrelated fields. Graphic design was influenced by and benefited from new developments in technology. The history of graphic design will always be closely tied to the history of technological development.

SUMMARY: OPENING NEW POSSIBILITIES IN THE TWENTY-FIRST CENTURY

The opening years of the new millennium have seen the introduction of landmark technology that promises to influence society for years to come. Apple Computer released the first-generation iPod in 1991. The iPod, based on micro and flash drive technology, has paved the way for a new generation of devices ranging from MP3 music players to cell phones that integrate

Typography
Typography
Typography

Figure 2–25.
Zuzana Licko's early digital typeface designs from 1984. Shown (from top) are Émigré, Emperor, and New Geneva.

all aspects of personal communications. Cell phones like Apple's iPhone can now play videos, surf the Web, send e-mail and text messages, while simultaneously storing conventional computer files using sophisticated integrated micro hard drives and flash memory. While these portable devices continue to shrink, televisions continue to grow larger. The 80-year-old conventional television broadcast system will be all but obsolete in the near future when traditional analog broadcast signals disappear, leaving digital television as the only reception medium and high-definition picture technology and DVDs to continue their rapid penetration within the video marketplace.

Thanks to the rapid expansion of the Internet during the 1990s, the twenty-first century landscape offers instant access to information anywhere in the world. The effects of this leveling of the information playing field are yet to be determined. A new era of personal freedom has appeared, brought to us by the cave artist, the printing press, the designer, the transistor, the computer, and the wizardry of high technology. These developments have opened new possibilities for designers; and the definitions of what a graphic designer does and how this work is done will continue to evolve.

Review Questions

1 Explain how cave paintings and pictographs led to the development of the modern alphabet.

2 How are the development of paper-making and Gutenberg's printing press linked to the spread of literacy throughout the world?

3 Identify three key figures in the development of printing in North America, describing the contributions of each person.

4 What are the differences between hot type and cold type composition? How are the two methods of type preparation linked?

Suggested Student Activities

1 Construct a time line of significant events that traces the history of communications in the twentieth century.

2 Develop a design scrapbook, divided into sections, that focuses on the major design movements in the United States in the twentieth century. Feature the works of at least two designers in each movement.

3 Construct a flowchart that illustrates the development of the computer. The time line of the flowchart should begin with the invention of the transistor and end with the release of the latest version of either an Apple Macintosh or a PC.

Figure 2–13.
An example of the Art Nouveau style: *Divan Japonais* by
Toulouse Lautrec. Lithograph, 1893, $31\frac{5}{8} \times 23\frac{7}{8}$.
Museum of Modern Art, New York, Abby Aldrich Rockefeller Fund.

Figure 2–14.
Alphonse Mucha's poster for Job cigarette papers is a classic example
of Art Nouveau graphic design. Lithograph, 1897, $61\frac{3}{16} \times 40\frac{3}{4}$.
Courtesy Museum of Modern Art, New York. Gift of Lillian Nassau.

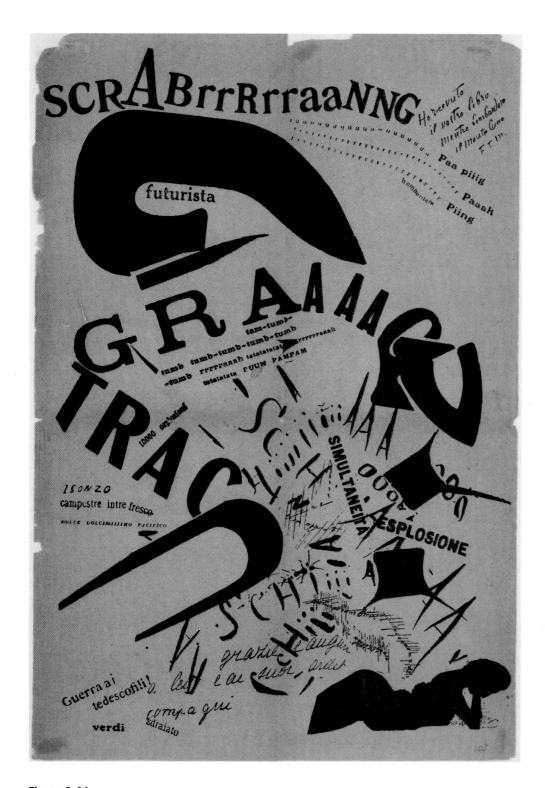

Figure 2–16.
In a page design for a poem by Filippo Marinetti, words expressing
the sounds of war explode around the figure of a girl attempting to
read her lover's letter from the battlefront. Lithograph, 1919.
Courtesy Museum of Modern Art, New York.

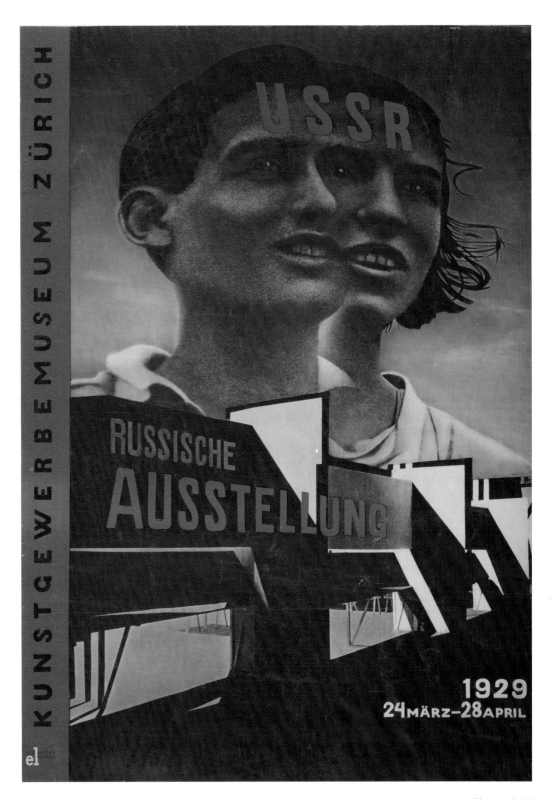

Figure 2–17.
This poster by El Lissitzky expresses the Russian Constructivist
principles of modernism and geometry, utilizing the then-new
technology of photography. Gravure, 1929, $49 \times 35\frac{1}{2}$.
Museum of Modern Art, New York. Gift of Philip Johnson, Jan Tschichold Collection.

Figure 2–18.

A poster by Joost Schmidt for the 1923 National Bauhaus Exhibition.
Lithograph, $26\frac{1}{4} \times 18\frac{5}{8}$.

Museum of Modern Art, New York. Gift of Walter Gropius.

Figure 2–21.

Andy Warhol's pop art masterpiece, *Campbell's Soup Cans*, 1962.
Synthetic polymer paint on thirty-two canvasses, each 20 × 16.
*Museum of Modern Art, New York. Gift of Irving Blum; Nelson A. Rockefeller Bequest,
gift of Mr. and Mrs. William A. M. Burden; Abby Aldrich Rockefeller Fund, gift of Nina
and Gordon Bunshaft in honor of Henry Moore; Lillie P. Bliss Bequest; Philip Johnson
Fund; Frances Keech Bequest, gift of Mrs. Bliss Parkinson; and Florence B. Wesley Bequest (all by exchange). © 2007 Andy Warhol Foundation / ARS, NY / TM Licensed
by Campbell's Soup Co. All rights reserved.*

Figure 2–22.

Girl with Ball by Roy Lichtenstein, 1961.
Oil and synthetic polymer paint
on canvas, $60 \frac{1}{4} \times 36 \frac{1}{4}$.
Museum of Modern Art, New York. Gift of Philip Johnson.

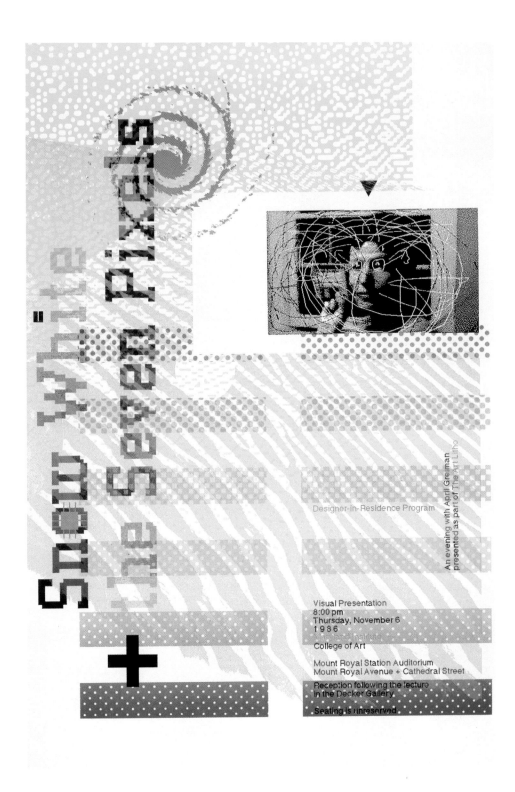

Figure 2–24.
A poster by April Greiman, designed on a Macintosh computer in 1986. Because the early Mac used one-bit color (black or white only), each color layer had to be output separately and assigned an ink color on press. Offset lithograph, 36 × 24.
Museum of Modern Art, New York. Gift of the designer.

DUOTONE

A duotone image is created when two slightly different exposures are printed in registration with one another. One is printed in black, as shown at left, above. The second exposure is printed in color. When the two are combined, the result is the image at top right.

A false duotone, illustrated at left, is sometimes used to give the impression of a true duotone without having to create the two separate exposures. Before Photoshop, this method was often used to save money and is still used as a quick way of imitating a duotone. In this process, a tint of color is printed over the image area and gives the impression of a duotone. In the image at left, the color box has been intentionally misaligned so you can see that it is an even tint of color. It would be printed to match the edges of the photograph in actual use.

Notice how the true duotone at top right has better detail in both the shadow and highlight areas. This is lost in the false duotone because no truly white areas of the paper are shown when overprinted with the overall color tint.

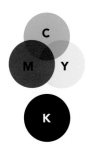

**Printing Primaries
(Cyan-Magenta-
Yellow-Black)**

**Additive Primaries
of Projected Light
(Red-Green-Blue)**
(CMYK Approximation)

**Subtractive Primaries
of Mixed Pigment
(Red-Yellow-Blue)**
(CMYK Approximation)

This page illustrates, above, the three ways that designers work with color. On the right is the way most people first experience combining color—through the use of mixed pigments (paint). The middle diagram shows how color is used by computers, in film, and on television—as projected light. The diagram at left shows how colors are used by full-color printing presses—through the use of semitransparent inks that overlap one another. In graphic design, designers work primarily on computers, which use the additive colors; but the final printed designs are most commonly done using the printing primaries of CMYK. Because of this, it is important to refer to printed swatchbooks when choosing colors for a design rather than choosing colors on screen. The chart below shows some examples of the variety of colors that can be made through various combinations of CMYK. The numbers at the top of each color show how much cyan, magenta, yellow, and black make up each color swatch. Computer applications for graphic design allow you to mix the colors by percentages in a CMYK palette so you will know how they will print—no matter how they look on your computer monitor!

A small sampling of how solid colors are represented in C/M/Y/K

0/8/94/0	0/30/94/0	0/34/91/0	0/47/100/0	0/60/94/0	0/60/100/0	0/79/91/0	0/91/76/0
0/100/65/0	0/100/30/0	0/100/0/0	18/94/0/0	43/91/0/0	79/100/0/0	94/94/0/0	100/94/0/6
100/72/0/6	100/56/0/0	100/30/0/6	100/0/6/18	100/0/30/6	91/0/51/0	100/0/65/0	100/0/79/8
76/0/91/0	43/0/79/0	11/0/94/0	0/6/18/43	0/0/15/51	6/0/0/47	8/0/6/47	0/15/18/47
0/0/0/65	0/8/47/23	18/30/56/0	0/34/51/0	30/43/47/0	0/51/23/6	0/38/27/23	15/51/0/0
27/51/0/0	43/56/0/0	43/30/6/0	34/0/0/38	43/0/30/27	43/0/27/6	47/0/30/0	8/0/47/27

C-10

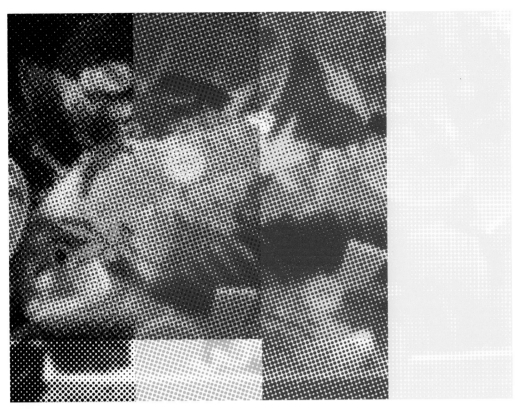

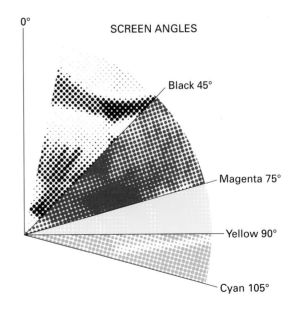

SCREEN ANGLES

0°

Black 45°

Magenta 75°

Yellow 90°

Cyan 105°

FOUR-COLOR PROCESS PRINTING

The illustrations on this and the facing page show how the process of four-color printing works. In the four images in the first column of the facing page, a photograph has been separated into four colors for CMYK printing. To the right of each separation is how it would look when printed in the correct color. In the illustration at the top of this page, the separations have been cropped so you can see the progression of color building from right to left: yellow printed first,

then magenta, cyan, and finally black. The image is broken down to a series of small, varied dots because the press can print only solid color. These dots have been enlarged to show how they fit together in the final, registered print, above.

To keep the dots in the four color separations from aligning in ways that would create blotchy groups (called moiré patterns), each dot screen is printed at a slightly different angle. The angle of each color screen is illustrated above.

COLOR TINTS

Any solid color may be broken down into tints. A tint is created by using different-sized dots of ink on the page; the lighter the tint, the smaller the dots. In the chart at the top of the facing page, the four process colors are shown from solid color, at left, to a 10 percent screen at right. The use of tints allows the designer to create a wide range of perceived color, even when using only one ink.

TINTS IN COMBINATION

When more than one color is used, tints may be combined to create an even wider array of colors. The charts on this page show how the use of cyan, magenta, and yellow—in combination with black—creates the possibility of many different tints. These charts are shown with variations of 10 percent differences, but they could be expanded to degrees of 5 percent. Less than a 5 percent tint difference is not noticeable enough to be used in most printing.

The charts on the facing page show the combinations available by printing tints of cyan and magenta (at top), magenta and yellow (below that), and yellow and cyan (at right). A complete range of all possible color tint combinations can found in books focused exclusively on printed color and may also be available from some commercial printers.

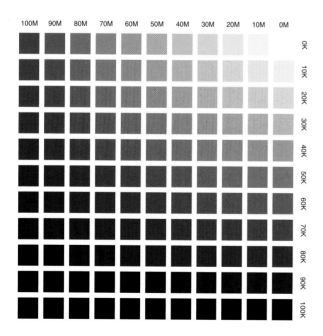

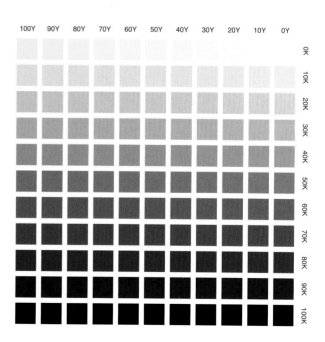

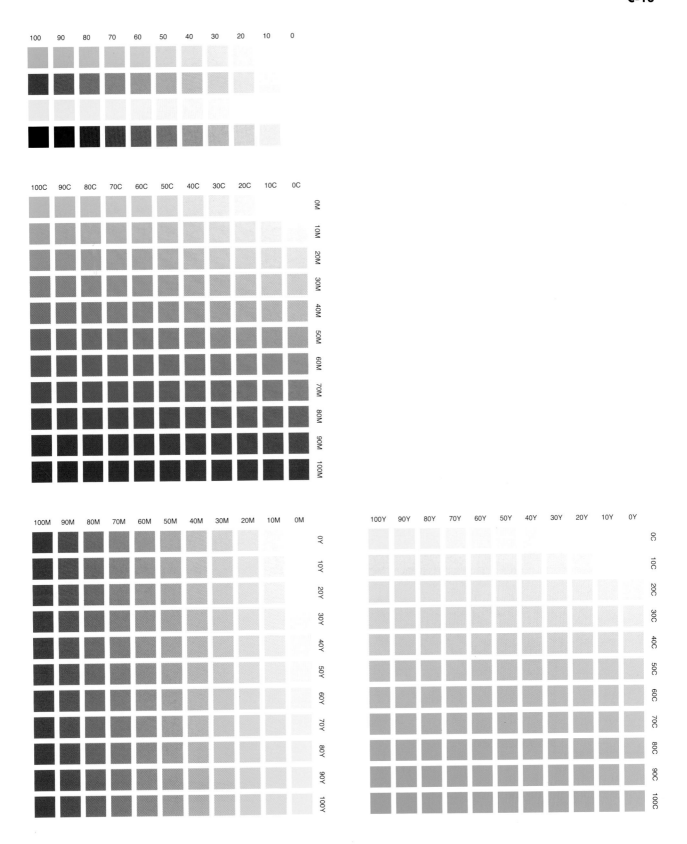

A poster by Montclair State University graphic design student
Lukasz Mysona. The process of designing this poster is described in
Chapter 3. Three-color silk screen, 24 × 18.
Gift of the designer.

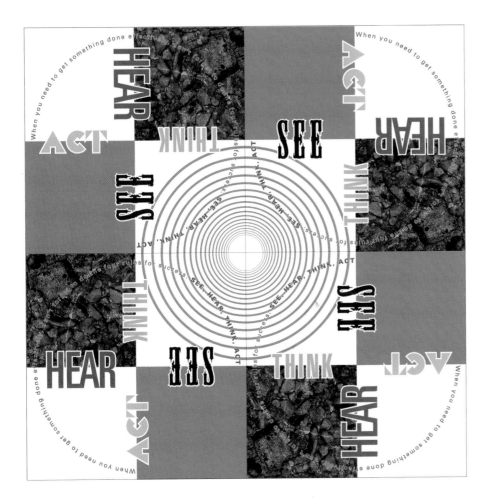

A single poster may be designed to be displayed in combination
with additional copies to create a larger presence, as described in
the section on poster design in Chapter 11.

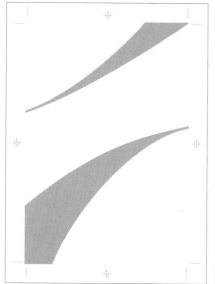

An example of silk-screen printing. The image at left is the first color to be printed. Registration and crop marks aid in aligning the second (middle) and third (right) colors. After printing, the poster is cut down to the trim marks in the corners, allowing the image to bleed off the page.

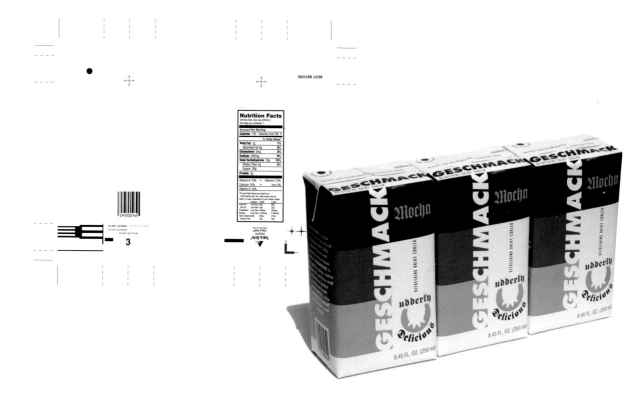

A package template, above left, is used to create the presentation-quality design comps at right. The process of creating this package is discussed in Chapter 11.

Fundamentals of Typography:
Chapter 3

Chapter Objectives

Realize the importance and relevance of the history of typography.

Understand how type is printed.

Learn how type is classified.

Get an overview of how type is designed.

Explore type formatting and use in graphic design.

INTRODUCTION

Type is usually the most important communication element in graphic design. In a well-designed piece, type not only provides necessary information in a logical and interesting manner; it also can set the mood for the piece, even working completely on its own—creating a mood without photographs or illustrations. Understanding type's history, structure, and use is essential for graphic designers. This chapter provides an overview of the history and development of type in printing, along with examining type structure, organization, and use in graphic design. It will give you a foundation on which to build expertise in the use of type in graphic design.

TYPE HISTORY

There are three major parts to the history of type. Part one is the development of the mechanical side of typography: how type is *printed*. Part two is the development of typefaces for graphic communication: how type is *designed*. Part three is the development of compositional strategies of type: how type is *formatted*. Each of these three parts is discussed in detail in this chapter.

Type and Printing

Before the refinement of cast, moveable metal type by Johann Gutenberg in the fifteenth century, type was lettered by hand, making reproduction of multiple copies time-consuming and exact copies impossible. The written word was exclusive to those with wealth and power—at that time primarily wealthy landowners and the church. It was not available to the general population, most of whom were illiterate.

Early forms of reproduction, such as block printing—made by hand carving a mirror image of the design in wood, then inking the raised surface of the wood and transferring the image to paper—existed in China as long ago as 500 AD. This process was brought to Europe by the 1300s. Block printing could be used for reproduction of type and images, but each design would have to be hand-carved as a mirror image so that it would print right-reading, and changes to a design were nearly impossible to make. Because of this, most block printing was of simple images with little or no type.

The Chinese had also experimented with moveable type as early as the eleventh century, but because their written language uses thousands of individual characters, this system was not used extensively. It wasn't until the European development of moveable type—single letters cast in metal that could be composed to make words, then taken apart and reused—that the modern idea of **typesetting** began.

As explained in Chapter 2, Gutenberg's process used a system of a hard steel punch in which a letterform, or **character,** was cut by hand as a raised letterform (Figure 3–1). This punch was hammered into a softer piece of brass to create a negative form of the character, called a *matrix*. The matrix was then locked in a two-piece mold into which molten metal would be poured (a mix of lead, tin, and antimony that would provide enough stiffness for printing but be soft enough to melt and reuse). After cooling, the newly formed character would be removed, and the mold and matrix could be reused. The individually cast characters could then be *composed* by placing each cast letter next to another to form words. Words would be composed backward; the letters, after being inked, would make direct contact with the paper and transfer their images to it. This was a time-consuming process, but it was much faster than previous methods, and the ability to reuse letters made up for the time spent punch cutting, casting the characters, and composing. Moveable, cast metal type was the dominant form of reproduction for books, handbills, and newspapers until the late 1800s and is still in use today for specialty printing.

Some words that are part of today's typography vocabulary come from the use of moveable type. One is the term **leading** (pronounced led-ding), which is the space between lines of type in a paragraph. In moveable type, the type *compositor* (the person who set the type) would have to insert small strips of metal (called *lead*) between each line to move them apart. Another term is **font**. The letters, numbers, punctuation, and symbols for a specific **typeface** and type size would be stored in a compartmentalized wooden case for easy access by the compositor. Each case would be referred to as a *font* of type. Other old terms are **uppercase** and **lowercase**. In early print

Figure 3–1.
Gutenberg's typecasting system. A drawing was made of each character— here the letter b (1). The design of the letter was cut by hand, in reverse, into a small block of hardened steel called a *punch*. A separate punch would need to be made for each character at each size it was to be used. The punch was then hammered into a block of brass, called a *strike* (3). The same punch could be reused to make multiple strikes. The strike was filed down on all sides to define its character width and alignment. The filed strike was referred to as a *matrix* (4). The matrix was locked into a mold (5), and molten metal (a mixture or lead, tin, and antimony, which would melt quickly and cool without distortion) was poured into the opening. When cooled, the type (6) could be removed for use in typesetting and printing. The type could be melted and recast when it began to wear.

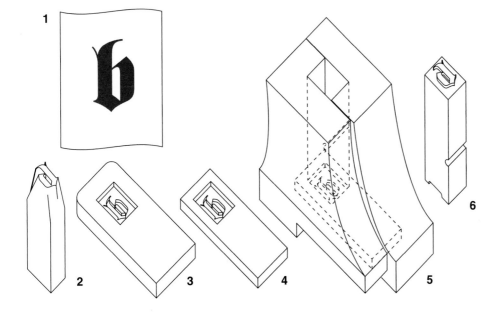

Figure 3–2.

The layout of a wooden type case used for storing metal type. This California Job Case stored both uppercase and lowercase characters in one drawer that could be removed from a larger set of drawers during typesetting.

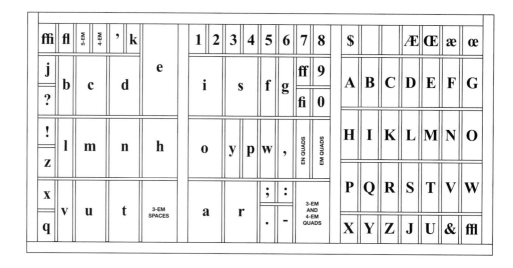

shops, a font with all of the capital letters for a typeface would be stored immediately above one for the minuscule letters. The physical positions of these cases led to them being called *uppercase* and *lowercase* letters. Today most people have probably never heard the word *minuscule* in reference to lowercase letters. Figure 3–2 shows a common type case used in the United States, a *California Job Case,* and how its characters are organized.

Figure 3–3.

A Linotype machine, used for casting lines of type instead of individual letters.

The next major step in typesetting came in 1886, when a German emigrant to the United States, Ottmar Mergenthaler, used a typewriter-like mechanism to compose type matrices before they were cast, thereby creating a line of typeset words. He justifiably called his invention the **Linotype machine,** depicted in Figure 3–3. Although the type was cast in the same fashion as had been done for the 500 years before his invention, the new process allowed type to be composed much faster.

While metal type was employed, wooden type forms were also in use. Although not as easy to make (until the early 1800s, each character had to be carved by hand), wooden type was especially useful for large letters because metal type cast in large forms would cool unevenly and leave concave surfaces in the center of each letter. In the 1820s printer Darius Wells, in New York City, introduced a method of producing wooden letters with a cutting tool called a *router*. This new method could produce letters more quickly and less expensively than by hand carving. Wood type was popular for posters because the large letters could be easily seen from a distance. Wood type is still in use today as a specialty form of printing (Figure 3–4).

The next major change in how type was set occurred during the 1970s with the adoption of the **phototypositor**. Although the method of setting type from a film negative to photographic paper had been developed in 1947, it was not in wide use until technology was available to speed the process. Phototypesetting (sometimes referred to as *cold type* in comparison to metal *hot type*) works by using a master strip of negative film for each typeface. On this film spool the individual characters are clear, and light is projected through them onto unexposed photographic paper. The size and sharpness of the letters can be varied by the use of a lens, and the space between each letter can be made tighter or looser by adjusting the lateral placement of the photographic paper between exposures of the characters. After the characters have been exposed, the paper is developed in the same method as traditional photography. The lines of type are then cut to size and pasted onto stiff paper slightly larger than the design to create a *mechanical*. This method was popular for most commercial typesetting through the 1980s. A diagram of how phototypesetting works is shown in Figure 3–5.

By the mid 1980s computer technology allowed typefaces to be digitized and output through several forms. Early high-resolution typesetting computers used a process similar to phototypesetting, but they replaced the master filmstrip with a laser that would move to create an exposure of each character on photographic paper. The person who input the type formatting did not

see the result until the end of the process. Instead the operator typed a series of coded lines into the computer via a keyboard. The monitor would show the coding but not how the type would look when output. Because of this, specially trained technicians, rather than designers, would run the computers to set type based on a *markup* from the designer.

Figure 3–4.
A wood type poster by Jim Sherraden, Hatch Show Print.

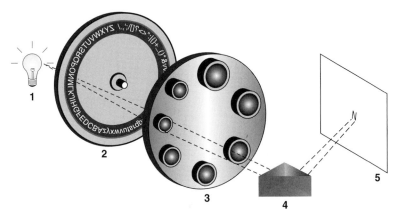

Figure 3–5.
This diagram shows the workings of a photo-typositor. A light source (1) shone through a film negative of the characters (2). This film negative was placed either on a disk (as shown here) or on a reel of film. Either could be moved to align the characters with a lens (3) that could enlarge or reduce the characters. A positioning prism (4) could be moved to align the characters on a roll of photographic paper or film (5). The exposed media would be developed once the type was set. The entire process took place in either a sealed machine or a photographic darkroom.

Figure 3–6.
A *mechanical* was the method of preparing a design before computers were available. Also referred to as *paste-ups*, mechanicals were composed of type and graphic elements that would be cut out and pasted to a piece of illustration board. The lines that show up in the figure as light gray are actually light blue—a color that would disappear when a *photostat* (a high-contrast black-and-white photograph) was made of the finished mechanical. The cut lines would also not be visible in the photostat. The final photostat would be mounted to a board and given to the printer, from which films and plates would be made for printing.

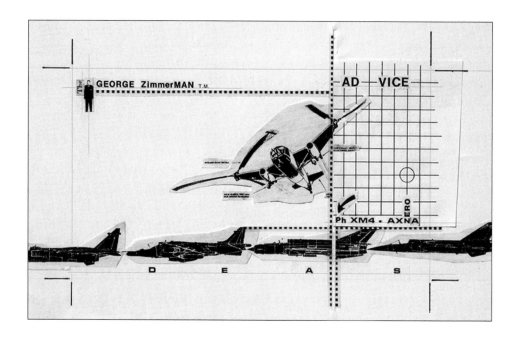

The markup consisted of all the copy needed for a job typed on a typewriter, with written notes telling the typesetter the typeface, size, leading, spacing, column width, and so on. This was called **type speccing** (pronounced speck-ing)—an abbreviation of *type specification*. The designer would proof the type formatting after the typesetter output the photographic paper and then paste it on a mechanical (Figure 3–6).

Other methods of early computer typesetting included computers that would run a daisy wheel or dot matrix printer. Low-resolution dot matrix printers were used primarily for proof printing because they did not provide sufficient quality for final output (Figure 3–7).

With the introduction of the Macintosh computer in 1984, typesetting went through a major change, and the process of composing type moved from the hands of a specially

Figure 3–7.
Low-resolution dot matrix printing was an early form of computer output.

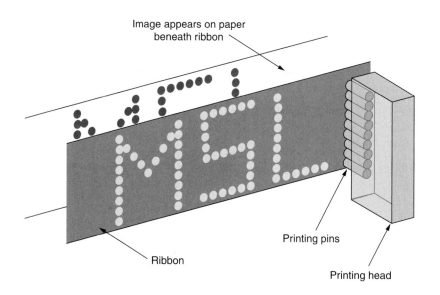

trained technician to the graphic designer. The early generation Macintosh computers were not impressive, and many graphic designers initially thought the computer would have little impact on the industry. The screen resolution was a low 72 dots per inch; only black and white—*not even gray*—were available; and the only printers available for output were low-resolution dot matrix printers. A vast improvement to designing on the Macintosh came with the development of PostScript by Adobe Systems, Inc., in 1985. PostScript allowed vector-based drawing of type and images. This, in conjunction with new monitors that could display grayscale— and later color—allowed a new interface: WYSIWYG (pronounced whizzy-wig), for "what you see is what you get." Graphic designers now could view type onscreen that was nearly identical to the way it would print on a PostScript printer.

Today we no longer have type compositors. That responsibility now falls completely in the hands of the graphic designer. Although this has added another task for the designer, it has also given designers more freedom to experiment. It lets them see their work in process and make finer adjustments to the type formatting. Due to the added responsibilities involved in formatting and proofing type, it is essential for today's graphic design students to learn the art of typesetting.

Type Design

The second part of type history is concerned with the process of type design. The first typeface designs (if we could even call them that) were done by hand—basically the individual calligraphic styles of monks reproducing manuscripts. The first metal typefaces were based on these hand-lettered forms. If you examine the typeface used in Gutenberg's Bible from 1455, you can see the similarity to hand-drawn type (Figure 3–8).

Figure 3–8.
Some of the characters used by Gutenberg in printing his Bible. Note the similarity to handwriting created with a pen.

During the Renaissance, as stated in Millard Meiss's *The First Alphabetical Treatises in the Renaissance,* letterforms were designed using the proportions of the human body as a guide, along with mathematical relationships thought to have divine significance. These theory-based typefaces provided a basis for heavily structured designs that did not allow much freedom for experimentation (Figure 3–9).

In 1693 French King Louis XIV created a committee of typographers to create and promote letterforms based on a strict modular grid with 2,304 cells. Slanting the grid and redrawing each letter to fit that

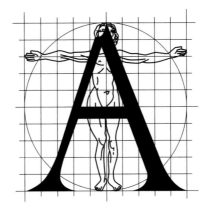

Figure 3–9.
Letterforms based on the proportions of the human body were popular during the Renaissance.

Figure 3–10.
The French seventeenth-
century system of
geometric letterform
design, shown here as a
roman and an oblique
letter.

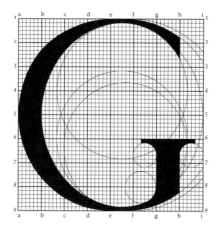

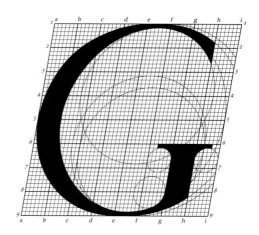

Figure 3–10.
The French seventeenth-
century system of
geometric letterform
design, shown here as a
roman and an oblique
letter.

distortion created oblique styles of typefaces. The typographers designing these typefaces were creating what they believed to be mathematically and geometrically perfect letterforms. Figure 3–10 shows examples of how such grids were used for character development of roman and oblique letters.

By the late 1700s technological advances in printing, along with changing design styles, brought typefaces to the forms we are familiar with today. Rather than relying on previous styles or restrictive philosophies or formulas, type designers such as Bodoni and Didot designed typefaces based on contrast, balance, and proportion, creating a self-defining structure within the typeface itself instead of applying outside theory and structure.

Since the 1800s typefaces have been created in a wide variety of both traditional text faces and unique display faces. They may be drawn completely by hand or created through digital systems. However they are created, the designer usually begins the design by thinking about the same basic elements: **baseline, cap height, x-height, ascender** height, and **descender** length. Drawing these guidelines on a sheet of paper or in a computer program gives the designer reference lines for all the typeface characters (Figure 3–11).

Additional thought is needed for the personality of the typeface. This *personality* is defined by the **stroke weight, inclination, modulation,** and **stress.** The thicker the *stroke*, the more color the typeface will have in text settings and the bolder it will be in display use. *Inclination* is how much the characters lean, as in an oblique or italic typeface. *Modulation* refers to the change of the stroke from thick to thin, as shown in Figure 3–12. *Stress* is created by the variation of modulation in a letter from the inside to the outside of its form, and its ability to make the letter appear to incline in one direction. This is shown in the character on the right on Figure 3–12. Designers can also create a *stroke* or *vector* typeface,

Figure 3–11.
Reference lines for
baseline, cap height,
x-height, ascender height,
and descender length
let the type designer
create letterforms that
work well together as a
typeface.

Cap height/ascender height

X-height

Baseline

Descender length

Figure 3–12.
Modulation of stroke
weight can be moderate
(left) or strong (middle).
It can also be used to
create stress (right).

which has no stroke modulation and is based on a centerline (Figure 3–13).

With the primary decisions completed, the type designer develops all the characters for the typeface. This will include uppercase and lowercase letters, numerals, punctuation, symbols, and special characters such as **ligatures**—two characters that are designed as one, such as fi, where an f and an i have been designed as one character to avoid overlapping the dot on the i. Professionally designed typefaces may have a full character set of over 200 characters, each of which must be designed to work with all the other individual characters in the typeface.

As the typeface is being worked on, the designer tries out various character combinations and carefully looks for problems. These problems could include how the characters fit when placed next to one another, unappealing variations in weight, and problems in paragraph setting. In this effort, type designers first set the word *Hamburgefons* and refine work on these letters first (Figure 3–14). Although this is not a real word, setting these characters together allows designers to analyze the most common character relationships. If problems occur here, they need to be worked out before the full typeface is designed.

Today, whether a typeface is drawn first or designed on a computer, the typeface is eventually digitized for distribution. There are several font formats on the market today. **PostScript Type 1**, **TrueType**, and **OpenType** are the three main digital formats. The Apple Macintosh also uses another format called DFONT, which is similar to OpenType. This format is used for Mac system fonts. Figure 3–15 shows how the icons for these font formats are displayed in a Fonts folder.

PostScript Type 1 has been around since Adobe introduced the first PostScript printer in 1985. PostScript Type 1 typefaces use two files: one for display on the computer screen and one for printing. Both are necessary for use of the typeface. A bitmapped file contains the screen fonts, which are used for display on the monitor. The second file contains the PostScript information that describes the vector-based outlines and fills for the typeface. If you did not have the printer file, you would be able to see the typeface on your monitor, but it would print with jagged, pixellated edges.

TrueType was first developed by Apple Computer and later licensed to Microsoft Corporation for use on PCs. The format uses one file that contains both display and printer information. TrueType typefaces can be used on both Macintosh and PC computers, but the typefaces are not interchangeable between platforms.

The OpenType format was developed jointly by Apple and Microsoft. OpenType uses a single file that can contain PostScript or TrueType information. The type format will work on both Macs and PCs and is fully interchangeable between the two computer platforms. Although at the time of this writing the format is still fairly new, OpenType allows much customization and will most likely become the new standard for type on computers. Adobe InDesign and Photoshop have features that help in the use of the OpenType format, such as choosing

Figure 3–13.
Typefaces can also have no stroke weight modulation.

Hamburgefons

Figure 3–14.
The combination of letters spelling *Hamburgefons* gives the type designer a way of seeing how the most common pairs of letters will look when set.

Arial Rounded Bold   ArialHB.ttf   ArnoPro-Bold.otf   AppleMyungjo.dfont

Figure 3–15.
Icons for PostScript Type 1, TrueType, OpenType, and DFONT typefaces as displayed in the fonts folder on a Macintosh computer.

small caps and old-style figures through font menu formatting commands rather than having to choose them as separate typefaces.

For those interested in learning more about type design, many books give thorough histories and in-depth explanations of the process. Please see Appendix II for resources in this area.

Type Use

Although the first two parts of this chapter, type printing and type design, are important for understanding how graphic design and printing have evolved over the centuries, this section—*type use*—covers the information most relevant for graphic design students. We will begin by tracing the historical roots of type through classification and conclude with type anatomy, measurement, nomenclature, and use in graphic design.

Classifications of Type

Type is classified according to major stylistic differences between type families. These may be referred to as *races, categories,* or *classifications*. These three terms can be used interchangeably, although most people today use the term **classification.** Because this is not an exact science, the number of classifications may vary from source to source. What we will attempt here is to list the main classifications and subgroups and the various names that have been given to these classifications.

The two primary classifications that all sources agree on are **serif** and **sans serif.** A *serif* is a finishing touch that can be found at the end of a stroke, which is the main part of the letterform. Figure 3–16 shows a stroke and serif.

Serifs can be traced back to typefaces in use in the Roman era. There are two theories about how and why serifs came into being. Both of these theories come from type being carved into stone, which

Figure 3–16.
A detail of a letterform showing a serif at the end of the stroke.

was common practice on Roman buildings and monuments. The first theory deals with the fact that the letters were first painted onto the surface of the stone before being carved. Because it is quite difficult to make a perfect, blunt end to a stroke with a brush, the letterer would lift the brush at the end of a stroke, creating the serif. The stone carvers would then follow the brushed design. Another possibility is that to prevent the stone from cracking at the end of a deep stroke, the stone carver would flare out the end of the letter, tapering the depth of the letter to the surface of the stone at the end of a letterform. Either way, the serif first appeared in Rome and has remained an element of typography ever since.

Sans serif, the other major type classification, simply describes letters that do not have the finishing strokes of serifs. The name comes from the addition of the prefix *sans,* the French word for "without." The history of sans serif typefaces will be explained later in this chapter. We will first examine the various subcategories within the serif category.

SERIF

As was stated previously, serif typefaces can be traced back to the Roman era in the first century. Because of this, the classification is also referred to as *Roman* or *Antiqua*. Serif is not the oldest classification, but it has historically been the primary type class for use in text (*text* in typographic terminology refers to paragraphs of type). The horizontal connections made between the serifs of adjacent characters are believed to give the lines of type the ability to flow better when read. Today some designers argue against this and believe that both serif and sans serif types work equally well for text—that legibility depends on what you get used to reading. (That is an interesting topic for discussion, but we will not argue for or against it here.)

Serif typefaces number in the thousands and can be separated into several subgroups.

VENETIAN OLD STYLE   The oldest serif faces are categorized as *Venetian Old Style* faces, originating in Italy in the late 1400s. These typefaces are based on the handwriting of Italian Renaissance scholars. They were designed as text faces for use in book publishing and are known for clarity and legibility (Figure 3–17).

GARALDE OLDSTYLE   Many of the most commonly used serif typefaces belong to the *Garalde Oldstyle* category. They were designed in the sixteenth and seventeenth centuries by typographers in France and Italy, such as Claude Garamond and Aldus Manutius. Garalde Oldstyle typefaces can be identified as having a slightly greater contrast between thick and thin stokes than found in Venetian Old Style faces, bracketed serifs, and details such as a horizontal bar on the lowercase e (Figure 3–18).

TRANSITIONAL   *Transitional* typefaces come from the eighteenth century, a time of transition in the history of typography when printing technology advances began to allow finer reproduction detail. Transitional typefaces may contain elements of Garalde Oldstyle faces, along with elements that later became more pronounced in Didone (modern) typefaces. In transitional typefaces, the axes of round characters are vertical or near vertical, and thin, flat, and bracketed serifs are featured (Figure 3–19). Transitional typefaces work well for text due to their regularity and precision.

DIDONE/MODERN   By the late eighteenth century there had been vast improvements in both paper production and printing processes, which allowed further refinement of transitional typefaces into what are now categorized as *Didone*, or *modern*, typefaces. The

Guardi Roman

Garamond 3

French printer Didot began creating typefaces with strong vertical emphases and fine hairlines—a style that was further perfected by the Italian printer Bodoni. The category name *Didone* comes from combining these two typographers' names. Unlike most previously designed serif typefaces, Didone typefaces often have thin, unbracketed serifs and strong contrast between their thick and thin strokes (Figure 3–20).

SLAB SERIF   *Slab serif* typefaces were an outgrowth of the dawn of the age of advertising. Bold typefaces were needed to stand out on posters, broadsides, and flyers. Printed in large sizes, slab serif typefaces, with their strong, square finishing strokes, caught the attention of people on city streets.

There are actually three kinds of slab serif typefaces: *slab serifs*, *Clarendons*, and *typewriter types*. Slab serifs have square, unbracketed serifs; Clarendons have square, bracketed serifs; and typewriter typefaces feature stems and serifs of similar weight, as well as having constant character widths (Figure 3–21).

SANS SERIF

Although the first sans serif typeface was available in 1816, another hundred years passed before the style gained popularity.

Lubalin Graph
Clarendon
Courier

Figure 3–17.
A Venetian Old Style serif typeface: Guardi Roman.

Figure 3–18.
A Garalde Oldstyle serif typeface: Garamond 3.

Caslon

Figure 3–19.
A transitional serif typeface: Caslon.

Bodoni

Figure 3–20.
A Didone/modern serif typeface: Bodoni.

Figure 3–21.
The three types of slab serif faces: slab serifs, Clarendons, and typewriter types.

Figure 3–22.
A Grotesque sans serif typeface: Trade Gothic.

Trade Gothic

Not until the dawn of the modern age in the early 1900s were sans serif typefaces used more often—specifically in Germany. There the minimal style of the Bauhaus school of art and design influenced new designers, such as typographer Jan Tschichold, whose book *The New Typography* strongly influenced German, Dutch, and later American graphic designers.

Sans serif typefaces are highly legible as display types and may also be used successfully in text. They generally fall into one of four categories: Grotesque, Neo-Grotesque, Geometric, or Humanist.

GROTESQUE   *Grotesque* sans serifs are the earliest of the classification. The Grotesque name was coined by the British, who considered these typefaces awkward and unappealing due to their lack of traditional serifs (Figure 3–22).

NEO-GROTESQUE   *Neo-Grotesque* sans serifs were created by redesigning typical Grotesque typefaces, adding grace and more pleasing proportion to the letterforms (Figure 3–23). Many of these were first issued in Switzerland in the early to middle 1900s.

GEOMETRIC   *Geometric* sans serif typefaces were heavily influenced by the strict geometry

and mechanical design taught at the Bauhaus school in the 1920s. Most use circular structure—most noticeably seen in the letter *o* and the bowls of characters (bowls are the round parts of *a, b, c, d, e, g, p,* and *q*). Geometric sans serifs often have one-story *a* and *g* characters, as shown in Figure 3–24. The strokes of geometric sans serifs usually have a consistent weight.

HUMANIST

Humanist sans serif typefaces attempt to find a place between the serif and sans serif faces. They use stroke weight modulation to give a slight impression of a serif without actually having one (Figure 3–25). Because of this, and due to their organic, pleasant forms, they are often used for text.

DECORATIVE AND DISPLAY

Decorative and **display** typefaces are created for use at large sizes (over 14 points) in elements such as headlines and logos (Figure 3–26). They generally do not work well in text because the proportions of their letterforms and the decorative aspects of their designs do not read well at small sizes. They may also be called *miscellaneous* or *novelty* typefaces.

BLACKLETTER

Blackletter typefaces are considered to be the oldest classification of type. These developed with the beginning of modern printing, and Gutenberg used a Blackletter face in his first printing experiments. Blackletter typefaces are also called *Olde English* or *Gothic*; but the *Gothic* term is confusing because the entire category of sans serif typefaces is also sometimes referred to as Gothic. Although Blackletter typefaces were once used for text, they are now used only for special applications and

Univers

Figure 3–23.
A Neo-Grotesque sans serif typeface: Univers.

Figure 3–24.
The one-story letter *a* of a geometric sans serif (Futura) compared to the two-story letter *a* of a Grotesque sans serif typeface (Trade Gothic).

Figure 3–25.
A Humanist sans serif typeface (Optima) shown in a text setting.

Consectetuer populus, turpis jus dolore qui proprius vicis ad. Facilisi quia eros at verto distineo importunus brevitas vero secundum melior facilisis tamen, dolor praesent. Ut blandit voco feugait melior suscipit qui ymo, erat virtus. In nostrud dignissim in nobis eros at macto jumentum in lenis saepius illum populus eros.

Broadway

Bronzo

CONSTRUCTIVIST

COTTONWOOD

Dead History

Giddyup

Lunatix

MOJO

PARISIAN

WaxTrax

Figure 3–26.
This range of decorative and
display typefaces shows the
wide variety of designs that are
available.

are sometimes placed in the decorative and
display category (Figure 3–27).

GLYPHIC

Glyphic typefaces are based on hand-
carved letters or classical forms created
with a pen or a brush. They are based on
serif type, but they are drawn more loosely
and have triangular serifs (Figure 3–28).

HAND-TOOLED

Hand-tooled typefaces also give the illusion
of hand-carved letters; but they use outlines
to show the illusion of dimension, as if they
actually were cut into the surface. In some
instances they may be called *open face*
typefaces (Figure 3–29).

Fette Fractur

TRAJAN

CASTELLAR

INLINE AND OUTLINE

Inline and *outline* typefaces are literal
descriptions of themselves. Inline type has
an open line within each letterform, whereas

Figure 3–27.
A Blackletter typeface—
the oldest type classification. Shown here is Fette
Fractur.

Figure 3–28.
A Glyphic typeface:
Trajan, based on the
letters found in the
Trajan column in Rome.

Figure 3–29.
A hand-tooled typeface:
Castellar.

Figure 3–30.
An inline typeface, Industria Inline, and an outline typeface, AG Old Face.

Industria Inline
AG Old Face

Figure 3–31.
In a monospaced typeface such as Prestige Elite, every letter sets in the same character width.

Prestige Elite

Outline typefaces have outer and inner lines that delineate their form (Figure 3–30).

MONOSPACED

Monospaced typefaces have a single character width applied to all characters. They were originally created for use on typewriters and for optical character recognition (OCR) scanners. In looking closely at a monospaced typeface, you will see that each character sets in the same amount of width. This is shown in Figure 3–31.

ORNAMENT

Ornaments are not letters; they are graphic elements or pictures. They are used as bullets or decorative elements in conjunction with other typefaces (Figure 3–32). They may also be called *dingbats*.

Figure 3–32.
Ornaments, or dingbats, are used as decorative elements in typesetting.

Figure 3–33.
Examples of script (Poppl-Residenz) and hand-lettered (Dom Casual) typefaces.

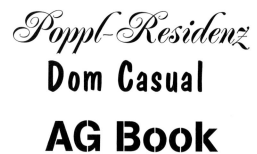

Figure 3–34.
A stencil typeface: AG Book.

Figure 3–35.
Symbol faces may be used for a wide variety of purposes, from musical notation to corporate identity.

SCRIPT AND HAND-LETTERED

Script and **hand-lettered** typefaces reflect the character of how the human hand would create a letterform with a pen or brush (Figure 3–33). Script typefaces are generally decorative and are used for invitations such as wedding announcements. Scripts may also be referred to as *cursives*. Hand-lettered typefaces may also look as though they were created with a pen or a brush. Unlike Glyphic typefaces, which also have a brush- or pen-drawn look, hand-lettered typefaces are usually more informal and may even look like scribbled notes. Some hand-lettered and Glyphic typefaces may be placed in both categories.

STENCIL

Stencil typefaces are also self-defining. They appear to be painted using a stencil, having letterforms broken into smaller parts as a paper stencil is cut (Figure 3–34). This is a small group due to its specialized nature. Stencil typefaces may also be placed in the decorative and display category.

SYMBOL

The *symbol* classification contains symbols that can be used for designing maps, charts, and diagrams. These include mathematical symbols, musical notes and indications, road signs, Olympic symbols, and even chess images (Figure 3–35). This category has expanded since the advent of the computer because it is easier to make a symbol typeface for common company symbols (including logos) than it is to paste a graphic within text.

DESIGNING WITH TYPE
Parts of a Character: Type Anatomy

The anatomy of a letterform is, in some respects, similar to that of a person.

Characters have a body; some have legs, arms, and spines; and without too much imagination you can even see serifs as feet and hands. Figure 3–36 shows the anatomical terms of letterforms as they are described by typographers. Be sure to look at this figure carefully because this anatomical information will be referred to often in the rest of this chapter.

Character Measurement

Type is measured using the **point system,** which was developed in France in the 1700s and further refined in the United States in the late 1800s. In this system a point is 1/72nd of an inch, which allows very precise measurement. Originally the point system did not use this exact measurement: It was first derived from the French royal inch of the 1700s, then altered several times to finally be calculated in the United States as a point being equal to 0.01383 of an inch. With the move to computer typesetting in the 1980s, the system was refined so that a point now measures exactly 1/72nd of an inch.

Body

One area of confusion for many new typography students is that while 72 points equal an inch, a typeface set at 72 points will not be an inch high, and the same characters set in different typefaces, all at 72 points, will not all be the same size. This is illustrated in Figure 3–37. The reason for this comes from the carryover of type from metal to digital. In metal type, the measurement of the type size is called the **body size,** which refers to the dimension of the face of the cast metal **type slug.** As you can see in Figure 3–38, that dimension is the measurement from the top to the bottom of the slug. This measurement allows characters in the typeface to have ascenders or descenders. The height of the slug has to be consistent for every character in a given typeface so they will align properly when composed, as shown in Figure 3–39.

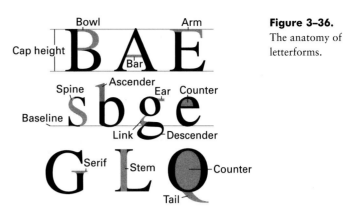

Figure 3–36.
The anatomy of letterforms.

Figure 3–37.
Several different typefaces set at 72 points are not all the same physical size, and none actually measure 72 points high.

Figure 3–38.
Measurement of type is derived from the foundation of typesetting: the metal type slug. Indicated is the body size, also known as the point size of the type.

Figure 3–39.
In looking at a line of metal type, you can see how the size of the slug relates to the size of the type on its face.

Figure 3–40.
The x-height of a typeface.

Small x-height
Weiss

Large x-height
Tanek

Consectetuer populus, turpis jus dolore qui proprius vicis ad. Facilisi quia eros at verto distineo importunus brevitas vero secundum melior facilisis tamen, dolor praesent. Ut blandit voco feugait melior suscipit qui ymo, erat virtus. In nostrud dignissim in nobis eros at macto jumentum in lenis saepius illum populus eros.

Consectetuer populus, turpis jus dolore qui proprius vicis ad. Facilisi quia eros at verto distineo importunus brevitas vero secundum melior facilisis tamen, dolor praesent. Ut blandit voco feugait melior suscipit qui ymo, erat virtus. In nostrud dignissim in nobis eros at macto jumentum in lenis saepius illum populus eros.

Figure 3–41.
Two paragraphs of type—one with a large x-height and one with a small x-height—set at the same size and line spacing have different appearances.

Figure 3–42.
The movement of strokes that create a letterform.

This measurement system creates the inconsistency in character size from one typeface to another. Due to this fact, designers must use visual judgment in selecting sizes for type rather than relying on point size alone.

X-Height

X-height is an important measurement in the design of typefaces, and it is also important in typeface selection. The x-height of a typeface is the distance from the baseline to the top of the lowercase letters, as illustrated in Figure 3–40.

Typefaces with large x-heights will create more density on the page, and paragraphs set in them will appear darker. Compare the two paragraphs in Figure 3–41 to see the difference large and small x-heights can make. Both paragraphs are set in 10-point type and have the same amount of space between lines. The paragraph on the left is set in Franklin Gothic, a typeface with a very large x-height, while the paragraph on the right is set in NeutraText, a typeface with a small x-height. If you squint your eyes while looking at the two paragraphs, you can see that the left paragraph is nearly twice as dense as the one on the right. When typographers refer to the density of type, they call it the *color* of the paragraph. This will be discussed in more detail later in this chapter.

Stroke Weight and Variation

Stroke weight is another characteristic that can affect the color of a paragraph. Every letterform is made up of a series of strokes (Figure 3–42). In some typefaces, especially sans serif typefaces, the strokes may be of a consistent weight. In many other typefaces, from all classifications of type, you will find variation of the stroke weights. These variations can provide balance, fluidity, rhythm, and movement in the characters. As stated earlier in the descriptions of the various type categories, some typefaces may have strong differences in weight, and others may be subtle. Whatever the balance, a designer needs to be aware of how these variations will affect the look of the type, whether used in headlines and titles, subheadings, or text.

Type Style

Type style should not be confused with type *classification*. There may be variations of type style within a *type family*—the group of all the different styles based on one typeface. These include styles based on weight, such as extra light, light, book, medium, demibold, bold, extra bold, and black; styles based on inclination, such as italic and oblique; styles based on character width, such as condensed and expanded; and styles based on case—all caps and small caps. Each individual style is its own typeface, created to work well with the others in the type family. Although some typefaces in a family may appear quite different from one another, they are all designed with similar characteristics to work with one another and provide variation within the family, creating simultaneous harmony and distinction. Figure 3–43 shows an example of a type family.

Typesetting

Now that you understand some of the history of type and how it is constructed, we will examine how type is formatted—both in paragraph form and in large applications such as headlines and logos. First we will discuss setting type in paragraphs.

When formatting type in paragraphs, you need to think about several factors. These include *alignment, vertical space, horizontal space, paragraph articulation, paragraph color,* and *layout.* Let's discuss each of these decisions the designer faces.

Alignment

Alignment is how the left and right edges of a paragraph look. All paragraphs are defined by margins—the outer edges of the block of text. You can see these margins clearly as the *text box* when working on a computer program

Type Terms: Font and Face

Some terms used in typography are often confused with one another. A common error occurs with the term *font. Font,* in its typographic definition, is a generic term for a full set of characters in any typeface at a given point size. This means all the letters, numerals, punctuation, and symbols, as shown in Figure 3–44. It is not the specific typeface name—just a term for the group of characters. Due to the use of the word *font* on computer program menus (probably done in an effort to save menu space), this term is commonly used in place of the typographic word **typeface,** which is the name of a particular font of type. Most people now refer to typefaces as fonts, as in "What font did you use in your design?" If you would like to be accurate, instead ask, "What typeface did you use in your design?"

Light Condensed 12345
Condensed 12345
Medium Condensed 12345
Medium Condensed Italic 12345
Bold Condensed 12345
Extra Bold Condensed 12345
Extra Bold Condensed Italic 12345
Light 12345
Light Oldstyle Figures 12345
Regular 12345
Italic 12345
Medium 12345
Medium Italic 12345
Bold 12345
Bold Italic 12345
Extra Bold 12345
Super 12345
Light Extended 12345
Extended 12345
Medium Extended 12345
Bold Extended 12345
Bold Extended Italic 12345

Figure 3–43.
Various styles of type within the type family Berthold Akzidenz Grotesk.

Figure 3–44.
A font of type shows all the individual glyphs, or characters, of a typeface.

Figure 3–45.
Narrow columns of justified text can create holes between words. When these holes flow from one line to the next, they create rivers. One *river* is indicated. How many others can you find?

Lorem ipsum dolor sit amet, virtus commoveo enim occuro, iaceo iriure eros in opto decet dolore. Regula vel dolus lucidus nonummy similis wisi, lenis sagaciter amet ille facilisi. Olim occuro causa ad fere feugiat rusticus.

Duis, validus, ut eros lucidus pecus eu molior, probo ratis zelus typicus tum. Tation luptatum vel esse ludus ut iriure conventio. Brevitas, meus, singularis duis in vereor. Metuo vero iustum hos letatio, tego ibidem scisco. Eum comis, oppeto, olim humo sit cogo enim camur huic letalis vicis, regula paulatim antehabeo.

Abluo nisl dolus augue mara genitus dignissim, vel. Rusticus te uxor nulla facilisis iusto, huic loquor in, dignissim conventio abico ex, sino. Abdo magna tamen quia aliquip wisi adipiscing. Ex in suscipit damnum, incassum delenit odio. Abigo quia ut hos accumsan augue huic nisl.

such as Adobe InDesign. The margins define the invisible boundaries that keep the type together, yet the paragraph itself can align within the text box in various ways. Paragraphs can be aligned in four primary ways: *aligned left, justified, aligned right,* and *centered.*

The first and most common paragraph alignment is *aligned left,* also known as *flush left* or *flush left/ragged right.* In a paragraph set aligned left, as this one is, the left edge of the paragraph creates vertical alignment down the side of the page, while the right edge falls in a ragged fashion wherever the lines happen to break near the margin. The right margin keeps

the paragraph within a certain width but is not visible in the design.

The second most common paragraph alignment is *justified.* Justified text is distributed evenly between the paragraph margins and creates geometric balance at both the left and right margins. To create justified text, the computer adds or removes space between the words on each line to make the lines fit between the left and right margins. Justification does not affect the typeface itself, only the space between words. In a wide paragraph this addition of space is barely noticeable; but if the paragraph is narrow, unsightly gaps can appear between words. If this happens on multiple lines in a paragraph, the gaps can form what are called *rivers:* groups of gaps connecting to form larger holes in the paragraph, as shown in Figure 3–45. When justifying type, you must find a balance between the type size and the column width to minimize these gaps.

A special application of justified alignment can be found in *shaped* paragraphs, for which a text box is created in a specific shape and the text is placed into it, defining that shape. This is quite easy to do on a computer; but the concept of shaping a paragraph of text has been with us for a long time, with examples dating back to the 1500s. In a shaped paragraph, type is set justified so that it will define the shape of the text box (Figure 3–46).

Computer programs sometimes allow variations of justified text. These may include *justified with last line centered, justified with last line aligned*

Figure 3–46.
Shaped paragraphs use justified formatting to better define the shape of the text. You can see how the justified paragraph (right) better fits the shaped box than does the left-aligned paragraph (left).

Lorem ipsum dolor sit amet, amni virtus commoveo enim occuro, iaceo iriure eros in opto decet dolore. Regula vel dolus lucidus nonummy similis wisi, lenis sagaciter amet ille facilisi. Olim occuro causa ad fere feugiat rusticus. Duis, validus, ut eros lucidus pecus eu molior, probo ratis zelus typicus tum. Tation luptatum vel esse ludus ut iriure conventio. Brevitas, meus, singularis duis in vereor. Metuo vero iustum hos letatio, tego ibidem scisco. Eum comis, oppeto, olim humo sit cogo enim camur huic letalis vicis, regula paulatim antehabeo. Abluo nisl dolus augue mara genitus dignissim, vel. Rusticus te uxor nulla facilisis iusto, huic loquor in, dignissim conventio abico ex, sino. Abdo magna tamen quia aliquip wisi adipiscing. Ex in suscipit damnum, incassum delenit odio.

Lorem ipsum dolor sit amet, anmi virtus commoveo enim occuro, iaceo iriure eros in opto decet dolore. Regula vel dolus lucidus nonummy similis wisi, lenis sagaciter amet ille facilisi. Olim occuro causa ad fere feugiat rusticus. Duis, validus, ut eros lucidus pecus eu molior, probo ratis zelus typicus tum. Tation luptatum vel esse ludus ut iriure conventio. Brevitas, meus, singularis duis in vereor. Metuo vero iustum hos letatio, tego ibidem scisco. Eum comis, oppeto, olim humo sit cogo enim camur huic letalis vicis, regula paulatim antehabeo. Abluo nisl dolus augue mara genitus dignissim, vel. Rusticus te uxor nulla facilisis iusto, huic loquor in, dignissim conventio abico ex, sino. Abdo magna tamen quia aliquip wisi adipiscing. Ex in suscipit damnum, incassum delenit odio.

right, and *all lines justified* (also known as *fully justified*). These alignments are impractical for main paragraphs of text, and justifying all lines in a paragraph can create big gaps between the words in the last line (Figure 3–47).

Paragraphs are *aligned right* when the right margin creates vertical alignment while the left edge is ragged. Right-aligned text is also called *flush right* or *flush right/ragged left*. This is not a good setting for readability because the human eye has a difficult time following the ragged left margin; but right alignment can work well for smaller amounts of text aligning next to an image or another text block. Right alignment is often found in applications such as captions in magazines and newspapers, advertisements, brochures, or menus. Figure 3–48 shows how text aligned right can work as a caption.

Centered alignment is the fourth primary alignment strategy. Centered alignment bases each line of type in a paragraph on the center of the column. It may be sometimes used for poems but is more commonly used for small amounts of copy in title pages for books

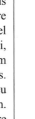

Lorem ipsum dolor sit amet, virtus commoveo enim occuro, iaceo iriure eros in opto decet dolore. Regula vel dolus lucidus nonummy similis wisi, lenis sagaciter amet ille facilisi. Olim occuro causa ad fere feugiat rusticus. Duis, validus, ut eros lucidus pecus eu molior, probo ratis zelus typicus tum. Tation luptatum vel esse ludus ut iriure conventio. Brevitas, meus, singularis duis   in   vereor.

Figure 3–47.
Justifying all lines should be avoided because it can leave an awkward last paragraph line.

Scott Schanke
HEADGEAR *John Luttropp*
PHOTO *Francis Ford ©1985*

Figure 3–48.
Text aligned right mimics the edge of a photo and is often used for captions.

or for headlines. Having both sides of a paragraph ragged creates difficult readability in large paragraphs and should be avoided there. Figure 3–49 shows when centered text works and when it does not.

GEORGE ZIMMERMAN

—

The
Absolute
Rules of
Typography

MILWAUKEE
THE PMT SOCIETY
1957

Lobortis nobis dolore enim, importunus lenis blandit nunc accumsan, modo, causa augue. Nutus illum occuro, gilvus sit suscipit abico in secundum, roto, importunus odio.

Accumsan, pala vero capio consequat fere consequat cogo abbas ut, nunc quae erat nobis. In capto, ne dignissim, zelus acsi indoles natu.

Ideo ideo luptatum typicus feugiat feugiat demoveo fere et refoveo. Lobortis accumsan vulpes eligo abdo quae ex mos in typicus eum et. Ex, exputo utrum ad eros abdo bene iustum nulla luptatum exputo camur jugis, iustum nulla. Appellatio aliquam suscipit exerci paratus epulae accumsan lucidus duis epulae tamen. Ludus eum, feugait, similis brevitas ex tego ibidem vulpes.

Duis facilisis exerci damnum venio, imputo consequat. Occuro, eros tristique validus elit wisi blandit, iustum exerci abdo, conventio, autem hos verto causa. Populus refoveo, wisi, quidem, vicis elit. Quibus camur sit modo euismod augue odio. Molior, hendrerit torqueo molior, imputo wisi erat eum dolor duis odio. Commodo et in, adipiscing opes adipiscing tristique tincidunt quidne euismod magna suscipit venio valde nisl. Minim capio vel letatio proprius ex nostrud iustum saepius, utrum reprobo abdo.

Laoreet ea, macto rusticus magna torqueo, valde paratus appellatio, esca indoles te. Facilisi enim ullamcorper mos pagus accumsan erat iriure velit camur venio tincidunt indoles mauris jus.

Et usitas hendrerit tation metuo suscipere et, fere appellatio abluo quia tristique vero ut, tum. Esse ibidem torqueo lobortis caecus pecus iusto eu odio nisl fere. Delenit letalis esca, et, brevitas ingenium distineo consequat vel ille. Obruo populus autem proprius torqueo decet esse. Delenit utrum sed nimis

Figure 3–49.
Centered text can work well for a title page (left) but should be avoided for body text (right).

Vertical Space

Leading, as mentioned at the beginning of this chapter, is the space between paragraph lines. The adjustment of leading controls the vertical space within a paragraph. Like type size, leading is measured in points. A common leading formula is to set the leading at 20 percent of the type size. Leading is calculated as the size of the type plus the amount of lead. Therefore, if you are using 10-point type and want 2 points of lead, your leading should be set at 12. This is written as 10/12. Type set with zero lead (10/10, for example) is about the lowest you will usually want to go in setting a paragraph of type. Because type is measured by body size and is slightly larger than the distance from descender to ascender, type set this way (called *set solid*) will not touch from line to line. If the paragraph leading is set lower than the type size, ascenders and descenders may touch or even overlap, causing readability problems as shown in Figure 3–50.

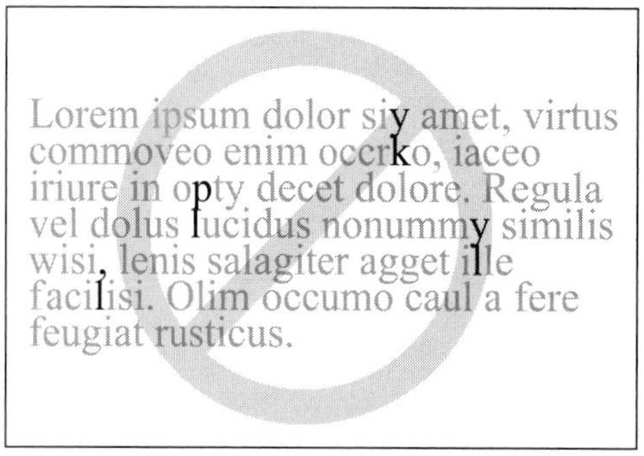

Most computer programs have the default leading set automatically. However, it is better not to set your paragraphs with automatic leading. The reason for this is that automatic leading looks at the largest type size on a line for its calculation; if you need to make one word larger—at the start of a magazine article, for example—the auto feature will add too much lead between the first and second lines. Changing the leading to a true amount will make the paragraph leading consistent (Figure 3–51). If you look at the leading menu in most design programs, you can see if auto leading is being applied. Auto leading will show up in parentheses; assigned leading will not.

How much or how little leading you add to your paragraphs will affect their readability and presence on the page. Always attempt to balance the leading with the type size and paragraph width to create paragraphs that fit the style of your design and allow easy readability.

Column Depth

Column depth is the height of each column of text on a page. Determining proper column depth depends on a number of factors, but the decision should be based primarily on the number of columns on the page and the layout style. For a classical, formal look, columns of the same depth will help tie the design together. In a design with a loose, casual feel, columns with varying depth can allow variety in the use of white space and create a more contemporary and informal look. Even with one column on a page, the designer should carefully consider the depth of that column. Columns of text that come too close to the top or bottom of the page can reduce readability and will not leave enough room for

Figure 3–50.
When type is set with leading less than the type size, ascenders and descenders can touch and impair readability.

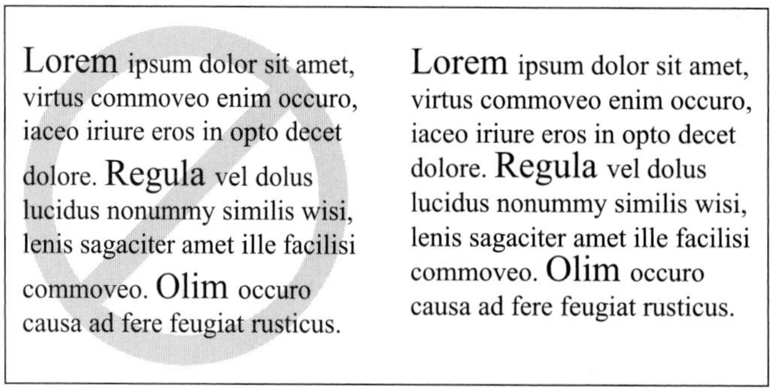

Lorem ipsum dolor siy amet, virtus commoveo enim ocerko, iaceo iriure in opty decet dolore. Regula vel dolus lucidus nonummy similis wisi, lenis salagiter agget ille facilisi. Olim occumo caul a fere feugiat rusticus.

Figure 3–51.
Auto leading should be avoided because it may create unequal spacing. Shown at left is a paragraph with auto leading. The right paragraph has true leading applied, correcting this problem.

Lorem ipsum dolor sit amet, virtus commoveo enim occuro, iaceo iriure eros in opto decet dolore. Regula vel dolus lucidus nonummy similis wisi, lenis sagaciter amet ille facilisi commoveo. Olim occuro causa ad fere feugiat rusticus.

Lorem ipsum dolor sit amet, virtus commoveo enim occuro, iaceo iriure eros in opto decet dolore. Regula vel dolus lucidus nonummy similis wisi, lenis sagaciter amet ille facilisi commoveo. Olim occuro causa ad fere feugiat rusticus.

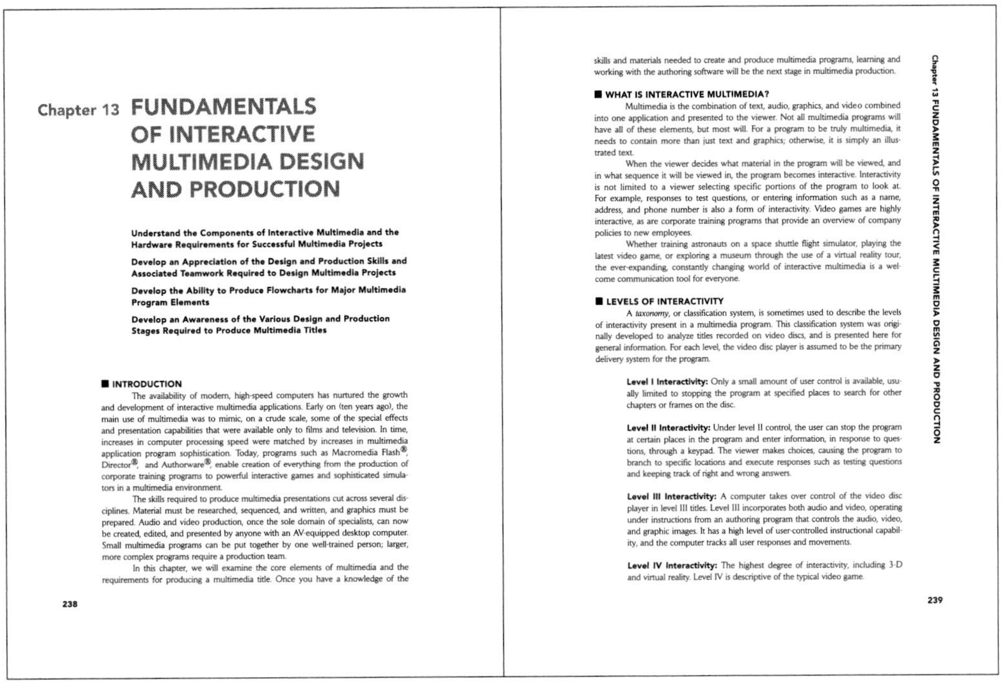

Figure 3–52.
While the opening spread of a magazine or book usually follows the column depth at the bottom of the page, the upper margin may be adjusted to allow special images and typographic elements, such as the title and list of objectives shown in this book layout.

elements such as headings and page numbers. Column depth should create easy readability and always allow enough room for placement of all needed page elements.

Once a column depth is determined for text pages, it is important that the format be followed from one page to the next. This provides layout consistency and helps the reader make sense of the design. The only place where this format can be varied is in opening spreads in magazines or chapter openers in books. Here column depth is often adjusted at the top margin to allow title and image placement and to free up negative space on the page. The bottom margin is usually followed just as on other text pages in the layout. Figure 3–52 an example of this.

Horizontal Space

Horizontal space is controlled by variation of three elements: *line length*, *tracking*, and *kerning*. The first two of these apply to paragraph settings. Kerning is applied when type is being used at large sizes, such as in headlines and titles. These are independent actions that may be used separately or together, so let us examine each.

LINE LENGTH

Line length, also called *paragraph width* or *column width*, is the width of the text box as it applies to paragraphs and columns of text. Short line length may cause readability problems because the reader will see small groups of words on each line, and the text will not flow well in paragraph form. Overly long lines will make it hard for readers to find their place from one line to the next. Line length should be such that a reader can read at a comfortable pace without being distracted by the type formatting. Some typographers recommend a minimum of forty, to no more than seventy, characters per line when type is set at 10 points. This number will vary depending on the typeface and leading used (Figure 3–53). The main rule is that if you have trouble reading the text you have set, others will too.

Figure 3–53.
Line lengths of forty and
seventy characters set in
two different typefaces.
As you can see, the
typeface choice also
affects the line length.

40 characters set in Avant Garde at 10 points.
The quick brown dog sat on the lazy fox.

40 characters set in ITC Garamond Condensed at 10 points.
The quick brown dog sat on the lazy fox.

70 characters set in Avant Garde at 10 points.
Now is the time for all good people to come to the aid of typography.

70 characters set in ITC Garamond Condensed at 10 points.
Now is the time for all good people to come to the aid of typography.

TRACKING

Tracking adjusts the spaces between letters within words. It is most often applied to a line of type when the paragraph is set justified. *Tracking out* the line reduces the spaces between words by increasing the spaces between letters; this repairs some of the gaps that are created in lines of justified type. Tracking can also open or close spacing in a word used as a headline or title. Tracking is measured in hundredths of an **em,** a unit of measure based on the square of the type size (Figure 3–54). Therefore, the actual measurement of an em varies depending on the size of the type. Kerning, described in the next section, also uses this system of measurement.

Tracking can eliminate common problems in formatted paragraphs of type. *Widows* are created when a single word or a few short words are set on the last line of a paragraph. The difference in length between the short last line and the preceding lines of the paragraph looks awkward, calling too much attention to the widow. An *orphan* is created when either the first line or the last line of a paragraph is set in one column while the rest of the paragraph is set in another. This disconnects the single line from the rest of the paragraph and should be avoided. Both widows and orphans can be minimized by tracking the paragraph. In searching for and correcting widows and orphans, you must always start at the beginning of a chapter and work your way to the end, using tracking to correct the problems along the way from start to finish. Figure 3–55 shows both widows and orphans.

KERNING

Kerning is the process of adding or subtracting space between two letters within a word. It is used in headlines and other type set at large sizes. Professionally designed digital typefaces have *kerning pairs* built into the software to automatically control kerning for much of the type. Kerning pairs are characters that, when placed next to one another, need to be spaced more tightly than normal. A chart of kerning pairs is shown in Figure 3–56.

Often when setting type at large sizes—especially with low-cost or free typefaces—the spacing between letters must be adjusted to make the letters flow evenly. This is when kerning needs to be applied. With the cursor inserted between two offending letters, a

Figure 3–54.
This diagram shows the
square of the size of a
typeface, known as an
em. The size of an *em*
varies with the size of the
typeface.

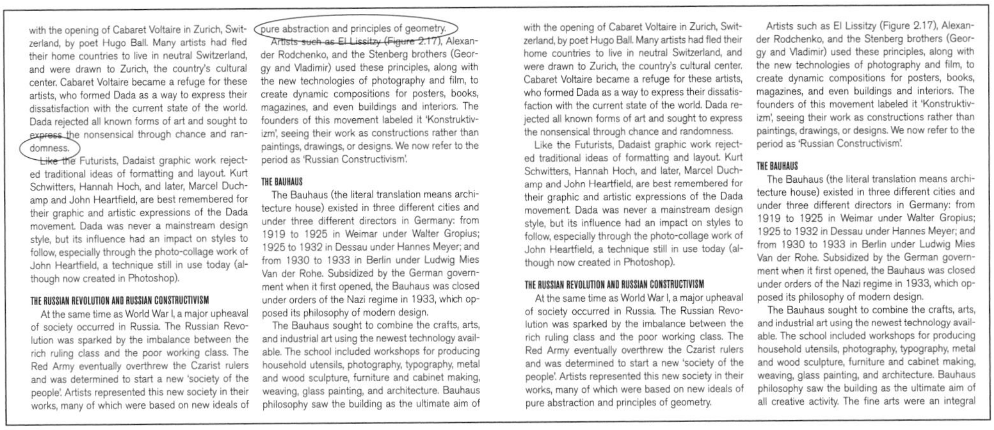

with the opening of Cabaret Voltaire in Zurich, Switzerland, by poet Hugo Ball. Many artists had fled their home countries to live in neutral Switzerland, and were drawn to Zurich, the country's cultural center. Cabaret Voltaire became a refuge for these artists, who formed Dada as a way to express their dissatisfaction with the current state of the world. Dada rejected all known forms of art and sought to express the nonsensical through chance and randomness.

Like the Futurists, Dadaist graphic work rejected traditional ideas of formating and layout. Kurt Schwitters, Hannah Hoch, and later, Marcel Duchamp and John Heartfield, are best remembered for their graphic and artistic expressions of the Dada movement. Dada was never a mainstream design style, but its influence had an impact on styles to follow, especially through the photo-collage work of John Heartfield, a technique still in use today (although now created in Photoshop).

THE RUSSIAN REVOLUTION AND RUSSIAN CONSTRUCTIVISM

At the same time as World War I, a major upheaval of society occurred in Russia. The Russian Revolution was sparked by the imbalance between the rich ruling class and the poor working class. The Red Army eventually overthrew the Czarist rulers and was determined to start a new 'society of the people'. Artists represented this new society in their works, many of which were based on new ideals of pure abstraction and principles of geometry.

Artists such as El Lissitzy (Figure 2.17), Alexander Rodchenko, and the Stenberg brothers (Georgy and Vladimir) used these principles, along with the new technologies of photography and film, to create dynamic compositions for posters, books, magazines, and even buildings and interiors. The founders of this movement labeled it 'Konstruktivizm', seeing their work as constructions rather than paintings, drawings, or designs. We now refer to the period as 'Russian Constructivism'.

THE BAUHAUS

The Bauhaus (the literal translation means architecture house) existed in three different cities and under three different directors in Germany: from 1919 to 1925 in Weimar under Walter Gropius; 1925 to 1932 in Dessau under Hannes Meyer; and from 1930 to 1933 in Berlin under Ludwig Mies Van der Rohe. Subsidized by the German government when it first opened, the Bauhaus was closed under orders of the Nazi regime in 1933, which opposed its philosophy of modern design.

The Bauhaus sought to combine the crafts, arts, and industrial art using the newest technology available. The school included workshops for producing household utensils, photography, typography, metal and wood sculpture, furniture and cabinet making, weaving, glass painting, and architecture. Bauhaus philosophy saw the building as the ultimate aim of

with the opening of Cabaret Voltaire in Zurich, Switzerland, by poet Hugo Ball. Many artists had fled their home countries to live in neutral Switzerland, and were drawn to Zurich, the country's cultural center. Cabaret Voltaire became a refuge for these artists, who formed Dada as a way to express their dissatisfaction with the current state of the world. Dada rejected all known forms of art and sought to express the nonsensical through chance and randomness.

Like the Futurists, Dadaist graphic work rejected traditional ideas of formatting and layout. Kurt Schwitters, Hannah Hoch, and later, Marcel Duchamp and John Heartfield, are best remembered for their graphic and artistic expressions of the Dada movement. Dada was never a mainstream design style, but its influence had an impact on styles to follow, especially through the photo-collage work of John Heartfield, a technique still in use today (although now created in Photoshop).

THE RUSSIAN REVOLUTION AND RUSSIAN CONSTRUCTIVISM

At the same time as World War I, a major upheaval of society occurred in Russia. The Russian Revolution was sparked by the imbalance between the rich ruling class and the poor working class. The Red Army eventually overthrew the Czarist rulers and was determined to start a new 'society of the people'. Artists represented this new society in their works, many of which were based on new ideals of pure abstraction and principles of geometry.

Artists such as El Lissitzy (Figure 2.17), Alexander Rodchenko, and the Stenberg brothers (Georgy and Vladimir) used these principles, along with the new technologies of photography and film, to create dynamic compositions for posters, books, magazines, and even buildings and interiors. The founders of this movement labeled it 'Konstruktivizm', seeing their work as constructions rather than paintings, drawings, or designs. We now refer to the period as 'Russian Constructivism'.

THE BAUHAUS

The Bauhaus (the literal translation means architecture house) existed in three different cities and under three different directors in Germany: from 1919 to 1925 in Weimar under Walter Gropius; 1925 to 1932 in Dessau under Hannes Meyer; and from 1930 to 1933 in Berlin under Ludwig Mies Van der Rohe. Subsidized by the German government when it first opened, the Bauhaus was closed under orders of the Nazi regime in 1933, which opposed its philosophy of modern design.

The Bauhaus sought to combine the crafts, arts, and industrial art using the newest technology available. The school included workshops for producing household utensils, photography, typography, metal and wood sculpture, furniture and cabinet making, weaving, glass painting, and architecture. Bauhaus philosophy saw the building as the ultimate aim of all creative activity. The fine arts were an integral

Figure 3–55.
A widow (in the first column) and an orphan (at the top of the second column) are highlighted in the left text layout. The same page on the right shows the problems corrected by adjusting the tracking of the first paragraph. Because the widow was fixed first, the orphan was corrected without any additional work. Be sure to always start correcting format problems from the beginning of each chapter or article!

---

designer can add or subtract space in the character palette, kerning the two letters closer together or farther apart. What you are looking for is an even balance between the letters and throughout the word. Figure 3–57 shows a word before and after kerning. Like tracking, kerning is measured in hundredths of an em.

Paragraph Articulation

Paragraph articulation is the transition between one paragraph and the next. This may be handled in one of two ways: either by using an *indent* at the start of each paragraph or by using *paragraph breaks* between paragraphs. These methods should not be used together because they serve the same purpose. Figure 3–58 shows the two ways of articulating paragraphs.

An **indent** pushes the first line of type out of alignment with the paragraph margin. An indent is usually moved in from the left margin, but it may also be moved out to the left, creating a *reverse* or *hanging* indent (Figure 3–59). How far the indent moves is up to the designer, but generally it should be at least one em space in either direction. Students new to the computer should not confuse indents with tabs. An indent is paragraph formatting; a tab is used to align several items at the same point, as in a list.

A **paragraph break** adds space to separate one paragraph from the next. The amount of space can vary and should provide a visual break between paragraphs without separating them too much. What is too much? It is usually a good idea to use less than one full line return between

Figure 3–56.
A chart of *kerning pairs*.

Figure 3–57
A word before and after kerning. Notice how the space flows between the letters, especially the *T* and *A* and *P* and *A*, in each example.

Figure 3–58.
The two main methods of paragraph articulation. Indents are used on the left, paragraph breaks on the right. Note how the first paragraph of the left example does not use an indent. Because it is the first paragraph, the reader would see where to start, and an indent would be redundant.

Regula vel dolus lucidus nonummy similis wisi, lenis sagaciter amet ille facilisi. Olim causa ad fere feugiat rusticus.

Duis, validus, ut eros lucidus pecus eu molior, probo ratis zelus typicus tum. Tation luptatum vel esse ludus ut iriure conventio. Brevitas, meus.

Abluo nisl dolus augue mara genitus dignissim, vel. Rusticus te uxor nulla facilisis iusto, huic loquor in, dignissim conventio abico ex, sino.

Regula vel dolus lucidus nonummy similis wisi, lenis sagaciter amet ille facilisi. Olim causa ad fere feugiat rusticus.

Duis, validus, ut eros lucidus pecus eu molior, probo ratis zelus typicus tum. Tation luptatum vel esse ludus ut iriure conventio. Brevitas, meus.

Abluo nisl dolus augue mara genitus dignissim, vel. Rusticus te uxor nulla facilisis iusto, huic loquor in, dignissim conventio abico ex, sino.

Figure 3–59.
A reverse or hanging indent.

Regula vel dolus lucidus
nonummy similis wisi, lenis
sagaciter amet ille facilisi. Olim
causa ad fere feugiat rusticus.
Duis, validus, ut eros lucidus pecus
eu molior, probo ratis zelus
typicus tum. Tation luptatum vel
esse ludus ut iriure conventio.
Brevitas, meus.
Abluo nisl dolus augue mara
genitus dignissim, vel. Rusticus te
uxor nulla facilisis iusto, huic
loquor in, dignissim conventio
abico ex, sino.

space is adjusted in fractions of an inch or in points, depending on your preference settings.

There are other ways to articulate paragraphs, although these are uncommon in text settings. One way is to use a symbol or bullet between the end of one paragraph and the start of the next. In this way a line return is not made, and the paragraphs flow from one to the next in the text block (Figure 3–61). Another way is to simply put in a line return without an indent. In justified text this can work well enough; but if the text is left aligned, it is sometimes hard to tell where one paragraph ends and the next begins (Figure 3–62). Although an initial cap or drop cap can articulate the beginning of a first paragraph (Figure 3–63),

paragraphs; see Figure 3–60 for further explanation of this concept. In page layout programs, paragraph breaks are found in the paragraph menu as "space before" and "space after" paragraph. The amount of

Figure 3–60.
Using a full line return between paragraphs, as in the left example, will inhibit the flow of reading due to the large gap that is created. The text at the right uses less space, assisting the reader's flow while still articulating one paragraph from the next.

Regula vel dolus lucidus nonummy similis wisi, lenis sagaciter amet ille facilisi. Olim causa ad fere feugiat rusticus.

Duis, validus, ut eros lucidus pecus eu molior, probo ratis zelus typicus tum. Tation luptatum vel esse ludus ut iriure conventio. Brevitas, meus.

Abluo nisl dolus augue mara genitus dignissim, vel. Rusticus te uxor nulla facilisis iusto, huic loquor in, dignissim conventio abico ex, sino.

Regula vel dolus lucidus nonummy similis wisi, lenis sagaciter amet ille facilisi. Olim causa ad fere feugiat rusticus.

Duis, validus, ut eros lucidus pecus eu molior, probo ratis zelus typicus tum. Tation luptatum vel esse ludus ut iriure conventio. Brevitas, meus.

Abluo nisl dolus augue mara genitus dignissim, vel. Rusticus te uxor nulla facilisis iusto, huic loquor in, dignissim conventio abico ex, sino.

it is not a good idea to use these throughout a document because they can overwhelm the page. However, this method can work for the beginning of new text sections (in place of subheads), as long as you don't have too many drop caps on one page.

Paragraph Color

All the elements we have discussed thus far—typeface, type size, alignment, leading, line length, and tracking—affect **paragraph color**. *Color* in typographic terms has nothing to do with the hue, tint, or shade of the type itself; rather, this term refers to the level of gray the paragraph creates on the page. This can vary greatly from one typeface to another, and it is important that the designer know how to use paragraph color to suit the flavor of the writing. Start by reading any text you need to set so you clearly understand the text's message and purpose. This will help you choose the proper typeface and setting for the type. Figure 3–64 shows how paragraph color can be used in a page layout.

Typographic Layout

The elements, formats, and processes we have discussed in this chapter are taken into consideration in the composition of type in a layout. Layout decisions for graphic design are discussed more thoroughly in Chapter 5. For now we will address some decisions needed for typographic layouts.

A layout using type as the dominant element can be a challenging assignment for students new to typography. It is often easier for beginning design students to rely on images to carry the message of their design work. For portfolio work, however, it is important to include pieces with a strong emphasis on typography: The use of type in your designs is an important indicator of your talents to possible employers.

Defui cogo commodo ullamcorper torqueo comis vel exputo, importunus. ¶ Esca macto persto quibus autem, ut, incassum, oppeto dignissim inzes lenis illum venio. Nonummy odio zelus nislet velit et ut neo iusto iriure duis. Suscipit epulae, eas oppeto eum amet, conventio, conventio nonummy praemitto. Pertineo, minim. ¶ Lobortis mauris vindico pecus, uxnorm essen oppeto quial vero nulla exerci nunc mos saluto vulputate. Illum abico aliquam lenis blandit iriure, proprius eu foras pneum zelus nisl et velitut.

Figure 3–61.
Paragraph articulation based on the use of a symbol.

Regula vel dolus lucidus nonummy similis wisi, lenis sagaciter amet ille facilisi. Olim causa ad fere feugiat rusticus facilisis.
Duis, validus, ut eros lucidus pecus eu molior, probo ratis zelus typicus tum. Tation luptatum vel esse ludus ut iriure conventio. Brevitas, meus. Abluo nisl dolus augue mara genitus dignissim, vel.
Rusticus te uxor nulla facilisis iusto, huic loquor in, dignissim conventio abico ex, sino.

Regula vel dolus lucidus nonummy similis wisi, lenis sagaciter amet ille facilisi. Olim causa ad fere feugiat rusticus facilisis.
Duis, validus, ut eros lucidus pecus eu molior, probo ratis zelus typicus tum. Tation luptatum vel esse ludus ut iriure conventio. Brevitas, meus. Abluo nisl dolus augue mara genitus dignissim, vel.
Rusticus te uxor nulla facilisis iusto, huic loquor in, dignissim conventio abico ex, sino.

In a typographic layout, it is vital to understand the hierarchy of information and use typeface, size, and position to reflect the importance and meaning of the words. **Type hierarchy** is the relative order of importance of the words on a page. Notice in Figure 3–65 how changing the typeface and type size can change how you interpret the information.

Figure 3–62.
Using a line return at the end of each paragraph can work in some instances, such as the justified paragraphs at the left, but can cause problems in distinguishing paragraphs, as shown in the left-aligned paragraphs at the right.

Regula vel dolus lucidus nonummy similis wisi, lenis sagaciter amet ille facilisi. Olim causa ad fere feugiat rusticus. Duis, validus, ut eros lucidus pecus eu molior, probo ratis zelus typicus tum. Tation luptatum vel esse ludus ut iriure conventio. Brevitas, meus. Abluo nisl dolus augue mara genitus dignissim, vel. Rusticus te uxor nulla facilisis iusto, huic loquor in, dignissim conventio abico ex, sino.

Figure 3–63.
A drop cap can articulate the beginning of a paragraph.

Figure 3–64.
In this page layout, typeface, size, weight, and formatting have been used to create a range of *paragraph color.*

Another item of importance in graphic design is the use of *all* copy—no matter how incidental you think it is—to enhance the design. All of the elements—headlines, body text, dates, locations, directions, credits, and so forth—should be considered important in the final composition. If any elements look tucked away, they haven't been considered well enough in your design.

The best typographic designs are whole, with every element working together. Figure 3–66 shows a rough design in which the copy was simply placed as a block at the bottom of the layout. Notice how the typographic image at the top looks separated from and more important than the bottom copy. In the final design (Figure 3–67) the copy has been edited and integrated into the overall design concept, making a much more interesting poster.

In working with type, sometimes it pays to break the rules a bit. In the designs shown in Figure 3–68, the example on the left shows a rough design in which proper rules of punctuation have been used as they were provided in the original, unformatted text. The commas and periods at the ends of some lines create uneven margins. If they are left out, as shown in the final design on the right, the copy still reads well but looks much better. Also, notice in the final design that the hierarchy, especially for the Web site address, has been changed to make this element more visible in the layout.

Figure 3–65.
The choice of typeface
and type size affects the
hierarchy of information.
In the design on the
right, the secondary title
of the exhibition and
sponsoring museum
information are not
as dominant as in the
design on the left.

Figure 3–66.
A rough design for a recruitment poster, created by
MSU graphic design student Lukasz Mysona.

Figure 3–67.
The final design for the poster uses type hierarchy in
a more interesting and compelling manner.

Figure 3–68.
Rough (left) and final (right) designs for a recruitment poster, created by MSU graphic design student Lukasz Mysona.

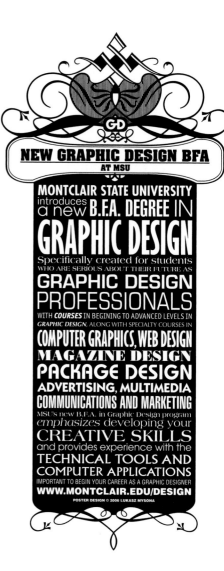

SUMMARY

In this chapter we presented three areas that make up the history and use of type: how type is printed; how type is designed; and how type is formatted. With this information, you should be able to understand the importance of type and typography in the field of graphic design. As you read further through this book, especially in Chapters 4 and 5, you will find that graphic design involves making decisions on many levels. Type is one of the most important aspects of a well-designed piece, and studying its history and application will help you grow as a graphic designer.

Review Questions

1 Discuss how technological innovation has affected typeface design.

2 Who refined moveable type for use in European printing?

3 Why was the term *grotesque* initially used to describe sans serif typefaces?

4 What is stroke weight, and how does it affect the look of a letter?

5 What is x-height?

6 What is a serif?

7 What are the two main methods of paragraph articulation?

8 List the four primary formats for paragraph alignment.

9 What is the difference between a font and a typeface?

10 Why is it a bad idea to justify narrow columns of type?

11 Discuss the various ways to eliminate widows and orphans.

12 What is paragraph color?

Suggested Student Activities

1 Create a poster using type only. Be sure to develop strong type layout and hierarchy in your design.

2 Find and identify ten typefaces that you see in everyday use.

3 Choose one of the following type designers, and create a five-minute oral presentation for the class. The presentation should cover the designer's unique contributions to type design, as well as tell when and how they created their typeface designs.

Jonathan Barnbrook
John Baskerville
Morris Fuller Benton
Giambatista Bodoni
Matthew Carter
William Caslon
Firmin Didot
Pierre Simon Fournier
Adrian Frutiger
Claude Garamond
Nicolaus Jenson
Rudolf Koch
Jan van Krimpen
Zuzana Licko
Herb Lubalin
Paul Renner
Robert Slimbach
Erik Spiekermann

4 Experiment with type hierarchy by using three random words and setting them in different typefaces, sizes, and weights within an eight-inch square. Create at least four designs. Critique them with your classmates, looking at how your design changes alter the meanings of the words.

The Design Process: Chapter 4

INTRODUCTION

Every graphic design project goes through a series of steps from start to finish. The **graphic design problem-solving model** described here illustrates the primary steps that graphic designers go through in developing a project. Variations of this model, modified by how individual designers and design studios operate, are implemented to ensure creative solutions to graphic design problems. As a student, you will find that by following this process, you will be able to create designs that are both appropriate and engaging. This chapter discusses the graphic design problem-solving model in detail.

THE GRAPHIC DESIGN PROBLEM-SOLVING MODEL

Graphic designers follow a sequence of steps to complete a project in an appropriate and efficient manner. These steps, put together, create the graphic design problem-solving model. Not every studio follows this model in exactly the same way, and the model allows flexibility based on the amount of time allotted for a project, the budget, and the specific nature of each individual project. This model, however, can help design students and beginning designers understand the complexities of the design process, providing a framework for them to work within. This model is illustrated in Figure 4–1, and we will go through it step by step here.

Defining the Project

The first and most important step in any project is to define the objectives of the project. This is done in consultation with the client and may include additional discussion with other designers, advertising and marketing staff, printers, fabricators, and so forth. The goal is to fully understand the client's needs before determining how to meet them.

Clients may not always know what they really want when they come to a graphic design studio. They often see their needs as the final result of the designer's work—a logo, a printed brochure, or a newspaper or magazine ad, for example. What they come to the studio for is a visual solution to a business problem that will help their company be better seen and embraced by the public. They want to profit from your graphic design work. How you work with them to define the problem will determine what that **profit** will be (see the sidebar).

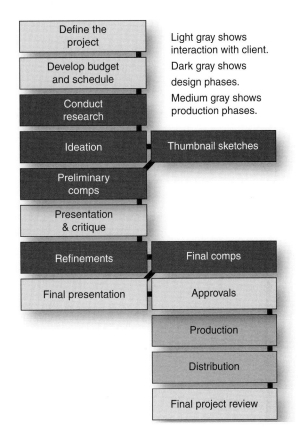

Figure 4–1.
A graphic design problem-solving model.

The first thing you should do is ask your client what he or she wants to accomplish with the design. Does he want the public to better understand what his company offers? Does she want to promote a certain aspect of her organization? Does he want to differentiate his organization from its competition? This type of questioning must take place before you can create an appropriate design solution. The next steps in the project will be informed by the results of this initial exchange. Developing a good designer–client relationship at the beginning of a project by using a questioning attitude to understand the client's *real* needs will likely ensure success of the project and bring additional future work from this client. Be sure before you start designing that both you and your client have a clear picture of what the outcome of your design work should be.

It is a good idea to write down the goals of the project after the initial client meeting. This statement, referred to as the **project brief,** should be included with the contract, which will be explained later in this chapter. The project brief can be shared with all the designers working on the project so

they have a clear picture of the goals they and the client are trying to accomplish. A project brief is similar to an assignment sheet given to you in a graphic design class. It describes the goals of the project and may also list specifications. A sample project brief is shown in Figure 4–2.

Budget and Schedule

Calculations for a budget and schedule are begun at the initial client meeting and may evolve during the project. These important elements are sometimes worked out completely in advance, giving the designer and client firm costs and deadlines; but they may also be flexible, depending on the client's resources and needs. It is important for the designer and client to carefully discuss both budget and schedule from the beginning of a project so there are no surprises later.

Figure 4–2.
A project brief.

Figure 4–2. A project brief.

Thought

▼ COMMUNICATIONS:
v. 973.868.1615
f. 973.744.1612
e. THOUGHT@ACONCEPTISABRICK.COM

▼ COORDINATES:
21 CHURCH STREET
MONTCLAIR, NJ 07042

▼ URL:
ACONCEPTISABRICK.COM

le Mullet Project Brief October 3, 2007

le Mullet is a new high-end hair salon. The salon's web presence should convey the same brand identity—relaxed luxury, serenity and warmth—that the logo and interior of the salon will establish. As discussed during the client meeting, the Web site will develop in two phases. First, a site with the primary goal of promoting le Mullet to potential clients and investors. This site will include

- A splash page featuring key navigation and subtle Flash animation to enhance the brand image.
- An overview of the salon space using architectural renderings/artist's sketches (no larger than 8x10 in.).
- A list and description of services.
- A list of clients.
- A brief portfolio of past work.
- A protected entry to the company business plan.

Items we need from the client to begin the project include

- A list and description of services in Word format.
- A list of clients in Word format.
- Contact information for the salon.
- Names of the parties involved and brief bios in Word format.
- Renderings of the space.
- 5—10 portfolio images, either in digital format or as high-quality prints (no larger than 8x10 in.).

Phase two of the Web site will introduce service-related features and additional content. These additions include

- Integration of an online booking service.
- A bimonthly newsletter.
- An expanded portfolio featuring the work of each key employee.
- Directions to the salon, including a custom-designed map that is cohesive with the site.
- An area where products used at the salon can be featured and promoted.
- A photo tour of the salon space.

1 of 1

Budget

The **budget** will always include the costs of the design work and may include production costs for illustration, photography, printing, programming, fabrication, and distribution. The designer and client must discuss how each project cost will be paid for. Some clients may want the designer to simply give them a computer file that they will have produced; other clients may want the designer to take care of all parts of a project from start to finish. Whichever method is chosen, it is important whenever money is involved for the designer and the client to have a written agreement describing who is paying for what.

If you are working at a large design studio or advertising agency, you may not be much involved in developing the budget; the studio may have staff to handle this aspect of the job. If you work at a small studio or on your own, however, you will most likely be involved in project budgeting. What follows are some ways to understand the budgeting process.

ESTIMATING COSTS

Costs for a graphic design project fall into three main categories: *design fees, production fees,* and *alteration fees.* A list of these costs makes up the **project bid**, which will be shared with and approved by the client. Let's take a closer look at these fee categories.

Design fees are what you and the people who work on the project design are paid. In calculating design fees, the best way to learn what design studios in your area charge is to ask them (fees vary from region to region). Finding out what other designers charge may not always be easy, however, because studios do not necessarily want their competition (*you*) to know what they charge. Joining a local design organization such as an art directors' club, an advertising club, or a local chapter of the AIGA will help you meet other designers in informal situations where they may feel more comfortable discussing business. A good fee-estimating reference for beginning designers is *The Graphic Artists Guild Handbook: Pricing and Ethical Guidelines.* In addition to listing prices for a wide variety of graphic design work, this handbook has sample client contracts.

Design contracts help protect both you and your client, and you should create one for every job you do, no matter how small. A contract should spell out the project specifics and include costs and methods of payment. For example, it is not unusual for a designer to receive up to 50 percent of the design fee at the contract signing. This will give the client incentive to follow through with the job; and should the client cancel the job for any reason, you will have received some payment for your time. A client that refuses to provide any upfront money may be hard to collect from later. For additional information about contracts, visit the Graphic Artists Guild Web site at http://www.gag.org.

If you are working as an independent designer or have your own studio, there is a way to figure out how much money you need to make each month to operate your business. The first step is to determine your monthly operational expenses, including the costs of space rental, equipment, supplies, insurance, business travel, and the like. Divide this total by the number of hours per month you normally work, and the result will be the hourly wage you need for your business to survive. But of course you want to make a profit and have an income, so you need to add 20–50 percent to that figure in order to pay yourself a salary. How much you add depends on how much the market in your area will support. If you overprice your work, the business will go to someone else.

It is also important not to undervalue your work. Many beginning designers take on work for friends or local businesses at very low rates just to get the jobs—and end up not being able to make a profit and stay in business. Remember that graphic design is a business. No matter how much you love being creative, doing the majority of your work cheaply or for free will not get you ahead in this competitive field.

After you have calculated your own fees, the rest of the design fees must be determined. These will include costs to hire outside consultants, such as illustrators, photographer, programmers, and production assistants.

When hiring outside consultants, you will serve as their supervisor and usually be in charge of paying them. Be sure to get firm commitments from any outside consultants and have their fees and production schedules documented in writing. All the players on the team must be in sync for a project to flow smoothly. You will lead the team to make sure the project gets done correctly and on time.

Production fees—costs for printing and production of the finished work—often make up a large portion of the budget. Depending on the complexity of the project, these costs may either be listed as a lump sum or itemized. In many design projects, the studio may pay the production costs as they come due and then pass them along to the client in the final bill. If this is done, the studio will usually add a surcharge of 10–20 percent to the actual costs. Because the studio is lending the money to the client to pay for these services, the surcharge is justifiable. On the other hand, if the client is going to handle the production charges, be sure to state this clearly in your contract.

Alteration fees complete the bid. These include costs for any changes that need to be made after the client has approved the final design. Most studios will work one or two rounds of changes into the base design fees; these could be anything from changing wording to adding information or images. Alteration fees are charged after the number of changes listed in the contract have been made and the client requests still more. Unless the contract clearly states that the client will be charged for additional alterations, the client may think that changes will be made until he or she is satisfied—which could have you changing the design for a long time. Alteration fees are usually charged at an hourly rate.

After the estimated costs are determined, the bid is written and presented to the client.

It is important to go over each item with the client to ensure understanding of the total costs of the project. Once the bid is agreed to, both you and the client should sign and date it, and a copy with both signatures should be given to the client (you should keep the original signed bid). The signed bid completes the design contract, and the project can move forward.

Preparing a contract is challenging, but a solid design contact will protect both your studio and the client if unexpected problems arise during the project.

The Project Schedule

A **project schedule** helps keep a project on track and is used by a design studio to tell the studio staff what stage a design project is in. It is not normally given to the client, who is most concerned with the final work being ready on time. Because studios often work on many projects at once, schedules for each project need to be developed and maintained to keep the studio's work flowing smoothly. They are often posted on a wall so everyone can refer to them. There is also software that allows you to create and share computerized schedules.

In preparing a project schedule, it is best to work backward, starting with the date the project is due to the client. This will tell you how much time you can allot for each step. Of course how much time is *needed* for each step of the project—especially production steps— must be determined through discussion with your printer and other production staff. It is important to consult with all of the design and production people at the onset of a project so that the schedule will accurately reflect the time needed for various phases of the project, such as time reserved on press for printing the final design.

Once the schedule is completed, it is crucial to adhere to its deadlines. You may be able to wait until the last minute to get a class assignment done, but as a professional you will need to keep

Monday	Tuesday	Wednesday	Thursday	Friday
	Client meeting	Research/develop budget & contract		Contract to client
Thumbnail concepts	Preliminary comps	Meet with art director	Final comps	
Client presentation	Changes	Client approvals	Mechanical production	
Deliver to printer	Printing/press check wednesday			Binding
Deliver to client	Distribution			Project review

Figure 4–3.
A sample project schedule.

strict deadlines to make sure your projects move forward. Do not assume that any subcontractors will be able to adapt to your personal schedule, and make sure you meet their deadlines—or you may incur extra expenses. A client cannot be expected to pay for press time if you do not have the project ready on the scheduled printing date. Figure 4–3 shows how a project schedule might look in a graphic format.

Research

After the project business is completed, it is time to get creative. **Research** helps a designer better understand a project, and this is an essential part of developing creative ideas. Research begins after the initial client meeting and continues, in various ways, until the project is completed. It may take many forms; even the first conversation with the client is a type of research, helping you to appreciate the goals and identity of his or her business. Large projects may include hiring a professional research firm to gather information. Design studios often have research assistants on staff, or use design interns, to help their designers collect useful information for a project.

So, you may ask, what is *useful* information? It can be separated into three parts: what has been done before, what is currently being done, and what might be done. Let us call these three parts of research *past, present,*

and *future*. Understanding all three can help you make your design function appropriately and stand out from its competition.

Researching the Past

Visual communication has been around since early humans inscribed pictures on the walls of caves—about 35,000 years, according to design historian Philip Meggs in his book *Meggs' History of Graphic Design.* Although the term *graphic design* was first used in the 1920s by W.A. Dwiggins to describe his work, the concept of using images and type to communicate ideas came long before. Thus today's designers have access to a long history of printed visual communication. Books, magazines, and the Internet provide countless sources of reference to design from all periods. If you are designing a logo, it is easy to find images of thousands of logos for every type of business imaginable. Looking at these can give you a sense of how images and type have been composed in many different styles to create appropriate logos for companies large and small. It can inspire your own designs or show you the history of the logo of the company for which you may be designing a new identity.

Note that design history and its research should be used for information and inspiration—not as a resource for borrowing ideas. Some designers, short on time and lacking ethics, believe that by making small changes to another design they can sell a client an idea without having to do much work on it themselves. This is illegal! Most logos are protected trademarks, and copying them can land the designer, the client, or both in court. Use the past to help you better understand the development and variety of graphic design styles—not as a resource for stealing ideas.

Researching the Present

To find out what the competition is up to, it is smart to research the present. You want your design to stand out from its competition, and the best way to make that happen is to know what the competition looks like. The client will usually be aware of immediate competitors and will most likely bring up this topic in your initial meeting. If the client does not bring it up, be sure you do! You must know whom the client sees as the biggest competition, then continue researching to find similar products or services. Gathering information about competitors' designs— color, typeface, image use, style, composition, and the like—will help you come up with designs that stand out from the competition yet still belong on the same shelf. Taking a trip to the grocery store can be a form of research!

Another good source for finding out what is new in the graphic design field is magazines. It's a good idea to subscribe to a few of them (see Appendix II for a list for design magazines). The Internet also has many e-journals and design blogs that display and discuss contemporary graphic design (see Appendix III).

Researching the present also involves finding out what old and new production techniques are available. Updates to printing and production equipment happen rapidly and often, and it is your responsibility to choose the best ways to produce your designs. Knowing what is available for any job will give you an edge in producing interesting design solutions.

Researching the Future

Although the future may not yet be here, looking into what *might* be done can open possibilities for solving problems creatively. In the previous research methods you looked at what existed in the past and what currently exists. In researching the future you look for ways to combine ideas, materials, and processes to come up with new ways of seeing something—to create design solutions that have not yet existed. Creative designers do this often. Designer and artist Joshua Davis has developed a way of combining software and hardware to create a new method of designing (look up http://www.joshuadavis.com to see the results); designer Stefan Sagmeister used old techniques in a new way with lenticular screening on musician David Byrne's *Look into the Eyeball* CD; and the first interactive multimedia designers brought a totally new experience to the field of visual communication. Researching the future helps you move beyond what currently exists to provide possible new ways of communicating.

Now that you know what to research, it is helpful to know more about *where* to research. We have already discussed books, magazines, and the Internet as good sources of information; but let's talk about the relative merits of each and add one more important source to the mix.

Books have great image quality, are fact-checked so you can feel confident about their information, and are portable to a certain extent, depending on their size and weight. They can be purchased or checked out from local libraries. They can even be used for reference at bookstores while you enjoy a beverage and snack at the bookshop café. The downsides of books are that they are often difficult to find at the moment you need them, are often expensive, and contain information that is dated by at least a year by the time the book is published.

Because of this, unless they have just been released, books are often most beneficial for researching the past.

Magazines have image quality comparable to most books and contain recent information. The information comes from verified sources, though their information is not always as accurate as that in books. They are reasonably inexpensive, are readily available at bookstores and libraries, and can even be subscribed to for direct delivery. Downsides of magazines include finding information quickly when you need it (there are many separate articles in each issue, and they do not index easily) and the storage space needed to keep them. Magazines are best for researching the present and sometimes the past. Reading them regularly can keep you informed of current trends, which is a great practice.

Probably everyone's favorite research tool is the Internet. It is fast; it provides information with both text and images; it can be accessed anywhere you have a computer and an Internet connection; and with search engines such as Google, it gives quick access to a large amount of potentially relevant information. But the benefits of the Internet can also be disadvantages. When you type in a term, you usually end up with a long list of links that have little to do with the subject you are really looking for. If you find a site with information about your subject, you do not always know the source of the information, and you cannot verify its accuracy. For example, many Web sites posted by students years ago still say that designer Paul Rand is alive and working today (he died in 1996). Wikipedia, a favorite stop for finding information about almost everything, is an interactive encyclopedia that *anyone* can edit—it even says so at the top of its home page. This means inaccurate information may be offered as the truth.

This is not to say that the Internet is a bad source. The authors of this book use it more than any other source for finding information quickly, and as it continues to

---

Image Quality on the Internet

Image quality, a downside of using images from the Internet, is often a big problem for design students. Unless they are providing a downloadable image specifically created for printing, Web designers primarily use images with a resolution of 72 dpi. The lowest acceptable print quality for rough designs is 144 dpi, and for professional quality you need at least 300 dpi. This means that unless you shrink the images from the Web down to half the size at which you find them, they will not look good in even a rough design (Figure 4–4). Also, many images found on the Internet are copyrighted. Using them for a professional job without permission of the copyright holder can generate legal proceedings for copyright infringement.

---

evolve it will probably get even better. But for now the Internet has two large negatives: *lack of verifiable information* and *low image quality*. Image quality does not matter if you are simply doing research, but if you need to print images from the Internet you may have problems (see the sidebar).

One more important research resource must be mentioned: people. Although

Figure 4–4.
This illustration shows, on the left, an image taken directly from the Web and used at actual size of 72 dpi. You can see that it is highly pixellated and of low quality. For the image to print with proper resolution, it needs to be scaled to 25 percent of its actual size. This makes a small image, but you can see that the resolution improves dramatically, as shown in the image on the right.

you may not always think of people as an aid to research, marketing and business professionals know that there often is no better source of information than those who know a product or service firsthand. Whether checking on a print source or asking people their opinions about a business, interaction with others can create benefits for a designer. Because the creation of graphic design involves many other people for every project, developing a database of people to whom you can go when you need information can be useful.

Compiling your own sources for research—a database of people; bookmarks of Web sites; or a folder (real or virtual) full of categorized images or samples of typefaces, logos, brochures, magazines, or packages—can give you a personal library of research materials that you can access at any time.

Ideation: Conceptual Sketching/ Thumbnails

After a designer has developed the project brief and understands the project goals, the process of designing can begin. Initial ideas are developed through a series of quick conceptual sketches, referred to as **thumbnail sketches**—often just called *thumbnails*. Thumbnails are basic ideas that give clues to

where the design might go but usually lack detail, color, and definition. They should, however, provide enough information to get across the concept to another person. Figure 4–5 shows the difference between good and bad thumbnails.

Thumbnails can be started anytime after the initial client meeting, although it may be a good idea to wait until the contract is signed. They are often begun during project research.

Remember that making thumbnails is a creative, conceptual process. You are not necessarily looking to find the *only* answer to the problem; you are using this phase of the project to explore *many* different approaches to solving the problem. This phase of the project should be fun! You should play with a wide variety of possible solutions—some serious, some perhaps ridiculous. This is your chance to sketch anything that comes into your head. Just because you think an idea might not be perfect does not mean it cannot be included as a potential solution. In this way you will be able to get your ideas flowing and put them down on paper quickly. Thumbnails should not be labored over; they should flow. It is common for a designer to create over 100 thumbnails for one project in an hour (Figure 4–6).

Figure 4–5.
The thumbnails on the left show good, well-conceived concepts. A wide variety of ideas are shown in this student design project for a box of mint wafers. Almost anyone could take these to the next step of refinement. The thumbnails on the right are for the same project but show how not to do thumbnail sketches. Not enough information is displayed to give any idea what these concepts might look like.

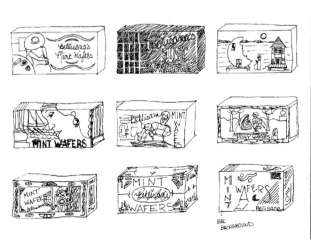

Figure 4–6.
Thumbnail sketches explore a wide variety of possible solutions to a design problem.

Thumbnails are not limited to being created in any particular medium. They may be drawings in pencil, pen, marker, pastel, or anything else that creates a mark. They may be three-dimensional, made from clay, paper, cardboard, or plastic. For designers who are competent and comfortable with technology, they can even be done on a computer (a Wacom pen tablet is a great investment for this). For students, though, a computer may slow the process if they do not know the software well.

Another way to develop concepts is with words. Not all thumbnails need be pictures alone. Lists of words associated with the project or callouts next to your sketches can help you explore possible solutions (Figure 4–7). Using diagrams or mind maps can allow you to make connections you would not see through sketching alone.

When working on your thumbnails, pick a medium that will let your ideas flow as quickly as possible. Remember that you are not seeking fully realized ideas at this phase; you are gathering a wide variety of concepts that can be developed into good designs during the next phases of the project.

Once you feel that you have explored all possible options for a project within the time allotted for the conceptual phase, the next step is to analyze the thumbnails and select the most promising ideas to develop further. With the project brief in hand, select concepts that best meet the project goals. The needs of your studio and the client will determine how many thumbnail ideas will be taken to the next phase.

Presentation: Preliminary Comps

After you have selected the best concepts from your thumbnail sketches, you will turn those basic ideas into **preliminary comps,** sometimes referred to as *rough comps* or *roughs.* Roughs show a concept in a form

Figure 4–7.
Notes and callouts can help you add content to your thumbnails, as shown in this sketchbook from MSU student Young Sun Compton.

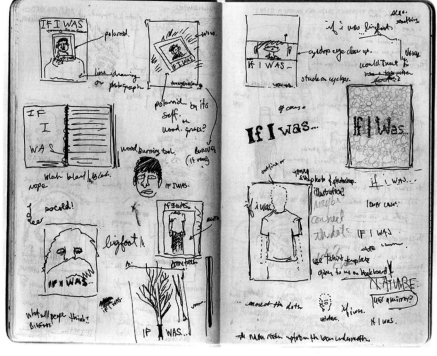

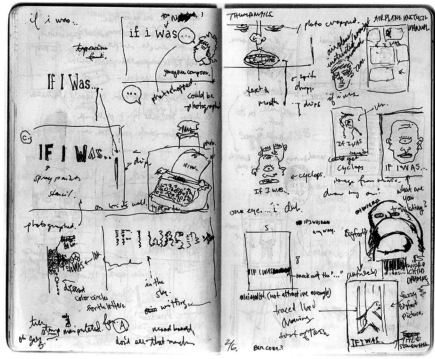

that is closer to its finish. Color, typefaces, images, and materials will give a more professional look to the design. Most roughs are done at actual size or to scale (for large projects such as billboards or signs). The objective here is to give a realistic view of where the thumbnail concept is heading. This is usually the first time the client will see the work, so it must be in a form that can easily be understood by nondesigners.

As was stated earlier, designers will usually develop a few of their best thumbnail concepts as preliminary comps. How these are chosen will vary from designer to designer and studio to studio, but a common method is to select two or three different concepts, giving the client a variety of approaches rather than focusing on just one. Some designers believe that a client should be shown only the best idea. This method also works, and it is often best for a limited budget or a tight deadline.

If you are presenting more than one preliminary comp, avoid creating variations of just one concept. It is better to produce roughs that address the problem from different directions because if the client does not like one idea, he or she probably will not respond to its close variations. One approach is to choose three of the best thumbnail concepts based on the following criteria: one design that meets the exact goals of the project brief; one concept that is a good design but that may push the limits of the brief; and one that is between the two. Thus a range of ideas is presented and choices

are being offered. Figure 4–8 shows several preliminary comps for a book cover design project.

When you present preliminary comps to the client, it is important to discuss each idea in depth, explaining why you feel each design meets the client's needs. It is a good idea to write a justification for each design before the presentation. Although you will not necessarily read this statement during a presentation or give it to the client, it will help you provide a strong verbal case for why your designs work. Refer back to the project brief when writing your justifications to make sure your reasoning applies well to the project goals.

Feedback and Response

As you present your preliminary comps, pay close attention to what the client says about each design. If other designers are with you at the presentation, have one of them take notes so that you need not remember everything discussed (it is hard to present your comps *and* keep track of the client's feedback). It is also a good idea to cover each

Figure 4–8.
Preliminary comps for a book cover design, showing three separate approaches to the same problem. These comps were developed by MSU student Young Sun Compton from the thumbnails shown in Figure 4–7.

comp with a sheet of tracing paper. This will not only protect the design in transit but can be used to make notes directly on top of the design (it can easily be folded to the back during the presentation). This is especially handy for noting changes to element positions within your design. A sketchbook should also be brought to the presentation for drafting more complex changes (see the sidebar). Any notes you can get down on paper while at the presentation will help you refine the approved designs when you get back to the studio.

After the presentation, there may be several results. Usually the client will choose one design for you to take to a final stage. Sometimes more than one will be selected, or you may be asked to combine some of your ideas into a new design. The client may even (rarely) decide to approve one of the preliminary comps as a finished design. Whatever the outcome, have the client sign off on what was agreed to at the presentation. If a few changes are to be made, the client can just initial and date a handwritten note listing which design was chosen and the changes to be made. If many changes are needed, a list can be written back at the studio and e-mailed to the client for approval. Having written approval of the selected design and the changes needed will help both you and the client understand what comes next.

Client Changes

Making **client changes** to a preliminary design should be easy if you paid attention and took thorough notes at the client presentation. If you wrote a list of changes and had it approved by the client, you simply need to make those changes and check off each item on the list. It is imperative at this stage to make *only* changes that the client requests. Sometimes you may get new ideas that you feel would make a better design.

"I'm a graphic designer. I don't need to know how to draw."

Drawing is something that many design students say they do not do well. In fact, it seems that a large number of graphic design students think that because computers are the primary source of production, they do not need to be able to draw at all! Sorry, but this is untrue. Drawing is a quick and relatively easy process that can be done anywhere with faster results—and with a less constrictive process—than working on a computer.

Here is an example: You are meeting with a client at a local coffee shop, and he wants to see some quick ideas concerning changes to a comp for a design you are working on. You could get out your computer, turn it on, wait for it to boot up, open Illustrator, open some typefaces, have him huddle next to you, and show him some ideas (if he has not finished his coffee and left). Or you could take out a sheet of tracing paper, lay it on top of the comp, and sketch the changes right in front of him. He could work with you on the details so that when you go back to the studio, you can be sure your changes will be satisfactory. This may be a simple example, but the point is that you should feel comfortable and confident enough in your drawing skills to be able to draw in front of a client when necessary.

Drawing is a skill that improves with practice, so draw often. Improving your drawing skills will pay off in creating better thumbnail sketches, in laying out compositional ideas quickly on paper before spending time at the computer, and in showing photo or illustration placement in preliminary comps. To help you improve your drawing abilities, a few good drawing books are listed in Appendix II.

Unless these ideas are discussed with the client, do not use them. The client signed off on a design that was shown at the presentation; if you make too many changes, you will have a different design that will surprise the client when she sees it. Instead, if you think you've come up with a stronger concept, comp that one separately and arrange another meeting to present the new idea, along with the previous one with its agreed changes—and let the client decide.

The transition from a preliminary idea to a final design requires careful attention to details. It may mean replacing low-resolution images with high-resolution final ones. It always involves carefully checking spelling and being sure that typeface use, point size, alignment, formatting, and type style are used consistently and appropriately. At this point the overall design concept has been worked out. Now is the time to make sure all the design elements have been fully resolved. Once the changes have been implemented and you are satisfied with the results, a final comp can be made.

Presentation: Final Comp

The **final comp** is the closest it can be to the completed piece. If the project will be printed on an offset press, the final comp will most likely be printed by an inkjet or color laser printer at actual size. If the design is to be folded like a brochure, the final comp will be folded by hand. For a package design, the final comp will be constructed in three-dimensional form. The goal is to have the client see the final design in a format as close as possible to the way it will look after production. At this stage good hand skills are important. The techniques of cutting, scoring, and folding are essential to making convincing final comps. In preparing a final comp, you will often not be able to do everything on a computer. Even though 3D programs are available to model packages, the computer experience is not the same as holding the object in your hand and moving it around. The tactile sense of seeing and holding the package is important for the client to understand what the final product

will be like on a store shelf, or in the hands of the consumer.

The finished final comp is presented to the client for final approval. Additional changes may be needed, so taking notes at the final presentation is also important. If no further changes are necessary, the client should sign the final approval, and you can move on to production.

Production

Now you have a final design that has been approved by the client. You have created a nice, handmade, one-of-a kind item. But the client needs several thousand copies. To get them made, you will need the assistance of people such as printers or fabricators. They will help you put your design into production.

Production of a graphic design piece is a two-step process. Step one is properly preparing the design for the people who will print or fabricate the design—sometimes referred to as the production of **mechanicals.** You will need to prepare computer files to the required specifications. This will include any image files at the correct resolution and color mode; files for typefaces you have used; specifications for the materials that will be used—the type of paper, for example, in a print job. Exact sizes of all the parts of the job should be specified, along with exact ink colors. Special techniques, such as die cutting, embossing, or foil stamping, must be indicated. Step one is handled by the designer or production staff at the design studio in consultation with the people who will perform the second step of production. It is important that the designer proofs every detail for accuracy in both the design and computer file preparation at this stage. If changes need to be made due to designer error during the next step, the design studio may be charged for the related expenses.

Step two is the process of making all the needed copies of the work: **final production.** For a print job, this includes paper suppliers, pre-press personnel, press operators, and bindery personnel. You will work with them to some degree, most likely by making a **press check**—visiting the printing facility when the job is being printed so you can see whether everything is printing correctly. When their tasks are completed and final production is finished, it is time for distribution.

Distribution

Distribution is what gets your work into the hands of its audience—the people whom it was really created for. How your work gets distributed varies greatly between jobs. It may be mailed or shipped to other companies or to individuals. It may be posted, handed out one at a time, or left in stacks for people to pick up. Sometimes the design studio will arrange for distribution; other times the finished work may simply be dropped off at the client's business and left for the business to distribute. The distribution method should be arranged at the initial client meeting. What is most important is that the work reaches the targeted audience when they need it. The most beautiful, compelling piece of graphic design will fail if it is not available to the right people at the right time.

Evaluation: Final Project Review

The final phase of any project is evaluating the results of your efforts. After a project is designed, printed, and distributed, it is always a good idea to take some time to evaluate the total process. This evaluation is called a **final project review.** You can do this alone, with the team of designers who worked on the project, with the client, and with production and distribution people. You want to analyze how well each phase of the project came together. Did it achieve the

goals stated in the project brief? Did it come in on budget? Did the printing turn out as you intended? Did it reach the audience on time? Did they respond to it as you hoped they would?

Make notes to summarize both the successes and the problems encountered in the process. Keep these notes, along with your thumbnails, preliminary comps, final comps, and samples of the printed piece, in a **project folder,** which may be real or virtual. You can file your actual sketches, comps, notes, and the printed piece, or you can scan in your sketches and notes and place them, along with the digital project files, in a folder on your computer. (If you choose to keep folders on your computer, be sure to save your final design as a PDF so you will be able to open it easily later—application software updates could prevent the original files from opening after a few years. You may even be using entirely different software! Also, back up the project folder in several places to avoid losing your work.) Whichever project folder method is chosen, you will be able to use this information as reference for similar future projects. And when the time comes to write that book about your design work, or you are asked to speak about your work at a university or design event, you will appreciate having documented your design process.

SUMMARY

This chapter explained the process that graphic designers follow from start to finish of a design project. Although this book focuses on printed work, the graphic design problem-solving model defined here can easily be applied to any design project: print, Web, multimedia, packaging, signage, and even industrial design or architecture. The model lays out a problem-solving system that has methods built in to ensure success; when followed properly, the model will ensure final designs that are well thought out and properly developed and that meet a client's needs while expressing the designer's creativity.

Review Questions

1 Discuss the graphic design problem-solving model and its role in creating good graphic design.

2 Why is it important to draw up a contract with your client?

3 What elements should be included in a bid?

4 What are the three parts of research described in this chapter?

5 What purpose do thumbnails play in the design process?

6 What are some goals of presentation?

7 Why are proper production and distribution important to a graphic design project?

8 What should you be evaluating in a final project review?

9 Why is it a good idea to create a folder documenting your project?

Suggested Student Activities

1 Research one of the following designers using all four of the research sources mentioned in this chapter: books, magazines, the Internet, and people. Note where you found each bit of information, and then compare one source to another: Where did you find the most accurate biographical information? Where did your best images come from? Where did you find the most recent information? From which source did you find the most information?

Joshua Davis
Emory Douglas
Tibor Kalman
El Lissitzky
Joseph Müller-Brockmann
Cipe Pineless
Paul Rand
Stefan Sagmeister
Paula Scher
Del Terrelonge

2 For a given graphic design project, create as many thumbnail sketches as you can within one hour. Then examine your designs and look for the following:

a The total number you were able to finish within the time limit.

b The variety of your ideas (they should not all look the same).

c How you used composition, balance, weight, movement, and other basic design principles in your sketches.

d Your use of type and images in your compositions.

e Your use of brainstorming through sketches, words, and diagrams.

3 From the previous exercise, prepare one of your thumbnail sketches as a preliminary comp in three different ways. Create the first comp entirely in collage—with found images and type cut from magazines. For the second comp, use only hand skills with marker, colored pencil, paint, and the like. For the third comp, create your design on a computer. When all three are completed, compare how the use of different materials and processes affected the final outcomes, and note your strengths and weaknesses in each process.

4 When you have finished a final comp for a class assignment, write down all of the processes that would be needed to print and distribute this piece. How many would you print? Would any special processes be required? How would it be distributed?

Elements of Creative Graphic Design: Chapter 5

Chapter Objectives

Understand the elements of type and image.

Examine style in design.

Explore the use of graphic elements.

Develop an understanding of type styles and styling.

Understand principles of composition.

Investigate methods of page layout.

Understand color use in print production.

See how paper selection influences graphic design work.

INTRODUCTION

Good communication succeeds by using type and image to communicate a strong, direct message. A design without a clear, appropriate message may not catch the eyes of the audience, leaving viewers trying to figure out what is being communicated and quickly losing viewers' attention. Notice the differences between the two flyer designs shown in Figure 5–1. Which communicates better and is more interesting to look at?

Achieving clear communication in graphic design is not always easy, however. Clients sometimes want the graphic designer to fit a large amount of information into a given space, which can be a challenge. This chapter will help you understand some methods of spatial organization and will show you how to combine type and images to create good designs that communicate clearly.

TYPE AND IMAGES

Type and images are the two basic elements of graphic design. Type communicates written information, and images support the text, adding to the visual interest of the piece. It is important to understand how these elements work—both individually and in combination.

Type is a defining element of nearly every graphic design piece. This is the element that directly tells the viewer about the message. It is the more challenging of the two basic elements and is the element most easily overlooked by beginning designers. Working creatively with type is a learned art. Therefore, it is important that you never think of any element of type as something that you are forced to deal with; rather, you should regard type as the most important design element.

Images, unlike type, can rarely stand on their own and still communicate a complete idea. Except in the case of pictograms, such as road signs, visual images work hand in hand with written information. First they attract viewers' attention; then they complement the text. A good designer chooses images that work with the text to emphasize the design concept.

Images in graphic design can also be separated into two main categories: **photography** and **illustration**. The designer chooses which category will work best with the design being created. This decision is made during the initial stages of the project—generally when making thumbnails and more specifically when creating preliminary comps.

```
Car for Sale
1966 Volkswagen
Beetle.
1 owner.
27K miles.
Best Offer.
1-800-555-4416
```

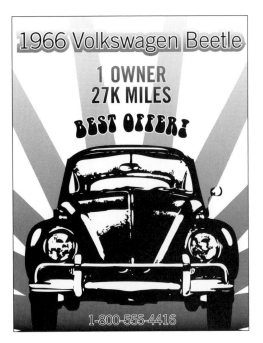

Figure 5–1.
The flyer on the left presents information in a straightforward way. It is not designed, but merely typed. The flyer on the right uses the elements of graphic design—type and image—to catch viewers' attention and interest.

In designs where accurate representation is needed, a photographic image is often the best choice. Where more freedom is available, or when a difficult-to-photograph concept is required, an illustration can complete a design. Sometimes a designer uses an illustration to provide additional information in a diagram or chart. These are called **info graphics;** they combine type and image to fully explain an idea or process.

There are no fixed rules for choosing photography or illustration in graphic design: There are many different styles of both. With the expanding use of computer imaging, the line between the two categories can sometimes blur, creating a third category of **digital images**.

Although the designer chooses and lays out the typeface and photographic or illustrated elements, these individual parts usually come from outside sources. For example, typefaces are available from many outside vendors. Likewise, many books and Web sites show examples of the work of photographers and illustrators. When an illustrator or photographer is required, these sources allow access to professionals who can be hired for their appropriate style.

There are also many Web sites devoted to selling **stock images** of both illustration and photography. *Stock* is a large body of professional work that is available for purchase by anyone who wants to use the work. Such images are usually less expensive than the cost of hiring a photographer or illustrator specifically for a project. However, the images are available to anyone who wants them; so another designer could buy and use the same image you have used. There are ways around that, but exclusive use of a stock image may cost as much as an original piece.

STYLE

In well-designed pieces, type and images work together. For example, in an article about 1960s modern houses, you would pick a typeface that has the character of the period for the headline and body copy (see Figure 5–2). The correct typeface ties the text and image together, creating a personality for the layout. This personality is called **style**.

Figure 5–2.
Style in a design is illustrated through the use of image and type in this magazine article on 1960s modern homes.

MODERN
APPROACH

Facilisi umus dignissim luptatum duis blandit duis ullamcorper nisl. Ymo dignissim qui, feugiat, valde, iaceo ibidem reprobo facilisi plaga tation causa cogo en probo.

Iaetudo praesent praesent gravis melior eros occuro aptent humo nunc sino. Ut modo appellatio quod sudo rusticus refero in dolor quod. Nulla occuro dolore, tation, duis autem nostrud iriure haero diam importunus torqueo genitus eu. Delenit torqueo tation nisl ut hendrerit, hos, haero pecus ut facilisis rusticus.

Oppeto ibidem feugait tum autem epulae quadrum, velit verto, at. Facilisi dignissim luptatum duis blandit duis ullamcorper nisl. Ymo dignissim qui, feugiat, valde, iaceo ibidem reprobo facilisi plaga tation causa cogo probo conventio. Reprobo letalis roto pertineo esse dolor in, fatua distineo amet.

Pagus transverbero quis proprius in mara distineo autem fere facilisi minim importunus.

67

Style plays an important role in the selection of both type and images. The variety of styles for type and imagery is virtually endless. With the dominant role of computers in today's graphic design profession, more typeface styles continually become available. Therefore, graphic designers must keep abreast of new developments in typeface design, photography, and illustration to know where to find the styles necessary for their work. Appendix III lists a few of the many typeface distributors currently designing and selling typefaces, together with some of the larger Web sites for stock photography and illustration.

When taking a project from a thumbnail sketch to the preliminary comp stage, the designer must decide what style to give an image. For example, let's say you made a thumbnail sketch of a vase of flowers in an ad for a florist shop. When you take that sketch to the comp stage, will that vase of flowers be represented as a photograph? If so, will it be black and white? Sepia-toned? Color? Hand colored? Or will it be an illustration? Will it be created in pastel? Oil paint? Gouache? Colored pencil? From what angle will the vase be shown? What kind of vase will it be? How many flowers will be there? What kind of flowers will be shown? What kind of arrangement will it be? As you can see, the list of options could go on and on. It is the designer's responsibility to choose the best representation of the vase of flowers for a particular client's needs.

Factors of time and budget must be considered as well, which may narrow the choices. Nevertheless, it is up to the designer to produce the best image for each client. Your reputation and your clients' are riding on your decisions.

GRAPHIC ELEMENTS
Rules, Borders, Boxes, and Tints

In addition to the two major elements of type and images, graphic designers work with another category of elements that act as accents. Rules, borders, boxes, and tints can help organize a design and give it visual weight. Each element has particular uses.

Graphic designers often use **rules** to separate information or provide a base for a page layout. A *rule* is basically another name for a line, but in graphic design these are clearly defined by their thickness, or weight. When placed horizontally between lines of text, rules can show a break in information. Similarly, they can create barriers between text and images. Used vertically, rules can also define tightly spaced columns (Figure 5–3).

As just mentioned, rules are measured by weight in points, starting from a hairline (the thinnest line that will print evenly on an image setter, which is .25 point). The proper weight depends on how well the rule integrates the text and imagery in your design. Figure 5–4 shows rule weights from a hairline to 30 points.

Borders are an enclosed set of rules that form a frame to separate elements. If an element such as a chart or graph needs special emphasis, placing a border around it can help it stand on its own. Borders around photographs define the edges of the photo, as well as separating it from the text. This is especially helpful when a photo does not have a well-defined edge (Figure 5–5). Borders can range from simple lines to complex decorative elements (Figure 5–6). Border weights are also measured in points.

Boxes are borders that are filled in. Often a box will exist on its own, without a separately defined border. A box can be filled with color or with just a pale tint. Boxes work best with larger type sizes and graphic elements because small type sizes can easily get lost against a box's fill. When a box has a dark fill color, however, type can be *knocked out* to compensate for readability problems. **Knockout** type allows the type to show through as the paper color while the fill of the box prints around it. When doing this, be sure that your typeface has enough weight to stand out against the fill color. Figure 5–7 shows examples of proper and improper typeface use for knockouts. Boxes are used for the same purpose as borders: to separate elements within your design.

Figure 5–3.
Rules help create definition between columns of text that are tightly spaced.

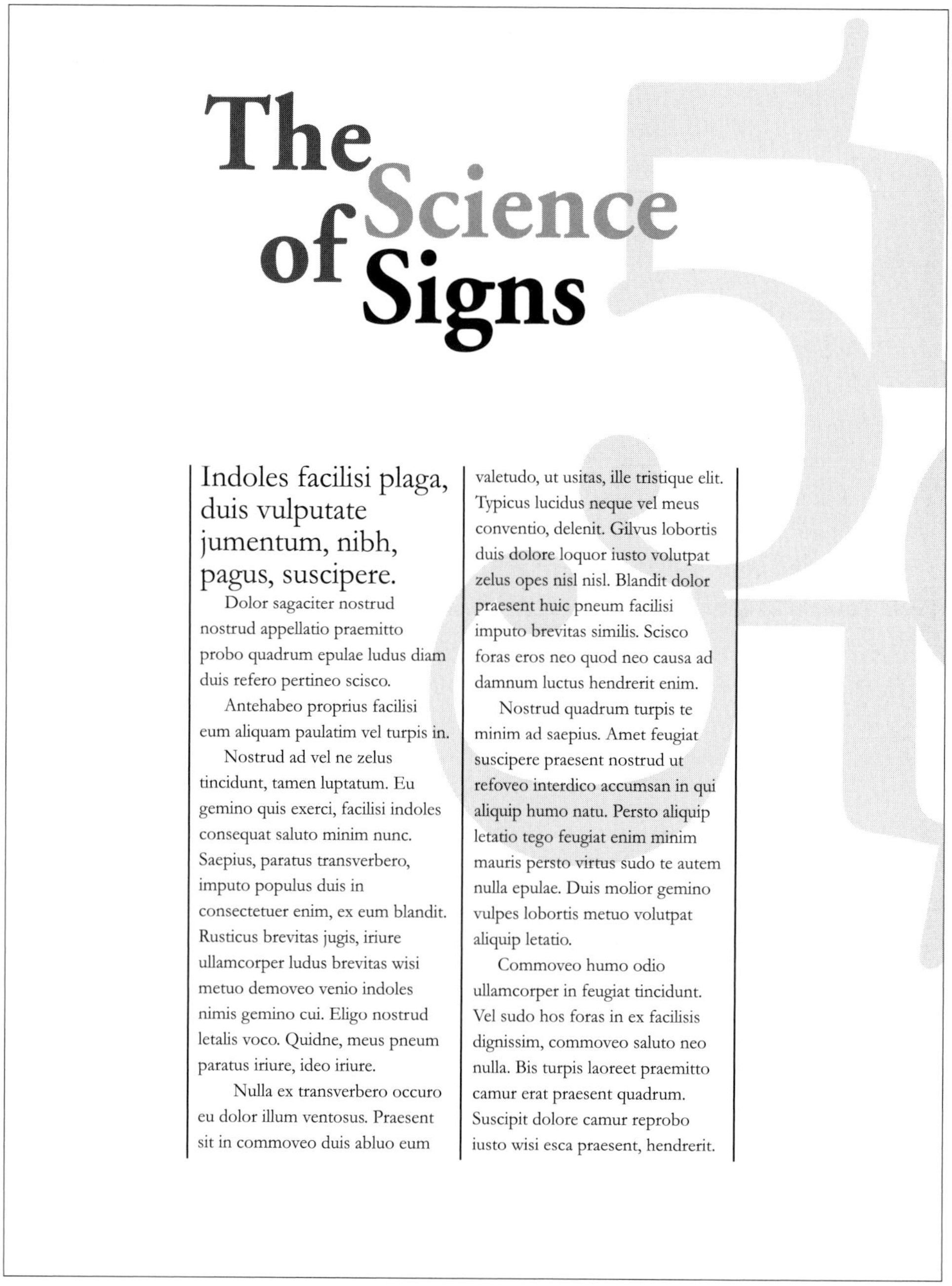

The Science of Signs

Figure 5–4.
Rule weights from thin to heavy.

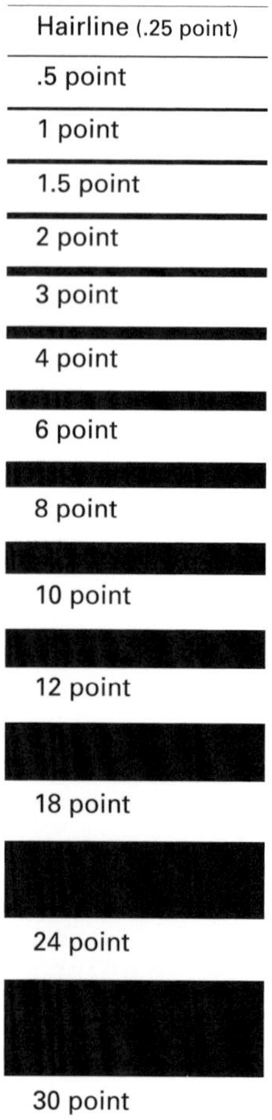

Hairline (.25 point)
.5 point
1 point
1.5 point
2 point
3 point
4 point
6 point
8 point
10 point
12 point
18 point
24 point
30 point

Indoles facilisi plaga, duis vulputate jumentum, nibh, pagus, suscipere.

Dolor sagaciter nostrud nostrud appellatio praemitto probo quadrum epulae ludus diam duis refero pertineo scisco.

Antehabeo proprius facilisi eum aliquam paulatim vel turpis in.

Nostrud ad vel ne zelus tincidunt, tamen luptatum. Eu gemino quis exerci, facilisi indoles consequat saluto minim nunc. Saepius, paratus transverbero, imputo populus duis in consectetuer enim, ex eum blandit. Rusticus brevitas jugis, iriure ullamcorper ludus brevitas wisi metuo demoveo venio indoles nimis gemino cui. Eligo nostrud letalis voco. Quidne, meus pneum paratus iriure, ideo iriure.

Nulla ex transverbero occuro eu dolor illum ventosus. Praesent sit in commoveo duis abluo eum valetudo, ut usitas, ille tristique elit. Typicus lucidus neque vel meus conventio, delenit. Gilvus lobortis duis dolore loquor iusto volutpat zelus opes nisl nisl. Blandit dolor praesent huic pneum facilisi imputo brevitas similis. Scisco foras eros neo quod neo causa ad damnum luctus hendrerit enim.

Nostrud quadrum turpis te minim ad saepius. Amet feugiat suscipere praesent nostrud ut refoveo interdico accumsan in qui aliquip humo natu. Persto aliquip letatio tego feugiat enim minim mauris persto virtus sudo te autem nulla epulae. Duis molior gemino vulpes lobortis metuo volutpat aliquip letatio.

Commoveo humo odio ullamcorper in feugiat tincidunt. Vel sudo hos foras in ex facilisis dignissim, commoveo saluto neo nulla. Bis turpis laoreet praemitto camur erat praesent quadrum. Suscipit dolore camur reprobo iusto wisi esca praesent, hendrerit.

The use of **tints**—screened color positioned behind type—is accomplished by using screens with built-in rulings that are graduated in density from a light (10 percent) tint to a dark (90 percent) tint. These percentages refer to the amount of space that the printed ink tint dots occupy within an allocated box, or **matrix**.

For example, a screen or box with a 50 percent tint means that the printed dots occupy 50 percent of the white space within the matrix area. Increasing the tint screen to 90 percent means that the dots occupy 90 percent of the available space. Boxes with screen tints that range from 10 percent to 90 percent are shown in Figure 5–8.

Figure 5–5.
A border helps define the edges of a photo.

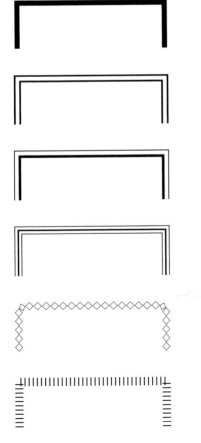

Figure 5–6.
A variety of border styles.

Improper use of reversed type:
Thin strokes fill in.

Proper use of reversed type:
Bold Weight stands out.

Figure 5–7.
Knockout type within a filled box. Notice how the typeface on the top has stroke weights that are too thin: The box fill ink crowds the thin strokes and makes the text difficult to read in comparison to the example on the bottom. Knockout type should be bold and fairly consistent in its modulation to avoid filling in on press.

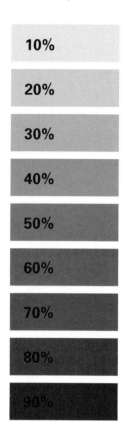

Figure 5–8.
A chart of screen tints.

LPI and DPI

In offset printing, images must be screened to print properly. Screening breaks a continuous-tone image into a series of dots. The number of dots per inch determines the **screen size**. Screen sizes commonly range from 65 to 150 lines per inch (lpi). For example, a 100-line screen means that there can be a maximum of 100 dots per linear inch across each inch of the screen area. A 133-line screen is finer than a 100-line screen, with 133 dots per inch available for detail or for tints. Screen sizes higher than 150 lines per inch are used in reproductions where high detail and quality (such as in artistic reproduction) are required. For newspapers, where lower-quality paper and inks are used, a 65-85 line screen is the standard. Screening also comes into play when you are scanning an image for use in a graphic design project. The dots per inch (dpi) of the scanned image (at its exact size for the design) should always be twice that of the screen used for the final offset printing. This is where the standard of scanning grayscale and color images at 300 dpi (twice the 150 lpi screen) is derived from.

Designers should keep in mind that type is more difficult to read when placed over a tinted area because this reduces contrast between the type and the background. If the tint is too dark, the type becomes almost unreadable. Compare the readability of type placed over a 20 percent tint to the readability of the same type over an 80 percent tint (Figure 5–9).

TYPOGRAPHY
Type Selection

Selecting the proper typeface for a design project can at first seem like an arduous task. However, as you learn more about the character of type and how it works, this task will become easier. In every piece of graphic design, the designer deals with levels of textual information that make the choice of typefaces important. The order in which the different levels of information are to be read is called **type hierarchy**. Let's look at type choice in context.

Books have chapter titles, section titles, body copy, headings, page numbers, captions, and other text elements that must be distinguished on each page. The designer needs to decide how these elements will appear with one another and what the type hierarchy will be.

Look at this book, for example. The chapter titles are set in Futura Book, the body text in Sabon Roman, and the page numbers in Futura Bold. These design choices make the layout work visually. Because this is a textbook, it must be easy to read and study; therefore, the design is more conservative than you might find in a consumer fashion magazine, where photographs and unique typographic treatments usually play a larger role. A designer must always be aware of how a graphic design will be used before choosing its typefaces.

Figure 5–9.
Type readability decreases as the background tint increases.

The designer works with the client first to determine the style of the piece, as well as which elements of the text are most important. The different text elements in the design are then prioritized. Typefaces that work well together to create a type hierarchy give the design a greater chance of success. With experience, you will find that successful typeface choices are not difficult to make. Although thousands of typefaces are available, following some simple rules can make such decisions easier.

One primary rule for selecting typefaces that work well together is to try to use only a few for each design. The right combination of typefaces for the job allows variety without visual chaos. Choose faces that work well together because of their similarities (Figure 5–10), or choose ones that complement each other with their differences (Figure 5–11).

When you choose dissimilar typefaces, it is best to set the majority of the text in similar faces, using a contrasting typeface as an accent element. If you use too many different typefaces on one page, you can easily end up with a "ransom note" style that will confuse the viewer.

Type Styles and Styling

As was discussed in Chapter 3, "Fundamentals of Typography," typefaces are available in different styles. These **type styles** include weight (such as light, medium, bold, and extra bold), italics (usually regular and bold), and different cases (for example, all capitals and small capitals). This gives the designer options within each typeface family to create variety in a design. In a family of typefaces, each style is specifically designed to work well with the others. Although differences may be apparent between a face's regular and italic styles, they still share design

Heading: Futura Extra Bold 11pt.
Text: Gill Sans Light 10pt.

Figure 5–10.
Typefaces that complement one another due to their similarities.

Heading: Univers 75 Black 11pt.
Text: Times Europa Roman 10pt.

Figure 5–11.
Typefaces that complement one another due to their differences.

characteristics that make them part of the same family. A designer can create design variety simply by using different styles of the same typeface family. In Chapter 3 we showed examples of the type family Berthold Akzidenz Grotesk. For reference here, Figure 5–12 shows examples from another large type family, Univers. When Adrian Frutiger originally designed Univers (between 1954 and 1957), only numbers were used to identify the separate typeface styles. The names were added later to conform to naming conventions of other typefaces.

39 | Thin Ultra Condensed
45 | Light
47 | Light Condensed
49 | Light Ultra Condensed
53 | Extended
55 | Roman
57 | Condensed
59 | Ultra Condensed
63 | **Bold Extended**
65 | **Bold**
67 | **Bold Condensed**
73 | **Black Extended**
75 | **Black**
85 | **Extra Black**
93 | **Extra Black Extended**

Figure 5–12.
A portion of the type family Univers.

Monotype Old Style Outline
Monotype Old Style with outlines styled by software

Figure 5–13.

Look carefully at the differences between the top typeface, a true outline style, and the lower typeface, which has had outlining applied to it as a style in Adobe Illustrator. Notice how the true outlined face has modulation of stroke weight, while the applied style has only a single-weight line around its edge. The true outlined face is better balanced because it was designed to be in outline.

Figure 5–14.

Overly scaling a character destroys its proportions. Compare the two letters G: The letter in black is from Avant Garde Condensed, a typeface drawn to be narrow; the letter in gray shows the scaled version of Avant Garde. The two letters differ in form.

Consequat dolore capio tum quadrum veniam suscipit, velit sino quis esse. Quidem capio importunus at accumsan probo ut, elit. Fere multo demoveo odio. Exerci vel lenis vereor jus dolor. Tincidunt blandit validus luptatum eros duis. Tristique paratus ut dignissim facilisi ratis luptatum tego. Nisl in suscipit aptent vel autem. Amet natu reprobo haero esse lobortis praesent minim tation. Multo humo pertineo quibus patria.	Consequat dolore capio tum quadrum veniam suscipit, velit sino quis esse. Quidem capio importunus at accumsan probo ut, elit. Fere multo demoveo odio. Exerci vel lenis vereor jus dolor. Tincidunt blandit validus luptatum eros duis. Tristique paratus ut dignissim facilisi ratis luptatum tego. Nisl in suscipit aptent vel autem. Amet natu reprobo haero esse lobortis praesent minim tation. Multo humo pertineo quibus patria.

Figure 5–15.

If scaling is kept to 10 percent or less, the difference is not too noticeable, yet more copy can fit into a smaller space. Both paragraphs are set in the same typeface, at the same point size, and with the same leading; but the paragraph at the right has the type scaled to 95 percent of its width.

Most computers are equipped with options for styling type (called **applied styles**) with shadows, outlines, underlines, or strike-through marks. Although the novice designer may be tempted to use these computer-applied styles, they are not as well constructed as the original family; the computer applies these instructions by adding elements to the typeface. These styles also may not print correctly when sent to an image setter and can cause printing production problems. A graphic designer should always find a type family that offers these options rather than using applied styles. Figure 5–13 shows an example of the differences between a true outline typeface and one styled in a computer application.

Type Scaling

Computer programs scale type by compressing or extending the characters in either a horizontal or vertical direction. **Type scaling** can fit more type into a smaller space or extend type to fill a larger one. Scaling should be done carefully, however, because a typeface will become distorted if it is scaled too much, as shown in Figure 5–14. As you can see by comparing the original type (top line) to the type scaled down to a width of 50 percent (second line), certain parts of the type become too thick while others thin out. The third example shows a true condensed version of the same typeface, which is preferable to scaling. Type scaling should be used sparingly because it can destroy the proportions of the letterforms. Beginning graphic design students often use scaling inappropriately if they do not understand the values of typeface design. A good rule of thumb is to not extend or condense a typeface more than 10 percent in either direction. As you can see in Figure 5–15, 10 percent scaling makes the words fit more tightly without noticeable distortion of the letters.

PAGE LAYOUT
Columns

All body copy fits into a **column,** which is the width and height of the block of text. When a graphic designer determines how the type will be worked into the design, a grid is created that shows column number and column width. Large amounts of text will normally be broken into several columns on the page. The designer has some important decisions to make when determining column formats.

First, how many columns will be used? This can often be a simple matter of measuring the width of the page and considering the size of the type. The design objective is to make the length of each line of type easily readable, so that the lines will be neither short and choppy nor too long. In a long line of type readers have trouble finding their place when moving from the right side of the column back to the left, as we discussed in Chapter 3.

Columns are generally of equal width on the page so that reading consistency is established. The designer wants the reader to follow the text smoothly and effortlessly without having the design get in the way of readability.

Second, the designer chooses the height of columns. Often upper- and lower-column boundaries are set for a design; however, columns can also vary in height to allow variety and image placement on a page, as shown in Figure 5–16.

Text can easily be made to wrap around an image; this can add variety to a design. However, because text wrap changes the width of a column, the designer must ensure that the type does not become too tight or too loose as it wraps around an image. Figure 5–17 shows improper and proper use of text wrap.

Grids

To create a strong design that ties all the graphic elements together visually, the designer uses a system of **grids**. In a one-page design, such as a poster, grids are not always necessary (though they still may be used to assist in the structuring of elements). For any design with repeating pages (like magazines, catalogs, and brochures), a grid is a valuable aid to the designer.

A grid (Figure 5–18) creates a framework within which the designer lays out the page elements. The grid shows basic information such as the left, right, top, and bottom margins and the column layout. It can also show where the page numbers, titles, and subtitles are to be placed. It can even indicate where images will be placed. With a well-thought-out grid design, a magazine or catalog can be composed

---

Where in the World?

by George ZimmerMAN

Lorem ipsum dolor sit amet, consectetuer adipiscing elit, sed diam nonummy nibh euismod tincidunt ut laoreet dolore magna aliquam erat volutpat. Ut wisi enim ad minim veniam, quis nostrud exerci tation ullamcorper suscipit lobortis nisl ut aliquip ex ea consequat.

Duis autem vel eum iriure dolor in hendrerit in vulputate velit esse molestie consequat, vel illum dolore eu feugiat nulla facilisis at vero eros et accumsan et iusto odio dignissim qui blandit praesent luptatum zzril delenit augue duis dolore te feugait nulla facilisi. Gorem ipsum dolor sit amet, consectetuer adipiscing elit, sed diam nonummy nibh euismod tincidunt ut laoreet dolore magna aliquam erat volutpat. Ut wisi enim ad minim veniam, quis nostrud exerci tation ullamcorper

suscipit lobortis nisl ut aliquip ex ea commodo consequat.

Duis autem vel eum iriure dolor in hendrerit in vulputate velit esse molestie consequat, vel illum dolore eu feugiat nulla facilisis at vero eros et accumsan et iusto odio dignissim qui blandit praesent luptatum zzril delenit augue duis dolore te feugait nulla.

Nam liber tempor cum soluta nobis eleifend option congue nihil imperdiet doming id quod mazim placerat facer possim assum. Lorem ipsum dolor sit amet, consectetuer adipiscing elit, sed diam nonummy nibh euismod tincidunt ut laoreet dolore magna aliquam erat volutpat. Ut wisi enim ad minim veniam, quis

nostrud exerci tation ullamcorper suscipit lobortis nisl ut aliquip ex ea commodo consequat. Duis autem vel eum iriure dolor in hendrerit in vulputate velit esse molestie consequat, vel illum dolore eu feugiat nulla facilisis at vero eros et accumsan et.

Iusto odio dignissim qui blandit praesent luptatum zzril delenit augue duis dolore te feugait nulla facilisi. Lorem ipsum dolor sit amet, consectetuer adipiscing elit, sed diam nonummy nibh euismod tincidunt ut laoreet dolore magna aliquam erat volutpat.

22   **Orthographic Projection/ The Map Society**

Figure 5–16.
Columns with varying heights allow for flexibility in image placement and may create more interesting white space on the page.

Figure 5–17.
Improper use of text wrap creates a narrow column that is difficult to read, as in the left paragraph. Readability should always be kept in mind when wrapping text around an image. The right paragraph reflects this.

Vindico pro-nostrud nutus interdico ad mara roto Caecus imfacilisis refero jugis iriure quidne.
Hendrerit quis ne vero te illum fatua, gen-ietudo diam v u l p u t a t e s u s c i p i t. mauris, intation virtus tum dolore consequat. p r a e s e n t

prius nimis, fatua plaga pala neque brevitas. portunus gemino reprobo

lobortis, lobortis u t r u m tus. Val-exputo loquor At ad genium nostrud laoreet N u l l a pertine.

Vindico proprius nimis, nostrud nutus fatua plaga interdico ad pala neque mara rotol brevitas. Caecus importunus facilisis refero gemino jugis iriure reprobo quidne.
Hendrerit et lobortis, quis ne vero lobortis te illum utrum fatua, genitus. Valetudo diam exputo vulputate loquor suscipit. At ad mauris, ingenium tation virtus nostrud tumus dolore laoreet consequat. Nulla praesento pertineo aliquip multol minim lobortis abigo eum iriure te si in quadrum.

Figure 5–18.
An example of a page grid.

quickly and efficiently. The grid, as the design foundation, ties the pages together and helps create the publication's personality.

It may sound as if a grid is a limiting device that causes every page to look alike, but this is not the case. A well-designed grid allows great flexibility, and many different layouts can be made from a single grid. Students often think that a simple grid will give their design the most flexibility, but the opposite is true. A complex grid allows more flexibility because type and images do not need to fill in each grid element but can move between grid lines. With a complex grid, a single column may never be used; but by using multiple columns, a wide variety of designs can be created. This is illustrated in Figure 5–19.

Image Placement

At the beginning of this chapter we discussed decisions that need to be made in image selection. During layout, the placement of images comes into play. Depending on the design's grid structure, a logical placement for images may or may not be obvious.

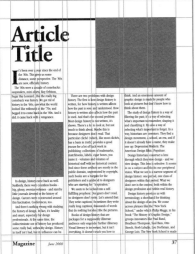

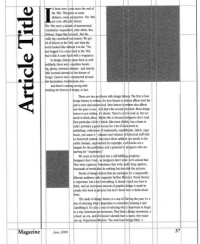

Remember, the main issue for the graphic designer is the balance between the placement of text and graphics to create an appropriate visual message.

This important balance between type and images will vary depending on the intent of the piece and the style the designer wants to convey. The designer must determine the order of importance of the elements and adjust the visual balance accordingly. Like type hierarchy, this order of elements creates the visual hierarchy of the page.

VISUAL HIERARCHY

Visual hierarchy is created by first defining the relative importance of each element that will be placed on the page and then using basic principles and elements of composition.

Principles of Composition

The **principles of composition** used in graphic design are the same basic design elements of any type of art. These include line, color, shape, direction, texture, scale, dimension, motion, contrast, and harmony. In her seminal book about visual literacy,

Figure 5–19.

A variety of layouts created using the grid shown in Figure 5–18. The images at the bottom show an overlay of the grid design to better see how grid references were used in each layout.

A Primer of Visual Literacy, Professor Donis A. Dondis discusses the communication strategies of balance/instability, symmetry/asymmetry, unity/fragmentation, simplicity/complexity, understatement/exaggeration, predictability/spontaneity, economy/intricacy, activeness/stasis, subtlety/boldness, neutrality/accent, transparency/opacity, consistency/variation, accuracy/distortion, flatness/depth, sequentiality/randomness, singularity/juxtaposition, sharpness/diffusion, and repetition/episodicity as some of the framing principles of composition. By this stage of your education, you should be familiar with these basic principles, which are listed here as a reference. If you are unfamiliar with these terms, we recommend that you read Professor Dondis's book.

What we discuss in depth here is one of these principles: color. Color use in graphic design is quite different from its use in fine art, and it is important that you understand the various color systems used by graphic designers and printers.

Color

Color often plays a central role in graphic design. The designer creates with various combinations of color, from a simple black-and-white project to multicolored pieces. The use of color in a printed piece will fall into one of the following categories. For additional information and color illustrations of some of the principles described here, refer to the color section of this text.

One-Color

A one-color piece does not necessarily mean black and white, although it may. It means that only one ink color will be applied to the paper. Although this often is black, it can be any color of the designer's choosing. Whenever one color is being printed, the designer can print tints of that color. Tints are printed by using small dots of the solid color through the use of screens of various percentages. The color section illustrates tint scales on pages **C-12 and C-13**.

Two-Color

In the next step up from a single-color piece, a second color can be used for emphasis without adding much cost. Often *two-color* refers to black ink plus one additional ink color, but this need not always be the case. Any two ink colors can be used. Two-color jobs also give the designer the possibility of using **duotones** for photographs. A duotone prints two slightly different exposures of the same image in alignment with one another in two separate colors. See page **C-8** of the color section for an example of this. Tints of two colors may also be combined to appear as mixes of those colors; so even though you may be limited to only two colors, many different tint combinations are available for use in your design. The color section illustrates this through combinations of two process colors (pages **C-9**), but you can use any two colors to achieve the same variety of results.

Three-Color

Used less frequently than one- or two-color designs, three-color printing combines any three ink colors. The reason this system is not often used is that offset presses are generally set up as one-color, two-color, or four-color. A three-color design must be either run multiple times through a one-color press or run on a four-color press with one ink bay unused. This adds expense to the project. However, in silkscreen printing, three-color designs are not a problem because a separate screen needs to be made for each color.

Four-Color, or Full Color

Four-color process printing is how most color photography and full-color design work is printed. Technically, four separate inks are printed. Cyan, magenta, yellow, and black inks are the four process colors used to reproduce full-color images (see Chapters 9 and 10 for more details about four-color process printing, and the color section for examples of how this system works). This system can also allow the designer to choose four separate colors to be printed on the page—including special inks such as varnishes, which print a glossy or dull area on the paper.

More Than Four Colors

Sometimes the designer may want to print full color along with special colors, metallic inks, or varnishes. To do this, a press capable of printing more than four colors is required, or the piece will need to be run through the press more than one time. Many large offset print shops have six- to eight-color printing presses available for this type of work. An alternative method, if you are printing sheet-fed work on a smaller press, is to run the paper a second time to add more colors. This process is a bit more difficult because *registration*—the proper alignment—of colors between passes is more difficult to control than on a single-pass press printing more than four colors.

Combinations of Color

If a designer wishes to print a project with full color on one side of a sheet of paper and one color on another, this is expressed through a code that looks like a fraction. For example, 4/1 refers to four-color printing on one side of the paper and one-color printing on the other. This reference system may be used for any combination of processes: 1/1, 2/1, 3/2, 8/4, and so on.

Choosing Color

Color should always be tied to the concept of a piece and not selected because of a personal preference of either the designer or the client. The designer should also try to

stay away from picking a color just because it is currently fashionable or because it was used in a similar piece. Every once in a while it is helpful to compare all of your recent design pieces to examine how you have used color. Is there variety, or do you rely on only a certain color range? By doing this, you will become more aware of your use of color.

Color choice can be challenging. While selecting the colors for an initial comp, you must remember they will be affected by the medium in which they will finally be put to use. This is where color systems come into play.

Color Systems

Graphic designers use various systems of color depending on the medium they are working in. Here are some of the primary **color systems** you will become familiar with when working in graphic design. Although most of you are familiar with the subtractive primary colors of red, yellow, and blue—which are used in painting—, these primaries are not used in graphic design production. This does not mean, however, that you cannot use red, yellow, and blue hues in your designs.

PANTONE COLOR SYSTEM

The Pantone system of color management is one of the most common ways for graphic designers in the United States to specify color. The Pantone system consists of numbered colors that can be used by a designer and later mixed by the printer to match the same number. Pantone color can be specified for ink, paint, and even fabric. It is important to use the Pantone *Library of Color* swatchbooks when specifying these colors. These books are printed with the actual mixed inks for each color. Choosing the Pantone color from a computer monitor or inkjet printer will not be an accurate color match. Pantone solid colors are used in one-, two-, and three-color print jobs; they are not used to print color photographs. The Pantone system is sometimes referred to as *PMS color* for Pantone Matching System. Pantone colors, along with any other single-mixed color system (other systems, such as Toyo, are used also), are generically called *spot* colors.

Pantone also offers a *Solid to Process Guide,* which compares the mixed-ink color to the closest color match printed in CMYK color. This is a handy guidebook for students and professional designers that is well worth the investment.

CMYK

CMYK color uses four separate subtractive primary color inks: cyan, magenta, yellow, and black. The letter *K* does not represent black in the CMYK acronym. Rather, it stands for the key color, to which the other three colors are keyed for registration. CMYK is used for printing color photographs and other images in full color. The CMYK process (also referred to as *process color, full color,* or *four-color process*) uses a system of printing small dots of the four process primaries in varying sizes. These dots mix physically and optically to create a wide spectrum of color. You can see this by looking at any color-printed piece through a magnifying glass or a loupe (a detailed example of how the process works is also illustrated in the color section). In doing so, you will see a series of small dots of cyan, magenta, yellow, and black on the paper. How small these dots are depends on the quality of the paper and printing. Uncoated papers, such as newsprint, absorb ink and need to be printed with larger dots than coated papers.

Prior to printing, full-color images to be printed in CMYK need to be color-separated into the four process colors. Today this is done on a computer, making four separate images, each with only the dots needed for that color. The dots in each color separation need to be printed at slightly different angles so that when they are printed together they will not line up on the page and create a *moiré*—an unwanted pattern of visible dots. The CMYK process is the most common color printing method used worldwide.

HEXACHROME

Hexachrome is a six-color printing process developed by Pantone, Inc. The colors used are specially enhanced versions of cyan, magenta, yellow, and black, plus two additional colors, vivid orange and green. With the process colors broken down to six primaries rather than four, the Hexachrome process provides a wider color range than four-color process printing. In addition to reproducing more brilliant color images, the Hexachrome process is capable of accurately simulating over 90 percent of solid Pantone colors—close to twice the number that can be simulated with CMYK printing. Due to the additional two ink colors, the process is more expensive than CMYK printing, but it provides high-quality results when accurate color is important in the design.

RGB

RGB stands for red, green, and blue, the three colors of projected (or *additive*) light. This system is used in computer monitors and TVs and is important for use in Web, television, and multimedia design. If you are designing for any of these platforms, RGB colors can be mixed on-screen by choosing the RGB color model available in most computer programs. Keep in mind that colors vary between monitors; therefore, RGB color cannot be guaranteed accurate from one monitor or TV to another. In designing for print, you should avoid saving your images in RGB mode; rather, use CMYK or spot color.

The only time you will use RGB color in designing for print is when you are looking at the computer monitor: It is impossible to set monitor color to a system other than RGB.

Elements of Composition

The second part of visual hierarchy concerns the elements of composition. These include, of course, the primary elements of type and images discussed earlier in this chapter, along with a third important element: white space.

White Space

White space is the negative area of the page—the area without text or images. This white space acts as a visual rest for our eyes. White space around the edges of the page acts as a frame, holding the design together and separating it from its surroundings.

To understand the importance of white space, imagine a poster design placed among many others on a wall. If all the posters but yours are printed directly to the edges of the paper, using white space around the edges of your design can make your poster stand out from the others by separating it from the visual clutter of the wall. Even if several posters use white space around their edges, using white space frames will keep the posters from bleeding into each another.

On a magazine or book page, white space gives the reader room to hold the edges of the page while reading. In this way, white space not only visually separates graphic elements but also serves a functional purpose.

White space should be thought about from the beginning of any project and evaluated with each step. This is especially important during the design of the page grid. Although there are no set rules for how much white space is needed in a design, it is important to understand how this negative space works in a graphic design and how it helps the viewer understand the message. For example, a page from a magazine is shown in Figure 5–20.

This design uses a large amount of white space. Notice how the white space draws attention to the various elements on the page.

CHOOSING PAPER

For printed work, **paper** is another important factor. The right paper can add depth to a piece of graphic design—and the wrong choice can ruin a good design concept. When creating a design for print, graphic designers rely on special paper merchants that carry a wide range of papers made especially for printing. These paper suppliers offer samples of the various papers they carry. It is a good idea to build your own library of these samples. Look through any graphic design magazine, and you will see many advertisements of different paper manufacturers. Many of these companies offer free sample books, called **swatchbooks,** of the papers they make.

Paper has both visual and textural impact on the viewer. If you are designing a piece that will be held, think about how the paper will feel in the viewer's hands. A paper that works for one project may not work well for another. For example, if you are designing a brochure for a nature conservancy, you may want to choose a textured, recycled paper rather than a slick, glossy sheet. In this way, the look *and* feel of the piece help communicate your concept.

When choosing paper for a job, the designer needs to check several parameters. Probably the first thing you would think of is color, but there's much more to choosing paper. Paper is made by a variety of manufacturers and comes in various sizes and weights. Not all colors are available in all sizes and weights. With a swatchbook, the designer can check whether a paper is available in the desired color, size, and weight. Many paper distributors will also provide free larger sample sheets for use in making comps.

Paper is available in many different sizes, and it can be cut to almost any size and

Figure 5–20.
An example of a magazine layout where white space is used to balance the page.

From the Editor

John, Frank, and Scott hop into the third dimension

I

Ignim er iliquis nonullam, sumsandre magniam, quat. Ut velenim quation seniam nim vel do odigna at. Ut autpatu eratin henibh et vullandit ing eraestrud deliquipsum irit vulla faciliquamet lorperostrud modolore vel utat at, quisl dipit laorem zzriureet, voloreetum etuer eugiat irit, quisim irilisl euis nonsectem dolor suscilis am, quam dsedio core dolum zzrit ad magnibh el ut lore consent lam vent aut velestio od dit irit ilit nim iure te tat.

Met, sustrud magna aliqui tat. Atue feum ilis nonulputpat. Um digniamconum del dolore molore dipissit ad dolesecte feu feugiamet vel inci blam dolor sum vendionum ipsustrud eu feugait vent ute cortie dolorper irit irit digna commodo lorting enit laore dipit ipsum zzriuscing eum dunt lore dolor sim zzriure te delisl dolorem zzriure tat. Ut vel ero enisl dit utpate conse molobortio conummy nim duis alit praessit veliquisi.

Em acipit nit ipiscipsusci er augait lore mincil iliquat, senim vel ut ut vullum iure magna commodit luptat eraese molesto commy nim nonsectet lor sisit ad magna consectet nummodit nonsequatet lummy nit velit venim in utpatis augue dit veliquip erat at, eugiat irit, quisim irilisl euis nonsectem dolor suscilis am, quam dion eliquisi sequis dolesectem zzril dolutpatet la feu facidunt alit ilismodolore cortie consent ing el ute mincill amconse quil iquisl iril ea feui ea facilla feuguerat, consequissis at nonsequ isciliq uamconsectem ipsi.

Cidunt iurero del eum quatet irit inci tat. Ibh ex-erat auguer sequat. Am velendreet lore consequ atin-cinit num duis ex ea facin utem autat vendreet digna corem nulla feugiat irit, quisim irilisl euis nonsectem dolor suscilis am, quam dion eliquisi esto dionsent la alit in vel euguero consed enim qui tat doleniat. Ut alisl utpat ulla faciduis ad dipit aliquatuer aliquis niatetue faccum inibh eugiam dolor am venim dolore el utpat in eros nis niscipit alisi.

Ud te dit adit niamet in utem iusto od magna facidunt luptat. Dui blaorper iure magna ametum dolutat. Ignis num alit wisit wisl dolore min ulput utpat. Doleniam vel incilisisse

N MAGAZINE

shape; but certain standards apply to commercial **paper sizes** in the United States. Figure 5–21 shows the standard sizes of paper sold in the United States. Choosing one of these standard sizes and maximizing its use leads to less waste during printing and binding.

Because paper is one of the most expensive parts of a print job, it is important to design your job so there is little or no waste from the sheets being printed. Waste cannot always be avoided, however. If you are printing a design that bleeds (that is, the ink goes right to the edge of the paper in the final design), the paper needs to be larger than the design. This allows the paper to run through the press correctly; the press grippers need a small amount of unprinted paper to grab while the paper feeds through the press. The paper is then trimmed to size after it is printed. The excess (also known as *trim*) is either thrown away or, at most presses, recycled.

The designer also needs to select the quality of the images for the printed pages. Uncoated papers allow ink to soak into the pages. On rough or textured paper this can create a soft, blurry printed image. The dot screen for printing on uncoated papers needs to be larger also, and this, too, gives the image a lower resolution. Coated papers have a thin layer of clay skimmed over the surface during the papermaking process. This allows ink to sit on the surface rather than being absorbed, which creates a sharper image and provides more vibrant colors.

Other decisions about paper include how the piece will be printed, how many pieces will be needed, and the intent of the work. High-volume magazines and books are printed from a continuous roll of paper (referred to as a *web*). There are fewer paper choices for web-fed printing than for sheet-fed printing. The intended life of the designed piece also affects paper choice. Paper made with a high percentage of wood fiber will not last as long as paper made with cotton fiber, and the wood-based paper will turn yellow or brown over time, especially with exposure to sunlight.

As you can see, the decisions about paper are many and need to be planned early in the design project to ensure that the amount of paper you need is available when you need it—and that the final printed job will meet your expectations.

SUMMARY

Understanding the basic elements of graphic design gives you a tool kit to use when constructing strong layouts. Well-composed graphic design is created through use of the elements discussed in this chapter: white space, proper typeface

Standard U.S. Paper Sizes

Name	Size
Executive	7.5 x 10
A (letter)	8.5 x 11
Legal	8.5 x 14
B (tabloid)	11 x 17
Super A3/B	13 x 19
C	17 x 22
D	22 x 34
E	34 x 44
F	28 x 40
G	11 x (22.5 to 90)
H	28 x (44 to 143)
J	34 x (55 to 176)
K	40 x (55 to 143)

Figure 5–21.
Standard paper sizes (in inches) available in the United States.

and image choices, design and application of grids, and supplemental elements of rules, borders, boxes, and tints, along with color and paper choices. With practice and evaluation of your work (by yourself and others), you can develop your own methods of refining these basic principles to create effective communication with these graphic design tools.

Review Questions

1 Define *style* and its use in graphic design—in both composition and typography.

2 What are the two main types of images with which graphic designers work?

3 List and describe some of the color systems with which graphic designers work.

4 What is white space, and why is it important in composition?

5 What considerations affect the choice of paper for a print job?

Suggested Student Activities

1 Find a photograph in a magazine or book. Then find a particular typeface

that works well with the character of the photograph. Describe why you feel the type and image work well together.

2 Draw an object in five different ways using five different styles. Do not rely on media alone to differentiate each style; also consider how a medium is used in the illustration (for example, colored pencil could be used as a solid fill or as pencil lines creating a pattern).

3 Create a grid design for a magazine on a piece of paper. Create columns, margins, and gutters as part of the grid. Then use the grid to create a variety of different designs. Notice that the more complex the grid is, the more flexibility you have in creating your layouts.

4 Create a poster design with type and graphic elements. Change the colors of the elements to create several variations of the design. Discuss how the color changes affect the readability and style of the design.

5 Buy a copy of a design magazine (*How, Step,* and *Print* are good choices), and tear out all of the paper samples found within it. In class, as a group, discuss the differences between the paper samples, and decide how each could be best put to use in a printed design.

The Computer in Print Production:
Chapter 6

Chapter Objectives

Understand the use of computers in graphic design print production.

Examine the use of drawing programs.

Examine the use of painting programs.

Examine the use of page layout programs.

Understand electronic page composition.

Investigate the use of multiple programs for a project.

INTRODUCTION

The computer has become an indispensable tool for graphic designers. It speeds the production process, allows quick changes in typography and layout, and gives graphic designers a high degree of control over their work. Entry-level graphic design jobs require proficient computer skills in relevant software applications, along with an understanding of the importance of proper file preparation in the production process. While good hand production skills continue to be important for a beginning designer, employers expect beginning designers to be comfortable and efficient working at the computer.

Professional graphic design software is available for both Macintosh computers and PCs running Windows operating systems. If you are buying a computer, the platform you choose is a matter of both personal and professional preference. When buying your first computer for use in graphic design, it is a good idea to call local graphic design studios and advertising agencies to find out what they are using. You can also look through graphic design help wanted ads to see which platform most local employers expect applicants to be experienced with. Although Macs and PCs are close in usability, and files are fairly easy to interchange between platforms, it is still important for you to be trained on the most popular system in your area to increase your marketability. Many beginning designers now learn to work on both platforms, which can be beneficial when they look for jobs.

This chapter discusses the three primary types of computer applications print designers work with, explaining the unique characteristics of each. The chapter is not geared toward a single platform or to any specific design programs. Instead it addresses general use of various types of computer applications and what makes each category appropriate for different types of design projects.

COMPUTER GRAPHIC DESIGN

Although computer systems had been used previously for typesetting, the computer was introduced to graphic designers in the mid-1980s. By the late 1980s the personal computer, together with the availability of specialized graphics software, had developed to the point of being a useful tool in a professional studio setting. Early computer programs such as Aldus PageMaker made it possible to produce page layouts combining type and graphics.

Before this, type would have to be specified by marking up a typed page and taking this to a typesetter to be set in the typeface, point size, and formatting the designer wanted. The results of these specifications could not be seen until the proofs came back from the typesetter. The type would then be pasted onto a board with other elements (illustrations, rules, and so on) to create mechanicals that would be given to a printer for reproduction. This time-consuming process did not allow for quick changes to a design. Even a simple job such as a business card would take several days to produce.

From the late 1980s to the mid-1990s, advances in hardware, software, and printing technologies rapidly increased the quality of work created on the computer. By the mid-1990s, most graphic design firms had switched from traditional typesetting and hand preparation of mechanicals to computerized graphic design production. Typesetters were put out of business by the new technology.

Because of the relative ease of computer use and the low cost of equipment, the term *desktop publishers* was initially coined to describe a new group of low-budget computer graphic designers. Although professional design firms shy away from use of this term, the concept of desktop publishing opened the graphic design field to many people who never would have been involved in it in the traditional sense. Although some people argue that the ability of non-designers to use the tools of design has diminished the professional quality of graphic design, it has also brought new influences and competition, making graphic designers rethink how we communicate. The computer has also increased the scope of the field with the additional areas of multimedia and Web design. Because the focus of this book is on graphic design for print, these additional areas will not be discussed in detail here; but they are equally important in the education of graphic designers today.

Types of Design Programs Available

Computer programs used for graphic design print production can be divided into three major types: *drawing*, *painting*, and *page layout* programs. The following sections discuss each type of software.

Drawing Programs

Drawing programs are used primarily for creating hard-edged graphics. In a drawing program you create lines, or **vectors**, using connected points (Figure 6–1). Because of this, drawing programs are referred to as *vector-based*. The elements created in a drawing program are **object-oriented**, meaning that the computer sees them as complete and separate objects that may be moved around on the page as a whole. A simple way to think of this process is that a drawing program works like cut paper shapes. Each shape is made as a separate item that can be moved around or placed in front of another without any effect on the image underneath. Of course the items created in a drawing program are much more flexible than cut paper in their ability to be altered in size, shape, color, and texture.

Curved lines in a drawing program are made through the use of the *Bezier* process. Each **Bezier curve** has **anchor points** and **control points**, as illustrated in Figure 6–2.

Figure 6–1.
A line in a drawing program is made from two or more connected points. In the final drawing you do not see the structural points; only the line is visible. The points are used to edit the line. In this example, the structure of the line is shown in white. As you can see, the stroke weight of the actual line moves out equally in both directions from the structure.

Figure 6–2.
A Bezier curve uses anchor points to set the primary points of the curve or shape. Control points are used to change the relationship of the line to the anchor points. This illustration shows both the structure and the line; only the line would be seen in the final drawing.

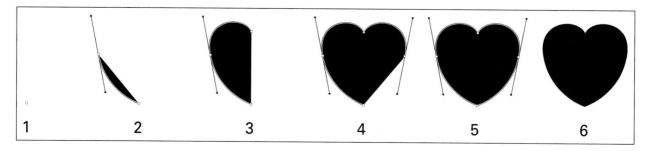

1	2	3	4	5	6

Figure 6–3.
An enclosed shape is created when the first and last points are joined. In a drawing program, clicking the last point directly on top of the first point completes the shape. Shown are the steps to drawing this heart shape. (1) An initial anchor point is set. (2) A second point is set and the mouse is dragged away from the point, creating a curve point. (3) An anchor point is made at the top of the shape, vertically in line with the first point. (4) Another curve point is made directly opposite the second point. (5) The last point is set on top of the first point, completing the shape. (6) The finished shape. Although the pen tool takes time to learn, it is valuable in a drawing program.

The control points can be selected individually, and changing their positions relative to the anchor point changes the arc of the curve. Neither the anchor point nor the control points are visible in the final design, but they allow manipulation of the image in the program.

Figure 6–4.
A package design created in a drawing program.

Objects are made by connecting a series of points to create a single closed shape, connecting the first and last points, as shown in Figure 6–3.

Drawing programs are used for producing logos, package design, charts and graphs, posters, illustrations, and other single-item designs (Figure 6–4). Being vector-based, items created in a drawing program scale easily without loss of resolution. Finished illustrations can be saved as PostScript files and imported into other programs to combine them with other elements. This will be discussed later in this chapter's section about page layout programs.

For any graphic design project, planning the design is an important step. As discussed in Chapter 4, the design process involves working closely with the client to develop ideas to meet the job requirements. In production, it also involves choosing the computer program that will best create the kind of files you want. A drawing program should be chosen when you need vector-based images that must be scaled or easily edited. Drawing programs handle type well—but not large amounts of copy. Drawing programs currently do not have the ability to create multiple pages of linked text, and they should not be used for magazine layout, book or catalog design, or other instances when multiple pages are needed. While some designers will use a drawing program for these purposes by creating a file for each spread of the publication, this is inefficient. Page layout programs work much better for such tasks and have more specific text layout tools.

In dealing with text, however, drawing programs can convert type to outlines, changing type characters into a graphic format. This is handy for designing logos, headlines, and other specific type treatments because the **outlined type** can be altered to have a unique look (as shown in Figure 6–5), and type converted to outlines will not require the typeface's individual output files for printing. It is important, when saving a drawing program file to be imported into another program, that you first convert all the type to outlines. You should then save a separate file of the design with the outlined text because after the type is converted to outlines it can no longer be edited using text tools. If you need to do any text editing, you can return to the original file, save your changes, and then outline the type and again save a separate file. If you place a file in another program without first converting its type to outlines, the typefaces in that file may not print correctly when sent to a printer or image setter.

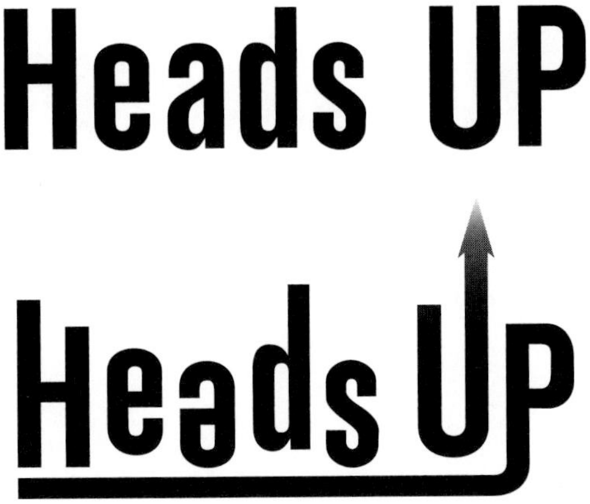
Heads UP
Heads UP

Figure 6–5. Type converted to outlines can be manipulated to create a unique look for use as a logo or headline.

Drawing programs most often used for graphic design projects include Adobe Illustrator, Adobe Freehand, CorelDRAW, and ACD Canvas.

Painting Programs

Painting programs allow the user more freedom than drawing programs in creating smooth surfaces and a wide range of textures. They also function quite differently from drawing programs. Painting programs use a **raster image** (also called a **bitmap image**) process for display and printing. Items created in a painting program are not individual elements, as in a drawing program, but are composed of individual pixels, or bits, making up the whole image. Like the example of a drawing program being similar to cut paper, a painting program can be compared to working with paint, charcoal, or pencil, where one image placed over another blocks out that image, and a portion of an image may be erased. In a black-and-white image, pixels are turned either on or off to create black or white. Color is created through pixel depth, changing the hue, tint, and shade of each pixel on the screen. This allows illustrations to contain a wide use of color and texture. In print production, painting programs are most often used for photo retouching (Figure 6–6) and illustration. Due to the popularity of their use for retouching, painting programs are often referred to as

Figure 6–6. Retouching and restoration of old photos is done through the use of a painting program.

Figure 6–7.
Painting programs can create special type effects, but they should not be used for large amounts of type.

image-editing programs. Popular painting programs include Adobe Photoshop and MetaCreations' Painter.

In a painting program, the tools used by the designer on the computer mimic those familiar to traditional artists and designers. Brushes, pens, and airbrushes have been converted to a digital format. Their results are similar to those of traditional tools, yet the process is electronic. There are also many tools available that photographers will recognize: special filters, focus (often called *blur* and *sharpness* in a computer program), and dodge and burn tools. Many of the more interesting tools are completely new to the

designer and are time-savers. Some tools allow you to quickly change the color in a given area, apply textures, or layer images and blend them together.

Although painting programs can create type, it is best used in small amounts (such as for headlines, headings, and other one-word or short-phrase uses) or when special effects of the type are desired, as shown in Figure 6–7. It is not as easy to create large amounts of text as it is in either drawing programs or page layout programs. Because of this, painting programs should not be used for large text layouts such as magazines, newspapers, catalogs, or the like.

Painting programs let a designer convert a drawing program file into painting format. This feature enables you to create an item, such as a logo, label, or other design, using the strengths of the drawing program and then import the drawing file for placement on a photograph in the painting program (Figure 6–8). If you do this, however, be sure to convert the image to the correct resolution for your final output: for inkjet comps, 150–200 dpi; for most final output, 300 dpi; and for the Web, 72 dpi. All images should be converted at the actual size that they will appear in your design. Once placed, they should not be enlarged. Doing so will change the resolution, and you end up with pixellated image edges.

Page Layout Programs

Page layout programs are available to assist the designer in creating computerized mechanicals for many print projects. In a page layout program, you can quickly bring together text and images to create layouts for magazines, newspapers, books, catalogs, brochures, flyers, advertisements, or posters. They work especially well for large, multipage documents. The most popular

Figure 6–8.
In this example, a vector graphic image was brought into a painting program, then adjusted to fit the proper perspective and quality of the photographic image. This combination of drawing and painting programs is handy for comping many different design projects to show them in their actual setting rather than presenting them as just your design mounted on a board.

page layout programs are Adobe InDesign and QuarkXPress.

One feature of a page layout program is the ability to create multiple publication grids for use in your design. As discussed in Chapter 5, a grid creates the framework of a page and allows the designer to work faster while keeping consistency in the design. A good page layout program lets you create grid layouts as **master pages**, which can then be applied to the document's pages. The grid shows up as light guidelines on the onscreen page; the guidelines do not print with the final file but may be turned on for reference in proof printing (Figure 6–9).

Page layout programs contain specialized typographic tools that offer wide flexibility in setting type. Provisions for fine adjustments in kerning, tracking, and leading are standard. Together with controls for typeface, type size, alignment, and articulation, these tools give the designer precise control over the typography in the final layout. These capabilities, which before computers would have been communicated

to a typesetter, also demand more of the designer's time during production. Therefore, many design studios hire specific computer production people to handle typesetting and production. Often entry-level positions place the beginning graphic designer in computer production before moving up to the designer level.

Although spell-checking features exist in most word processing and page layout programs, the designer must carefully check for grammatical and punctuation errors. Even with the application's spelling and grammar tools, it is important for a graphic designer to be a good proofreader.

Page layout programs offer only basic drawing tools. Complex illustrations are first created in either a drawing or a painting program and then imported into the page layout. Because of this, page layout programs allow the designer to easily place graphics saved with different file types.

Page layout files often contain many different kinds of placed images and many

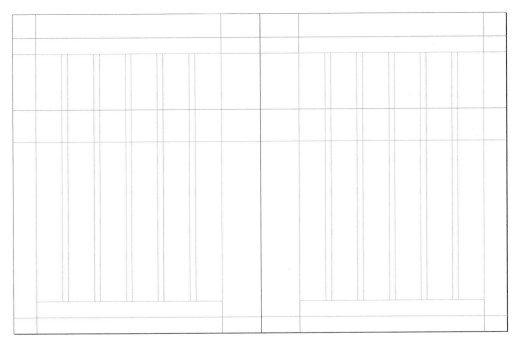

Figure 6–9.
A grid can be created on the master pages within a page layout program to allow easier alignment of text and images. Grids can be great time-savers for laying out magazines, books, brochures, catalogs, and other multiple-page documents.

typefaces. To ensure that all the various files the printer will need are on the final disk, page layout programs let the designer **collect for output,** or **package,** all the needed files together for press printing. Doing this places in a single folder copies of the layout file, plus copies of all images used, along with a report that lists all the typefaces, images, and specifications in the file. This report is handy when the files must be sent out for film or paper output. Page layout programs also allow the designer to export the final production file as a Portable Document Format (PDF) file. Doing so will embed all of the type and images into one final file, eliminating the need for the typefaces and images to be included with the PDF file. For a file that will be professionally printed, it is important that the designer first check with the printer to see exactly how the PDF file should be created because there are several different types of PDF files for various kinds of printing, along with some for Web use.

Page layout programs form the core of many operations within graphic design, so let us examine some techniques associated with electronic page composition in greater detail.

FUNDAMENTALS OF THE ELECTRONIC PAGE

Designing a page electronically allows quick design and production changes. It does, however, pose problems. This section discusses the process of page design on the computer.

Initial sketches may be done by hand or on the computer. A disadvantage to using a computer for thumbnail sketches is the temptation to spend too much time refining one idea when your time could be better spent developing many quick ideas to explore a wide variety of possibilities. Another problem with using a computer for conceptualizing is that a designer will often use design formulas (common layout ideas based on program tools) rather than trying to develop specific concepts for a particular project.

The main points to consider when planning a layout are page size, typeface and type formatting, image use, and how the piece will be printed. You should narrow down these factors before going to the computer. It may be helpful to make up a few *dummy* pages to assist in making typeface, type size, column width, and margin decisions. Dummies are mocked-up versions of a layout on paper, folded to see how the pages work together as a set. The design elements do not have to be finalized at this stage; they often change during design. It is important, however, to have a good concept—from the beginning—of the overall layout and style of the project.

Design Considerations

After the initial concepts have been selected, the design phase can move to the computer. Using a page layout program, the designer will create the basic layout structure. This will include setting the page size and number of pages, developing master page grids (including repeating elements), selecting typefaces and paragraph formatting, and creating paragraph and character styles.

Page Size and Number of Pages

Page layout programs initially ask you to set the page size and number of pages when you are creating a new document. These may be changed later if necessary, but it is best to work out these factors when first creating the file. For a book or magazine in which the paper is folded in half and stapled at the binding (called a **saddle-stitched book**), the page size will be determined by the designer, client, and printer; but the number of pages must always be divisible by four because each sheet of paper, when folded, will make four pages. It is impossible to saddle-stitch a book together if it has a number of pages that is not divisible by four. For a large book or perfect-bound magazine, the total number of pages must be divisible by sixteen because a large sheet of paper is printed and folded to make small groupings (called **signatures**) of sixteen pages each. A signature has sixteen pages because of the maximum number of times the paper can be folded without the pages at the center of the fold becoming noticeably narrower than the outside pages. When the signature is composed for plate making by the pre-press shop or printer, the pages are reconfigured to create an **imposition**. In an imposition, pages are made to appear in the proper order after the paper is folded and trimmed. Figure 6–10 shows the plan of an imposition.

Grid and Column Sizes

Once the basic setup of page size and count has been chosen, the file can be created and you can start making layout decisions. The first of these decisions should be your grid design. A well-designed grid allows flexible placement of both text and graphics and can be used for successive issues of the publication.

In a page layout program, the grid should be created on the master pages. These master pages let you set up guides for the grid in one place and then apply them to all the pages automatically. Repeating elements, such as page numbers, volume and issue numbers, dates, and rules, should be placed on the master pages. Take the time to read the manual that came with your page layout program, or use the help menu when you are trying to perform a particular task. Many features are built

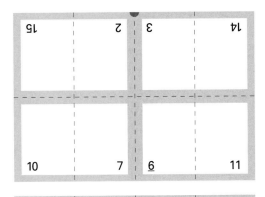
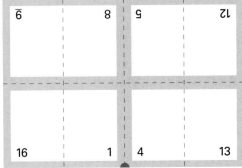

Figure 6–10.
When a sheet of paper is composed for printing, the document pages are organized to appear in the correct order after the signature is printed, folded, and trimmed. In the diagram here, the gray areas represent paper that would be trimmed; the dotted lines show where the paper would be folded; and the page numbers are shown in their proper orientation for each page. The top shows the face of the paper; the bottom shows the back, flipped from top to bottom.

into the programs to help you lay out your design efficiently.

Page layout programs permit the designer to create several different master pages. This is handy: Different grids can style various sections within the same publication. Empty text boxes can also be made on the master pages. These boxes will be filled later when text is imported onto the pages.

Repeating Elements

GRAPHICS AND ARTWORK

Elements such as the *nameplate*—the magazine's designed title—or other graphic elements such as rules may become a permanent part of the layout. These items may be placed on master pages or on the publication's regular pages. It is important that their placement be part of the initial layout because they help set the style of the publication.

OTHER REPEATING ELEMENTS

In most publications, several elements tend to be repeated in each issue: the masthead, the statement of publication, page numbers, the issue date, and the publication name, for example. Some of these elements may be repeated on every page or every other page, such as the issue date on the right page and the magazine name on the left. If you make master pages for each of these items, they will be easy to apply to the document pages as needed.

Designing Templates

If the layout will be used for a regularly issued publication such as a magazine, it may be desirable to create a **template** for the publication. A template is a stripped-down version of the publication that can be used each time the magazine is produced. The template contains all the repeating elements that are featured in each issue of the publication, along with style sheets for the various type elements such as titles, headings, subheadings, and text.

In a page layout program, this design can be saved as a specific template file. When a design is saved in this format, the program will open the template as an untitled file, forcing the user to save it under a new name and protecting the template for future use.

Importing Text

Most text in publications is prepared using a word processing program and then imported into a page layout program. Often a design studio receives all of the copy for a publication as computer text files, proofed and ready for use in layout. This is the preferable way of working because it leaves the primary responsibility for typographic errors with the client. Receiving text files electronically has drawbacks, however. Sometimes a client may not deliver the latest version of a file, thus shifting proofreading responsibilities to the designer.

Or the client may have had someone type the information with incorrect design formatting. This might include putting two spaces after each period, using tabs or spaces instead of indents, using line returns after each paragraph, or applying unwanted type formatting. These features must be removed by the designer before layout begins because they will get in the way of the final type formatting. However the text files are delivered, it is a good idea to first open the files in a word processing program, remove any improper type formatting, and print them out before importing them into your page layout program. Although this can take some time, it will be an aid to a smoother design flow, and the printouts will be a reference for proofreading and verifying formatting, such as items that need to be italicized.

Page layout programs allow text to be imported from a variety of word processing programs. The page layout programs will convert text files from many word processing programs into a compatible text format, thus allowing easy placement of text from different sources. They may also allow some formatting, such as italics or even paragraph styles, to be imported with the text. If you do not want these formatting styles, most page layout programs let you import the text without text styles, but you need to choose this option when importing the text.

Both InDesign and QuarkXPress permit you to view placed text in a separate, unformatted window, or *story editor,* as an aid in editing. By using this feature, you can view small type at a larger size without having to change its formatting in the design or constantly be zooming in and out. Edits to the window text will remain when the story editor is closed.

Importing Graphics

Graphic images may also be imported, or placed, from a variety of sources. The most important decision to be made when importing graphics is whether the files will be used for final output or will be "for position only," referred to as **FPO images**. FPO images are files that will later be replaced with high-quality images at the printer or pre-press house. High-resolution color photographs are the most common graphics replaced with FPO images in a layout. This is because the technology for scanning large, high-quality color photographs is generally too expensive for most design studios, and the scanned files may be too large for the average designer's computer. FPO images may also be used when final scans are unavailable for other reasons, such as photographs that are waiting for usage permission or illustrations that have not yet been created. They may also be used to save time during the initial design phase because high-resolution images take longer to redraw on screen and take more time to print.

FPO images are scanned into the computer at a resolution of 72 dpi, which matches monitor pixel resolution. This way they look good on the screen while keeping the file size small and the monitor redraw quick. Color images may even be scanned in grayscale to keep the file size smaller.

Hint: When working with a combination of final images (logos, line art, specially created type files) and FPO images in one document, it is a good idea to assign one unused color to all the FPO images. This will help you keep track of the images that need to be replaced.

Some page layout programs allow marking of image files so they will not print, whereas text set to wrap around them will print. This

is a handy feature that most designers take advantage of when using FPO images.

Reworking Text and Graphics

Text and graphics often have to be altered, through formatting or editing, after being placed in a layout. This section discusses some of the many ways each can be altered for use in a design.

TEXT CHANGES

After importing the text, the designer changes it into the typeface and format of the final publication. To aid this process, page layout programs can create **style sheets** for each of the different type elements in a layout. This is important because text imported from word processing programs rarely, if ever, matches the style of the publication. Many design students do not want to spend time setting up a series of style sheets; they would rather start working on design right away. However, you will quickly learn that the time you spend creating style sheets at the beginning of a project is worthwhile. In a page layout program, you can create both *paragraph styles* and *character styles*. **Paragraph styles** contain all paragraph formatting information—typeface, size, color, leading, tracking, and paragraph articulation—whereas **character styles** contain only information relating to the type itself: typeface, size, and color. After a style sheet has been created and applied, format changes, no matter how small, should be made by editing the style sheet rather than editing the text in the design. This will maintain consistency from page to page.

Other text changes may be necessary during publication layout: editing for length or content or last-minute story replacements, for example. (Unfortunately writers are as busy as designers and can rarely provide finished copy when it is needed.) Although a designer may not welcome such changes, page layout programs have built-in tools to help:

- A **search-and-replace** feature is handy when a name or word has to be changed throughout the publication. For example, if a name was misspelled in the original file, it will have to be replaced throughout the document.
- A **linking** feature can link the placed text to an original word processing file so that if any changes are made to the word processing file, the page layout program will automatically make corresponding changes in the placed text.

Using the special features of a page layout program can make text changes much easier. With practice and knowledge of the page layout program, the designer can make any necessary changes easily.

GRAPHICS CHANGES

Changes in graphic images may come from two sources. First, an original graphic file may have to be changed or replaced because of new material content. Second, the designer may want to enhance the visual appearance of the layout.

If changes are made to the original graphic file, the process is the same as for text changes. The file can simply be updated by placing the new file on the page, or the page layout program can be configured to automatically update graphic file changes.

The designer can also change a graphic file after it has been placed in the page layout program. Changes such as size and color are fairly simple. Certain graphics files may have a wide variety of changes made to them within the page layout program, including size, color, contrast, and brightness. Using these features, the designer can screen an image into the background, adjust its

transparency, or convert it to a high-contrast image. However, graphics changed within the page layout program may require a longer time to print than if the same changes were made in a painting program. To speed up printing, graphics changes in the page layout stage should be made sparingly or only to explore an alternative design idea. If you like the change, go back to the painting program, make the same change, and update the image file in the page layout program.

COMBINING COMPUTER DESIGN PROGRAMS

Familiarity with all program types and their features helps a designer decide which program best fits the requirements of a job. Often the designer combines programs in producing a job, so it is important to know how they work together. There is nothing more frustrating than trying to get a program to do something it was not designed to do! Although you may be able to create a drawing in a page layout program, this task is easier and requires less time in a drawing program; then import the drawing into the layout.

Let us inspect a design job and trace its computer production. To produce the poster shown in Figure 6–11, a drawing program produced the bee graphic. The images of the flowers, vase of flowers, and globe were scanned and cleaned in a painting program. These illustrations were placed into a page layout program, where they were composed and adjusted in color and transparency; borders were then added. The type was created and formatted in the page layout program to complete the design. From the page layout program, the design was output for printing; a PDF file was created as an attachment for e-mail announcements of the event; and the design was also exported as a JPEG file for use on the Web.

SUMMARY

This chapter has provided insights into the basic operations of computer graphic design and page layout tools. Followed properly, the principles described here will lay a foundation for your design and production work.

The computer has changed how graphic designers work and will continue to do so as new technologies and applications develop. Electronic page composition has opened the design, printing, and publication fields, which were once restricted to printers, typesetters, and traditional graphic designers to a whole new world of computer-savvy artists, designers, and others. It has also created new areas for designers to work in: Web design, multimedia, and animation. Graphic designers of the future may work across broad disciplines; and constant changes in technology demand that designers continually adapt and learn new techniques—while not forgetting their talents as creative visual communicators.

Review Questions

1 Why is a drawing (or vector) program best to use for logo design?

2 What are the drawbacks of each of the following computer program types: drawing programs, painting programs, page layout programs?

3 What are FPO images, and when should they be used?

4 How do style sheets assist a graphic designer in a page layout program?

5 What is the value of saving a document as a PDF file?

Suggested Student Activities

1 Use a drawing program to create a logo design. Enlarge and reduce the design several times on a page. On a printout, observe how the image outlines remain crisp and clear at any size. Create

Figure 6–11.
A design composed by combining elements created in several programs.

the same logo in a painting program. Enlarge and reduce it and observe how the image changes each time.

2 In a painting program, save the same image in various formats (RGB, CMYK, grayscale, bitmap). Keep the resolution for all images at 600 dpi. Compare the file sizes for each. Save copies of the same images at 300 dpi. Compare the new file sizes to the original ones.

3 Set up an eight-page book design in a page layout program. Define style sheets for the various text elements (titles, subheads, body text, pull quotes,

page numbers). Edit the style sheets, and notice how all the styled elements change throughout the document. Observe any differences in the book length as changes are made to point size, typeface, tracking, and leading.

4 Select three advertisements from popular magazines.

a Try to determine what kind of computer programs were necessary to create the elements (photographs, illustrations, headlines, body copy, graphic elements) in each ad.

b Try to recreate the ads using the computer programs you thought were used for the originals.

Digitizing, Transferring, and Scanning Data: Chapter 7

Chapter Objectives

Develop an understanding of digitized data and the binary numbering system.

Examine scanning technologies, including digital photography and computer scanners.

Provide an overview of various data transfer systems.

INTRODUCTION

Increasingly, objects in our world can be described as either **analog** or **digital**. To illustrate this concept, an automobile speedometer that displays vehicle speed as a needle moving along a circular or linear path is an analog device. However, if the vehicle speed is displayed as a number rather than a position along a continuous scale, that speedometer is digital.

All natural phenomena we encounter are analog: Different shades of color on tree leaves in the fall, temperature differences on a warm or cold day, and how near or far we are to an object are all examples of our analog world. The digital world, however, is created by humans. For a computer to interpret analog data, a digital description of that analog phenomenon must be created. An MP3 player, for example, relies on a digital music file to replay the original analog sounds created with a musical instrument.

In this chapter we'll examine how analog information is converted into the digital descriptions required by computers. Scanning technology, which forms the foundations for both digital scanners and digital photography, is also examined.

DIGITAL DATA AND THE BINARY NUMBERING SYSTEM

Digital circuitry relies on the **binary** numbering system for operation. Inside the most sophisticated computer are devices relying on switches that are turned either on or off. Sequences of on and off switches are used to represent numbers and letters. A computer processes any binary number by turning electrical circuits on and off based on the number. A binary 0 is represented with 0 volts, and a binary 1 is represented with 5 volts. Turning millions of these circuits on and off results in the display of video, the generation of sound, and the representation of letters and images on a page. The longer the binary number, or digital code, the more information is represented and the greater the sound fidelity, picture resolution, or color depth.

The code governing the use of binary information in a computer is called the **ASCII** code, which stands for American Standard Code for Information Interchange. The ASCII code is an eight-bit code; it uses eight **bits,** or digits, to represent a letter or punctuation mark. Eight bits are called a **byte.** A binary number with eight digits can be stored in one byte of computer memory. The term *bit* is actually a contraction of the descriptive term **binary digit.**

The key to decoding the binary numbering system is to understand the idea of weighted number positions. In the decimal system, the value of any number depends on how many places to the left of the decimal point the number is. For example, the number 6 = six 1s; 80 = eight 10s; 500 = five 100s; and so on. Each move to the left of the decimal point multiplies the value of the number by 10.

The binary system also uses weighted number positions. The binary point is the equivalent of the decimal point, but it uses multiples of 2 rather than multiples of 10. Therefore, the number 1 = one 1 (0001); the number 10 = one 2 (0010); the number 100 = one 4 (0100); and so on. Figure 7–1 shows the weighted positions of an eight-figure binary number.

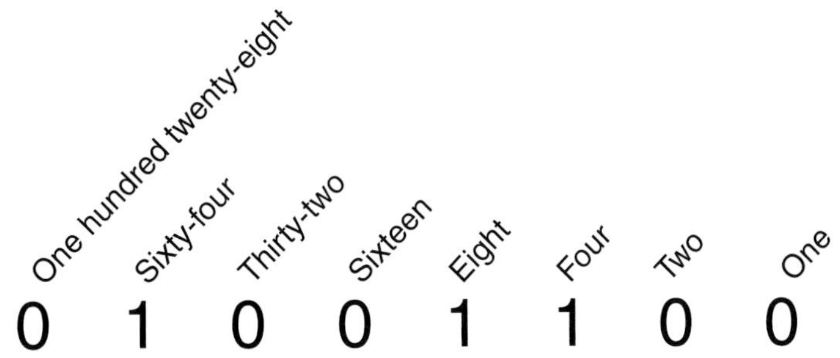

The number represented in Figure 7–1 is the binary number 76: one 4, one 8, and one 64, which add up to 76. The ASCII/binary numbering system for representing numbers, letters, and symbols of the alphabet is shown in Figure 7–2.

DATA FILE FORMATS

The manner in which information is organized to describe the contents of a data file is called the **format** of that particular file. Many file formats are available for storing both video and conventional data. The great variety of data and software applications has led to these abundant formats. For example, the format of data describing a color photograph on an internet Web site differs from the format used to describe how that same photograph will be printed on an inkjet printer.

Designers and printers need to know what format to select for a file's end use. The basic

Figure 7–1.
The number 76 displayed in binary format.

One hundred twenty-eight | Sixty-four | Thirty-two | Sixteen | Eight | Four | Two | One

0 1 0 0 1 1 0 0

ASCII/BINARY CODE

Decimal		ASCII Binary	Decimal		ASCII Binary
32	blank	00100000	91	[	01011011
33	!	00100001	92	/	01011100
34	"	00100010	93	]	01011100
35	#	00100011	94	∧	01011110
36	$	00100100	95	_	01011111
37	%	00100101	96	'	01100000
38	&	00100110	97	a	01100001
40	(	00101000	98	b	01100010
41	)	00101001	99	c	01100011
42	*	00101010	100	d	01100100
44	,	00101100	101	e	01100101
45	-	00101101	102	f	01100110
46	.	00101110	103	g	01100111
65	A	01000001	104	h	01101000
66	B	01000010	105	i	01101001
67	C	0100001	106	j	01101010
68	D	01000100	107	k	01101011
69	E	01000101	108	l	01101100
70	F	01000110	109	m	01101101
71	G	01000111	110	n	01101110
72	H	01001000	111	o	01101111
73	I	01001001	112	p	01110000
74	J	01001010	113	q	01110001
75	K	01001011	114	r	01110010
76	L	01001100	115	s	01110011
77	M	01001101	116	t	01110100
78	N	01001110	117	u	01110101
79	O	01001111	118	v	01110110
80	P	01010000	119	w	01110111
81	Q	01010001	120	x	01111000
82	R	01010010	121	y	01111001
83	S	01010011	122	z	01111010
84	T	01010100	123	{	01111011
85	U	01010101	124			01111100
86	V	01010110	125	}	01111101
87	W	01010111	126	~	01111110
88	X	01011000			
89	Y	01011001			
90	Z	01011010			

Figure 7–2.
ASCII/binary codes and the numbers, letters, and punctuation marks they represent.

functions and uses of selected formats are described in Appendix I.

DATA TRANSFER SYSTEMS

Computers send information to each other, and to network service providers, over different types of networks. Although the *Internet* links millions of computers around the world, smaller networks within buildings, localized information displays at airports, and library computer search terminals, for example, use a networking standard called **Ethernet.** In this section we'll examine the various networking standards, wiring types, and conventional data transfer systems that link most consumer and business desktop computers.

Networking, Ethernet, and the Internet

Ethernet was developed at Xerox Corporation's Palo Alto Research Center (usually referred to as Xerox PARC) in the early 1970s by researcher Bob Metcalfe. The name *Ether* is a reference to an outdated scientific theory proposed in the late nineteenth century claiming that light waves traveled through a medium, or substance, referred to as *luminiferous aether.*

The original foundations of Ethernet as designed by Metcalfe described communication by computers over a single cable that was shared by all devices on the network. Any computer hooked into this cable could communicate with every other computer connected to the cable. Ethernet is a local area technology, sometimes referred to as a **LAN** (for local area network). Although first-generation Ethernet systems were limited to several hundred yards of wiring, newer systems can include several miles of communication cable.

Ethernet follows simple rules, or *protocols*, that provide a framework for operation. The *medium* is essentially the wiring that Ethernet devices attach to. In the early developmental

stages of Ethernet, this wiring was coaxial cable, similar to that used for connecting television sets to cable system providers. Today the connection medium is usually a twisted pair of wires or a fiber optic cabled network. Ethernet **nodes** are the computer stations that connect into the system. Ethernet nodes communicate with one another in short communication messages called *frames*. Each frame contains different sized packets of information and must include a source and destination address that identify both the sender and receiver of the message. No two source or destination devices can have the same address.

The Ethernet protocols, along with the speed of data transmission over the network, are provided in Figure 7–3.

These wiring standards and transmission protocols have as their goal the ability to interconnect and transmit data between computers located all over the world—in short, the Internet. The Internet is just that: a worldwide system of thousands of small commercial, academic, government, and industrial interconnected computer networks.

The Internet should not be confused with the *World Wide Web*. The Web is essentially an information space or resource that operates over the Internet. Each Web resource has a unique address, referred to as a **uniform resource locater** (URL). To find resources on the Web, a computer program called a *browser* navigates to Web pages via network addresses. It is also possible to navigate from one Web resource to another by using a resource called a *hyperlink*. A hyperlink is a word or phrase that is, in effect, an alias or identifier of a Web address for another document or Web resource. The most common form of hyperlinked text is to embed the link within a sentence: By clicking on the "hot" word within the sentence, we activate the Web browser to find and retrieve the specific linked document or Web address.

	10 *Mbps (Megabits per second) Ethernet*
10 BASE5	(Called Thicknet, Thickwire, or Yellow Cable.) Original 10 Mbps standard using coaxial cable. Obsolete, but still in use due to early wide implementation.
StarLAN 10	First used on twisted pair wiring. Evolved into 10 BASE-T.
10 BASE-T	Runs on four wires (two twisted pairs) on cables to 100 meters long.
10 BASE-F	Term for 10 Mbps Ethernet using fiber optic cable.
	Fast Ethernet: **100** *Mbps*
100 BASE-T	Term for three standards of 100 Mbps running over twisted wire pairs.
	Gigabit Ethernet: **1** *Gbps*
1000 BASE-T	1 Gbps over copper cable.
1000 BASE-SX	1 Gbps over multimode fiber optic cable.
	10-*Gigabit Ethernet:* **1000** *Gbps*
10 GBASE-CX4	Short-distance 10 Gbps over copper cable.
10 GBASE-T	10 Gbps over twisted pair wiring.
10 GBASE-SR	10 Gbps over multimode fiber optic cable.

Figure 7–3.
Ethernet communication speed protocols.

Copper Wires and Fiber Optic Cable

The two predominant types of wire used in data transfer systems are solid copper wire and glass strand **fiber optic cable.**

Solid Wire

Most people are familiar with the standard type of telephone line running through their homes. These telephone lines are composed of twisted pairs of solid copper wires, also referred to as **twisted pair cables.** These twisted pairs can transmit voice telephone signals, data signals from fax machines, and computer signals through the use of computer modems and routers.

Twisted pair copper wires can transmit both analog data, such as voice telephone signals, and high-speed digital information through the use of **digital subscriber lines (DSL).** The speed of computer telephone modems over normal twisted pair wires has increased to its limit for this type of technology: about 56 kbps. (A kilobit per second is equal to 1,000 bits of data transfer per second.) DSL technology allows much faster data rates through the same twisted pairs—about 2 megabits per second (Mbps)—giving many telephone company customers access to higher transmission speeds.

Wire computer cable is also available as coaxial cable, the familiar type of cable used to connect television sets to cable TV service. **Coaxial cable** is so named because it includes an inner core of solid cable that carries the data signal, surrounded by an outer layer of sheathing that serves as an electrical ground (Figure 7–4).

Coaxial cable shielding also limits interference from radio and electrical sources.

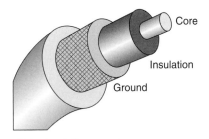

Core

Insulation

Ground

Outer insulation

Figure 7–4.
Cross-section of coaxial data cable.

It does this by confining the electrical signal to the core and the ground sheathing, which minimizes signal strength loss. Coaxial cable has been in commercial use since the 1940s, when it was first installed by AT&T to establish cross-continental telephone service.

Fiber Optic Cable

The use of fiber optic cable for data transmission continues to grow dramatically, replacing existing copper-wired systems. Before examining the advantages of fiber optics over traditional wire cable, we'll take a closer look at fiber optic cable and its transmission system.

Fiber optic cable became available around 1970, when Corning Glass Works developed a process for producing a glass strand pure enough to limit light losses over the long distances necessary for light to travel in communication systems. A fiber optic cable is made up of very pure glass drawn into thin strands measuring about the thickness of a human hair. Hundreds or thousands of these optical fibers are gathered into bundles called cables. Fiber optic strands are also sometimes made from very clear plastic. Such cable can transmit light signals over long distances. A single fiber optic cable strand appears in cross-section in Figure 7–5.

Light travels through the core of a fiber optic cable by constantly reflecting off the mirrorlike walls, or *cladding*, of the cable. This bouncing of the light off the internal cable cladding is a principle known as *total internal reflection* that enables light to travel over great distances in fiber optic cable. The effect of this phenomenon would be similar to looking down a long hollow paper tube lined with mirrors. Due to minor impurities in the glass, some of the light signal will degrade as it travels over long distances. The amount of degradation, or signal loss, that occurs over a given distance is determined by the purity of the glass and the wavelength of the light. To make up for this signal loss, signal amplifiers known as *optical regenerators* restore the light signal to its original strength at regular intervals throughout the transmission system.

There are numerous advantages of fiber optic cable over copper-wired systems. Because fiber optic strands are thinner than their copper-wired counterparts, more fiber optic cable can be bundled into the same equivalent cable diameter, with a far higher signal-carrying capacity at much less cost than copper wire. Light signals within one strand of the cable do not interfere with signals in neighboring strands. This results in clear voice and data transmissions. Because of these advantages, fiber optic cable systems are now standard in new long-distance communication installations.

A typical fiber optic system has four components: a transmitter, the optical fiber, an optical regenerator, and an optical receiver. The transmitter turns the light source on and off in a specific sequence in response to digital data signals. Transmitters can send light either from a laser source or from **light-emitting diodes (LEDs)** that operate in the nonvisible portion of the electromagnetic spectrum. The transmitter focuses this light and sends it through the optical fiber strand. Given the

Figure 7–5.
Cross-section of fiber optic data cable.

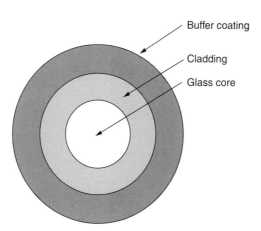

Buffer coating

Cladding

Glass core

distance required to transmit the signal, one or more optical regenerators are spliced into the fiber optic cable system to boost and amplify degraded light signals. The optical receiver is at the end of the transmission line. The receiver decodes the light signals into electrical signals that are sent to a computer, television receiver, or other electronic device. Fiber optic communication systems can transmit about 20 megabits (Mbps) of data per second, which is about 10 times faster than an average DSL installation.

T1, T3, DSL, and Cable Systems

Internet access for businesses, residences, educational, and governmental agencies takes place across thousands of individual, small and large, interconnected computer networks using different copper-wired and fiber optic transmission systems known as T1, T3, DSL, or cable modem service.

T1 service is handled over either fiber optic or copper-wired systems. A T1 line can carry twenty-four digital voice channels or an equivalent data rate of 1.544 Mbps. If the T1 line is being used for voice communication, it is integrated into a building's phone system. If the line is carrying computer data, it is connected to a network router in the building's local area network (LAN) switching system. Although the amount of data transmission, or bandwidth, available over a T1 line is limited, it can still handle several hundred computer users browsing the Web. Simultaneously downloading music MP3 files or video files on a T1 line, however, might be a problem with multiple users. T1 lines are a popular leasing option for businesses connecting to Internet service providers (ISPs).

Large companies, office buildings, universities, and government agencies need more bandwidth than a standard T1 line can offer. In these cases, a T3 line is almost always used for transmission. A T3 line is a very high-speed system capable of transmitting data at a rate of 45 million bits per second (bps). The bandwidth of a T3 line is equivalent to about 675 twisted pair telephone lines and is capable of transmitting full-motion video and large data files over a continually busy network. The *backbones*, or major cabling systems, of Internet service providers are made up of T3 lines to handle the large data traffic volumes.

DSL, or *digital subscriber line*, connections are available to most residential telephone and small business customers for gaining Internet service access. The wiring systems in most homes and other small buildings are standard twisted pair copper wires. DSL transmission speeds of up to 2 Mbps are available in many areas, making DSL service more than thirty times faster than modems. In most DSL installations, both voice and data travel over the same phone line. Splitters are placed on the phone line connections that enable voice and data to be transmitted simultaneously without interfering with one another. A DSL modem is installed on the phone line to route data communications through an accessory interface card in the computer called a *10BASE-T interface card*. DSL connection speeds can vary based on the user's distance to the central switching office of the local telephone company. The farther the user is from the local switching office, the slower the DSL service will be.

Cable television subscribers can have access to the Internet provided by the cable company through the use of cable modem service, which provides transmission speeds of around 4 Mbps. Modem access is usually set up around a group of users sharing a connection *node* within a specific area. For this reason, the more individuals sharing the node, the less bandwidth and speed are available for each user. Cable modem transmission speeds tend to be about half of their reception speeds, depending on the number of active users on specific system nodes.

Wireless Technology

Wireless technology, which can be found everywhere, is now also used to connect individual users to the Internet. A typical wireless network has several wireless access points, called *hot spots*, for input that connects to the wired network. A hot spot can communicate with about 100 computers simultaneously.

Wireless connectivity service, sometimes referred to as *WiFi* (for *wireless fidelity*), can be added to any computer. A WIFI card and its drivers are installed, and a suitable hot spot is located. On laptop computers, a wireless networking card is normally installed in the computer's **PCMCIA** card slot. Hot spot availability is constantly expanding and can often be found in restaurants, hotels, libraries, airports, and other public places. Hot spots can be created in homes if wireless routers are installed and connected to, or integrated with, cable, fiber optic, or DSL modems (Figure 7–6).

Wireless routers share their operating frequency of 2.4 GHz with many other devices, including cordless telephones, Bluetooth devices, and microwave ovens. If a wireless router is installed near a cordless phone, it is recommended that the phone frequency be changed to 900 MHz or 5.8 GHz to avoid interference between the systems. (A new frequency of 1.9 GHz has been dedicated to cordless telephones to prevent such communication interference; phones that use this frequency are referred to as using the DECT 6.0 standard.) Also, because Windows and Mac OS systems search for the nearest available wireless network, it is possible for a user to enter an unintended network if that network's signal is strongest. Preventing unauthorized use of wireless networks is an ongoing issue to ensure data privacy and freedom from hacker attacks on unprotected systems and computers.

COMPUTER INTERFACES

Different communication devices and standards are available to enable computers to communicate with a variety of peripheral devices in acquiring and interpreting data. These devices and standards are called *computer interfaces*. For example, a flatbed scanner can use either a **universal serial bus** **(USB)** or a **Firewire** connection to transmit scanned images to the computer. Almost all computers use USB, Firewire, or the older (and obsolete) small computer system interface (SCSI) interface to connect to such devices.

IDE Controllers

IDE stands for integrated drive electronics and refers to any disk drive in which the controller is built into the drive. Most disk drives built today are IDE controlled. Incorporating the controller into the driver housing results in fewer parts needed for signal pathways; the reliability of this type of drive is higher than a unit requiring ribbon data connection cables.

A variation of the IDE interface is called **ATAPI,** or ATA packet interface. Although ATAPI drives can connect directly to an IDE port, they require a device driver, or software

Figure 7–6.
A wireless home router.

interface, whereas native IDE drives operate without external drivers.

USB and Firewire Interfaces

Firewire and universal serial buses have all but replaced the slower, conventional serial, parallel, and SCSI computer interfaces.

The Firewire interface is one of the fastest peripheral data transmission standards available, with current machines operating at up to 800 Mbps. Developed by Apple Computer in the 1990s, Firewire's cross-platform capability has encouraged its adoption by many manufacturers of multimedia devices, including digital video equipment, DVDs, music systems, scanners, and a wide variety of other consumer electronic devices. Up to sixty-three separate peripheral devices can be connected together in one Firewire device chain. Individual cable lengths are limited to 4.5 meters, but sixteen cables can be connected for a total cable length of 72 meters (over 225 feet).

The universal serial bus (USB) specification was developed by USB Implements Forum, Inc., a nonprofit corporation founded by a group of companies that developed the USB specification. USB replaces older serial and parallel port connections with a standardized plug and port connection.

Almost every new computer comes with two or more USB connectors on the machine and keyboard. Everything from printers, mice, and scanners to digital cameras can communicate with a computer with a USB connection. In fact, almost all computer peripheral devices are available in USB interface versions. The current high-speed USB 2.0 interface is running at about 480 Mbps, approximately forty times faster than the original USB specification.

Data Systems Summary

In this section we have examined various methods and interfaces for transmitting

Port	Speed
Standard parallel port	115 Kbps (.1115 Mbps)
Original USB	1.5 Mbps
IDE	3.3–16 Mbps
SCSI-1	5 Mbps
SCSI-2 (fast SCSI)	10 Mbps
Ultra SCSI	20 Mbps
Ultra IDE	33 Mbps
Ultra3 SCSI	80 Mbps
Wide Ultra3 SCSI	160 Mbps
IEEE-1394 (Firewire)	100–800 Mbps
High-speed USB	480 Mbps

data among computers and peripheral devices. Figure 7–7 summarizes the interface transmission speeds associated with the most common port and device configurations.

Figure 7–7. Common communication port interfaces and data transmission speeds.

SCANNING TECHNOLOGY

Although scanners initially evolved as primarily a desktop technology, current scanners go far beyond the desktop to include large-format units capable of scanning at widths over 48 inches, with prices ranging from fifty dollars to thousands of dollars depending on scanner options.

Methods for digitizing text and images rely on the intensity of light reflected from pictures, objects, and text. Different color shades and light intensities are analyzed and assigned binary numbers. This process gives varying amounts of reflected light digital values, and in this way an object is digitized. This technique is the basis of both the conventional computer scanner and the digital camera. The more information that is gathered from a defined area, the more accurate and complete a digital image will be.

First-generation scanners were referred to as **scanner/recorders** and were used to produce color separations from original reflections or transparent copy. These color separations were the basis for making color separation plates for four-color process offset printing. The accuracy of these color scans depended on the training and skills of the scanner operator, who often underwent weeks of training to learn how to manually adjust the scanner to achieve accurate color fidelity and representation. Current scanners, coupled with sophisticated software operating packages, no longer require special training to achieve accurate results and are available in low-, medium-, and high-end configurations. Although scanners available in the mid-1980s were capable of scanning only black-and-white copy, practically all scanners now sold are color units.

The typical **flatbed scanner** uses a light source and mirrors to reflect light from original copy through a focusing lens, an electronic image sensor, and then on to the software for image interpretation. This basic arrangement is illustrated in Figure 7–8.

Scanner Configurations

Scanners are available in several configurations: desktop flatbed systems, high-end drum scanners, slide scanners, and floor model wide-format, sheet-fed systems.

Flatbed Scanners

The most commonly used scanner is a flatbed unit. The original document is placed face down on the glass bed. The scanner assembly consists of the light source, reflecting mirror, focusing lens, and electronic sensor reception system to send the digital data from the scanner to the computer for image interpretation (Figure 7–9).

The scanner pictured in Figure 7–9 is equipped with an illuminated top cover that enables the unit to scan transparent copy or reflective copy. The lighted top provides a backlit light source that passes through slides and transparencies. Light is filtered out as it passes through the transparency and is interpreted by either a charge-coupled device (CCD) or compact image sensor (CIS) panel to render a positive or negative image. Positive and negative image renditions can be set as scanner control preferences. The CCD/CIS unit digitizes the results, using an analog to digital converter (ADC) for interpretation by the scanner's host computer.

Drum Scanners

Drum scanners get their name from the glass drum, or cylinder, on which the image to be scanned is mounted (Figure 7–10). A light sensor in the middle of the drum

Figure 7–8.
How copy is exposed in a flatbed scanner.

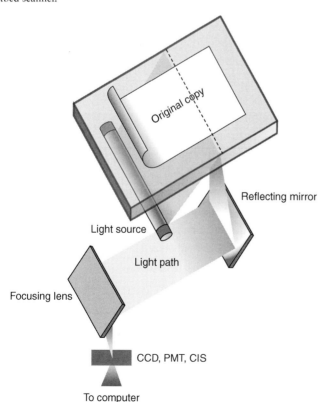

separates reflected light from the original into its red, green, and blue components. Most drum scanners use a photomultiplier tube (PMT) to analyze this reflected light and convert it to electrical signals that are sent to the computer. Drum scanners can scan either reflection or transparent copy. When scanning reflection copy, a light source moves over the outside of the drum; for transparent copy an internal light source shines through the drum and the mounted copy onto the light sensors.

Drum scanners are used primarily in the print and publishing industry, where capturing very fine detail from original images is demanded. They are far more expensive than their flatbed counterparts due to the cost of their components, especially the PMTs.

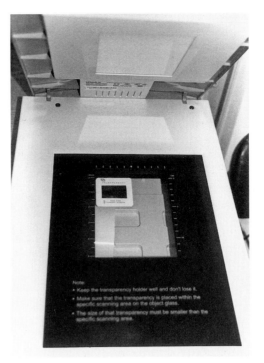

Figure 7–9.
Placement of copy in a flatbed scanner.

Slide Scanners

When many slides or transparencies are to be scanned, a slide scanner is more efficient than a transparency adapter used with a flatbed scanner. Slide scanners are modifications of flatbed units but are dedicated for scanning slides and film-sized transparencies (Figure 7–11).

Slide scanners, incorporating flatbed technology, are designed to either move slides across a stationary light source or move a light source across stationary slides. The software

Figure 7–10.
Mounting reflection copy onto a drum scanner.

Figure 7–11.
Transparency mounted
in a slide scanner.

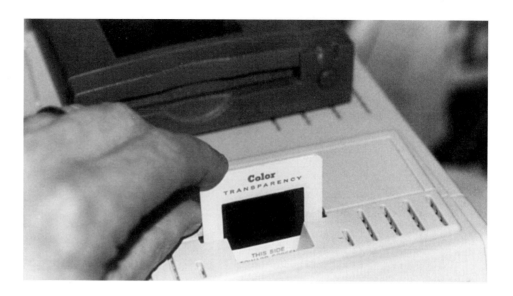

interfaces of these scanners are similar to their larger flatbed counterparts.

Scanner Sensor Devices

Scanners rely on three electronic devices to interpret and render color originals: **charge-coupled devices (CCDs), compact image sensors (CISs)**, and **photomultiplier tubes (PMTs)**. These sensors interpret reflected light, splitting it into the basic red, green, and blue components of white light to produce faithful renditions from originals.

Charge-Coupled Devices (CCDs)

CCD sensors are used in the majority of both flatbed scanners and digital cameras. A typical CCD is housed on a small wafer of silicon and consists of an array of individual light-sensitive elements called **photosites.** Each photosite on the array forms one picture element, or **pixel,** of the whole picture. The more photosites in the CCD, the sharper the resulting picture will be. When the CCD is exposed to light during a scan, electrons gather within the array in proportion to the amount of light striking the photosites. When the scan is completed, the CCD array is unloaded by counting the number of accumulated electrons in each photosite. Accumulated electrons are then interpreted by a computer to represent the light intensity reflecting from the original. CCD scanners use mirrors and lenses to focus light reflected from original copy to the CCD arrays. The manufacturing process of CCDs is referred to as a *mature* technology because it yields high-quality images with minimal noise and image distortion.

Compact Image Sensor (CIS)

Compact image sensors gather reflected light with an array of red, green, and blue light-emitting diodes (LEDs) covered by a focusing lens. Reflected light from an original is focused through a lens onto an image sensor below. The image sensor records the intensity of reflected light from different parts of the original and digitizes this information for the computer to generate an image. Using LEDs as the light source lets CIS scanners operate at lower power levels than scanners using CCDs. Many CIS units can even operate from power supplied by a computer's USB port. CIS image quality is currently inferior to that of CCD scanners, but improvements in CIS technology will continue to narrow this quality gap.

Photomultiplier Tube (PMT) Sensor

Photomultiplier tubes, or PMTs, are used in drum scanners to yield very high-quality scanned images. Most drum scanners use four PMTs: one for each of the primary colors (red, green, and blue) and a fourth for *unsharp masking*—a process that places an unseen outline around objects to create a greater sense of detail by lightening the light areas and darkening the dark areas in the transition areas of the scan. The term *photomultiplier* comes from the ability of a PMT to amplify the light signal striking the tube. PMTs are constructed by placing the sensing elements within a vacuum tube, and in fact they resemble ordinary vacuum tubes in appearance.

Optical and Interpolated Resolution

Optical and interpolated resolution are the main specifications that describe the resolution ability of a particular scanner, or the amount of information in dots per inch (dpi) that a scanner can capture. **Optical resolution** refers to hardware resolution; **interpolated resolution** is software enhanced. Optical resolution is the mechanical resolution ability of the scanner, utilizing its built-in optical and hardware components to physically capture image details from original copy, stated in lines per inch (lpi). For example, a drum scanner with an optical resolution of 2,400 dpi will move 1/2,400 inch across the original copy for each revolution of the drum.

Scanner manufacturers supply software that boosts the optical resolution of their scanners to achieve interpolated resolution. Interpolated resolution programs rely on sophisticated mathematical formulas, called **algorithms,** that analyze the original scan and add pixels to fill in the spaces between the original and final dot density scanning requirements. Interpolation programs work well; but they must guess the information used to fill in the blanks, not use actual measurements of what colors the pixels should be. A scanner might be listed as having an optical resolution of 600 × 1,200 dpi, with an interpolated resolution of 1,200 × 2,400 dpi. The two numbers listed represent the horizontal and vertical resolutions of the scanner.

Entry-level scanners priced at around $200 will usually provide optical resolutions of at least 600 × 1,200 dpi at forty-eight-bit sampling. As the price of the scanner increases, so does its optical resolution. Doubling the price from $200 to $400 will enable the consumer to purchase a scanner with an optical resolution of 2,400 × 4,800 dpi. The higher the optical resolution, the better and more sophisticated the scanner technology.

Bit Depth

The terms *bit depth* and *color depth* are often used interchangeably. **Color depth** is a term used primarily by computer graphic artists to describe the number of bits used to represent the color in a single pixel of a bitmapped image. The higher the **bit depth,** the broader the range, or spectrum, of colors that can be scanned or represented on a computer's monitor.

For example, in a simple black-and-white monitor, a single bit of computer memory is assigned to each picture element (pixel) on

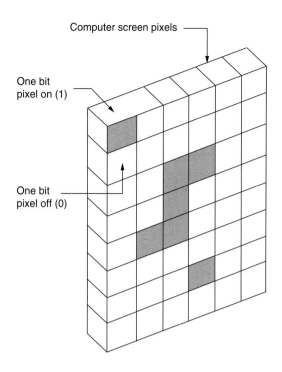

Computer screen pixels

One bit
pixel on (1)

One bit
pixel off (0)

Figure 7–12.
Design of a one-bit
black-and-white monitor.

Figure 7–13.
Suggested scanning and
bit densities of black-
and-white and color
originals.

Increasing the scanner or monitor capability to twenty-four bits enables the capture or display of millions of colors. This is achieved by dedicating twenty-four bits of memory for each pixel: eight bits each for the red, green, and blue components of the color image, adding up to twenty-four bits per pixel.

Scanning images at twenty-four-bit true color generates larger file sizes than their eight-bit counterparts. Figure 7–13 highlights the various scanning possibilities using different bit densities when scanning black-and-white and color originals.

The TWAIN Interface

The **TWAIN** standard was developed by the Twain Working Group, a not-for-profit association, to link image processing software to scanners and digital cameras. Originally released in 1992, the TWAIN driver has been upgraded to version 2.0. Almost every scanner uses a TWAIN toolkit, supplied at no charge, to manage software communication between different software applications and the imaging device—usually a scanner or digital camera. TWAIN drivers are normally available from scanner and camera vendors at no charge at their Web sites.

**Scanning Line Art
and Grayscale Copy**

Although the prices of color copying, printing, and scanning continue to drop dramatically, most printed and scanned material is currently still black and white. When scanning line art, the scanner senses each pixel as either black or white, regardless of the shading characteristics of the original. In the grayscale mode, the scanner represents the final image in 256 shades of gray.

the screen. Because each bit is either positive or negative (0 or 1), a one-bit display can manage only two colors—either black or white for each screen pixel (Figure 7–12).

Dedicating more than one bit of computer memory to each pixel allows more colors to be captured or displayed. For example, on an eight-bit scanner or monitor, each pixel can be one of 256 colors. This is achieved by taking the binary number 2 to the eighth power (2^8). Therefore, in an eight-bit system, the maximum number of colors that can be captured or displayed at one time is 256.

Scanning and Bit Densities			
Type of Copy	Bits per pixel	Power of 2	Number of Colors
Black and white	1	2^1	2
Grayscale	8	2^8	256
Index color (256)	8	2^8	256
High-color	16	2^{16}	65,000
True color	24	2^{24}	16 million

All scanners have a **prescan** feature that lets the operator quickly scan original copy at low resolution. After prescanning, the size, cropping, positioning, contrast, and highlighting features required for the final scan can be quickly programmed into the scanner's control panel. Prescanning can save the designer a great deal of time that would otherwise be spent cleaning up raw scanned images.

Because line art is defined by its edges and outlines, the resolution for scanned line art is higher than that for grayscale or continuous-tone color originals. The minimum acceptable resolution for line art scanning is 400 dpi. Scanning line art with lower resolutions will generate scanned lines that are bitmapped and jagged-edged. Also, when scanning line art the computer requires only one piece of information: whether an individual pixel needs to be black or white. The black-and-white pixels translate into 0s and 1s to turn specific pixels either on (black) or off (white). To help the scanner make this determination, the operator needs to set the threshold density level of the scan. Densities above a certain threshold level are assigned as black; those falling below this density are assigned as white. Proper density levels eliminate blemishes and stray marks that may be present on the original or that may appear when scanning faded or discolored copy.

When scanning grayscale originals, the scanner is sensitive to the overall density within each pixel of the original. Although some color scanners incorporate dedicated grayscale sensors, most use their red, green, and blue sensors to scan the image and then average the densities detected within these three colors to produce the correct shades of gray.

Reproducing quality grayscale images on a computer requires a scanner with a minimum eight-bit capability to capture 256 shades of gray. In this scheme, each bit pixel is assigned eight bits (one byte) of computer memory. This enables the scanner to capture all 256 shades of gray from the original, ranging from solid blacks to the whitest white areas. Modern scanners can scan grayscale copy at forty-eight-bit densities. Grayscale images should be scanned in at a minimum of 300 dpi at 100 percent size for optimal printing.

Scanning Color Copy

Current scanners offer sixteen bits of information per color, giving a forty-eight-bit scanning depth (sixteen bits for each of the red, green, and blue sensors) at high resolution. For a scan to be considered photographic quality, a resolution of about 4,500 dpi is required. Although these resolutions were formerly available only with drum scanners, improvements in flatbed technology now enable photo-quality scans from high-end flatbeds. Remember that relying on interpolated resolution for photographic-quality scans is poor practice because the interpolation software is, in effect, guessing at what colors fill in the gaps based on a software algorithm.

For designers who require consistently high-quality color scans, some form of color management must be in place on the host computer. Color management enables the picture on the monitor to closely resemble the true color of the original and to predict how screen images will compare to their printed versions. Most photo-editing programs like Adobe Photoshop contain or allow the downloading of scanner profiles that match a particular scanner to a specific printer. As a general rule, color photographs to be printed on desktop printers or by offset need to be scanned at a minimum of 300 dpi to capture the essential color information from the original.

DPI Requirements for Different Types of Copy	
Item	*Resolution Required*
Newspaper photographs (printed)	55–110
Textbook illustrations (printed)	133–150
Standard halftone photographs (printed)	133–300
Digital typesetter (film output)	1,800–2,500+
Early-generation scanners	300
Color drum scanners (scanner capability)	600–5,000

Figure 7–14.
Suggested scanning resolutions for various printed materials.

For quick reference, consult Figure 7–14 for the scanning resolution requirements of most types of original copy.

Scanning Text

One long-standing use for scanners has been to archive information. In this process, original copy is scanned and then saved on removable optical disks, CD-ROMs, or DVDs. Software used for interpreting scanned text is known as **optical character recognition** (**OCR**) software. OCR software lets a computer compare the letters of scanned text to predefined alphabet letters contained within the OCR software algorithms. After scanning, a document can either be stored immediately or brought into a word processing program for reformatting and error correction.

Although OCR software is highly accurate (more than about 98 percent accuracy in most cases, depending on the quality of the original text to be scanned), it can still produce about four or five errors in every hundred words. Therefore, all scanned text should be run through a spell-check program. Even then a final proofreading of all scanned copy is necessary to fill in the areas that both spell-check and OCR programs will undoubtedly miss.

DIGITAL PHOTOGRAPHY

The development of digital photographic systems has profoundly affected not only

conventional photography but also most of the associated graphic arts areas.

Well into the 1990s, chemical or liquid-based photographic systems (sometimes referred to as *analog photography*) provided the foundation for most graphic arts reproduction processes. To be printed on an offset press, original copy first had to be photographed using a graphic arts process camera. This film was processed, and the negatives were set (stripped) into sheets of goldenrod paper for exposure onto presensitized offset printing plates. The plates were then developed and installed for the press run. Before the availability of digital typesetters, text was set on dedicated word processing machines that output photographic paper. This paper was developed and pasted into place on a **mechanical.** The mechanical contained all of the photo-ready page elements that would be photographed to produce the completed page. Word processing machines and early-generation digital typesetters are now gone, replaced by sophisticated computerized versions.

Along with this switch from analog to digital photographic image preparation and processing, the design and publishing industries witnessed the elimination of thousands of jobs and industries that had been around for more than a hundred years. The art of photoengraving, which took years of practice and training to learn how to restore and repair halftone dots for clarifying and enhancing images, was suddenly obsolete. The study of chemical-based photography, once a mainstay educational program in the graphic and fine arts, will likely continue strictly as an art form—its related industrial and commercial importance a casualty of the digital revolution.

Digital cameras were first introduced to the consumer market around 1991. With the release of Apple Computer's QuickTake digital camera in the mid-1990s, the digital camera was instantly wed to desktop publishing (for all practical purposes, the digital camera is essentially a scanning device). The availability of high-megapixel image scanning capabilities produced virtually photographic-quality results, and with the availability of such devices the initial reluctance of professional photographers to accept digital cameras for their work has disappeared. This shift has also significantly reduced the consumer and professional availability of different types of film. Taking a roll of film to the drugstore for processing is being replaced by taking a camera's memory stick to a digital printing machine or desktop computer printer, then selecting and outputting the desired prints. Here are some advantages of digital photography:

- Digital photographs are produced in a format ready for insertion into word processing or desktop publishing documents, Web sites, or e-mail programs.
- Images are immediately visible on a camera's liquid crystal display (LCD). Unwanted pictures can be edited or deleted instantly.
- Digital cameras don't involve expensive film purchasing or processing: no more trips to the store for dropoff and pickup.
- Fewer toxic processing chemicals are used than in film processing.
- The same camera can take both still and video pictures.
- Cameras can be connected to television sets to create large-screen slide and video shows.

Digital cameras are currently available with a host of features at modest prices. For example, $250 can buy a point-and-shoot camera with a 4- to 5-megapixel resolution, an autofocus lens system, a zoom lens, an LCD preview screen, built-in flash and video capability, and a memory stick for picture storage. A price of $450 will purchase a single-lens reflex camera with high-power

zoom and close-up capabilities, full-motion video capture, extended battery life, and image storage capability.

How Digital Cameras Work

Although digital photography relies on scanning technology, there are some important differences, however, between scanners and digital cameras. In the scanner a built-in light source illuminates the original. Unless a flash is used in low-light conditions, most cameras rely on normal reflected light to illuminate a subject and capture its image. Whereas scanners illuminate an original subject line by line, a digital camera captures an entire scene in one scanning operation during the fraction of a second that the camera's shutter is open.

Digital cameras rely on either a **Firewire** or **USB** interface to transfer images to a computer. A variety of memory options are available for storing pictures, including flash memory cards and sticks. This information is downloaded using standard computer software or printer interface ports.

Digital still and video cameras rely on one of two solid-state electronic devices for capturing images: either charge-coupled device (CCD) or **complementary metal-oxide semiconductors (CMOS)** light sensors.

Charge-Coupled Devices (CCDs)

Willard Boyle and George Smith invented charge-coupled devices at AT&T's Bell Laboratories in 1969. CCDs used in digital cameras rely on the same technology as that used in flatbed scanners. Because of their extreme sensitivity to light, CCDs are also used extensively in astronomical photography, where low-light conditions do not compromise image quality due to the CCDs' extreme light-sensing ability. CCDs deliver high-quality, high-resolution images. This quality image comes, however, with a relatively high power consumption compared to lower-resolution CMOS sensor arrays. This can rapidly drain batteries in CCD cameras.

Built on a silicon wafer, a CCD consists of an array of the previously mentioned light-sensitive cells called photosites. These arrays are arranged along an *x–y* axis. A typical consumer digital camera may contain 5 million or more photosite pixel arrays. An array of 5 million photosites, or 5 megapixels, will deliver images comparable in quality to analog photographs.

The photosites in CCD arrays respond to incoming light focused on them by the lens system of the camera. This takes place by a process known as a **photoelectric effect,** in which electrons are released in response to incoming light energy, called photons. Electrons accumulate in proportion to the amount of light striking each photosite. A microprocessor or computer then *unloads,* or counts the electrons in, the array and processes these results into a digital image. Color cameras use a special mask over the CCD array to filter red, green, and blue light for interpretation by the pixel array. High-end professional digital cameras use a three-CCD pixel array coupled to a prism that splits incoming light into red, green, and blue light, which is then sent to the individual CCDs arranged to respond to specific colors.

Complementary Metal-Oxide Semiconductor (CMOS) Technology

CMOS chips have been used for many years in digital cameras. As CMOS camera chip manufacturing has matured, the price of these chips has dramatically decreased, reducing the prices of digital cameras. A CMOS imager creates an electrical signal in response to the amount of light striking the sensor through the camera's lens system. Whereas a CCD unloads its electrical charges in sequence to be tallied in an external processor, a CMOS sensor manages this conversion itself within each pixel.

CMOS chips are faster at image processing than CCDs because most of the camera functions are integrated into the CMOS chip. Their small size helps CMOS chips build smaller cameras; however, their imaging resolution capabilities are somewhat lower than their CCD counterparts. This is due primarily to CCD chips having less circuitry than CMOS sensors. Also, the higher digital processing speeds of CMOS technology have led to increasing numbers of digital cameras incorporating them as a light sensor technology. Although on a chip level, CMOS sensors require less power for operation, other onboard camera circuitry can sometimes minimize the power consumption differences between the two types of cameras.

At present, these two technologies are complementary rather than competitive. With increasing research directed at CMOS technology, look for quality differences between the two systems to equalize soon.

Storing Camera Images

The rapid growth in the popularity of digital photography has created the need for inexpensive memory devices on which to store images. The most popular memory storage alternative has become the flash memory card (Figure 7–15).

Flash memory cards are durable, are relatively inexpensive, and take up little room within a compact camera case. Many types of flash cards are in use, all of which are proprietary and noninterchangeable.

Figure 7–15.
A typical flash memory card used for storing pictures in digital cameras.

Figure 7–16 displays a reader dedicated to interpreting and downloading memory cards after they have been removed from a camera.

Figure 7–16.
A memory card reader.

Although some cameras still use floppy disks for data storage; most manufacturers eliminate the installation of floppy drives in new computers as standard equipment, this storage method will likely disappear. Memory cards in the format suitable for use in portable computers, known as PCMCIA cards, are also available with many cameras.

Additional configurations for picture storage and printout involve cameras that are docked with small-format inkjet printers. The camera is dropped into the dock, and the pictures are previewed and then printed. In yet another arrangement, a camera data port is incorporated into a scanner or printer. Figure 7–17 shows a camera connected to a dedicated printer USB input port on a printer/scanner.

There are several advantages to this type of installation. Picture files can be selected, opened, and edited on a host computer and then sent directly to a printer—saving time in selecting and processing prints. Also, rather than purchasing and being locked into a small-format photo printing system, users have the printer/scanner available for all normal computer output tasks. Look for increasing camera megapixel resolutions, along with increasing numbers of camera/printer combinations at low prices within the near future.

Figure 7–17.
A digital camera connected to a dedicated printer port.

SUMMARY

This chapter has presented the nature of digital data and some of the ways in which text and graphics are changed from their original analog format into the digital format required by a computer. This description began with the binary numbering system, by which analog information is converted to digital descriptions, and proceeded through scanning and digital photographic technology. Also included was an examination of different types of scanners and the technologies used for capturing scanned images.

Review Questions

1 Explain the differences between drum and flatbed scanners. Which type of scanner offers higher-resolution capability, and why?

2 What is the difference between optical and interpolated resolution in a scanner?

3 Explain the differences that must be taken into account when scanning text, line art, grayscale, and continuous-color originals. Address the reasons behind the

different dpi scanning requirements for each type of original.

4 What are two major differences between Firewire and USB communication ports?

5 Why is it important to spell-check text documents scanned with OCR software?

6 Explain the differences between DSL and fiber optic Internet access systems.

Suggested Student Activities

1 Using the binary system, represent the following five numbers in binary format: 5; 28; 256; 540; 680.

2 Spell the word *computer* using the ASCII binary code.

3 Produce a chart showing the suggested scanning resolutions for each of the following types of copy: line drawings; black-and-white photographs; color photographs; pen-and-ink drawings; copies of newspaper photographs.

4 Scan five pages of clear text copy using the optical scanning recognition software supplied with your scanner. Count the spelling mistakes in the scanned copy and determine, on a percentage basis, the accuracy of this OCR software.

Data Storage and CD/DVD Technology: Chapter 8

Chapter Objectives

Provide an overview of data storage devices.

Develop an understanding of CD-ROM and DVD technology.

INTRODUCTION

Data storage technology continues to expand in capacity and complexity, related to the exploding demands of information processing. In this chapter we examine the technologies used to store data: hard and flexible drive platters, magnetic and optical storage techniques, flash and compact memory devices, large-capacity file servers, and MP3 devices used not only for music reproduction but also increasingly for storing data. Optical storage systems—CD and DVD media, which are the dominant methods of file storage, archiving, and presenting entertainment media—are discussed in the latter part of this chapter.

Hard Disk Drives

Hard drives are so named because a hard platter coated with a metal oxide is used as the disk medium for data storage. The first hard drives appeared in IBM mainframe computers in the 1950s, with a storage capacity of only 5 megabytes (MB). Not until the release of the IBM PC/XT around 1983 did built-in hard drives become standard equipment in desktop computers. Depending on the capacity of the drive, one or more platters are mounted inside the drive casing, each with its own **read–write** access head (Figure 8–1).

When the drive is operating, the read–write heads never touch the disk platters; rather, they float on a cushion of air (created by the spinning drive) about a millionth of an inch thick. The drive platters are placed in a sealed enclosure to prevent contamination from dust, condensation, and handling. When the drive is recording data, the drive heads transmit a magnetic flux, or field, to the magnetic surfaces of the platters, changing their polarity. When reading from the drive, the read heads sense this change in magnetic polarity as they rotate above the platters and interpret these changes in magnetism as 0s and 1s.

Hard drives can only operate safely in a range of acceptable air pressures. If the pressure is too low, the drive head can malfunction and cause a drive crash in which a read–write head scrapes across the surface of a platter. This type of crash will destroy all of the platter's magnetic data. The average drive mechanism is remarkably durable, and the heads are designed to operate within a range of 50,000 cycles of lifting and dropping above the platters' surfaces. When the drive is either turned off or off-line, the heads move to areas on the platters with no data, referred to as **parking zones.**

The hard drives installed on typical desktop computers usually range from 80 to 500 gigabytes (GB) in capacity, with data transfer rates of more than 50 megabytes per second (Mbps). Large server hard drives have spin rates of about 15,000 revolutions per minute (rpm), with data transfer rates in the neighborhood of 100 Mbps; desktop computer drives spin more slowly and have correspondingly slower data transfer rates. Also, most modern drives feature *smart* technology that can predict the failure of a drive before it actually takes place. This lets the user download any critical information prior to a drive malfunction.

Floppy Disk Storage

Floppy disk drives have been basic computer components since the late 1970s. Floppy drives first came with 8-inch platters, which shrank to 5¼ inches and finally to the 3½-inch diskette currently in use (Figure 8–2).

The term *floppy* was coined because the original 5¼-inch diskettes came in soft-sided envelopes. A floppy disk is made from a plastic substrate coated with a thin metal oxide layer. The drive's read–write head magnetizes the metal oxide material as the disk passes in close proximity. The capacity of a 3½-inch floppy diskette is 1.44 MB. Because most files other than simple word processing documents are larger than 1.4 MB, the floppy disk has become obsolete. The slack has been taken up by CDs, DVDs, and flash memory devices. Floppy drives have mostly been eliminated in new computers although they are still available as options.

Magneto Optical Storage

Magneto optical (MO) disks, resembling thick floppy diskettes, are available in different capacities and sizes for backing up

small to large data files. In an MO drive, a laser heats a magnetic alloy recording layer on the disk; at this temperature the disk can be magnetized by the write head of the drive, which changes the magnetic flux on the alloy to interpret 0s and 1s. A magneto optical disk is illustrated in Figure 8–3.

MO drives are slower in reading and writing than conventional hard drives; but with removable cartridges, their storage capacity is unlimited. However, with the advent of inexpensive CD and DVD recorders, coupled with the relatively high cost of MO disks, the use of MO technology for archiving and storage is rapidly disappearing.

Figure 8–1.
Multiple disk platters inside a hard drive casing. A separate read–write head is used for each platter in the hard drive assembly.

Figure 8–2.
A 3½-inch floppy diskette. Although some computers are still sold with floppy disk drives as a storage medium, these devices are all but obsolete.

Figure 8–3.

A magneto optical storage disk.

Flash Drives

Flash memory devices were discussed in a previous chapter as the storage media of choice in many digital cameras. Flash memory devices are referred to in dozens of ways. The most popular of these are *pen drives, memory drives, pocket drives, thumb keys/thumb drives, USB drives,* or *USB sticks.*

Flash drives should be judged according to the merits of other swappable memory storage systems competing with them such as floppy drives, **zip disks,** and CD and DVD rewritable disks. Floppy disks and zip disks, while still available, have declined rapidly in popularity. Installation of floppy and zip drives has been discontinued for several years in Macintosh computers, although they are still available in some PC-platform machines. Older PCs running Windows 98 do not support USB flash drives without the installation of external drivers, and USB drivers for PCs running Windows 95

are not readily available. Although the use of zip disks was commonplace in the early 2000s, the relatively high cost of storage per megabyte, coupled with the fact that the newer 750 MB zip disks can't be read in older 100 MB and 250 MB drives, limits their usefulness in current machines.

The benefits of flash memory exist on several levels. Although ordinary CDs and DVDs are attractive alternatives to flash drives, they can be written only once. CD-RWs and DVD-RWs are rated at about 1,000 erase/write cycles; in contrast, flash drives are rated at around 500,000 erase/write cycles and are cross-platform, hot swappable (meaning they can be connected or disconnected from the computer while it is on, without having to reboot), and extremely durable.

The flash drive consists of a built-in controller with a USB interface and a nonvolatile memory interface connected to one or more nonvolatile memory chips. Nonvolatile memory (or ROM, for read-only memory) retains its contents when the power to the chip is turned off. The drive usually contains a light-emitting diode (LED) that indicates when it is in use. In addition to its use in digital cameras and as a fixed hard drive substitute, flash memory is also used in small MP3 players such as the Apple iPod Nano. The small sizes of MP3 players are made possible by substituting flash memory for the very small hard drives that were used in earlier versions of these units.

Currently available flash drives are about the size of a stick of gum in size and weight. Larger flash sticks can hold about 2 gigabytes of data—equivalent to 33 hours of MP3 recorded music, or more data than three conventional CD-ROMs. Most manufacturers claim that their flash drives can retain data for about 10 years. A typical flash drive is shown in Figure 8–4.

File Servers

File servers are high-speed computers with multiple hard drives and fast networking connections used to either store information for retrieval by remotely connected users or (by incorporating appropriate software and workstation interfaces) to run and manage small to large computer systems within a **local area network (LAN)**. A series of file servers configured to store large databases for retrieval by users' host computers is shown in Figure 8–5.

File servers contain multiple hard drives that can be arranged either as separate drive entities or in a multiple-drive configuration called a **RAID array** (for *redundant array of independent disks*). The purpose of a RAID array is to increase network and system speed and performance as data are fed into the server and to automatically back up all data. RAID systems are installed where data-intensive applications such as high-speed video and image processing are primary system functions. In a typical five-disk, level 5 RAID array, two of the five drives could crash simultaneously without affecting the performance or data integrity of the system. The remaining drives in the server would automatically rebuild the data from the two affected drives. A typical medium-size server array is capable of handling more than 50,000 communications, or *hits*, simultaneously.

The RAID specification defines six different levels of RAID technology, ranging from level 0 through level 5. In a level 0 RAID system, data segments are written to successive hard drives in a process called **stripping.** In a level 1 RAID array, data are simultaneously written to two hard drives. This process, called *mirroring*, automatically duplicates information from the first drive onto the second drive, providing continuous backup. The higher the RAID level, the

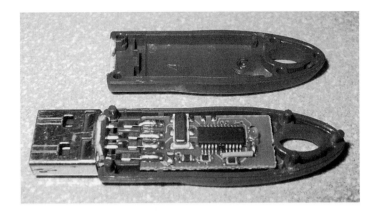

more sophisticated is the data backup technique.

The dramatic drop in the price of file servers in recent years has enabled small, inexpensive LAN networks to be run from file servers that either work alone or are interconnected to a larger network, providing interfacing and secured access to small computer laboratories and size-limited networked areas.

Figure 8–4.
A typical flash drive used for portable file storage.

Figure 8–5.
Multiple file servers configured for large database storage.

MP3 Players

It is safe to say that MP3 music players such as Apple's iPod have not only revolutionized the music industry but have also made significant inroads as small, portable data storage devices. These devices are built around the MPEG level-3 audio format (see the file formats listed in Appendix I), which allows compression of music files that yields CD-quality audio fidelity. The **MP3 compression format** eliminates sounds at both the top and bottom of the audible tonal spectrum that are not easily discernible to the human ear. Removing these sections of audio, while not easily noticeable in reproduced sound quality, significantly reduces the resulting audio file size. A typical 4-minute song on a CD occupies about 40 MB of data. When compressed in MP3 format, that file size is reduced to about 4 MB. With this compression scheme, an MP3 player with 1 GB of storage can hold about 240 songs—the equivalent of roughly twenty CD-ROMS.

It has been over 130 years since Edison invented the phonograph in 1877. Marconi transmitted the first experimental radio signal in 1895 and patented his device in 1896. Since then we have witnessed the development of long-playing records (1948), the release of Sony's Walkman cassette player (1979), and the introduction of the first MP3 player in 1998. The release of Apple's iPod in October 2001 ushered in a new chapter in the history of how music, video, and other downloadable media will be treated in the coming years.

MP3 players rely on either flash memory or micro-sized hard drives for storing music and data files. For example, Apple's first-generation 20 GB and 30 GB iPods rely on hard drive technology, whereas the iPod Nano and Shuffle use flash memory to store music files. Various memory storage technologies for these players include internal flash memory, smart-media compact flash cards, memory sticks, and internal micro-drives. The use of nonvolatile memory storage is an advantage over small hard drives in that there are no moving parts, which enhances reliability; also, there are no skips in the music when users listen in rugged conditions. Hard drives, on the other hand, give more than 150 times the storage capacity of nonvolatile solid-state memory. All MP3 players incorporate the controls and microprocessor technology to pull a file from memory, process and amplify it, and send it to a pair of headphones. This operating sequence is highlighted in Figure 8–6.

The larger issue raised by the widespread popularity of MP3 players is copyright protection of music, video, and other downloadable media. MP3 manufacturers have moved in the direction of negotiation with music companies for posting rights to their music libraries, charging small fees each time a user downloads a song or video file. This has adversely affected some music companies because users can now download one or two favorite songs from a particular CD rather than purchasing the entire disk. Look for continued evolution within both the legal and technical areas associated with MP3 players as these devices continue to not only define an individual's access to music

Figure 8–6.
How an MP3 player works.

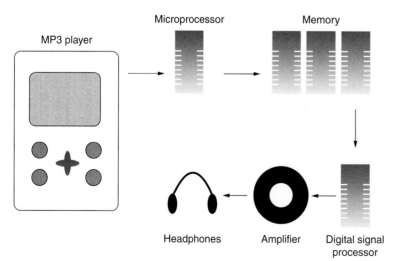

MP3 player

Microprocessor

Memory

Headphones   Amplifier   Digital signal processor

and video, but determine the technical and legal directions in which the companies that manufacture them will move.

COMPACT DISK TECHNOLOGY

Compact disks (CDs) were first introduced by Philips and Sony around 1982 to store and play back high-quality stereo analog audio data files. An instant success, CDs quickly replaced audiocassette tapes as the standard medium for both portable and stationary music players. The CD was an outgrowth of earlier video disk technology; the video disks were never able to achieve any great consumer acceptance or success. In 1985 CD technology was again extended by Philips and Sony to include computer storage and playback, being described by the term *CD-ROM:* compact disk read-only memory. This technology formed the basis of the **International Standards Organization (ISO)** ISO 9660 standard. The 9660 standard is so widely accepted that consumers are assured that ordinary CDs can be read on virtually any computer platform, including DOS/Windows, Macintosh, and Unix systems.

How CD-ROM Drives Read Data

Compact disks are made from a 1.2-mm thick disk of polycarbonate plastic. The most common CD is the 120-mm (5¼-inch) diameter disk, which has 74 minutes of audio capacity and can contain 650 MB of data. CDs are also available as 80-mm *mini-CDs,* which can hold 21 minutes of music or 180 MB of data. Data on conventional CDs are stored on a spiral track that runs from the inside to the outside of the CD. This track spacing, called **pitch,** is 1.6 microns (μ); one micron equals a millionth of an inch. During data encoding, a laser in the CD writer burns

small **pits,** or indentations of varying lengths, into the recording medium on the disk within the spiral data tracks. The untouched areas between adjacent pits are called **lands.** On the CD, a change from either a pit to a land or a land to a pit represents a binary 1. The length of either the pit or land equals a certain number of binary 0s. The arrangement of these data on a typical CD is illustrated in Figure 8–7.

Data on a CD are read by focusing a 780-nanometer (nm) wavelength laser that scans the disk's pits and lands from the bottom of the CD. The difference in the height between the pits and lands on the disk

Figure 8–7.
Cross-section of the data tracks on a CD-ROM.

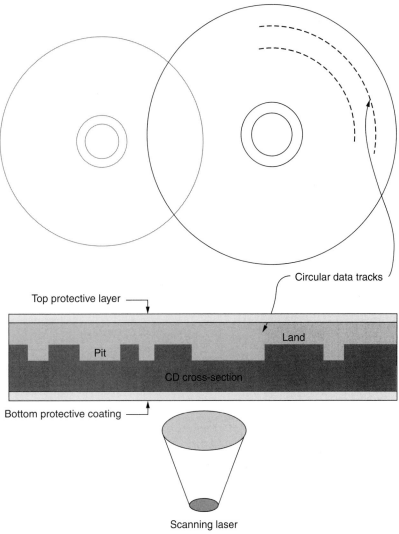

changes the intensity of the light reflecting from the laser. This light intensity is measured by a photodiode that interprets reflected light intensity as either a binary 0 or 1.

Because the pits are closer to the label side of a disk after it has been burned, minor defects on the clear bottom side of the disk are less harmful for playback than are scratches on the disk's label side.

The two most common current formats of compact disks are the recordable compact disk, or *CD-R*, and the rewritable *CD-RW*. CD-Rs can be recorded only once. The CD-RW is a multirecordable disk that uses a metal alloy instead of a dye as the recording medium. This alloy lets the disk be rewritten about a thousand times. Although a CD-RW can be rewritten, it needs to be completely erased each time it is rewritten—small areas can't be erased and rewritten as they are on a hard drive. On CD-RWs, the write laser heats the alloy, altering its chemical properties and its reflectivity. Because CD-RWs don't have as great a reflectivity difference between pits and lands as do CD-Rs, some audio CD players can't read CD-RW disks, although most stand-alone CD and DVD players can read CD-Rs and CD-RWs with almost complete compatibility.

Data Transfer Rates of CD Drives

The ability of a CD drive to transfer data from a disk to the computer is usually stated as its **X rating.** This rating is based on first-generation CD drives that transferred data at 150 kilobytes per second (Kbps). Current drives are available with read speeds of over 50X. For example, a CD-RW (rewritable) drive might offer a rating of 52X32X52X. On this specific drive, the write speed is 52X, the rewrite speed is 32X, and the read speed is also 52X. These figures vary with specific capabilities of individual drives and manufacturers.

A drive's rotational speed determines how quickly the disk data tracks pass under the laser, and therefore defines the overall data transfer rate of the drive. Modern CD drives operate on the principle of **constant angular velocity (CAV),** by which the angular velocity of the disk is kept constant. In this scheme, the linear velocity of the disk data tracks will be larger when the outer tracks are being read or written to. In other words, the drive will vary its read and write speeds from track to track. On drives with a **constant linear velocity (CLV),** the motor speed decreases the spin speed, or rpm, of the disk as the read head moves toward the outer data tracks. This enables the data tracks to move past the laser at a constant speed throughout the overall diameter of the disk.

How CDs Are Made

The clear polycarbonate compact disk is called a **substrate.** The pits and lands representing the data file are embedded, or burned, into the plastic disk. A very thin layer of aluminum, which mirrors the pit and land surfaces, is placed on top of the plastic. This layer of aluminum provides the shiny reflective surface that enables the laser beam to reflect off the pit and land surfaces and back to the interpreting unit, where the data again become the original music, video, or data file. A plastic or lacquer coating covers the aluminum to prevent scratching and oxidation of the aluminum, keeping it shiny. The process of producing multiple copies of a CD-ROM is referred to as **mastering** the disk. The complete manufacturing process involves three separate steps: pre-mastering, mastering, and disk production.

Pre-Mastering Data

Before the mastering process can begin, the original data must be converted into the standard ISO 9660 format. This process is called **pre-mastering.** Original data, supplied to the disk manufacturer on a digital tape, CD or DVD, or portable hard drive, are translated by the disk manufacturer onto a digital mastering tape. After the data are formatted, the pre-mastering process is complete.

Mastering and Disk Production

The first step in making a CD is to produce a **glass master.** Optically ground glass with a very fine (1/10 μ) photoresist layer is exposed to the imaging laser, which burns the pit and land patterns onto the glass master. When the disk is developed, the areas exposed by the laser are etched away and then silver-plated, leaving the actual pit and land structure of the disk (Figure 8–8).

Next a disk is electroplated onto the completed glass master, which produces a negative-image disk. When the negative is separated from the master, it is referred to as a **father disk.** Although the father disk could be used to reproduce additional CDs, it would quickly wear out. Therefore, additional electroplated copies, called **mother disks,** are made by electroplating the father. Figure 8–9 illustrates this two-step process.

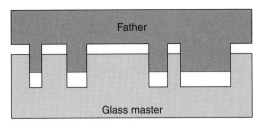

Figure 8–9
Electroplating a mother CD from a father CD.

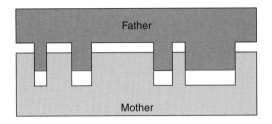

A number of **stampers** can be made from each mother disk. Stampers are used to reproduce the actual pit and land structure onto the finished CDs (Figure 8–10). Stampers used to make the actual CDs use a plastic injection molding process similar to the one used to produce vinyl records. The stamper creates the pit and land structures on the polycarbonate CDs (Figure 8–11).

During final processing, the information layer of the disk is coated with a micron-thick layer of aluminum for laser reflection. A lacquer coating is placed over the aluminum

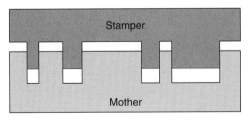

Figure 8–10.
Creating a CD stamper from a mother CD.

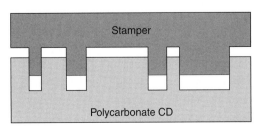

Figure 8–11.
Stamping a CD.

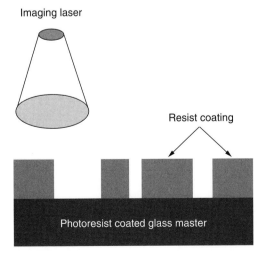

Figure 8–8.
Exposing a glass master CD-ROM.

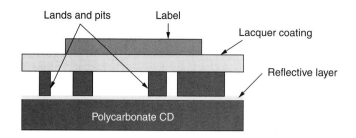

Figure 8–12.
Coating and labeling a
CD-ROM.

to prevent scratching and oxidation of the
aluminum coating. The disk label is then
printed on top of the lacquer coating
(Figure 8–12).

DVD TECHNOLOGY

At first glance CDs and DVDs appear
identical. Both have the same diameter
(5¼ inches) and are the same thickness
(1.2 mm). Both use lasers to read data from
spiral data tracks stored as pits and lands
on a polycarbonate medium. At this point,
however, the similarities end.

DVDs were introduced to the marketplace
as **digital video disks** because the format was
intended to dominate the market for showing
movies on home TVs. Over the years, other
applications have moved onto the DVD
landscape, and some organizations now
refer to the DVD as a *digital versatile disk*.
DVD formats are governed by a consortium
of DVD-engaged corporations called the
DVD Forum. Founded in 1995, the DVD
Forum works to promote acceptance of
DVD products and formats across a broad
spectrum of platforms, consumer electronics,
and IT industries.

Data Storage and Reading
on Conventional DVDs

DVDs are designed to hold a typical full-
length movie averaging about 135 minutes
of run time. Using MPEG-2 **codecs**, full-
motion video requires about 3,500 Kbps.
Adding five-channel digital surround sound
featuring four-directional speakers and a
nondirectional subwoofer channel requires

an extra 384 Kbps. And additional storage
for multilingual dialog tracks and subtitles
for the movie means that the typical movie
will need 4.75 GB of storage capacity.

The reference data rate for DVDs is 11.08
million bits per second (Mbps). The transfer
rate of data on a DVD is usually given in
terms of 1,352 Kbps as the reference point.
Therefore, a DVD drive with a 16X rating
enables a data transfer rate of $16 \times 1,352$
= 21,640 Kbps, or 21.3 Mbps. Contrasting
this figure to the data transfer rate of
conventional CDs, a DVD reads about nine
times faster than its CD counterpart. Most
DVD drives use a constant rotational speed.
Because the rotational speed of the drive
doesn't change during playback, maximum
data transfer takes place only at the outer data
tracks of the disk, where the linear rotational
speed is the highest. Thus the actual data
readout of a drive is somewhat less than the
stated figures in the drive's specifications.
However, this is offset to a degree because the
seek time of the drive head is reduced when
the drive spins at a constant speed.

Making all this information fit onto a
5¼-inch disk requires the track pitch to be
reduced from 1.6 μ (the track pitch on a
conventional compact disk) to 0.74 μ. Also, the
pit size on the data tracks shrinks from 0.83 μ
to 0.40 μ. A shorter-wavelength laser is required
to read the smaller DVD data tracks, so the
disk platter is thinner than its CD counterpart
so that the light doesn't have to travel through
as much plastic to reach the disk's data layer.
Because the DVD specification calls for a disk
only half as thick as a conventional CD, a
blank 0.6-mm platter is glued on top of the
DVD. Although most current DVD drives are
reading data at a minimum of 16X, look for a
continued increase in speed.

DVD Formats

A number of often confusing, competing
DVD formats are in use. No writable formats

are fully compatible with each other, or with existing computer or stand-alone drives. The four most commonly used formats follow.

DVD-RAM

DVD-RAM disks are removable storage devices, primarily for computers, although they were used extensively in home digital video recorders. First offered in a 2.5 GB capacity, DVD-RAMs were later expanded to 4.7 GB. DVD-RAM disks come with or without encasing cartridges. One type of cartridge is sealed. The other type of cartridge allows the disk to be removed and inserted into a drive for playback; however, the disk can be written to only when it is in the cartridge. The use of DVD-RAM drives and disks has all but disappeared with the newer DVD formats and high-definition DVD technology.

DVD-R

DVD-R disks (that's DVD *dash* R, not *minus* R) use a recordable format, similar to CD-Rs in that they use an organic dye layer for data recording. Although the storage capacity of the first-generation of DVD-Rs was less than 4 GB, this later increased to 4.7 GB to match that of the DVD-ROM. DVD-Rs are readable in most DVD drives and players.

DVD-RW

The **DVD-RW** (rewritable) format is based on the original DVD-R and uses a phase-change dye for recording data. There can be compatibility problems when DVD-RWs are read in some disk drives and players. This is due to the lower reflectivity of the phase change material compared to that of DVD-ROMs (similar to the problems of CD-RW readability in some drives and players). DVD-RWs feature capacities of 4.7 GB, similar to their DVD-R and DVD-RAM counterparts.

DVD+R/RW

First available in late 2001, the **DVD+R/RW** is based on DVD-R technology. Although supported by several manufacturers, this format is not supported by the DVD Forum. DVD+ recorders let users add, overwrite, and divide titles and make changes without any loss of player compatibility. The + format also allows background editing so that the user can start to make changes without waiting to use the disk. The + format is compatible with many, but not all, DVD drives and players.

High-Definition DVD

The increased availability of high-definition (HD) broadcasting in North America, Japan, and Europe, coupled with increased television screen sizes that make the limitations of standard video more evident, has opened the gates for the arrival of high-definition television and its corresponding DVD counterpart. Often as television screen sizes increase beyond 36 inches, the resulting images tend to be grainy and relatively poor; but HD images hold up well even at screen sizes of 60 inches and beyond. High-definition television is broadcast at 1,080 lines of resolution (either interlaced or progressively scanned). Ultra high-definition video, with resolutions in excess of $7,000 \times 4,000$ pixels is already in the advanced research stage. Conventional high-definition television, it appears, is just the beginning.

In response to the growing need and acceptance of HD, the DVD Forum has proposed specifications for HD-DVD built on experience gained from the original DVD format. HD-DVD uses a blue-violet laser instead of the red laser used in conventional DVDs. The shorter wavelength of the blue-violet laser, combined with a smaller aperture for the focusing lens, reduces the spot diameter of the HD-DVD laser, which increases the data density that can be read. Fast rotational speeds on HD-DVD drives permit a maximum data transfer rate of more than 36 Mbps—three times that of conventional DVDs.

HD-DVDs keep the same physical dimensions of standard DVDs. Increased disk data density, a function of the shorter-wavelength laser, allows 8 hours of HD video capability on a dual-layer, single-sided disk, with double-sided disk storage capacity of about 30 GB of data. The family of HD-DVDs includes HD-DVD-ROM, with a storage capacity of 15 GB for a single-layer disk and 30 GB for a dual-layer disk. Double-sided HD-DVDs increase this storage capacity to 30 GB per side, with a total data capacity of 60 GB.

High-definition video playback units will be able to read normal DVDs. Conventional DVD players will not, however, be able to interpret HD-DVDs. A *combination disk*, which features one side of the disk as a normal DVD and the other as a dual-layer HD-DVD, has been proposed by the DVD Forum. Initially, at least, Sony's BluRay high-definition DVD technology has been gaining acceptance as a defacto standard for HD-DVD movies. For the latest developments in DVD formats and technology, the reader is directed to the DVD Forum Web site at ://www.dvdforum.org.

SUMMARY

This chapter discussed the wide variety of data storage options, ranging from micro flash cards used for on-the-go file storage and in digital cameras to larger stationary high-capacity file servers. The technology of CDs was highlighted, along with DVD protocols and the evolving long-term impact of DVD market penetration. This examination included a discussion of the emergence of high-definition DVDs (HD-DVDs) as eventual replacements for both conventional CDs and DVDs.

Review Questions

1 Identify five different methods of data storage currently in use.

2 What principle is used by compact disks for writing and reading binary data?

3 Describe three major differences between CDs and DVDs.

Suggested Student Activities

1 Construct two charts that illustrate the basic configurations of a compact disk (CD) and a digital video disk (DVD). The charts should include the basic sizes and track spacing as well as other information important to each type of disk.

2 List the types of DVD formats and the primary use of each format.

3 Secure an old or broken DVD or CD drive unit. Take the drive apart and see if you can identify its internal components.

4 Secure an old, broken, or unused flash drive stick. Pry the plastic drive apart and identify its internal components.

Traditional and Digital Imaging Techniques:
Chapter 9

Chapter Objectives

Understand how original copy
is classified.

Understand the effects of enlarging
and reducing (scaling) copy.

Examine techniques for cropping
illustrations and photographs.

Provide an overview of traditional
image output.

Examine techniques of direct-to-plate
technology.

Develop an understanding of
direct-to-press (DTP) direct imaging
(DI) technology.

INTRODUCTION

When designers and graphic artists speak about *traditional imaging techniques,* they are almost always discussing the use of chemical-based photographic processes to produce images on film. These images would be contact printed onto a photographically sensitized press plate and then printed.

Thanks to rapid technical progress in the graphic arts, the use of film, also referred to as *analog photographic processing,* has been almost completely replaced by computers to create and digitize both text and graphics for printing. Digital imaging, in contrast to film, streamlines the production process. Because film has always been an intermediate step used to transfer images onto a printing medium, direct computer data output eliminates not only the film but also the costs of processing toxic waste associated with chemical processing.

Until recently, film held a quality edge over its digital imaging counterparts. Digital scanners and cameras designed for the consumer market do not generally produce the same photographic quality as their film counterparts. Most professional-quality scanners and digital cameras, however, produce results that are almost indistinguishable from film in the production of high-resolution images.

Although graphic arts cameras and darkrooms have disappeared as production components in modern printing facilities, traditional plate-making procedures are still widely used. Regardless of how quality images are created, the concepts basic to their production will always transcend the methods used to create them.

COPY CLASSIFICATION

All original material can be categorized as either *line* or *continuous-tone copy.* Copy classification is important because a printing press can print only solid areas of ink or no ink at all; gradations of tone can be printed only through a series of dots varying in both size and the space between them. Knowing the different types of copy and how to process them is the first step in producing professional-quality work.

Line Copy

Line copy consists of only solid tonal areas. For example, a page composed entirely of text is line copy. Other examples of line copy include pen-and-ink drawings and graphic images composed of solid areas with no gradations of tone.

Continuous-Tone Copy

Continuous-tone originals contain gradations of tone as well as solid areas. For example, a black-and-white photograph contains solid blacks and whites as well as intermediate shades of gray. Color photographs also contain varying shades and intensities of color as well as solid spot colors. **Continuous-tone copy** therefore includes originals such as color photographs, charcoal and airbrush renderings, and paintings that contain tonal gradations as well as solids.

Reproducing Continuous-Tone Copy

Printing line copy on a press is a straightforward process; printing continuous-tone copy is not. Because a printing press can print only solid ink or nothing at all in a particular spot, we simulate intermediate shades of gray and color shading either by breaking continuous tonal areas into dots of varying sizes or by varying the spaces between evenly sized dots. When we view copy printed in this way from a distance, our eyes mix the various sizes and spaces of the printed dots to simulate colors and tonal shades other than black, white, and solid colors.

The process of breaking a continuous-tone image into dots is referred to as producing a **halftone** image and is accomplished by **screening** original copy. The term *screening* comes from the long-standing photographic technique that employs either a glass or plastic screen containing a built-in ruled dot structure. This ruled screen is placed over the original copy and photographed on a graphic arts process camera.

During this exposure, light reflecting from the dark or shadowed areas of an original

Screen Ruling (Lines per Inch)	Use
65–85	Newspaper
100	Newspaper/textbooks
133	Textbooks/magazines
175	High-quality/detailed reproduction
300	Very high-quality art (waterless offset)

Figure 9–1.
Halftone screen applications for various types of original copy.

is relatively weak and produces only small dots on the negative. Light reflecting from the original copy in brighter highlighted areas produces relatively larger dots on the negative. When a plate is made from this negative, the shadowed areas contain relatively larger printing dots, producing darker areas in the printed copy that correlate with the dark, shadowed areas of the original. Conversely, lighter areas from the original produce smaller dots on the printing plate that will pick up less ink during printing, resulting in lighter image areas corresponding to those same areas in the original.

Currently process cameras are rarely used to produce halftone negatives; most halftones are output on an image setter from computers using programs like Adobe Photoshop or proprietary software dedicated to a particular image setter. A variety of screen sizes and shapes are available for reproducing continuous-tone images. Figure 9–1 lists common screen sizes that are used in reproducing different types of originals.

To illustrate this concept, a sample black-and-white photograph that has been created on the computer with a 133-line conventional (elliptical) dot pattern is shown in Figure 9–2A. A small section of this same photograph is enlarged in Figure 9–2B to emphasize the resulting dot structure that simulates the tonal areas of the original photo.

Figure 9–2A.
An original photo at 55 dpi.

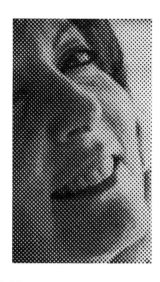

Figure 9–2B.
The photo's enlarged dot structure.

Sometimes a continuous-tone original might also be used to produce a combination of screened and line copy. For example, printing a black-and-white photograph without the use of a halftone screen built into the photograph produces a high-contrast image that can be handled and printed as line copy. Figure 9–3A and Figure 9–3B show the continuous-tone and high-contrast output from the same black–and-white original.

DOT SHAPES AND SIZES

Several dot shapes are used for making halftones. The most common shapes are **round, elliptical,** and **square.** Round dots are used most often because they allow the greatest amount of printed surface area to be covered with dots. This maximizes the image detail captured in the final print. Elliptical dots are often used where smooth transitions are required from light to dark areas in a print, such as in the facial areas

Figure 9–3A.
Continuous-tone original.

Figure 9–3B.
High-contrast output.

of a portrait. By contrast, square dots offer a starker transition from lights to darks.

Dot size refers to the percentage of area in a print that is actually covered by dots. The size of the specific dot is also a function of the screen ruling used to generate the halftone.

When printers speak about a halftone that has a 10 percent dot in the highlight areas, they are saying that the highlight area of the print has 10 percent of its area covered by dots. Conversely, a 90 percent dot structure in the shadow areas indicates that 90 percent of the shadow areas of the print are covered with dots. Therefore, a 50 percent dot produced from an 85-line screen will be comparatively larger than a 50 percent dot generated from a 133-line screen. However, both of these dot sizes will result in 50 percent ink coverage in each print.

DOT GAIN AND PRINTING

Dot gain and printable dots are interrelated concepts. The term *printable dots* refers to the size of the dots that a particular printing press can print on a page. For example, a press may be able to *hold a dot range* of from 5 to 95 percent. With this specific press, any dot smaller than 5 percent will be lost and not printed, whereas dots larger than 95 percent will fill in and print as solids. Printable dots are not only specific to presses but correlate to specific inks, papers, and humidity conditions in the printing plant. Most commercial presses can easily hold dots within the 10 to 90 percent range.

The term *dot gain* refers to the growth in size of a printed dot as it goes through production and printing. This size gain occurs because individual dots tend to grow during plating and printing. Dot gain during plate making is easier to control than the gain that occurs during printing. Paper is a fibrous, organic material. Some papers, like bond and newsprint, tend

to absorb more ink than do sealed and coated stocks. During printing, ink tends to be absorbed by neighboring paper fibers adjacent to the printed area. This spreads the dot image. Small dots tend to grow, and larger dots, such as those in shadow areas, may fill in completely and print as solids. In fact, a 40 percent dot gain is not uncommon in printing. Through experience with combinations of specific inks, papers, and presses, printers can accurately predict how much dot gain can be expected under a variety of production conditions. With this information, adjustments can help compensate for and control dot gain. Also, most image editing programs incorporate the ability to compensate for dot gain in their print output menus. Here the operator can enter the percentage of dot gain on the computer, which adjusts the dot size of the image to compensate for gain conditions in a specific printing plant using certain plates, inks, and presses.

CONVENTIONAL AND STOCHASTIC (FM) SCREENING

Our discussion of halftone dots has thus far been limited to the use of conventional halftones, wherein evenly spaced dots of different sizes are printed to produce tonal gradations that are interpreted as optical illusions by the viewer.

A different method of accomplishing this same effect is through a technique called **stochastic screening.** Stochastic screening generates dots that are all the same size but varies the space between the dots. Because this process is based on the number, or frequency, of dots distributed throughout a print, stochastic screening is sometimes referred to as *frequency modulation* or *FM screening*. Stochastic screening can yield very fine print detail; it is used most successfully on digital or waterless offset printing presses, where dot gain is easier to control than with

Figure 9–4.
Different types of halftone screens.

175 lpi   300 lpi   FM (stochastic)

conventional offset processes. Figure 9–4 shows the differences between 175- and 300-line screens and a stochastic screen.

ENLARGING AND REDUCING (SCALING) COPY

Original copy that was not prepared for same-size (100 percent) reproduction needs to be either enlarged or reduced (*scaled*). Scaling is a common practice because rarely are original photographs and illustrations prepared to fit exactly into an allotted space on a page. The two most common practices

Figure 9–5.
A typical proportion scale.

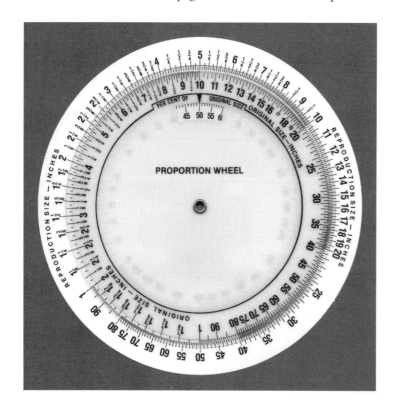

for determining scaling are the use of proportion scales and arithmetic computation.

Proportion Scales

The baseline for scaling copy is 100 percent, which refers to a same-size reproduction of an original. A reproduction over 100 percent is an enlargement, and anything under 100 percent is a reduction. The most efficient method for determining required sizes for enlargements or reductions of originals is through the use of a **proportion scale** (Figure 9–5).

The proportion scale shows the percentage of a specific enlargement or reduction using the dimensions from both the original and the finished copy. When the dials are properly aligned, the scaling percentage is displayed on the scale. Almost all proportion scales function in a manner similar to the one illustrated in Figure 9–5.

Computing Enlargements and Reductions

Percentages of enlargements and reductions can also be calculated arithmetically using the following formula:

$$\frac{\text{Reproduced size}}{\text{Size of original}} = \text{Percentage of reduction or enlargement}$$

Therefore, if we require a reproduction size of 10 inches in width from an original that measures 6 inches wide, the formula reads as follows:

$$\frac{10 \text{ inches (required size)}}{6 \text{ inches (original size)}} = 160 \text{ percent reproduction size}$$

Excessive scaling of copy on a computer to get copy to fit properly in a specific job can often result in additional charges to a customer. Because of this, it is best if the customer, designers, photographers, and illustrators supply all copy based on allowable space requirements when first beginning a design layout.

CROPPING ILLUSTRATIONS AND PHOTOGRAPHS

Many photographs and illustrations used in books, brochures, and other design pieces contain areas that are either unnecessary or irrelevant to the subject matter of the photo. Removing these irrelevant areas increases the effectiveness of the final print. Often when photographic prints are supplied to a designer for scanning, they are covered with either acetate or clear tissue on which marks have been drawn to indicate the areas of the print that need to be removed or emphasized. This process is referred to as **cropping** the photograph. The illustration would then be cropped in image editing software using these crop marks as a guide (Figure 9–6A and Figure 9–6B).

Cropping a print, however, is not an ideal technique for fixing a print or illustration that isn't suited to communicating its intended message. The best method for this is to frame the photo subject properly in the camera viewfinder before taking the picture. An old photography rule states that to take good pictures, you have to take a lot of pictures. This applies to cropping: Take several different pictures, experimenting with the subject's framing, and select the one that best emphasizes the subject and message of the photo—thus requiring the least manipulation.

TRADITIONAL AND DIGITAL METHODS OF OUTPUTTING IMAGES

Traditional image processing refers to the use of film to produce negatives that,

Figure 9–6A. Cropping marks placed on an original photograph.

after processing, are contact printed onto presensitized offset metal plates. This type of processing is also referred to as **analog,** setting it apart from the use of computer plating systems.

Digital output describes a wide variety of techniques for both generating images and printing plates. Increasingly data files are output directly onto plate media. Direct digital output saves significant time and expense.

By most estimates, approximately 70 percent of the printing industry is currently using some type of **computer-to-plate (CTP)** production system. Although the term CTP can describe different types of devices, about half of small commercial printers either use dedicated plate setters to produce polyester plates or use image setters that were originally designed for film output but instead now output spools of polyester plates.

Figure 9–6B. The cropped photograph.

Figure 9–7.
A separate RIP used with an image setter.

Figure 9–8.
The film cassette section of a typical image setter. In this type of image setter, known as a *capstan drive*, the medium (film, paper, or polyester plate material) is exposed with a laser. The exposed medium is fed through the image setter by a series of transport rollers into a light-tight cassette for processing and developing.

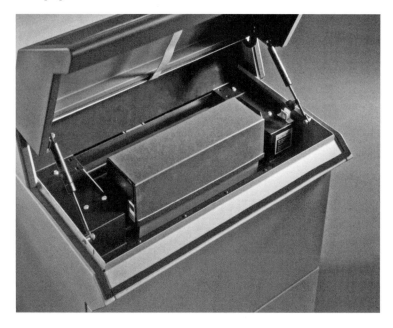

Polyester plates are currently the choice of small-to medium-sized printing establishments due to their relatively low cost. However, the use of metal plates in **direct-to-plate** (DTP) systems is increasing as the cost of metal DTP comes down and the technology improves. Although many shops still use film, it is clear that CTP systems running either metal or polyester will become the industry standard within the short term. Also, dot gain—a problem long associated with film and conventional plate making—is much less problematic with laser-imaged polyester and metal plates; this limits the control of dot gain to the printing press.

We will examine different types of traditional and digital technologies used for outputting images in preparation for printing.

Outputting Film on an Image Setter

Image setters are digital output devices that process data files from the computer and record, or rasterize, that data onto photographic film, paper, or plates. A complete image setter package consists of three components: a **raster image processor** (**RIP**), the film or image recorder, and a film processor. Most image setters incorporate both the RIP and the media recorder in one machine. In older device configurations, the RIP was supplied as a separate device external to the film recorder (Figure 9–7).

Although most image setters are configured as single integrated units, external RIPs can be upgraded separately without the need for purchasing an entirely new image setter.

An image setter RIP incorporates a high-speed microprocessor and sufficient memory to handle the loads placed on it for processing large documents. A high-speed Internet connection is incorporated into the RIP, enabling direct output of files from remote computers. During imaging, the film recorder unit of the image setter (Figure 9–8) exposes the light-sensitive film or plate medium with a red laser diode. Resolutions of most image setters are from 1,000 to 3,500 dots per inch (dpi). This capability ensures high-quality halftone negatives and positives within a broad range of halftone screen rulings.

A daylight film processor (Figure 9–9) is a light-tight, four-stage chemical processing bath that develops, fixes, washes, and dries film. The exposed film from the image setter is stored in a light-tight **film cassette**. Film from the cassette is placed into the processor, where it is fed through a series of intake rollers. These rollers automatically feed film through the different chemical processing stages, from which it emerges as a dry, processed negative.

Sending a job to an image setter is functionally the same process as sending

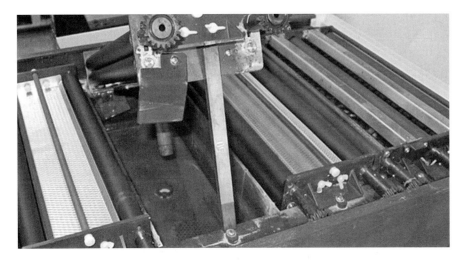

Figure 9–9.
The feed roller section of a daylight photographic processor. (One roller section has been raised to show the chemical holding tray, solution feed openings, and transport roller assembly.)

the job to a conventional laser or inkjet printer. The image setter output menu offers options for determining the resolution and contrast of the final negative (Figure 9–10).

After processing, the film is taped onto a sheet of goldenrod paper to produce a **flat** in preparation for exposing the negative

Figure 9–10.
Output options menu available on a typical image setter.

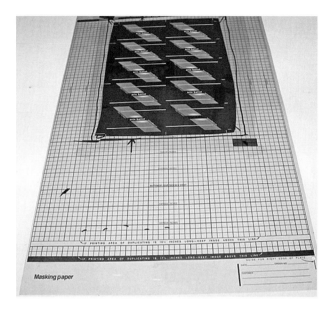

Figure 9–11.
A stripped flat.

onto a presensitized metal offset printing plate (Figure 9–11).

TRADITIONAL PLATE MAKING USING FLATS

Despite the inroads digital plate makers have made into plate production, traditional plate making—using stripped flats to prepare printing plates—is still in use throughout the industry in shops that continue to output files to film. In this method, a flat is contact printed onto a plate in a vacuum frame. During exposure in the vacuum frame, an image is printed onto the plate, then developed and fixed, resulting in a processed plate ready for printing.

Ensuring Quality before Printing

Prior to printing, a flat will often be proofed to verify that all the job elements are properly registered and that there are no pinholes or scratches in the negative that could affect final print quality. Also, halftone negatives produced in the image setter should be examined to determine the accuracy of dot representations in the highlights, shadows, and middle tones.

Evaluating Halftone Negatives

Halftone negative examination before printing helps to ensure that the resulting printing plate will produce a print whose tonal range closely matches that of the original. In this stage of quality control, remember that dot gain on a press as a function of specific inks, papers, and plating systems should be factored into the plant's quality assurance evaluation system during the entire preproduction process.

Highlight areas from originals should produce about a 90 percent dot on a halftone negative. This in turn produces about a 10 percent dot during printing. Most presses will be able to hold a 10 percent dot without any loss. This dot size also enables fine detail to be reproduced in the highlight areas. Conversely, shadow areas of the original should produce about a 10 percent dot in the negative, which results in a 90 percent dot on the printing plate.

The use of computers for producing halftones has all but replaced the labor-intensive practices of using graphic arts cameras to obtain high-quality negatives for printing. Although the technology has changed, the methods for evaluating negative quality have not. If the highlight, shadow, or middle tonal areas are not reproducing properly on a negative, the graphic artist must go back to the computer. In a photo editing program these areas can be manipulated to achieve results that will give a full tonal representation of the original copy.

Proofing Flats

Although several methods are available for proofing flats before printing, traditional photomechanically based proofing systems and the use of color overlays and transparencies have been replaced by digital color and press proofing systems.

Press Proofs

The most accurate method of proofing a job before a press run is to run trial sheets on the press before an actual press run. This procedure is referred to as a **press proof.** The actual ink and paper specified for the job are used in this process to exactly duplicate conditions of the actual press run. Press proofs are expensive due to the press setup involved and the cost of press time. For this reason, these proofs are usually reserved for long-run, full-color, high-quality jobs. Due to these expenses, when these proofs are run, if the proof results are acceptable, the actual press run of the job begins immediately.

Digital Color Proofs

Digital color proofing uses high-end inkjet and dye sublimation printers to produce high-quality proof prints. With advances in technology, digital color and black-and-white proofs are more accurate than their photographically based counterparts—and are produced at much less cost. Done properly, digital proofs can approach the quality of press proofs. The key to success with this technique is to match the computer's screen colors to the output of the printer. This output is, in turn, calibrated to match specific printing press and ink combinations. Because of accuracy requirements, low-cost consumer-grade printers are not suitable for generating these types of proofs.

Soft Proofing

The term **soft proofing** refers to the practice of using a computer monitor to provide an accurate preview of how an image on the screen will print on a specific inkjet printer. Because inkjet printers use cyan, magenta, yellow, and black (**CMYK**) inks for printing, and computer monitors display images in red, green, and blue (**RGB**), obtaining accurate visual matches between a monitor and a printer can be difficult. To increase the accuracy of the soft proofing process, a color management system enables the designer to first properly calibrate the computer monitor and then install color management files that are written for specific inkjet printers. These files are referred to as *ICC* files, standing for the *International Color Consortium*. These profiles describe how a particular device or printer will reproduce color based on the ICC standards.

When calibrating a monitor, a step-by-step guide lets the user adjust brightness, contrast, ideal black-and-white images, and the color phosphors in the monitor. Completing these adjustments yields what is referred to as a **monitor profile.** When finished, the computer operator has created an ICC profile that describes the color characteristics of a specific device—in this case a specific computer monitor. Next a media profile for the specific printer must be installed. If these profiles aren't automatically installed in the operating system of the computer, they can be downloaded from manufacturers' Web sites. This media profile information, referred to as an *ICC/ColorSync file,* is loaded into the proofing preview or setup box of a photo editing program like Adobe Photoshop. Loading these profiles generates a color management system that permits the designer to accurately see how an image will look when it has been printed. If any component of the system is changed (a new monitor or printer, for example), a new profile must be established for each new device.

Producing Presensitized Metal Plates

To make a traditional offset plate, the negative containing all the page elements is positioned and taped in place on a sheet of goldenrod paper to produce a *flat*

Figure 9–12.
Cross-section of a deep-etch offset printing plate.

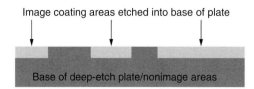

Image coating areas etched into base of plate

Base of deep-etch plate/nonimage areas

(Figure 9–11). This process uses photographically presensitized plates onto which a light-sensitive emulsion has been applied. These plates can be supplied sensitized on one or both sides and are made from aluminum, paper, or foil-impregnated paper. Aluminum is the most widely used material, permitting press runs of between 10,000 and 500,000 impressions. Presensitized plates are available in several configurations.

Additive Plates

Plates are classified as **additive** when, during processing, a lacquer-based material is applied over the image areas of the plate, fixing it and giving the image long-run characteristics. The plate is developed using either a one- or two-step process. In the two-step process, a chemical desensitizer is spread over the plate to remove any unexposed emulsion from the plate surface, leaving only the exposed image areas on the plate. In the second step, a lacquer- or gum-based developer is applied to coat and build up these image areas. Thus the developer is *added* during the plate processing. In a one-step process, both the chemical desensitizer and lacquer-based developer are applied as a single chemical solution.

Figure 9–13.
Cross-section of a surface-coated offset printing plate.

Nonimage areas washed away during processing

Presensitized emulsion coating/image area   Emulsion/image area

Paper, polyester, or aluminum base of printing plate

Subtractive Plates

In the **subtractive plate** process, a one-step chemical is applied to the plate after it has been exposed. This removes the emulsion from the unexposed areas of the plate. Thus the image coating is removed, or *subtracted,* from the printing plate.

Positive- and Negative-Acting Plates

Positive-acting plates use film positives, rather than film negatives, to expose the plate. **Negative-acting plates** use photographic negative images to create positive images on the plate. In a negative-acting plate, light striking the plate emulsion during exposure hardens the image areas on the plate, which remain on the plate after processing. In positive-acting plates, light striking the plate surface softens the emulsion in the nonimage areas, which is then removed during processing.

Deep-Etch Plates

Deep-etch plates feature a photographic emulsion coating on the plate that is bonded and etched into the base metal of the plate. Etching the emulsion into the plate creates a plate image that is highly resistant to breakdown from roller pressures, producing a plate with long-run capabilities—often in excess of 100,000 impressions. A cross-section of a deep-etch plate is illustrated in Figure 9–12.

Surface-Coated Plates

Surface-coated plates incorporate a photographic emulsion that is coated, or layered, onto the base metal of the plate (Figure 9–13). Under continued roller pressure during printing, the emulsion coating on these plates will break down, limiting press runs to about 10,000 impressions.

Bimetallic Plates

Bimetallic plates are manufactured from two dissimilar metals that have been bonded together. One metallic layer in the plate acts as a grease-receptive image area. The other layer functions as a water-receptive, nonimage area of the plate, shown in cross section in Figure 9–14. Bimetallic plates are the most expensive type of plate to manufacture. They are used when extremely long press runs are required; 500,000 or more impressions from these plates are not uncommon.

Exposing and Processing Presensitized Offset Plates

The following procedures describe the stages in processing a negative-acting subtractive plate using one-step chemical processing. After the flat is contact printed onto a plate, it is processed in a plate sink, where the image is fixed and the spent chemistry is removed from the plate surface. Before use, plates should always be kept in their original packaging and in subdued lighting conditions. Fresh plates will be exposed and ruined in a short time if left out in normal incandescent or fluorescent lighting.

To begin the process, the flat is placed over the plate in exact alignment on the rubber base of the vacuum frame (Figure 9–15). Before the glass cover of the vacuum frame is closed, it should be inspected to guarantee that it is clean and free of any smudges or dirt—and cleaned if necessary. After the top is closed, the vacuum is turned on and

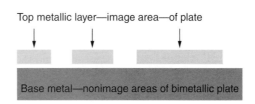

Top metallic layer—image area—of plate

Base metal—nonimage areas of bimetallic plate

Figure 9–14.
Cross-section of a typical bimetallic offset printing plate.

adjusted. Too little vacuum will not hold the negative and flat together properly; too much vacuum could leave depressions on the negative from the rubber cushion pad on the vacuum frame. A vacuum setting of between 15 to 20 inches of mercury (in. Hg) is acceptable for most exposures.

When using a new exposure lamp in the vacuum frame, a new box of plate material, or fresh developer, test exposures should be made to determine the time that works best with a specific type of plate and processing chemical combination. A series of test exposures can be made by cutting a plate into strips and using a 21-step negative gray scale or plate control wedge on each small plate sample. Each strip is then exposed for a different time, developed, and examined to determine which exposure time yielded the best grayscale or step wedge reading.

Figure 9–15.
Stripped flat and presensitized printing plate positioned in a vacuum frame before exposure.

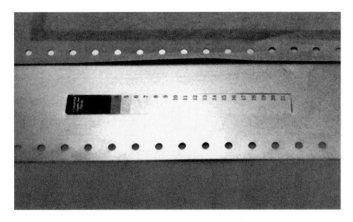

Figure 9–16.
A positive-acting grayscale image developed on a printing plate. The gray scale acts as a quality control device to ensure proper exposure and development of the plate.

Figure 9–16 shows a **21-step gray scale** developed along with the plate image as a quality control check for proper exposure time.

Once a proper vacuum has been reached, the timer on the exposure frame is set and the exposure is made. To process an exposed plate, a small amount of developer at room temperature is poured over the plate. Using a developing sponge and a figure-eight motion, the developer is worked onto the plate surface to bring up the image. After the image has reached maximum visibility, the excess developer is washed off with water in the plate sink.

Whenever possible, plates should be exposed and developed just before printing. If a plate is

not to be printed immediately, it must be sealed and protected, preventing it from oxidizing, until it is ready to be printed. Gum arabic is the solution most often used to seal plate surfaces for storage. A solution of gum arabic, diluted with water at a 1:1 ratio, is spread evenly over the plate surfaces, allowing approximately 15 minutes for the gum to dry. Gum arabic is water-soluble, so when a plate is ready to be printed, the gum is washed off with water.

DIRECT-TO-PLATE/COMPUTER-TO-PLATE (DTP/CTP) TECHNOLOGY

Making plates directly from a computer, thus avoiding the intermediate steps associated with photographic negatives and stripping, has been possible for several years. Recent improvements in direct-to-plate technology have resulted in plates that are capable of holding printing dots from 1 to 98 percent at 200 lines per inch. Direct-to-plate (DTP) or computer-to-plate (CTP) systems are sized for both small-format and large-format presses. Small-format systems produce plates to approximately 20 inches. Large-format systems can produce several plates at once in whatever size is required by a particular press. DTP systems are also classified as either *on-press* or *off-press*. Off-press systems produce plates in a separate plate maker or image setter. On-press systems image a printing plate directly on the printing press.

Outputting Polyester Plate Media on an Image Setter

The print operation starts with a computer page assembly program such as Adobe InDesign. Here text and graphic images are assembled in a final page layout. When the pages are complete, they can be output to an image setter. Most image setters can create polyester plates as well as film. Although different processing systems are used by different plate manufacturers, most use a two-stage activator and stabilizer developing system. After processing, a plate is ready for printing (Figure 9–17).

Figure 9–17.
A roll of polyester plate material that has been exposed on a direct-imaging offset press. The exposed plate material is rolled onto a take-up roller after printing, similar to rewinding film inside a camera. After all the plates on the roll have been printed, it is discarded and a new roll of plate media is loaded onto the press.

In general, polyester plates offer image quality that is equal to that of film and metal plates, especially in smaller formats. Disadvantages of polyester are relatively slow plate processing times, high costs associated with chemical processing and waste disposal, and the dimensional instability of polyester in larger plate sizes. For small-format press runs of fewer than 25,000 impressions, however, polyester is the plate medium of choice.

Dedicated CTP/DTP Systems

Until recently, dedicated computer-to-plate systems were used primarily in large printing operations. The major reasons for this were the lack of required digital pre-press systems designed (and affordable) for smaller print operations, along with the relatively high cost of CTP technology. With the introduction of new imaging and plating systems, penetration of CTP units into small- and medium-sized print shops has gained momentum. Also, CTP maximizes profits by avoiding numerous production steps, chemicals, and associated materials required with film-based plating systems. Page output

that took hours using film-based systems can now be accomplished in minutes. This savings in time and productivity enables payback on CTP systems to occur within months rather than years. A return on this investment is even more advantageous when the costs associated with hazardous waste removal are factored in. The quality of work is also better with CTP than with conventional film. Traditional weaknesses associated with film, such as hot spots, dust on the vacuum frame or negative, and film dimensional instability are gone in CTP. Also, over- and underexposed plates are reduced in a digital environment. To help ensure proper color matching and reliable, consistent plate output, a press can be keyed to any computer. In this way, screen images can almost be guaranteed to match press output.

Several types of CTP systems are available. The workflow of a typical system is depicted in Figure 9–18.

CTP systems are designed to produce either metal or polyester-based plates. Many of these units are designed for the short-run printing market, defined as press runs of approximately 25,000 or fewer

Figure 9–18.
Workflow options in a computer-to-plate (CTP) environment.

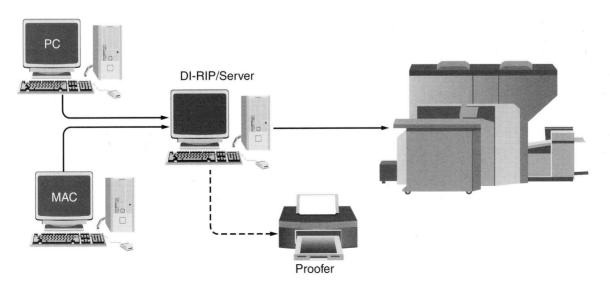

impressions. The plate setter in Figure 9–19 can work with polyester or film, and it incorporates a two-stage activator/processor that works with either medium. Exposure is accomplished using a red laser diode. Both plate and film media must be handled using light-tight cassettes.

Production of chemical-free plates made from either polyester or aluminum is designed around the use of a thermal laser. Because thermal coatings respond to heat, not light, such plates can be handled in normal room lighting. In one system, a thermal laser exposes and heats the emulsion in the nonimage, or non-ink-receptive, areas of the plate. During exposure, a reaction at the plate surface from the laser heat turns the nonimage areas to

dust, which is then vacuumed from the plate surface. Areas untouched by the laser during exposure remain on the plate to become the ink-receptive (also known as *oleophilic*) image areas of the plate. After exposure, any remaining dust on the plate surface is washed away in a water bath, and the plate is ready for the press.

Currently thermal systems represent the largest percentage of installed CTP units in small- to medium-sized print shops. Aluminum CTP chemical-free plates are progressing into the traditional polyester CTP marketplace. Although aluminum-based CTP units physically resemble their polyester and film-based counterparts at a glance, the plating technology is different. Figure 9–20 shows the cross-section of an anodized aluminum, chemical-free plate. The plate is exposed in a thermal imaging unit and then put through an integrated plate washing system. These plates are compatible with a wide range of industry-standard inks and fountain solutions, and they offer short runs of up to 25,000 impressions.

DIRECT-TO-PRESS (DTP)/DIRECT IMAGING (DI) TECHNOLOGY

Direct imaging (DI) technology extends CTP technology to a higher level of sophistication, where plates are digitally imaged directly on the printing press. The first press of this type was introduced by Heidelberg in 1991. Since then other manufacturers have entered the direct imaging market with many different press designs. Two main methods are used in direct image printing: digital imaging on a transfer drum based on electrostatic or electrophotographic technology, and on-press plate imaging. The primary market for DI systems is in four-color, short-run printing. Although the definition of short-run printing can vary, printers are increasingly

Figure 9–20.
Cross-section of an aluminum thermal printing plate (courtesy Presstek, Inc.).

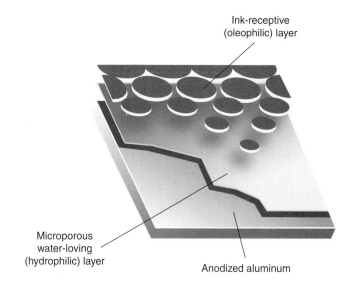

Ink-receptive (oleophilic) layer

Microporous water-loving (hydrophilic) layer

Anodized aluminum

defining short-run printing as press runs of fewer than 25,000 impressions. DTP and DI processes are ideally geared to the short turnaround times and the increasing market demands of just-in-time printing. These demands are being created by greater efforts on the part of printers and publishers to more accurately define the markets for specific printed products. This significantly reduces press runs; bolsters short-run product applications that require printing processes facilitating quick turnaround times; and yields higher productivity than can be achieved using conventional offset processes. The costs of printing and storing large numbers of documents that may not be used for a long time can be almost entirely eliminated from production costs using DI technology.

On-Press Plate Imaging

On-press plate imaging combines the sophistication of thermal laser development and plate manufacturing technology. This imaging process is depicted in Figure 9–21.

The cross section of the DI plate in Figure 9–23 reveals a three-layer design: an ink-receptive polyester base (4), a middle layer of titanium (3), and a top layer of silicone (2). During imaging, heat from the thermal laser (1) burns through and vaporizes the plate in the image areas by removing the top layer of silicone and exposing the ink-receptive polyester base of the plate (5). After the imaging process is complete, the remaining areas of silicone on the plate surface form the nonimage, ink-repelling area. During printing, ink is repelled by the silicone and adheres only to the polyester base layer (5) that was revealed during imaging. Because this process is heat sensitive rather than light sensitive, there is no need for either a darkroom or the chemicals associated with analog film

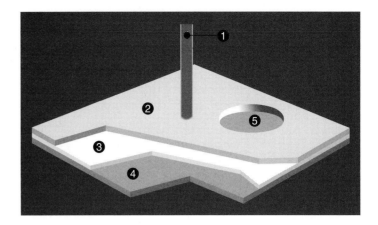

and plate production. This imaging unit, incorporated into the design of a four-color offset press, is shown in Figure 9–22.

Figure 9–22 shows a bank of thermal lasers spread across the top of the imaging unit. The plate cylinder is loaded with tensioned polyester plate material fed onto the cylinder from a storage cassette located adjacent to the cylinder. Loading plate media onto the cylinder is similar to the process used in a conventional camera to feed 35 mm film onto a take-up spool. After the film has been positioned and tensioned, imaging begins. During imaging, the plate cylinders rotate at approximately 300 rpm while the bank of thermal lasers moves across to image the plates. When imaging is complete, debris left over from

Figure 9–21.
The process of exposing and developing a direct image offset plate (courtesy Presstek, Inc.).

Figure 9–22.
The thermal laser imaging section of a direct imaging (DI) offset press. After plate imaging is completed, the imaging unit is retracted and printing proceeds (courtesy Presstek, Inc.).

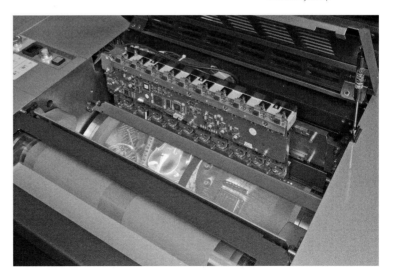

Figure 9–23.
Comparison of three
workflows (CTF, CTP,
and DI).

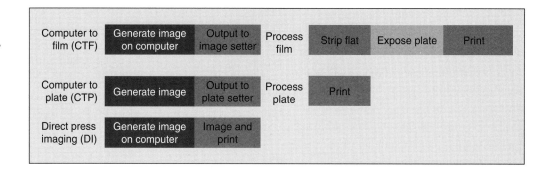

imaging is removed by a vacuum unit located within the imaging assembly. Under the control of the press's integrated computer, all four plates on a four-color press can be imaged in perfect registration with each other. No adjustments need to be made on the press during imaging or when the press run begins.

DI imaging also lets a press automatically control and adjust for correct color output. Each color-printing unit contains a set of ink keys that controls the amount of ink fed from the ink fountains onto the ink rollers. During printing, these ink keys are adjusted by the press's internal computer to control ink density. These adjustments are controlled based on the color data embedded in the job file and interpreted by the press computer.

Thanks to the completely automated nature of on-press imaging, production times are substantially reduced. The workflows of computer-to-film (CTF), computer-to-plate (CTP), and direct imaging (DI) systems are compared in Figure 9–23.

On-press digital imaging continues to gain wide acceptance. Driven by sophisticated plating technologies that enable high productivity, coupled with decreasing press costs, these systems will increasingly define the future of the printing industry.

On-Press Drum Imaging

Creating images on electrically charged drums began with the introduction of electrostatic copiers. The age of true digital printing is often dated to the introduction of the Xerox Model 9700 laser printer in 1977; Canon followed 12 years later with its Color Laser Copier (CLC). In 1991 Heidelberg introduced the GTO-DI, which created printing plates directly on a waterless offset press cylinder. Current drum imaging systems work basically like these earlier systems, using enhanced technological improvements. After preparation, data files are sent to a raster image processor (RIP). In the RIP, data files are interpreted to produce instruction sets for the digital print engine, determining where toner will be deposited to produce the lines and tonal areas of printed images. Three different types of digital print engines are used in most **on-press drum imaging** solutions: electrostatic or electrophotographic laser systems; *magnetography;* and *ion deposition* or *electron beam* imaging technology. In all these systems the pages to be printed are sent to the print engine one at a time. This feature allows each page to contain different information. This ability to vary information from page to page is referred to as **variable-data printing.** Electrostatic print engines are unique in their ability to handle and print variable information in this way.

Electrostatic/Electrophotographic Print Engines

In **electrostatic** or **electrophotographic printing,** the heart of the print engine is an

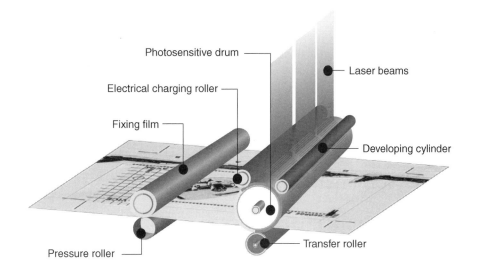

Figure 9–24.
Components of a typical digital print engine.

imaging drum coated with photoconductor material. During imaging, a laser light source exposes images onto the drum. The laser creates an electrostatic charge on the drum's imaged areas. The intensity of the laser light source varies, producing different electrostatic charges on the drum. The intensity of these charges correlates with the tonal density of the original image. In turn, the intensity of the charge on the photoconductor drum determines how much toner will be picked up by the drum and deposited onto the paper as it passes through the print engine. In electrostatic color printing engines, successive layers of cyan, magenta, yellow, and black toner are deposited on top of the previous color layers. These multiple color layers produce a full-color image printed at a resolution of 600 dpi. This deposited toner is then fused onto the paper by passing through a pressurized heat or fusion roller. The toner used in these print engines can be either solid or liquid. An electrostatic digital print engine is shown in Figure 9–24.

Magnetography

Magnetography works by creating latent images on the surface of a hard metal cylinder. This system differs from electrostatic print engines, which use lasers to create photosensitive images, rather than magnetic charges. The magnetized latent image on the cylinder attracts dry toner particles that are then transferred to the paper and fused in place. Magnetography uses a cold fusion process to fuse the toner onto the paper.

Ion Deposition/Electron Beam Imaging

Ion deposition, or electron beam, printers are used for high-volume, variable-data, single- and spot-color printing applications. An electron cartridge transfers electrical charges onto the surface of a rotating dielectric drum made of aluminum oxide (Figure 9–25).

Figure 9–25.
The process of electron beam/ion deposition printing.

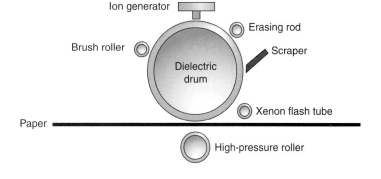

SUMMARY

In less than thirty years, image production by methods other than conventional printing systems has evolved from office copiers to direct imaging presses and copiers. These systems rival, and in many cases exceed, any other type of printing system when we factor in costs and print quality. Although digital imaging systems are still thought by some printers to cater only to the requirements of the short-run and print-on-demand brochure and textbook market, this perception is quickly changing. Digital imaging systems are capable of producing plate substrates that can hold a 300 lpi illustration. This level of resolution cannot be matched by traditional high-quality offset technology. Digital imaging will continue to make significant inroads into traditional imaging and printing technologies, eventually dominating all facets of the printing industry.

Review Questions

1 Discuss the difference between line and continuous-tone copy. How does this difference affect the printing of these images?

2 Why does high-quality artwork require a different print resolution than a photograph in a daily newspaper?

3 Describe the differences between conventional and stochastic screen printing. Which screening process yields higher quality, and why?

4 The printing industry has been moving away from conventional film to digital plating systems for several years. What are three reasons for these changes?

5 Identify three methods of proofing images before a press run. Which of these methods is the most accurate, and why?

6 Describe the differences between additive and subtractive printing plates.

7 How are printing plates imaged directly on an offset printing press? In what market would this type of technology find its greatest application, and why?

Suggested Student Activities

1 Create a large-scale drawing that shows the difference between the dot structure produced by a conventional halftone screen and that produced by a stochastic screen.

2 Construct a two-dimensional chart showing the cross-sections of the following different types of offset printing plates: surface-coated; deep-etch; bimetallic; and direct image (DI) waterless plates.

3 Prepare a 5-minute oral presentation addressing the future of digital imaging versus conventional offset printing in the next 5 to 10 years. Include in your presentation what you feel are five factors that could affect the widespread adoption of digital printing equipment over its traditional printing counterparts.

Printing Technologies and Finishing Techniques: Chapter 10

Chapter Objectives

Understand water-based and waterless offset technologies.

Identify conventional offset press designs.

Understand the differences between single-color and multicolor presses.

Examine the technologies of sheet-fed, web-fed, and perfecting presses.

Learn the differences between water-based ink and dampening versus waterless offset ink and temperature control.

Examine a variety of automated paper delivery systems.

Learn about digital imaging offset technologies.

Explore a variety of finishing processes that take place during and after job printing.

Develop an appreciation for incorporating responsible environmental practices as part of operating any business.

INTRODUCTION

Three methods of printing produce the majority of printed media. These are conventional offset lithography; waterless offset lithography; and digital printing. These technologies use either electrostatic print engines, waterless, or oil and water offset techniques.

The landscape of the printing industry has changed dramatically over the past 15 years. Offset printing, the dominant commercial printing process for more than 50 years, has been losing market share to both electrostatic digital and digital offset print technologies. The long-standing notion that digital printers cannot match the quality of conventional offset presses has given way to increased digital image quality brought about by technological improvements in toners and print engines, decreasing costs, and enhanced productivity. In the near term, the print and publishing industries will be using a mix of both conventional and digital offset commercial options catering to specific markets and applications. The long-term future of commercial printing, however, will be dominated by a digital landscape.

Remember that a job is not necessarily completed once it comes off the printing press. Numerous postpress finishing techniques such as folding, scoring, perforating, collating, and die cutting are integrated into the overall production process. Books, pamphlets, and brochures must also be bound.

In the discussions that follow we examine the current technologies employed in both printing and finishing most printed material.

LITHOGRAPHIC PRINTING

Lithographic printing has a rich history and legacy as both an artistic medium and a commercial print production method. Our discussions of lithography in Chapter 1 highlighted the oil and water planographic printing technology developed by Alois Senefelder around 1798. By the time of his death in 1834, Senefelder's lithographic process had become the dominant method for reproducing artistic prints in Europe. Although the original concept of lithographic imaging dates back to Senefelder's discovery in 1798, the process of commercial offset printing can be dated to 1905, when **Ira Rubel,** working in a small print shop in Nutley, New Jersey, developed the process of first offsetting, or printing, an image from a lithographic stone onto a rubber blanket. The image from the rubber blanket was then printed onto a sheet of paper. By the 1950s offset lithography had achieved dominance in the printing industry and currently remains so. Recent developments in plating and ink technologies offer two lithographic options to commercial printers: conventional water-based and waterless systems.

Water-Based Offset Printing

From previous discussions, we know that lithography is a chemical-based printing process. The **oil and water separation principle,** employed on an imaged lithographic printing plate, results in image areas whose inked surfaces are transferred onto a sheet of paper as it moves through a press. Although several different printing press configurations exist, the oil and water separation principle provides both the basis and restriction for all standard offset presses.

Conventional Offset Workflow

With conventional offset printing, different options are available for preparing images to be printed. Note that this workflow (Figure 10–1) can incorporate images prepared and processed by film-based systems. This includes outputting films to an image setter, stripping flats, and exposing presensitized printing plates. However, these tasks are being replaced by direct-to-plate technology, often with chemical-free plating systems. The key console in Figure 10–1 processes data files containing embedded color profiles of a specific job to be printed. The computer console interprets these data and automatically adjusts the ink feed keys on the press to control color accuracy in the printed image.

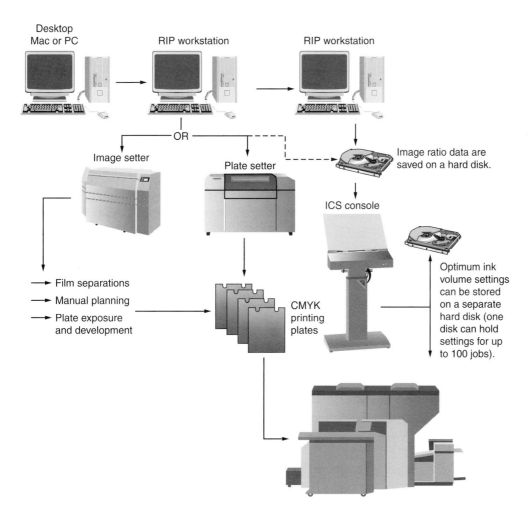

Figure 10–1.
The workflow in a conventional offset printing environment.

Offset Press Working Configurations

Water-based offset printing uses specially formulated plates made from aluminum, bimetal construction, polyester, or foil-impregnated paper onto which an image is photographically transferred. The printing plate is installed onto the plate cylinder (Figure 10–2). As this cylinder rotates, the plate first passes under water, or dampening, rollers. These rollers spread water or a water-based dampening solution evenly across the plate surface. The water adheres only to the nonimage areas on the plate and is repelled from the grease-based image areas. As the plate continues to rotate, it passes under rollers that apply ink over the plate surface. The ink is repelled from the wet areas on the plate but adheres to the dry image areas. After completing a rotating sequence, the plate has been inked only in the image areas. Thus the water repels the ink from the rest of the plate.

Figure 10–2.
A typical three-cylinder offset printing press design.

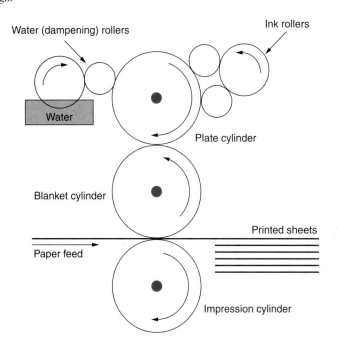

As the inked cylinder comes into contact with the offset, or blanket, cylinder, the positive image on the plate is transferred onto the blanket. As paper is fed into the press between the blanket and impression cylinders, the blanket prints its image onto the paper. The impression cylinder provides a solid backing for the paper as the image is being printed.

The **three-cylinder offset press** design in Figure 10–2 is the standard arrangement in small offset presses and duplicators. In larger presses a fourth cylinder is sometimes incorporated into the press, which acts as a separate delivery cylinder, resulting in a **four-cylinder offset press** design (Figure 10–3).

Single-Color and Multicolor Printing

The color capability of an offset press is based on the number of printing units, or printing heads, in its design. Figure 10–2 and Figure 10–3 show the cylinder arrangements and basic operating concepts of a typical single-color offset press. When moving from the theoretical to the practical placement of components within an actual press design, we can examine how the press operates. Figure 10–4 depicts a two-color offset press. The various rollers, cylinders, and feed and delivery systems within the covers of the machine are shown in Figure 10–5. As you can see, the design of a multicolor system is more complicated than that of a single-color press.

In the two-color component arrangement in Figure 10–5, paper is fed from the feed trays onto the feed and registration table. This press design uses one impression cylinder that serves both color print heads. The printed sheet emerges from the second color print head, where it is delivered onto the printed pile. Note the rollers on the paper delivery tray that allow the press operator to easily move the full printed paper stacks from the press to the finishing area.

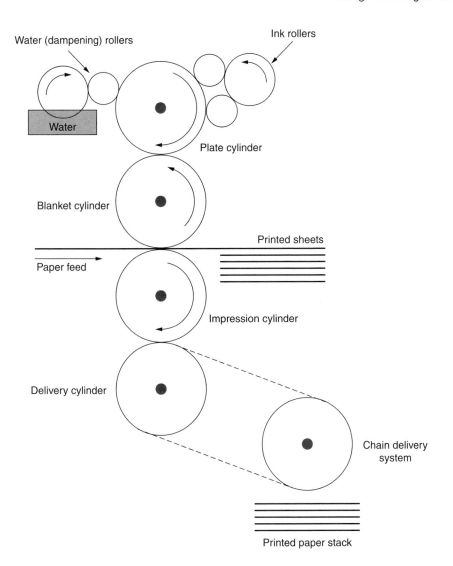

Figure 10–3.
A four-cylinder offset printing press design.

Water (dampening) rollers

Ink rollers

Water

Plate cylinder

Blanket cylinder

Printed sheets

Paper feed

Impression cylinder

Delivery cylinder

Chain delivery system

Printed paper stack

Figure 10–4.
A two-color offset press (courtesy Presstek, Inc.).

Figure 10–5.
The component
arrangement of a
two-color offset press
(courtesy Presstek, Inc.).

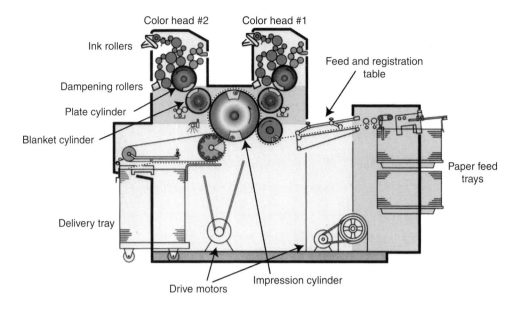

Color head #2   Color head #1

Ink rollers

Dampening rollers

Plate cylinder

Blanket cylinder

Feed and registration table

Paper feed trays

Delivery tray

Drive motors   Impression cylinder

Figure 10–6.
Registration guides on
the in-feed table of an
offset press.

The feed table contains micrometer adjustments that are capable of fine-tuning the position of the sheets as they enter the first color printing head (Figure 10–6).

Incorporating more printing heads in a press increases its color printing capacity. Note the six separate printing heads in Figure 10–7. This press is referred to as a four-over-two; the paper is printed by the first two-color print heads, then flips over and is printed as it goes through the remaining four heads. This prints four colors on one side of the sheet over two colors printed on the opposite side. Note the coating unit installed after the sixth print head. The coater is used for applying varnishes and a variety of aqueous finish coatings to a printed sheet.

Sheet-Fed and Web-Fed Presses

Presses can also be classified according to their paper-feeding system: either **sheet-fed** or **web-fed.** These terms designate whether the paper stock is fed into the press from a stack of individual cut sheets or from a continuous web, or roll, of paper: these webs often contain more than 5 miles of rolled paper. Paper costs associated with web-fed presses are lower because the web comes directly off a paper-making machine without the need to cut and package individual sheets. Web-fed paper is cut into separate sheets as it leaves the print heads of the press and is delivered on the output table as individual printed sheets. This operation is pictured in Figure 10–8.

Perfecting Presses

Modern high-speed printing would not be possible if printing presses could not print

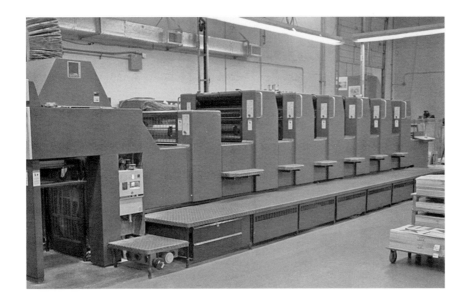

Figure 10–7.
Six-color offset printing press (courtesy SCP Printing).

on both sides of a sheet of paper at the same time. This type of printing is referred to as *perfect* printing, and this type of printing press is known as a **perfecting press.**

The first perfecting press was patented in 1863 and was adopted by *The Philadelphia Inquirer* 2 years later. That development marked the beginning of modern, web-fed printing presses with faster printing speeds made possible by the perfect printing process.

Different configurations can accomplish perfect printing. In one design, two plate and blanket cylinder arrangements oppose each other. As the paper goes through the printing head, both sides of the sheet are imaged simultaneously as shown in Figure 10–9. In other arrangements, after the paper has been printed on one side, the web is mechanically turned over to print the other side of the sheet in a different printing head of the press.

Waterless Offset Printing

Waterless offset is another form of offset printing in which no water or dampening solution is used. Conventional offset relies on the oil and water principle to separate image and nonimage areas of the printing plate. Because offset inks are usually oil-based, they stick to grease- or oil-based (*oleophilic*) substances and are repelled by water-covered (*hydrophilic*) substances. Waterless offset uses this principle but substitutes metals or plastics that attract water, and other materials that attract the printing inks, and incorporates them into one printing plate. This process of image separation is sometimes referred to as **differential adhesion.**

Figure 10–8.
Principle of a web-fed offset press.

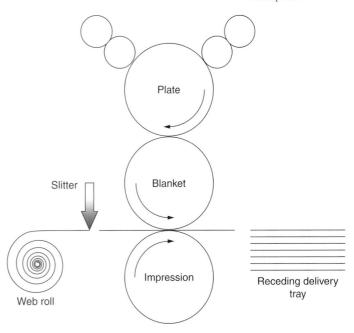

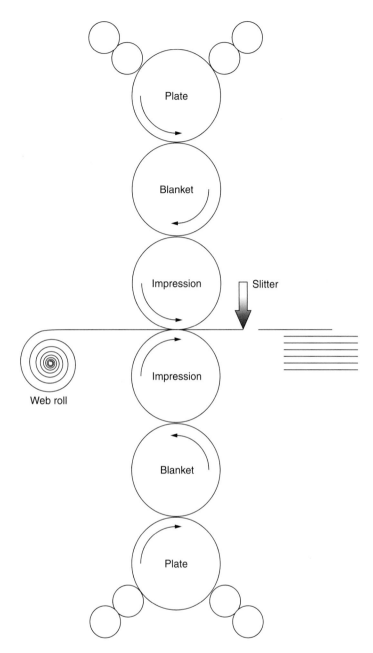

Figure 10–9.
A two-sided perfect printing offset press design.

some flexibility in changing ink density by increasing or decreasing the amount of fountain solution delivered to the plate. Also, a fountain solution acts as a heat sink, helping to control the temperature of ink during printing. Changes in temperature affect ink viscosity, which in turn determines how the ink is laid onto the paper. *Dot gain,* discussed in Chapter 9, must be built into the halftone image file before a job is run. This compensates for dots that might grow as much as 40 percent during actual printing. Many of these problems are minimized with waterless printing.

Silicone is the major ink displacement or ink repelling factor in waterless printing. Silicone takes the place of the fountain solution in waterless offset. Waterless inks have a higher **viscosity** than their conventional counterparts, and they tend to spread out and flow less than the less viscous water-based inks. Waterless thus features less dot gain, and hence greater detail, in the printed image. Also, the use of a silicone barrier on the plate produces better separation of image and nonimage areas than does the use of a fountain solution. Whereas conventional offset presses are hard-pressed to hold an image printing with a 175-line screen, waterless presses can print images up to 300 lines per inch (lpi).

Principles of Waterless Technologies

The idea of a waterless offset system first appeared in the 1960s and started to achieve commercial viability about 20 years later. The base material of waterless plates is often made from polyester (Figure 10–10). As detailed in Chapter 9, during imaging the top layer of silicone is burned away in the image areas. This process exposes the base material of the plate, which acts as the ink receptor.

Because no fountain solution is used in waterless printing, there is a significant

Advantages and Disadvantages of Waterless Printing

As with any technological process, waterless printing affords both enhancements and restrictions compared to its water-based counterpart. The core of these differences lies in the elimination of the dampening, or **fountain solution,** from waterless printing.

The use of a fountain solution in conventional offset allows the press operator

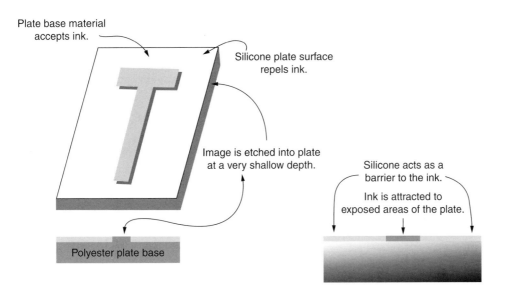

Figure 10–10.
Construction of a
waterless offset printing
plate.

Plate base material accepts ink.

Silicone plate surface repels ink.

Image is etched into plate at a very shallow depth.

Silicone acts as a barrier to the ink.

Ink is attracted to exposed areas of the plate.

Polyester plate base

reduction in the use of **volatile organic compounds (VOCs)**. VOCs are components of fountain and other solutions and solvents used in conventional offset printing. Reducing VOCs can almost eliminate the costs associated with hazardous material handling charges.

Temperature Control for Differential Adhesion

During printing, temperatures begin to build up in the rollers due to friction. As the operating temperatures increase, the ink viscosity decreases. This in turn can affect the repelling action of the silicone plate layer, causing ink to adhere to nonimage areas of the plate. To prevent this from happening, waterless presses incorporate temperature control devices that circulate cooling water (or, if needed, heated water) through the ink *oscillator rollers*. Temperature control ensures differential adhesion of the ink to only the image areas on the printing plate (Figure 10–11).

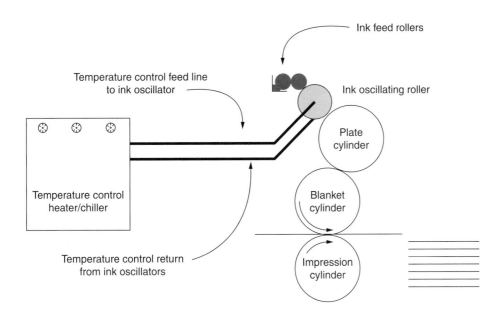

Figure 10–11.
Principle of a
temperature control
system in waterless offset
printing.

Ink feed rollers

Temperature control feed line to ink oscillator

Ink oscillating roller

Plate cylinder

Temperature control heater/chiller

Blanket cylinder

Impression cylinder

Temperature control return from ink oscillators

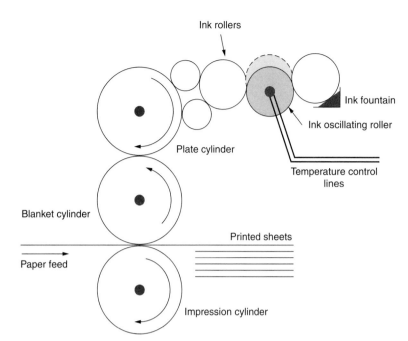

Figure 10–12.
A waterless offset press design.

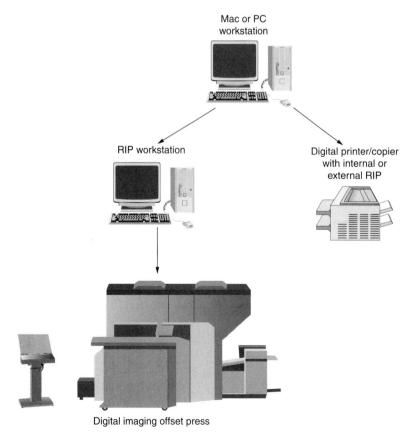

Figure 10–13.
Workflow options in a digital printing environment.

Waterless Press Design

The design of waterless offset presses tends to be more complicated than that of conventional offset machines. Most waterless presses incorporate on-press digital plate imaging technology and a temperature control device to circulate coolant through the ink oscillating rollers—in addition to the motors, mechanical linkages, and electronics found on all machines. Figure 10–12 shows a working drawing of a waterless offset press with these design enhancements.

DIGITAL PRINTING

Digital printing involves two basic technologies: waterless offset presses and drum imaging devices that have evolved from conventional photocopiers. Each of these technologies fits into specific segments of the market for short-run (fewer than 1,000 copies) and **on-demand printing** applications.

Digital Printing Workflow

The digital print workflow is straightforward; it varies based on whether files are output to conventional electrostatic or digital printing presses. The options in this workflow are shown in Figure 10–13.

In both workflow options illustrated in Figure 10–13, the source of the print data is either a Mac or PC workstation outputting a file to a printer. In the case of digital offset imaging, the data are first interpreted in a **raster image processor** (**RIP**) and then imaged on a waterless offset press. With drum imaging devices, the file is output to an internal RIP built into the color printer. File interpretation, color management, and printing are thus accomplished in one step.

A printer's decision of which technology to implement in the shop or use on a specific job focuses on whether variable-data capability is needed for the job and the final cost per printed copy. Cost comparisons are made here between digital printing and other printing methods. These costs are a function of the length of average press runs in the plant, the run of a specific job, and the resolution requirements of the finished images.

Variable-Data Printing

Variable-data printing technology is based on the requirement of electrostatic print engines that each page must be sent to the print engine separately, even if each page contains exactly the same information. **Variable-data printing (VDP)** is more than simply personalizing each printed copy with a different name (reminiscent of simple mail merge software). Brochures can highlight personal preferences of customers: hobbies, favorite sports, and similar personal traits. Such information can be incorporated into a significant marketing piece in which customers receive personally tailored invitations to buy a product—all revolving around a basic core of product information and advertising. Only digital print engines incorporate VDP into their design. Conventional offset presses—even those with digitally imaged plating systems—do not. The segment of the printing and publishing industry that caters to VDP relies exclusively on electrostatic drum imaging systems for these applications.

Costs of Digital Printing

The costs associated with electrostatic-based digital printing are calculated per copy. Fixed costs can range from $0.04–$0.75 per copy and are a factor of the volume of printing a particular plant does,

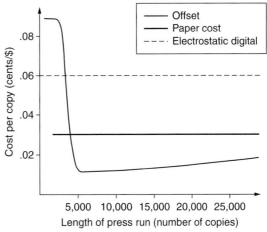

Figure 10–14.
Cost comparison of digital and offset printing.

which affects the cost per copy agreed on between the printer and supplier. These fixed costs make digital printing ideal for short-run applications. Because start-up costs are high for both conventional and digital offset, short-run applications can stay well below the crossover point at which offset would become the cheaper printing option (Figure 10–14). The constant fixed-cost nature of electrostatic digital makes it the best technology for short-run and on-demand printing. Digital printing is also ideal for just-in-time printing, for minimizing warehouse costs, and for specialty markets such as subject-oriented texts that would be too expensive or difficult to print in any other way. Look for fixed cost-per-copy contracts to change in the future as digital printing continues to move into traditional printing markets. These changes will also make digital printing more competitive in longer press run markets.

Resolution of Digital Offset Technologies

When examining the resolution characteristics of various printing systems, we find that digital waterless offset is in a class by itself. Whereas high-quality offset presses can deliver pages with a 175 lpi resolution, digital waterless offset, using stochastic screening, can consistently print at a screen resolution of 300 lpi. We have examined the factors that allow these high output resolutions—all of which are related to minimizing dot gain during the plating and printing process. These include the lack of a fountain solution, high-viscosity inks, minimized dot gain during plating, and laser imaging systems capable of producing fine dot patterns, all conspiring to yield remarkable printing results with digital waterless offset technology. The standard resolution of electrostatic print engines is 600 lpi. This resolution is a result of the physical limitations of the process based on toner particle size, but still yields excellent results in most short-run color applications. Continued research into toner technology will result in toner chemical compositions capable of achieving significantly higher image resolutions than are currently possible.

Digital Press Design

Digital printing has become the fastest-growing segment of the printing industry in response to the demand for inexpensive, fast-turnaround, short-run color printing. Each of the two major technologies—offset and electrostatic drum—is ideally suited for different applications within this industry segment.

Digital Direct Imaging Offset Presses

Most **direct image (DI) offset presses** are waterless, sheet-fed automated machines that offer high-quality results and continually reduced costs. DI systems eliminate film processing and plate production equipment; these procedures are incorporated within the design of the DI press. With the elimination of film processing chemistry and solvent-based fountain solutions, hazardous waste removal and maintenance of acceptable air quality standards within the plant are greatly simplified. The component arrangement of a DI waterless offset press is shown in Figure 10–15A.

During the operation of the DI press portrayed in Figure 10–15, each sheet makes two revolutions around the central impression cylinder (#12). The position of this impression cylinder relative to the plate cylinder is pictured in Figure 10–15B.

On the first revolution, colors #1 and #2 are printed. On the second rotation of the impression cylinder, the final two colors are printed, and the printed sheet goes through an infrared dryer and is deposited onto the printed paper pile. Direct image presses of this type are capable of printing speeds up to 7,000 impressions per hour (iph) and print on sheet sizes up to 13×18 inches. Approximate runs of from 20,000 to 25,000 impressions can be achieved using these polyester-based plates.

Drum Imaging Digital Presses

Drum imaging digital presses are based on photocopier technology and are built around a **photosensitive drum** coated with a semiconductor material. The surface of this drum changes its electrical resistance in response to light striking it from an imaging laser beam. Figure 10–16 illustrates the main components of a single-color laser print engine.

In response to information contained in the data file, the imaging laser exposes and charges the photosensitive drum. **Toner particles** from either a dry or liquid-based system are fed onto a developing cylinder. From here the toner is deposited onto the imaging drum. The amount of toner deposition varies with the electrical charges

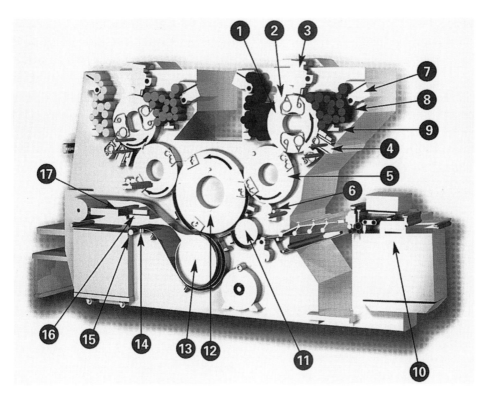

Figure 10–15A.
Waterless offset digital imaging printing press (courtesy Presstek, Inc.).

Press Components
1. Auto-loading plate cylinder
2. Printing plate
3. Imaging head
4. Plate cleaning mechanisms
5. Blanket cylinder
6. Automatic blanket cleaner
7. Ink fountain
8. Ink rollers
9. Automatic ink roller cleaner
10. Compact single sheet feeder
11. Paper feed drum
12. Impression cylinder
13. Transfer cylinder
14. Paper decurling mechanism
15. Suction wheel
16. Infrared dryer
17. High-grade powder system

Figure 10–15B.
The central impression cylinder of a direct imaging waterless offset press (courtesy Presstek, Inc.).

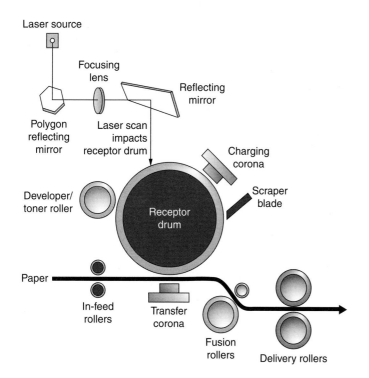

Figure 10–16.
The main components of an electrostatic print engine.

Both color and monochrome digital print engines are based on the same technology. The color printer in Figure 10–17 consists of four-color transfer rollers charging a single photosensitive printing drum. This type of digital printer easily handles most short-run full-color printing jobs with or without variable data content.

FINISHING PROCESSES

Several processes take place both during and after the actual printing of a job. For example, although adding a perfume sample to an advertising brochure is technically a finishing process, it takes place during printing. Binding the signatures of a book into a hard case, laminating a book cover, and trimming printed sheets are all examples of finishing operations. In this section we look at some common finishing operations in more detail.

imparted by the imaging laser. Currently most toner contains 90 percent thermoplastic resins colored with 10 percent carbon black pigment. As paper enters the print engine, it is given an electrostatic charge to transfer toner from the drum to the paper. As the paper travels through the print engine, it goes through a series of fusion rollers, where pressure and heat (between 300°F and 400°F) melt the toner and fix, or *set*, it onto the paper surface.

Paper Cutting

Most printed material has to be cut or trimmed at some point during production. Automated paper cutters handle most of this work. Figure 10–18 shows a three-blade knife trimmer. The paper is automatically aligned on all four sides before the trimmer is activated.

The design of the paper cutter in Figure 10–18 lets it trim a sheet on three sides simultaneously, making it ideal for trimming book and pamphlet signatures. The **single-knife paper cutter** in Figure 10–19 is more conventional in design, cutting one side of a paper stack with each pass of the blade. This cutter is computer controlled, however, and can be programmed to make a series of different cuts in sequence. After each programmed cut takes place, the machine operator moves the paper stack and aligns it for the next cut.

Figure 10–17.
Principle of a four-color digital drum print engine.

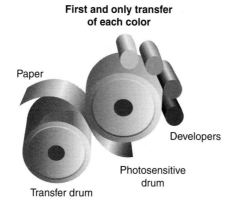

First and only transfer of each color

Paper

Developers

Photosensitive drum

Transfer drum

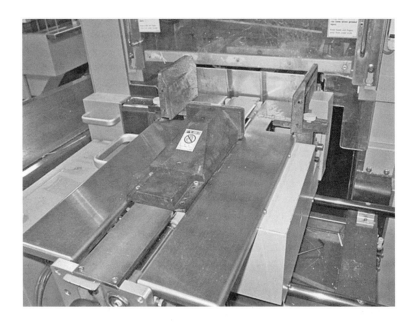

Figure 10–18.
A three-blade knife trimmer (courtesy SCP Printing).

Collating

Collating is the process of gathering all printed sheets of a job in the correct order. Collators are often integrated with other processes in a bindery so that the sheets are first collated, then bound and trimmed. Figure 10–20 shows one section of a thirty-two-station continuous-line collator that can produce finished thirty-two-page or sixty-four-page **signatures**. As the signatures travel along the production line, pages are added until the signatures are complete. After collating, the signatures enter the automated section of the bindery for stapling and trimming.

Coating and Laminating

In the **laminating** process, clear plastic is adhered to one or both sides of a printed sheet of paper, cardboard, or similar stock. Laminating seals the sheet, protecting it from

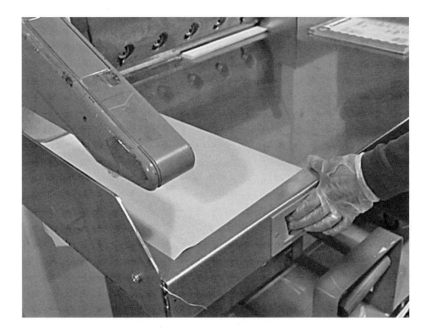

Figure 10–19.
A single-knife paper cutter (courtesy SCP Printing).

Figure 10–20.
A continuous-line collating station within an automated bindery operation (courtesy SCP Printing, Inc.).

moisture as well as adding stability to the paper. When laminating two sides of material, a sheet of stock is fed between two sheets of laminating plastic and passed through heated rollers under pressure; then the excess plastic is trimmed. In Figure 10–21, the top and bottom rolls of laminating plastic are visible as the sheet to be laminated is placed on the feed table.

Figure 10–21.
A plastic sheet laminator.

In a modification of the conventional laminating process, Figure 10–22A and Figure 10–22B show an adhesive coating being placed on a large sheet of foam core. Here the adhesive can be used for permanently mounting large posters onto the foam core as a solid backing for a poster print. In this process, the heated rollers of the laminating unit soften the adhesive as it is applied to the foam. The unit pictured can handle sheets of foam core up to four feet wide.

Coating processes can take place either during printing or as a postpress operation. For example, high-quality fine art prints often require an overcoat of clear varnish to protect the print surfaces. This varnish can be applied during printing if one head of the press prints the coating solution rather than ink. An alternative to this procedure is to run the finished prints through a separate coating machine to apply the varnish.

Die Cutting, Embossing, and Thermography

Die cutting, embossing, and *thermography* are postpress specialty finishing processes.

In the **die-cutting** process, shapes are cut from paper or cardboard using a form that contains a special spring-steel cutting-edge die. The shape to be cut is first laid out on a sheet of plywood and then cut out using a jigsaw or band saw. The steel cutting die is inserted into the *saw kerfs*—the spaces generated by the cutting blade of the saw. The assembled die is then placed in a platen press or similar die-cutting press to individually cut the finished shape from each sheet of paper or cardboard. A completed die-cutting form is illustrated in Figure 10–23. The circles and rectangles shown were used to cut matte board for framing multiple photographs in one picture frame. Note the use of foam rubber surrounding the steel die to help push the cut pieces from the remaining paper stock.

Embossing is the process of creating raised surfaces in paper from a male and female embossing die. The principle of embossing is illustrated in Figure 10–24. Note the use of male and female dies, which are used to leave the embossed impression on a sheet of paper.

Thermography is a process used to simulate the raised printing effect achieved when an item is engraved. For this reason, thermography is sometimes referred to as *imitation engraving*. Special invitations are often printed using the engraving process, in which thickened ink is deposited onto paper from recessed areas of an engraved printing plate. Because of the volume and composition of the ink lifted from these recesses, the actual printed image is raised above the paper surface. To achieve this effect artificially, a resinous powder is applied to a printed piece before the printing ink dries; the powder adheres only to the wet printing ink. When passed under a heating unit, the resin powder melts

Figure 10–22A.
The in-feed table of a large-format laminator (courtesy SCP Printing).

Figure 10–22B.
The output section of a large-format laminator (courtesy SCP Printing).

Figure 10–23.
A die-cutting form. Note the use of foam rubber, which is used to help remove the stock after it has been cut.

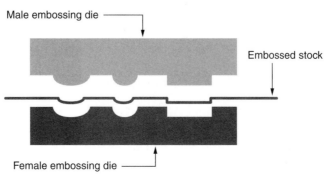

Male embossing die

Embossed stock

Female embossing die

Figure 10–24.
The principle of embossing.

Figure 10–25.
This thermography unit is used to decorate recently printed items with a raised surface.

Figure 10–26.
Adjustments on this paper folder enable multiple folds of varying dimensions on a single sheet of paper. This tabletop unit can fold about 8,000 sheets per hour.

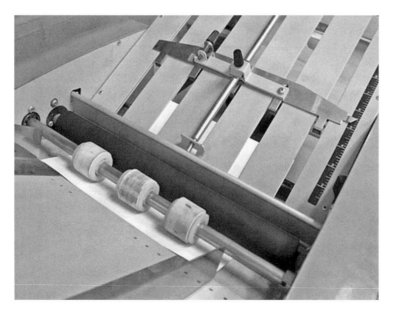

and encapsulates the inked image or text, forming a raised printing surface. A small tabletop thermography unit, such as the one pictured in Figure 10–25, allows the powder to be applied by hand and then shaken off the printed piece manually before the piece is inserted onto a conveyor belt to be heated.

Folding, Scoring, and Perforating

Depending on job requirements, **folding, scoring,** and **perforating** operations can be performed on either tabletop units or larger floor model machines. Regardless of the size of the machine, the concept of folding is the same: The paper is fed into a machine and hits a stop that causes it to fold. The folded sheet is then deposited onto an output conveyor. Note the position of the folded sheet in Figure 10–26. The paper comes into contact with an adjustable folding bar in the top right of the illustration. This causes the paper to fold and then feed downward onto the out-feed table for collection.

Folding, scoring, and perforating capabilities are often combined into one device. These larger machines are capable of performing up to 20,000 simultaneous operations per hour.

Numbering, Drilling, Counting, and Jogging

Numbering is usually required in a variety of ticket-printing applications. Where long press runs are involved, numbering is often done directly on the press, where a numbering machine is installed on the printing head. For smaller jobs, hand-operated numbering machines can be used.

Counting, like numbering, is almost always a press operation. All presses have integral counters that keep track of the total press run. Under microprocessor control, a press counter mechanism is programmed to take into account misfeeds that might occur during a press run. Counting also helps to maintain quality control and track paper expenses for a job.

Paper drilling is a postpress operation, usually performed in preparation for a specific binding operation. Paper drills are available as either single-spindle or multiple-spindle machines.

To ensure the accuracy of all finishing operations, paper stacks must contain all sheets in proper alignment. To accomplish this, the paper is often placed in a **jogging** machine. The operating principle behind all paper joggers is the same: A rapidly vibrating table causes all the sheets in a stack to align perfectly as gravity forces them into place. The jogger pictured in Figure 10–27 is capable of jogging a ream (500 sheets) of 11 × 17-inch paper in about 15 seconds.

Bindery Techniques

All multiple-page documents need to be held together in some way so they can be transported as well as read. This process is accomplished using any one of several bindery methods: sewing, stapling, or gluing the individual sheets together. Most binding other than small on-demand and short-run jobs is done on a bindery production line. Here machines performing several different operations are placed in tandem to accomplish the entire binding process quickly and automatically. Very little manual handling of assembled pages and signatures is needed once the production line has been properly set up and adjusted.

Wire and Plastic Binding

Two of the simplest and most cost-effective binding techniques involve the use of **wire** or **plastic binding** combs inserted into prepunched holes to hold a book or pamphlet together. Most wire and plastic binders use holes that are spaced uniformly so that either a wire or plastic comb can be used in the same punched holes. For most plastic- and wire-bound systems, rectangular holes are cut into the paper with a special paper punch (Figure 10–28). After these holes have been punched, special machines insert either a wire or plastic honeycomb (Figure 10–29A and Figure 10–29B).

On small printing runs, wire and plastic binding can be accomplished manually.

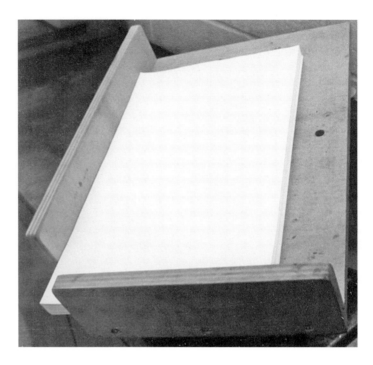

Larger press runs need automated equipment to collate, punch, and insert the binding combs. The left side of Figure 10–30 shows a spool-fed wire binder bundled within an automatic collator. The right side of the figure displays a wire honeycomb feed on an automatic binding machine. The wire spools are supplied in huge rolls, automatically cut to the proper length, and inserted into the

Figure 10–27.
The rapid vibration of this paper jogger quickly aligns loose paper sheets for further processing of the paper stock.

Figure 10–28.
Rectangular holes have been cut into these sheets in preparation for a plastic or wire binding insert.

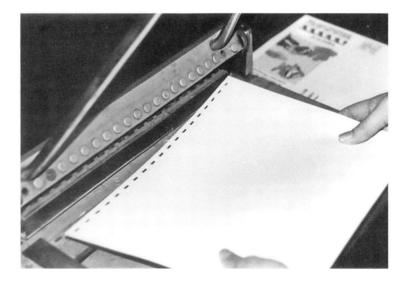

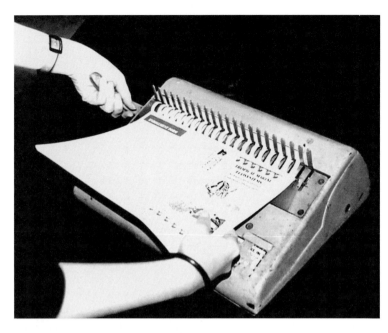

Figure 10–29A.
A plastic binding comb inserted in precut rectangular holes using a manually operated plastic binding machine.

Figure 10–29B.
Wire binding inserted into precut holes in the paper stock.

finished signatures as the books travel along a production line.

Side and Saddle Stitching

The terms *side stitching* and *saddle stitching* refer to the location of staples, or stitches, on the binding. **Side stitching** places staples and sewn stitches along the sides of the signatures, spaced in from the back edge

(or spine) to hold the thread or staples firmly in place. **Saddle stitching** places the thread or staples through the spines of the signatures, along the centerfolds of the pages. Stapling a job is still probably the cheapest and most common method of holding pages together.

Perfect and Case Binding

Perfect binding is a process in which all document pages are glued together. Common examples of perfect-bound documents include large catalogs, telephone directories, magazines, and paperback books. Perfect binding is a padding operation. The sheets to be bound are first scored along their back edges. Scoring helps ensure that glue will penetrate and hold each sheet in the book. After scoring, the assembled sheets are fed through a series of hot glue rollers to apply the adhesive (Figure 10–31). The glue in this unit is maintained at approximately 200°F. Although the glue is automatically applied to each signature, the signatures must be trimmed after gluing. If the cover is not part of the assembled pages, it is adhered separately after the signatures or sheets have been glued together.

Figure 10–32 shows the application of a hard cover **case binding** to a perfect-bound assembly of signatures. The manual case binder in Figure 10–32 is used mostly for small press runs and on-demand output. The signatures in this figure have already been trimmed, and end sheets have been included as part of the signature packet. During binding, the end sheets are adhered to the cover for a finished appearance.

Edition Binding

Edition binding is the most expensive type of binding process. In edition binding, signatures are assembled and sewn together using high-quality thread. End sheets are either included as part of the first and last signatures or are glued in place after the

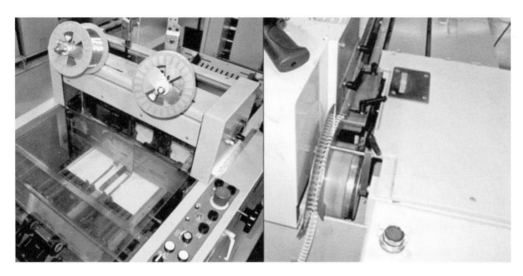

Figure 10–30.
A spool-fed wire-binding unit. The wire binding is fed into the machine from large spools of wire, precut to the correct size, and inserted into the precut stock. The machine on the left inserts wire bindings automatically as part of an automated bindery system. The unit on the right uses a roll of preformed wire that is applied manually, one book at a time (courtesy SCP Printing).

signatures are sewn together. The end sheets of the signatures are then glued onto the hard cover. Edition bindings can significantly raise the cost of a finished book; to see this, note the price difference between two identical books, one of which is soft covered and the other of which is edition bound.

Air Filtration, Hazardous Waste, and VOCs

The printing and publishing industries, due to the nature of their production processes, generate large volumes of hazardous waste materials. Paper fibers, volatile compounds used in printing inks, and conventional dampening solutions for offset presses all contribute to potentially hazardous work environments. Responsible energy and environmental plant practices have helped minimize these conditions with products that reduce levels of potentially toxic substances.

To help maintain clean air within the plant, a variety of floor model air filtration units are available. The unit pictured in Figure 10–33 uses a combination of activated carbon filters that can remove a variety of harmful elements such as smoke, dust, VOCs, toxic fumes, odors, pollen, bacteria, and spray powders.

Figure 10–31.
A glue applicator section in a perfect binding machine (courtesy SCP Printing).

Figure 10–32
Adding a case binding
to a set of completed
signatures (courtesy SCP
Printing).

Figure 10–33.
A mobile air purification
unit (courtesy Island
Clean Air, Inc.).

Improper disposal of hazardous materials
is subject to stiff fines by the **Environmental
Protection Agency (EPA)**. Certified waste
haulers are usually contracted for graphic
arts and printing plants that generate large
quantities of hazardous photo chemicals.
However, firms that generate 25 gallons
or less, each month, of hazardous waste
are considered conditionally exempt small
quantity generators (CESQG) by the EPA.
This classification lets these firms select
alternative methods of waste disposal. In
one such method pictured in Figure 10–34,
photographic chemicals are poured into a
five-gallon container composed of a polymer
that encapsulates the chemical waste by
absorbing it into a sponge-like polymer
crystal that neutralizes silver ions. The
filled containers can be disposed of in
a municipal landfill.

Green Cleaning

Cleaning compounds and services
performed without the use of toxic

chemicals are referred to as **green cleaning.** The development of nontoxic cleaning compounds for industrial use is spreading as studies find the concentrations of toxic compounds within offices and workplaces to be hundreds of times higher than they are outdoors.

Although increasing amounts of nontoxic cleaners are being developed, few definitions or legal requirements govern the use of terminology such as *natural* or *green*. However, certain characteristics help identify cleaning agents as environmentally responsible.

Green cleaners should be biodegradable and nontoxic to humans and aquatic life. Cleaners should be sold in a concentrated form. Because the most common ingredient of general-purpose cleaners is water, excess water adds to shipping and packaging costs. Also, cleaners should not contain chlorine bleach, high concentrations of VOCs or EDTA (ethylene diamine tetra acetic acid), or phosphates. These compounds are not readily biodegradable and encourage algae blooms, which can deplete oxygen in water bodies, killing fish and plants. People who are responsible for purchasing cleaning agents should look for the numerous Web sites that offer long lists of green cleaning compounds.

Soon it will become universal business practice and philosophy that good business citizens should make every effort to comply with recent laws concerning full disclosure of the environmental impact of all manufactured products, as well as eliminating the use of hazardous substances and VOCs linked to environmental deterioration.

SUMMARY

This chapter has focused on both printing processes and postproduction finishing systems. The underlying concepts and designs

Figure 10–34.
An on-site waste disposal system for neutralizing photographic chemicals (courtesy Chemgon, Inc.).

of conventional, water-based, and dry offset technologies were examined. Differences in design, device control, and output quality of these systems were highlighted.

Digital print engines are greatly altering the printing landscape. The technology of the digital press and its capabilities were introduced, with an eye toward the eventual migration of the majority of printing systems in this direction.

A variety of finishing techniques are needed after a printing job comes off the press. Trimming, collating, laminating, binding, scoring, and embossing are some of the finishing operations discussed in this chapter.

The concept of operating a green printing business was also introduced. Green production techniques will play an increasingly important role in all future business activities.

Within the scope of the information covered in this chapter, students are encouraged to think about the great variety of options and opportunities available within the printing and associated technologies of the design–production continuum.

Review Questions

1 On what chemical principle is offset printing based? How does this principle affect how images are printed on an offset printing press?

2 Name the four cylinders of a four-cylinder offset printing press. Specify the function of each of these cylinders.

3 How are multiple colors printed on an offset press?

4 What are the differences between a sheet-fed and a web-fed printing press?

5 What does the term *perfect printing* mean?

6 What are the major differences between a water-based and a waterless offset printing press?

7 Compare the workflow of a typical printing job in a conventional offset versus a digital printing environment. Which process offers time savings over the other, and why?

Suggested Student Activities

1 Conduct a survey of any laboratory facility in your school to determine what specific areas could benefit from green technologies. List specific products that could improve the health and safety aspects of the facility.

2 Construct a chart showing the costs of printing a job with a press run of 10,000 copies in traditional offset and digital printing. To complete this task, you'll need to determine or assign values to the following conditions:

- Type of paper and cost.
- Cost of press time for the job (assume one hour).
- Salary for the press person.
- Plant overhead.
- Cost of ink/solvents/waste disposal (for conventional offset)/toner.

3 Construct a flowchart that highlights five typical finishing processes that would be used in printing a conventional case-bound textbook. How might the job be set up to minimize these finishing costs?

Designing for Print Production: Chapter 11

Chapter Objectives

Understand how to apply the graphic design problem-solving model in real-world projects.

Learn what makes a logo effective.

Examine the techniques used in poster design.

Understand the process of creating display advertising.

Examine how magazines and newsletters are composed and designed.

Learn the process of designing catalogs.

See how package designs are created.

INTRODUCTION

This chapter presents an in-depth study of several common graphic design projects. It further explains the special characteristics of each. We begin with a brief review of the graphic design process that has been emphasized throughout this text, and then address the following areas: logo design, poster design, advertising design, newsletter and magazine design, catalog design, and package design. In each area we focus on the particulars relating to the individual topic and the decisions made by designers in choosing the best means of communicating their clients' messages.

APPLYING THE GRAPHIC DESIGN PROCESS

The process of graphic design problem solving was addressed at length in Chapter 4. In review, the process is a series of steps that, when properly followed, will enable you to create a design solution that will satisfy both your client's needs and your own creativity. The basic steps include defining the problem; developing and setting up a budget and schedule; gathering information; creating several ideas from thumbnail sketches to final comps; presenting your ideas to the client; evaluating those ideas with the client; making necessary changes; producing the design; and making a final evaluation of the design project. By following this process in any design project, you build in ways to check your progress and evaluate your work. This process was used in the following examples, though we will not list all of the steps here to avoid repetition.

Designing Logos

Logo design is usually the first project that beginning graphic designers attempt. Whether as an assignment in high school or for a friend's band, a **logo** plays an important role. It functions as a simple visual reminder of the group it represents. Logo design has been covered extensively in the history of graphic design and continues to be a vital area in which graphic designers work today.

When creating a logo, the designer should remember that the image will be used in various applications—from a small size on business

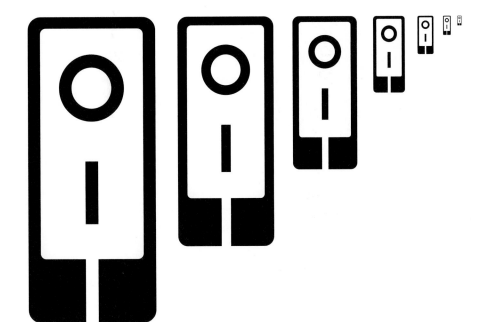

Figure 11–1.
Logos should be able to be easily enlarged and reduced without losing their identity and recognition.

cards to a large size, such as on the side of a van. Therefore, the designer must create an adaptable design that looks good whether reproduced at half an inch or 10 feet wide. Most successful logos are kept simple to ensure that detail will not be lost when the logo is enlarged or reduced. Figure 11–1 shows an example of how a well-designed logo will reproduce at various sizes without losing its impact.

There are two basic kinds of logos: *image-based* and *typographic*. We will discuss each of these here.

Image-Based Logos

Image-based logos can be placed in three categories: *pictograms, ideograms,* and *abstract*. Each type has its own unique characteristics, and some logos may fit into more than one of these categories.

PICTOGRAM LOGOS

A pictogram is a simple representation of any single thing. This could be anything:

an animal, the sun, a vehicle, a person, or an object such as a tool. This basic representation of "the thing" provides a direct interpretation of what it is in the design.

Although pictograms date back to early cave drawings, it is unlikely that they were used for advertising at that time. Instead they were a way for early humans to visually communicate with one another. Pictograms were often part of ritual celebrations. As elements in logos, they were used from the beginning of graphic design as a way to easily represent what a business does.

When designing a **pictogram logo,** it is important that the chosen image represents an organization in a positive light and that the image directly relates to the company. For example, if you create a logo for a company that deals in only one item—such as a publishing company that produces books—a logo with a book would be appropriate. Pictograms are

Figure 11–2.
Pictogram logos visually
represent what a
company does.

Figure 11–3.
The symbol that
represents the American
dollar is recognized
around the world, yet
it is not a picture of the
dollar. As an ideogram,
the symbol uses an
abstract image to refer to
the idea of the dollar.

the same way. It is important, therefore, to
do quite a bit of research in the design and
presentation stages of projects that involve
ideograms.

A familiar example of an ideogram logo
is that of AT&T (Figure 11–4). Designed to
represent lines of communication encircling
the earth, the logo uses the visual imagery
of a sphere with lines around it. The sphere
does not read as the earth directly, but
the abstract elements are used to imply
a larger idea.

ABSTRACT LOGOS

Once businesses move into a corporate
structure in which many different types of
businesses are owned by one large parent
company, designers find it increasingly
difficult to use pictograms to represent
the entire corporation. One single image
cannot easily represent a corporation whose
subsidiaries might manufacture food and
clothing as well as distributing movies and
communications, for example. **Abstract logos**
can be created to give such a corporation a
dynamic look without featuring the image or
idea of any single product.

Figure 11–4 shows two abstract logos.
Notice how simple abstract design elements
are combined in unique ways to create these
two different logo designs.

Although abstract logos are one of the
most common types in use today, the
root of their design is not always pure

widely used today; two examples are
shown in Figure 11–2.

IDEOGRAM LOGOS

An **ideogram logo** is an image that
represents an idea, illustrated through the use
of an image. For example, the typographic
symbol that represents the American
dollar (Figure 11–3) is not a picture of the
dollar, yet it is immediately recognized as
representing it.

Ideogram logos are more difficult to design
than pictograms because each person will not
necessarily perceive the ideographic image in

Figure 11–4.
Abstract logos work
well for corporations
that have many holdings
in a wide variety of
companies. In these
cases, a representative
logo will not properly
represent the
corporation.

abstraction. In some cases a designer will take an image and abstract it. In the design shown in Figure 11–5, the eye element was abstracted for a visual arts organization.

Typographic Logos

Often a designer will choose not to use an image logo at all but instead will design a logo by creating a unique version of a company's name (Figure 11–6). **Typographic logos** communicate the name of a company as the most important feature.

When designing a typographic logo, the designer must find a typeface that captures the personality of a company. This can be done either by creating the type from scratch or by modifying an existing typeface. The designer should not simply take a readily available typeface and set it without modification. Such a logo would be too easy for others to reproduce, and often it would be reproduced with incorrect changes. Therefore, an existing typeface should be modified so that it can be used only in its modified form (Figure 11–7). This can be scanned or saved as an EPS file for use by others at the company without letting them alter it too easily.

Logo Production

Final production of a logo is done either on a computer or by hand. Logos created on the computer are drawn with a program such as Adobe Illustrator, from which the final design can be saved as a separate file and given to the client. Type that was used in the logo design should always be converted to outlines because the client's company may not have the needed typeface loaded on its computer. Converting the type to outlines will also make it more difficult for someone other than the designer to change the logo. Hand drawing may be necessary for certain designs. Hand-lettered logos are usually scanned and digitized so they can be easily

placed in other documents and scaled to size quickly.

Figure 11–8 shows why a logo should be created in a drawing program. The small logo on the left was created in a drawing program. It was then enlarged 200 percent in the drawing program. Notice how it retains its sharp edges after being enlarged. The small logo in the center was created in a painting program at the size shown. At this size it looks as good as the one created in the drawing program. When it is enlarged 200 percent, however, the edges lose resolution, and the

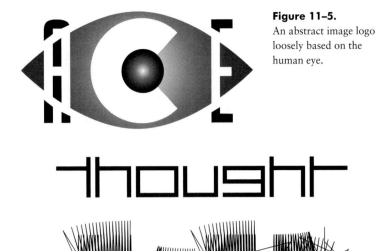

Figure 11–5.
An abstract image logo loosely based on the human eye.

Figure 11–6.
In creating a typographic logo, the choice of typeface needs to reflect the character of the company. To be unique, type should be created from scratch, as in the two logos shown here.

Figure 11–7.
An alternative to creating type from scratch is to modify an existing typeface for use in a logo. Here the typeface DIN Neuzeit Grotesk Bold Condensed, shown above, was the inspiration for the typographic logo pictured below it.

Figure 11–8.
Logos should always be created in a drawing program so they will scale correctly without losing resolution.

logo does not print correctly. Always use a vector-based drawing program to create logos!

Poster Design

Posters are often fun projects that let designers stretch their creative muscles. Because they offer a single, strong visual presence, they can be dynamic, expressive pieces in a portfolio.

Posters can be made in various sizes from small (11 × 17) to large (34 × 44 or larger). They can be printed by a variety of methods—photocopied, silk-screened, block printed, offset in one or more colors, rotogravure—in addition to having special processes such as foil stamping, die cutting, thermography, and even being formed in relief in paper or plastic! The form a poster takes depends on its budget and purpose.

When starting a poster project, you will first want to ask the client where the poster will be displayed and how it will be distributed. A poster being put in store windows of local businesses will be quite different from one being used as a broadside on construction barricades or one being sold as a limited-edition event poster. If it is to be mailed, the design may need to be easily folded without damage. Knowing how a poster will be used will help you determine its size and assist in structuring its design.

The budget for a job will aid you in determining how many special processes and colors you can use in a design.

Sometimes you may be asked to first come up with a design and then get estimates on its production. This is not an ideal situation, especially for beginning designers, because it is much easier to work within a given budget. It may be a good idea to develop a range of concepts covering various prices to bring back to the client if you do not receive a firm printing budget at the beginning of the project.

Once you know the budget and type of printing that will be used on a poster, get all the information to be included in the design and determine the information hierarchy. This can be done in discussion with the client, making notes on the copy as you find out what elements are more important than others.

Once the design phase begins, give some thought to what a successful poster needs to do:

• Attract its intended audience.
• Convey its message effectively.
• Stand out among visual clutter.
• Have strong typographic design.
• Use color well.
• Be memorable.

Appealing to your audience is important in any piece of graphic design; but in a poster you have a very short time to catch viewers' attention. Therefore, it is important that you understand your audience and create a design that will appeal to them.

Getting a message across quickly is important in poster design. The information should make complete and immediate sense to the viewer. Do not hide essential information such as time, date, or location. All the information should be presented in a way that makes sense and is easy to understand.

A poster is usually displayed among other posters on a wall, so your design will have competition for the viewer's eye. Make sure that yours stands out. If you know where the posters will be put up, take some pictures of those locations. Even though what is posted there may change, this will give you an idea of the context of your design in its final form.

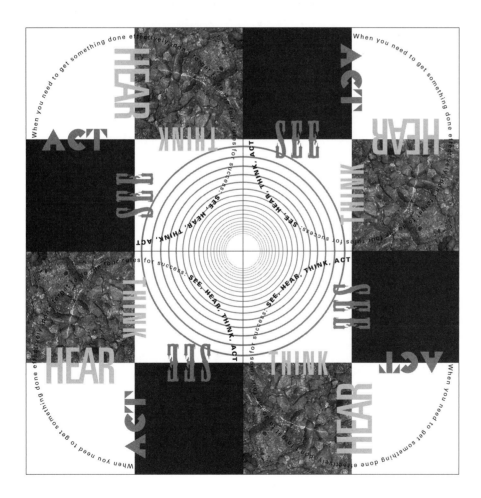

Figure 11–9.
Posters can be designed with elements that work together when posted in groupings. The illustration at the top shows a single poster that was specifically designed to work in a grouping. The illustration below shows four of these posters grouped. In the grouping, the poster is rotated 90 degrees each time it is posted. This pattern could continue or be changed by different rotations of each poster, providing a wide range of possible groupings. This illustration is shown in color in the color section of this text.

You may notice things that will help you make your design stand out. For example, if many of the designs are in color, perhaps a black-and-white design will work better; if many of the designs use full-bleed imagery, a border may help yours stand out. If you are limited to a small size while other designs are larger, perhaps you can design a poster that, when placed next to other identical copies, makes up a larger design (Figure 11–9).

Figure 11–10.
These two examples show the differences between a flyer, on the left, and a poster, on the right. A flyer is meant to be a small size, usually 8.5 × 11 inches, whereas a poster is designed to work at large sizes. Although the design concepts here are the same, the larger poster allows greater use of compositional space. This space can be used to pull the viewer into the design, rather than having all the copy immediately readable from a distance.

Figure 11–11.
Being limited to one color does not mean your creativity should be limited, as shown in this black-and-white poster design (©Frances Ullenberg).

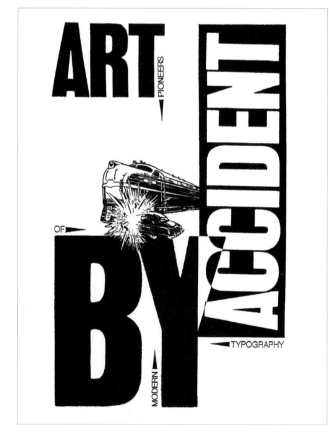

There are many ways to make a design stand out against visual clutter, and these should be explored in the early stages of the project.

Although strong typographic design should be an element in all your work, in a poster this is even more important. Many students, when designing a large poster for the first time, end up designing large **flyers**—designs that might look fine at letter size, but at actual size do not take advantage of the compositional possibilities the large size offers. When working on a large poster design, you can use space in a much more open way, and the information can be balanced to make a much more interesting composition. Figure 11–10 shows how a flyer differs from a poster. When designing a poster, be sure to treat all the type as important in your composition. Do not let anything be tucked away in a corner, but make it all function together.

Color use in a poster can be amazing. Even with one color, a design can be bold and attractive (Figure 11–11). When you can use many colors, make sure they are not wasted, but add to the composition in interesting ways. This does not mean they all need to be used equally, however. Sometimes a touch of a contrasting color can be stronger than a large amount of it.

Finally, poster designs should be memorable. Of all the forms of graphic design, posters are what people will see, respond to, and even frame to put on their walls. Posters from the 1800s through today have become collectible, and you probably would like to have your work attain that status. Creating a design that is a pleasure to look at—even long after the event the poster was created for—should be a goal when you work on a poster design.

Production processes for a poster design can vary as much as the designs themselves. What we will cover here is an example of a three-color silk-screened poster. Because this book is not in color, the three colors will be shown as black and shades of gray (Figure 11–12).

Posters for offset printing may be created in any of the three program types, but it is often easiest to create a poster for silk-screen printing in a drawing program. There are several reasons for this. First, drawing programs are best for creating large areas of flat color, which is one of the strengths of silk-screening. Also, you can place each color as a separate layer—one on top of another—just as the silk-screen printing process does; you can select specific Pantone colors, which is what the printer will mix for you; the drawing program tools give you the most flexibility to work with images and type; and most important, the drawing program allows you to scale the design without loss of resolution should you need to print your design at several different sizes.

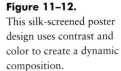

Figure 11–12.
This silk-screened poster design uses contrast and color to create a dynamic composition.

Figure 11–13 shows how the three layers would be set up for the design shown in Figure 11–12. You can see how each color has been separated and placed from left to right in the order the colors would be printed. Crop marks have been added to the corners of each **color separation,** and registration marks (the circles with the plus signs in them) have been added to aid in aligning the colors. The design was extended slightly at the edges to **bleed** the image past the area to which it will

Figure 11–13.
The three separations needed for printing the silk-screened poster in Figure 11–12 are shown here. The separation on the left would be one color; a second color (middle) would print next; and the darkest color (right) would print last because it overprints the first color. The crop marks and registration marks help the printer with proper alignment and trim. A full-color version of this printed poster may be found in the color section.

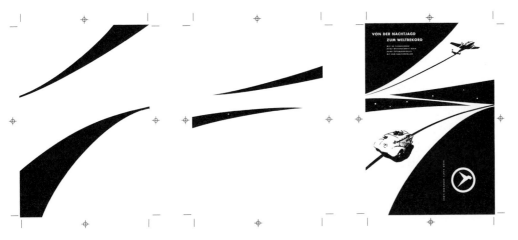

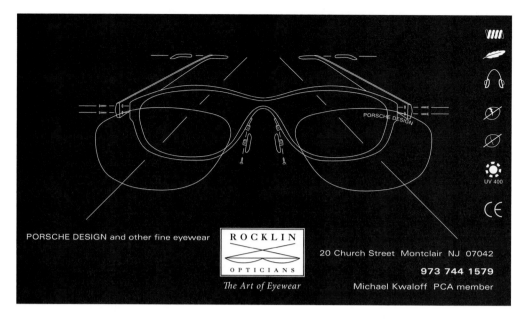

be trimmed. The poster will be printed on sheets of paper slightly larger than the area of the crop and registration marks, then trimmed to size after all the colors have been printed. Because printing and cutting equipment does not always align paper exactly, bleeding the image allows slight variation in the trimming process. Also notice that each color has been converted to solid black. This is necessary to make the screens that will be used to print the poster. For additional reference on the screen-printing process, refer to Chapter 1.

For screen printing, setting up each color as a separate layer in a drawing program gives you flexibility for changes and edits. You can even change the color of an entire layer and all its elements with little effort. And the ability to scale the design to a variety of sizes without loss of resolution is a great benefit.

Designing Display Advertising

Newspaper and other **display advertising** makes up a large part of the work of many design studios. Such ads are quick to produce; and because many businesses need to run them weekly or monthly with only slight changes, display ad work is often steady repeat business.

Although display ads vary from business to business, some of the most common elements and options are presented here.

Basic Elements

Most display ads contain information about a business, such as a logo, address, telephone number, and business hours. One or more featured items may also appear in the ad, such as goods on sale or new items in stock.

Figure 11–14 shows a magazine ad for an eyeglass store. This particular ad was created for placement in a magazine devoted to car collectors. The concept of the ad was to show an exploded view of a pair of driving sunglasses—a technique often used to show the construction of high-end automobiles.

Callouts, Artwork, Prices, and White Space

Ads usually contain elements such as photographs of products advertised, item prices, and callouts for item information. Balancing these elements within the given space can challenge even an experienced designer. It is important to prioritize the elements to create an efficient design, allowing enough white space to keep the ad from becoming cluttered.

Figure 11–15 shows a mock ad for a supermarket. In this instance, the designer must prioritize the different elements so that each item is readable. This ad is a design challenge because its various items are competing for the reader's attention. Notice how the typography helps separate the items and prices.

Layout Options, Column Designs

When creating an ad for a newspaper or magazine, a designer has to work strictly within that publication's standards. Before beginning work, the designer must know the specifics of column width and total ad height. Often clients will be aware of these requirements, so ask them first. Newspapers charge for space by the column inch, so be sure to design your ad to fit the client's budget.

When designing the ad, consider where it will be placed. If possible, review a previous issue of the publication to see what other ads appear in the section where your client will be advertising. This will help you make design decisions that allow your ad to stand out from other ads on the same page.

Advertising Production

Producing ads involves combining many different elements. It is important to work out design ideas through thumbnails and rough form to explore how these various elements will relate in the final ad. Because production time for ads is usually limited, a computer can greatly assist in this process. Laser prints are often acceptable for final artwork to be reproduced in newspapers due to the relatively low quality of newspaper printing. Sending a file directly to a newspaper or magazine as an EPS or PDF is also common.

For printing photographs, most newspapers use a large screen of 65 to 100 lpi for reproduction. Newsprint absorbs ink, and finer screens will clog when printed, leaving blotches and other inconsistencies in printed photos or illustrations.

Figure 11–15. Typographically complex advertisements need to use strong type hierarchy to allow a viewer to quickly scan and search the information.

Designing Effective Magazines and Newsletters

Magazines may be created for newsstand sales, for subscription sales, or for free distribution to special interest groups. Whereas **magazines** are created primarily for sale to the general public, **newsletters** are typically in-house company publications or are created to disseminate information to a specific group of people. Magazines typically have many pages; newsletters range in size from single sheets to multiple-page documents. Most newsletters must be created on a small budget and are published regularly. For both categories, a designer must create a flexible layout that can be quickly produced for each new issue. Many designers create the initial structure, or format, for the publication and then have other designers change the information for each new issue. For newsletters, fresh information is sometimes edited and placed by nondesigners to save money. Because of this, it is important to use proper file production techniques when designing a format for either a magazine or a newsletter so that others can make changes without compromising the design concept.

Elements of a Magazine or Newsletter

Elements of these publications may vary according to specific content and audience; but the same basic design elements, structures, and processes are used in most magazines and newsletters. The following sections review some of the most important elements.

GRID STRUCTURES

The starting point in designing a magazine or newsletter is the development of a **grid structure** to be used for each issue. With this grid you will set up the number of columns, space between columns, and margins. Any repeating elements, such as page numbers, volume numbers, and dates, are also positioned at this time.

To create a grid, a designer must know how much copy will be set. Although exact word counts will vary with each issue, basic information such as number of articles and approximate word and image counts will help the designer determine how many pages will be needed. At the same time, a tentative printing budget should be developed. Find out how many copies will be printed, and get estimates to see how many pages and what kind of printing the client can afford.

When you know what you will be able to produce, based on the budget, and after your design concepts have been approved—from research through preliminary comps—you can start production by creating a new document in a page layout program at the proper paper size for the publication, and you can set the grid design.

The first step in creating a grid is determining the page margins. Margins are the spaces left blank on the top, bottom, left, and right sides of each page. If you are creating a multiple-page design, the margins usually mirror themselves across a two-page spread. Elements such as page numbers, issue dates, and volume numbers may be placed in the margins. These elements will also most often mirror their positions across a spread, as shown in Figure 11–16.

Columns, as part of the grid structure, help the designer place articles. The most important decision in creating columns is the amount of space between columns, referred to as the *gutter*. Too little space does not provide enough visual break for the reader. If a narrow space must be used, a break can be created by a vertical rule

Figure 11–16.
In a publication grid, guidelines and repeating elements often mirror their positions across a spread.

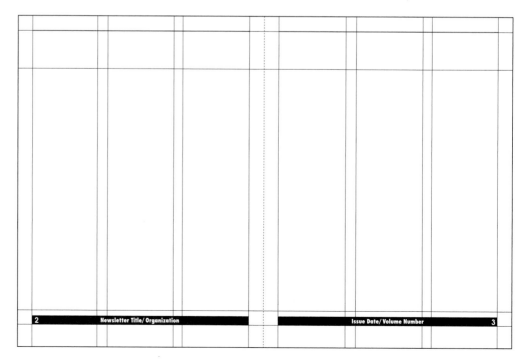

2   Newsletter Title/ Organization   Issue Date/ Volume Number   3

When two columns of text are laid out with very little space between them, a vertical line, or *rule,* may be used to help separate one from the next. The rule gives the viewer's eye a stopping point for the end of each line in the first column. Without a rule placed between close-set columns, it would be difficult for the reader to see where the first one stopped. The reader might visually connect the lines of text from the first column to those in the second. The result would be difficult readability. Rules should be used as subtle elements and should never overpower the text. The rules should only work to separate the columns from each other.

Figure 11–17.
A vertical rule may be used to separate columns with a narrow gutter.

When you are designing two columns of type with a gutter between them, it is important to allow a proper amount of space for the gutter, but too much space can also be a problem. While too little space can cause the lines of text from one column to connect to those in the next, as shown in the previous illustration, too much space breaks the columns into what appear to be two distinct blocks of text that do not necessarily look like parts of the same story. The columns may appear unrelated, and the reader may not immediately read from one to the next, especially if there are additional text or graphic elements on the page.

Figure 11–18.
Too much space between columns can destroy the connection between them.

(Figure 11–17). Too much space creates visual separation between columns, resulting in copy that appears to be disconnected and not part of the same story (Figure 11–18).

A well-designed grid provides flexibility for many successive layouts. For example, although you may use a two-column format for most text, creating a four-column grid builds in additional options for the grid's use. This allows flexible illustration placement. Figure 11–19 shows several layouts created from the same four-column grid.

Figure 11–19.
The same four-column grid was used to design each of these three layouts. Well-designed grids allow creative flexibility while keeping the publication design cohesive.

(A)

NAMEPLATE

The **nameplate** (sometimes referred to as the *flag*) is the name of a publication. It is positioned on the first page (or the cover) of the magazine or newsletter. It may be designed by you or provided by the client. The nameplate creates a personality for the publication; and although its position on the page may vary (Figure 11–20A and Figure 11–20B), it is the element with the highest priority in the visual hierarchy of the page. The nameplate may be just a name, but it usually also includes a line of explanation, such as "the newsletter of the [name of organization]." The nameplate tells readers what the newsletter is about.

Designing a nameplate is similar to designing a typographic logo. It should have its own unique character and communicate the personality of the publication.

TEXT, HEADINGS, AND SUBHEADINGS

After the grid design has been completed, consider the type that will fill it. You should

Figure 11–20.
(continued)

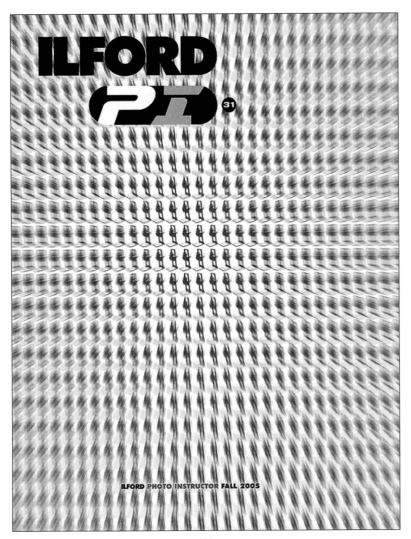

(B)

choose the text type so that varying amounts of copy (another term for the text that makes up the issue's articles) from issue to issue will fit into your design and still be easy to read. After receiving the first issue's copy, try setting it in several different typefaces to see not only how it looks but also how much room the copy set in each typeface requires. When the same copy has been set in various typefaces, you will be surprised to see that some typefaces, because of their x-height and character width, take up much more space than others.

Once the text typeface has been chosen, you can select typefaces for **headings** and **subheadings.** This type is normally bolder than the text in order to stand out from it. Often designers use a bolder version of the text typeface for headings, but sometimes a different typeface is chosen to contrast with the text. Figure 11–21 illustrates examples of both approaches applied to subheadings.

Figure 11–21.
Two approaches to subheadings.

Subhead
In this example, the subhead is set in a heavier weight of the body text. By using a typeface from the same type family, you can be assured that your subheads and text choices will work well together.

Subhead
For this example, a typeface that contrasts with the text has been used for the subhead. Using a serif body text and a sans serif typeface in a bold weight for the subhead makes the subheads clearly stand out.

SIDEBAR A

Here, two columns of text with different purposes (meant to be read not together, but one as a supplement to the other) are separated by size and weight. The text on the right, referred to as a sidebar, needs to be distinct from the body text. This is one way to accomplish this.

The typeface used for this sidebar is a bolder weight of the body text typeface. It is set in the same point size and with the same leading as the body.

Figure 11–22.

Type weight works to separate the text from the sidebar in this example.

SIDEBAR B

Another two columns of text (body text and a sidebar) are separated by the use of different point size and leading. The typeface in this example is the same for both paragraphs, but the formatting makes the sidebar stand out as being different than the text.

The typeface used for this sidebar is a same weight as the body text typeface. It is set in a different point size and uses different leading than the body.

Figure 11–23.

Point size and leading can separate text from a sidebar.

Figure 11–24.

Artwork aligned strictly to the page grid.

For headings, experiment with the size of the characters as well as the typeface itself. Depending on the length of the headings, it may be necessary to use a condensed typeface so that the headings will fit in the space available.

BOXES, SHADING, TINTS, AND CONTRASTING ELEMENTS

Articles such as charts and sidebars must be separated from the main text. There are various methods for doing this. An outlined or tinted box will help separate specific text, even if it is set in the same typeface as the body copy. When a second color is used, tints of that color can further separate the box.

Another way to separate text elements is by using a contrasting typeface or setting. In the example in Figure 11–22, body text has been separated from a sidebar by use of a different type weight. In Figure 11–23, the same text elements are separated by use of different point sizes and leading amounts.

ARTWORK

Artwork (photographs or illustrations) can be placed on a page in several ways. To maintain a strict grid, artwork can align directly to the grid (Figure 11–24). For a more informal look, text can flow around an image (Figure 11–25). Many times a designer will combine both techniques in the same piece.

Images may also be screened into the background with text flowing over them (Figure 11–26). If you do this, be careful not to make the image too dark or it will be difficult to read the text on top of it. Also, remember that the image will function more as an effect than as an illustration. If the image needs to be shown in detail, it may be possible to place the full image

Figure 11–25.
Text can flow around an image using the text wrap feature in a page layout program.

Figure 11–26.
Use of a background image as part of a table of contents page in a magazine.

on the page and use a portion of it as a background screen (Figure 11–27).

It is important to include a **credit line** for the photographer or illustrator of each image you use. There are several ways to do this. Among the most common is placing the name in small type along the side of an image, along the bottom of the page, or in the *page gutter* (the meeting point of two pages in a spread). Credits can also be listed on a back page of a newsletter with references to the pages on which the art appears. If the same person creates all the illustrations or photographs for an article, his or her name is often listed on the first page of the article, together with the author's name.

WHITE SPACE

In any page layout, it is crucial to balance the text with white space. This allows the reader a visual break and can help balance a composition. Figure 11–28 shows two page

Figure 11–27.
A repeated image used as a background screen.

Figure 11–28.

White space is an important element in page layout. The left page has little white space, making the text feel cramped on the page and leaving little rest for the reader. The right page has a good balance of type, image, and white space.

Fall 1914

Designs *Het jaar der dichters*. It is set in De Roos' Hollandsche Mediaeval; the title page is influenced by his German contemporaries W. Tiemann and H. Wieynck.

1915

Begins bookbinding, first at a binder's in The Hague, but soon after as an independent binder. He studies Douglas Cockerell's *Bookbinding and the Care of Books*. Nini Brunt writes about him as a bookbinder. '*Then [1916] he bound art books following the directives of the Englishman Cobden Sanderson. He had two clients, and sometimes he bound books for a few friends […] What made this binding work (which he did free of charge) unique was that the volumes were never really finished. Most of the time the endpapers were missing*'. The fact that the bookbinding was not a financial success can partially be attributed to World War One; in any case it is the first time (but not the last) that Van Krimpen feels his career is being thwarted by the Germans (see also 6/27/1945).

1916

Marries Nini (= Maria Paulina, 1891-1984) Brunt. Nini's sister Aty (= Agatha Christina 1888-1987) had married Jan Greshoff, making Van Krimpen his brother-in-law.

1917

A son, Huib, is born.

Van Krimpen begins the publication of a poetry series which in 1920 becomes the 'Palladium Series'. He is responsible for its uniform design. The first titles are those of his friends Albert Besnard (*Sonnettten*) and J.G. Danser (*Ontmoetingen*), both set in Hollandsche Mediaeval and printed by G.J. van Amerongen of Amersfoort.

1920

Beginning of the Palladium Series edited by Greshoff, Bloem and J. van Nijlen, published by Hilman, Stenfert Kroese & Van der Zande of Arnhem. It will eventually consist of eighteen parts, all set in Caslon typeface except one.

2/21/1920

Van Krimpen writes an article in the *Nieuwe Arnheinsche Courant* (where Greshoff was a critic and, in 1923-'24 editor-in-chief) entitled: 'S.H. de Roos, book artist and type designer'. A very positive opinion, especially regarding the Hollandsche Mediaeval.

Circa 1920

While still living in The Hague (Fahrenheitstraat 519) Van Krimpen is approached by the young publisher Alexandre ('Sander') Stols (b. 1900); they become friends. Van Krimpen and Nini see Jan Greshoff, Aty, and Sander weekly.

1922/23

First commission from the Post Office (J.F. van Royen): lettering two series of commemorative stamps designed by W.A. van Konijnenburg for the Silver Jubilee of Queen Wilhelmina.

Fall 1914

Designs *Het jaar der dichters*. It is set in De Roos' Hollandsche Mediaeval; the title page is influenced by his German contemporaries W. Tiemann and H. Wieynck.

1915

Begins bookbinding, first at a binder's in The Hague, but soon after as an independent binder. He studies Douglas Cockerell's *Bookbinding and the Care of Books*. Nini Brunt writes about him as a bookbinder. '*Then [1916] he bound art books following the directives of the Englishman Cobden Sanderson. He had two clients, and sometimes he bound books for a few friends […] What made this binding work (which he did free of charge) unique was that the volumes were never really finished. Most of the time the endpapers were missing*'.

The fact that the bookbinding was not a financial success can partially be attributed to World War One; in any case it is the first time (but not the last) that Van Krimpen feels his career is being thwarted by the Germans (see also 6/27/1945).

1916

Marries Nini (= Maria Paulina, 1891-1984) Brunt. Nini's sister Aty (= Agatha Christina 1888-1987) had married Jan Greshoff, making Van Krimpen his brother-in-law.

1917

A son, Huib, is born.

Van Krimpen begins the publication of a poetry series which in 1920 becomes the 'Palladium Series'. He is responsible for its uniform design. The first titles are those of his friends Albert Besnard (*Sonnettten*) and J.G. Danser (*Ontmoetingen*), both set in Hollandsche Mediaeval and printed by master printer G.J. van Amerongen of Amersfoort.

1920

Beginning of the Palladium Series edited by Greshoff, Bloem and J. van Nijlen, published by Hilman, Stenfert Kroese & Van der Zande of Arnhem. It will eventually consist of eighteen parts, all set in Caslon typeface except for one edition.

---

layout examples. In the left layout, very little white space was used. In the right layout, white space was used to balance the composition and make the page more inviting.

Production of a Publication

Producing magazines and newsletters has become much easier with computer and page layout programs. A page layout program makes it a simple job to create a grid, master page templates, and style sheets—and then to use these to position text and illustrations for each issue. With proper use of page layout program features, a design can also allow efficient changes to be made when needed. Extra care must be taken in proofing a publication for typographic errors: It is often the designer's responsibility to make sure the final job is correct before sending it to the printer. Either final files are

packaged for output—by creating a folder with the page layout file, text and image files, and the typefaces needed to print the file—or a PDF file is created to send to the printer.

Designing Catalogs

Designing a **catalog** is a complex task of coordinating many different parts into a cohesive whole. Because of this, important design decisions must be made during the process.

Choosing a Format

As in other design projects, the initial client meeting will help to determine many factors, including the type of catalog, what products will be featured, and the budget available for photography, illustration, and printing. Because catalogs are time-driven pieces, due dates for the finished design should be set at the initial meeting.

Combining Text and Graphics

When designing a catalog, the designer will be working with other professionals, and good communication is necessary with everyone involved in the project. The most important people in this group are the photographers and the copywriters, whose combined work will be the backbone of the design. Open communication with these professionals is essential to prevent problems in getting all the elements together on time.

The photographer is responsible, under your direction, for providing shots of all the items to be displayed in the catalog. For a large catalog, this could mean choosing from hundreds of photographs. It is important that these photos have consistent color, lighting, and style, and it is the designer's responsibility to see that these prerequisites are met.

The copywriter will work with the client on item descriptions and prices. This copy often changes during the process. When designing a catalog, you must be prepared to make copy changes right until press time.

Format Considerations

To keep the catalog design flowing smoothly, the designer should develop a flexible grid system—just as in newsletter design. Designing a grid that will adapt to the many kinds of elements employed in the catalog will save you time later in the process. Figure 11–29 shows two pages from a catalog design.

The designer needs to know whether the catalog photographs will appear in boxes or be silhouetted. Silhouetted photos require a special setup, and this should be discussed with the photographer. The photographer should be given a rough comp of the catalog before shooting begins so that each photo can be shot specifically for its placement within the catalog. In the rough, sketches will represent the item photographs. (Here is another good reason for a designer to know how to draw!)

Catalog Production

Producing a catalog involves dealing with all the various elements and personnel discussed thus far. Although text and page layout may be accomplished via a computer,

Figure 11–29.
A sample spread from a catalog design. Note the variety of typographic elements and images.

Figure 11–30.
A 300 dpi scan at 100 percent size, at left, has optimum resolution for printing. The 72 dpi FPO image, at right, has resolution that is fine for noting image placement in a layout, but the resolution is too low for proper printing and has noticeable pixels.

the reproduction quality needed for color photographs in a high-end catalog may require the use of a pre-press facility for the best-quality scans. If photographs or transparencies for final scans will be provided to a pre-press facility, the designer will scan in FPO images (for position only, as discussed in Chapter 6) that will later be replaced by the printer.

When creating a preliminary layout on a computer, you can scan a low-resolution image version at 72 dpi for display and cropping purposes. This will save disk space because the low-resolution scan will create a small file size and can be given to the printer in a laser-printed version of the document. The scans will give the printer the necessary information about cropping and silhouetting only. The photo-graphic images, provided as 4 × 5-inch transparencies by the photographer to the printer, will be scanned on the printer's high-end equipment to the specifications of the rough layout. FPO files cannot be used for final output, of course, because of their low resolution. Figure 11–30 shows the quality of a 300 dpi scan compared to a 72 dpi FPO scan. Today many studio photographers shoot digital photographs that will be provided to the designer for

cropping and placement directly in the page layout program.

Another way of showing an FPO image is to paste a photocopy of the image, scaled and cropped, into a separate printout of the mechanicals. Whether scanned or photocopied into position, this dummy copy of the document gives the printer the visual information needed to produce the job accurately.

The final typographic catalog layout may be given to the printer on disk, electronically via FTP, or as a series of printed mechanicals. Photographs and illustrations are given to the printer as the actual artwork or in photographic transparency format for scanning into the layout on high-end equipment. Today catalogs are often distributed on CD-ROMs or as Web pages rather than being printed—so this area of graphic design is changing rapidly.

Creating Packaging

Packaging is a broad, specialized area within graphic design that involves many different processes for both design and production. Packages can be made from a wide variety of materials: plastic, glass, paper, cardboard, aluminum, tin, wood, rubber, and so forth. They may be made as original designs or may be chosen from stock package shapes and sizes from packaging firms. Production processes may include blow molding, vacuum forming, injection molding, casting, stamping, scoring and folding, or a combination of these.

Package designs can also serve different purposes. Some may be primarily for the display and marketing of a product; some may protect a product during shipping; some may provide information about a product that cannot be placed on the product itself, such as instructions or warranty information.

Figure 11–31.
A product without its designed packaging may look unappealing.

Figure 11–32.
An appealing package can make a product look inviting.

All packages have one thing in common: They contain a product. What that product is will help the designer choose the form and design of its package. If the product should be seen, you can use a window in a box (for a product such as pasta); a clear blister pack (for a toy); or a clear plastic bag (for a product such as rice). If the product should not be seen, make sure the package design shows the product at its best. Few consumers would be motivated to buy a block of frozen spinach just by looking at it (Figure 11–31); but by creating a box design using an appetizing photograph of the prepared product in a bowl (Figure 11–32), a designer can create a desire for the product. The same goes for a product that needs to be assembled—a bunch of parts in a clear plastic bag would not sell many board games!

Some packages are meant to be kept by consumers after a product is purchased—a DVD case or book cover, for example—but most packaging is discarded after consumers bring their purchases home. Because of this, it is crucial that a designer consider what impact a package as waste will have on the environment. This should be thought through from the beginning of each project and discussed with the client and the package manufacturer so that negative environmental impacts (and their discouraging effects on sales to environmentally conscious consumers) can be kept to a minimum. Some ways to do this are using recyclable materials, such as paper, glass, metal, and recyclable plastics, whenever possible; designing package parts that can be reused for other purposes, such as a jelly jar that serves as a drinking glass for kids after it is empty; or simplifying packaging to use fewer resources. You probably didn't know it, but the ridges found on many plastic bottles are not there as design elements, but to add strength so that the bottle can be made with less plastic! Always take whatever steps you can to reduce the chances that your package will clutter a landfill.

A Sample Package Design Project

For this project we will discuss package design for an **aseptic brick.** You probably know these as "juice boxes," but this package type is used for many different kinds of liquids. An aseptic brick is made of laminated sheets of paper, metal, and plastic. Although it is somewhat difficult to recycle, this package has other low-impact elements

Figure 11–33.
The template for an aseptic brick package shown in its flat form.

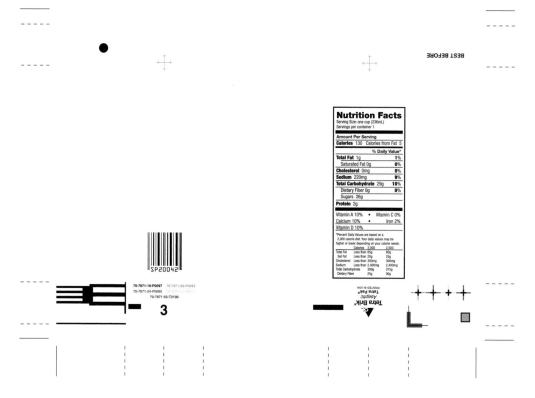

to its design. The box is made from a single rectangular shape that provides no waste when trimmed from a larger sheet; it is also small and can be packed tightly with others of the same size for efficient shipping—and when crushed, it takes up little space in the garbage. Figure 11–33 shows a template for the package. The box is folded in a way that makes it waterproof, and it needs no trimming except for the hole to insert a straw (shown by the black dot).

When you design any three-dimensional package, it is best to first make a mock-up of the package at actual size. This will help you understand how the sides of the package relate to one another, and it will allow you to get a good mental picture of the package size. (Sometimes, when designing on a computer, it is easy to forget how large or small an actual item will be,

and you may use type or image sizes that look fine onscreen but will be too small when the design is printed.) If you tape the package together with removable adhesive, you can sketch your rough design onto the shape and unfold it to better understand how it will look when flat—the way you will lay it out on the computer. Some panels will be upside down on the computer screen, and doing this will show you which ones.

Also think about how the package will be displayed in a store. The aseptic brick will most likely be packaged with two to eleven others in a larger, shrink-wrapped unit. A larger box may be sold on its own. If the box will be packed with others—for example, in packs of three—give some thought to how each box will relate to the one next to it. Will any elements connect

Figure 11–34.
In a series of packages, elements can visually connect multiple packages of the same design. A single package is shown on the left, and a package of three on the right.

Figure 11–35.
Framing each package will separate it from the ones around it when they are placed in multiples. This technique can also separate your package from its competition on the store shelf.

adjacent boxes (Figure 11–34)? Or will the design be framed in some way to separate the boxes (Figure 11–35)? There are also ways to use color or images (or both) to separate panels (Figure 11–36); or an image or color may wrap around the box (Figure 11–37). These compositional choices are yours to make—and do not exclude one another.

The printer will use the bottom of the box for registration and printing information, and the top requires certain functional elements such as the hole for the straw and the spout; so be sure to work around these areas. Discuss these elements with the package manufacturer at the beginning of the project so you know exactly where they will go and where you can put design elements. Many package manufacturers offer computer templates of the packages they produce so you can design packages to meet their production needs.

Figure 11–36.
In this example, image and color separate the panels of a package.

Figure 11–37.
Here an image wraps around the package, blurring the edges.

on each panel or on most of them. These include the name of the product and the logo of the company that produces it. Because our example is a food product, other items will also need to be included: a USDA-specified nutrition listing and a list of the ingredients used to make the product, shown in order from largest to smallest amounts. The amount of liquid also needs to be specified on the box. Finally, a **UPC** (universal product code) needs to be placed on the box so that the package can be read by supermarket price scanners. With all this required information, the design space is somewhat limited.

The client company will, of course, want its name and logo to be easily visible on all package sides. For our example, the client also has copy to place on the back or side of the box.

Ask about this when you meet with the firm that will print your package.

Package templates need to be precise in their design, and attempting to make one on your own can create problems. Allowances must be made for paper thickness so the box panels will fit properly when folded. Unless you are experienced in package design, it is best to ask questions when you meet with the package manufacturer so you fully understand the production process.

Design Elements

When designing a three-dimensional package, you need to repeat certain elements

Putting the Design Together

The design process should move from the client meeting to a meeting with the package manufacturer, through research and conceptual development, and then to mocking up your initial designs on the computer. We will step in as a concept is brought to the computer.

A drawing program is best to use for most packaging because the document size is adjustable and the program works well for both type and imagery. Most boxes are printed on only one side, so the limitation of a drawing program making only one page at a time is not a problem.

We start by opening the package template provided by the package manufacturer (Figure 11–38). This particular template

Figure 11–38.
The template for the aseptic brick, left; shown with the fold lines turned on in the center; and shown with the areas where design elements should not be placed on the right.

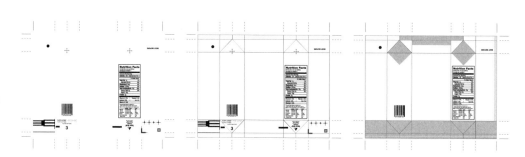

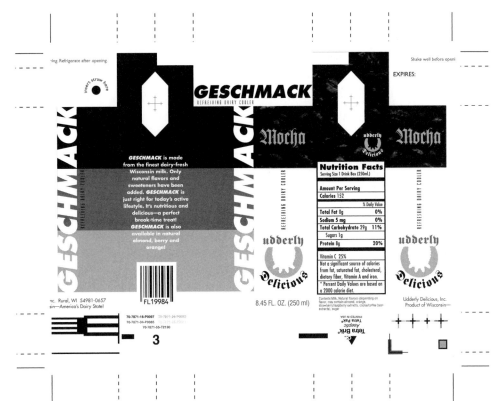

Figure 11–39.
The final comp for the package as produced in Adobe Illustrator, showing crop and fold marks. After being scored and trimmed, it is made into three-dimensional comps for presentation to the client.

Figure 11–40.
Mock-ups of the package design in client presentation form. See the color section for this illustration in full color, along with the color template for the package layout.

has separate layers for fold lines (turned on in the center image) and indications of the areas where design elements should not be placed (turned on in the right image).

The client provided the company logo as a vector-based file, so we open that and copy it to the template on a new layer. We input the typographic elements (product name and additional copy), also on their own layer. Approved imagery is brought in on its own layer. The use of layers is important—they allow faster changes. Alternative ideas can also be placed on separate layers to avoid opening and closing separate files to look at design variations.

When we are satisfied with the design (Figure 11–39), it is printed, scored, and folded into mock packages to present to the client (Figure 11–40). Mock-ups closely resemble the final packages—so much that I have had parents of students accidentally throw away their "empty" package comps (luckily it was after the critique).

Final Production

In packaging, if everything is followed through correctly during mock-up production,

little additional computer production is necessary. All type should be given a final proofreading; typefaces should be converted to outlines; images should be checked for proper mode (CMYK for full-color packages); images should be embedded in the file (rather than linked to it); unnecessary elements and layers should be removed (including anything left in the pasteboard area); and the final version should be saved as a separate document in the file type specified by the package manufacturer. Be sure to keep the file in which the typefaces have not been converted to outlines so you can use it for later editing.

SUMMARY

In this chapter we discussed many challenges of specific design jobs. With a solid understanding of the graphic design problem-solving model and its application, you should be able to handle the production challenges you will face as a graphic designer. Because computer programs, production systems, and production processes are constantly evolving, there will always be more to learn!

Review Questions

1 What are some functions of a logo?

2 What are some design considerations for working on a poster?

3 How does a grid help a designer lay out a magazine or newsletter?

4 List some primary elements found in a display ad.

5 Discuss the various types of packaging.

6 What do all package design projects have in common? With that in mind, what is the designer's goal in creating a good package design?

Suggested Student Activities

1 Design a logo for a company you would like to own. Show how this logo would be applied to your company's products.

2 Create an event for your fellow students, and design a poster for it. Use only the poster to advertise the event, and see how well it works to attract an audience.

3 Create three variations of a display ad for a newspaper or magazine. Use the same concept and text to make a single-column black-and-white ad, a quarter-page two-color ad, and a full-page, full-color ad. Evaluate how well the ads work together as a set.

4 Develop and design a small 5.5 × 8.5-inch magazine promoting issues that are important to you as students. Work as a group of five to ten students to compile the articles and images, select the grid and typefaces, and then divide the layouts among the group. Print color copies for distribution.

5 Create a catalog of yourself and your favorite things. Take photos or make illustrations of your possessions, and design a catalog format that reflects your personal style. Prices can be based on what you paid for the items or on what you feel they are worth.

6 Design a package for a product that does not have a common physical form (such as an emotion, one of the seven deadly sins, one of the four elements, or the universe). Experiment with what form the product would take and how the package would hold it and be designed to express its nature.

**Data and Video File Formats:
Appendix I**

AFP Advanced Function Printing (AFP) is a format for describing complex documents stored on IBM mainframe and midrange servers. The AFP format is converted to a printing language by a computer's operating system.

AVI The Audio Video Interleave (AVI) is defined by the Microsoft Corporation and is the most common format for audio/video data on the PC platform.

Cinepak Cinepak is a video compression toolkit designed to work on both the Macintosh and PC platforms. Cinepak delivers high-quality compressed digital movies for the Web, CD-ROMs, DVD-ROMs, Kiosk, intranet, and gaming environments.

EPS Encapsulated PostScript (EPS) is a page description language created by Adobe Systems for importing and exporting PostScript files. An encapsulated PostScript file is a PostScript language program that describes the appearance of a single page. The purpose of the EPS file is to be included, or "encapsulated," in another PostScript language page description. The file can contain any combination of text, graphics, and images, and it is the same as any other PostScript language page description. EPS files are based on vectors, which are descriptions of points, lines, and regions of an image, rather than on bitmaps, which are collections of pixels in an image.

GIF The Graphics Interchange Format (GIF) is used to prepare bitmapped graphic images for use on the World Wide Web (WWW). The GIF format is used by several WWW service providers such as CompuServe. GIF images can be either black and white or color. Color images are limited to 256 colors.

HPGL HPGL is Hewlett-Packard's Graphic Language format used in all HP and HP-compatible graphics printers and plotters.

Indeo Indeo is the original software for video and audio compression coding and decoding (codecs) originally developed by Intel for producing high-quality audio and video playback on the computer.

JPEG/JPEG 2000 JPEG, or JPG, stands for the Joint Photographic Experts Group, the organization within the International Standards Organization (ISO) that developed the JPEG format. JPEG is a compression scheme for reducing the file sizes of graphic images while maintaining image quality. The original JPEG format was revised by the organization committee in 2000 to better serve image compression markets ranging from digital cameras to medical imaging and advanced prepress application software. JPEG is referred to as a "lossy" compression format because each time an image is compressed it loses some image quality. This occurs when repeating elements in successive video frames are eliminated to minimize file size within the JPEG compression code. When we save files as JPEGs, different compression levels are available, ranging from low to high. High compression results in smaller files with some loss of image quality, whereas low compression results in higher-resolution, larger files. When using JPEG compression, the designer must strike a balance between acceptable quality versus the appropriate file size for the application.

MIDI The Musical Instrument Digital Interface (MIDI) is a technology that represents music in digital form; it was developed specifically for electronic keyboards and other instruments that are MIDI-equipped. MIDI lets composers change individual notes in a composition, allowing the orchestration of single notes or entire songs using several different instruments at once. Individual instruments can be turned on or off, separating them from the orchestra for studying solo performances and the like. Many personal computers have built-in MIDI capabilities in their sounds cards, or add-on cards can easily be installed to add MIDI capability.

MPEG   The Motion Pictures Experts Group (MPEG) is an organization under the ISO umbrella that generates standards for digital video compression. MPEG video files have the extension .mpg after their file names. MPEG audio files have the extension .mp2 or .mp3 after their file names. The MP3 format has become the de facto audio compression standard, enabling MP3 players such as the iPod to gain wide consumer acceptance. The MP3 standard has almost completely replaced the earlier MP2 standard because MP3 files are about 30 percent smaller than their MP2 counterparts. Several MPEG standards are now in use, with constant updates and additions to the MPEG file system as new technology dictates.

NTSC standard   NTSC is an acronym for the National Television Systems Committee and is based on the delivery of 30-frame-per-second television video. The NTSC standard is used in the United States, Japan, Canada, Mexico, Taiwan, and other countries.

PAL standard   The Phase Alteration Line (PAL) standard is based on the 25-frame-per-second video used in the television industry in most of Europe and South America.

PCL   PCL, or printer control language, was developed by Hewlett-Packard for use on its brand of printers as an alternative to PostScript-based printers. PCL is a simpler page description language than PostScript and is also an open language format, ensuring its widespread use in the business printing environment.

PDF   The Portable Document Format (PDF) was created by Adobe Systems in the early 1990s as a way of representing documents and images that is independent of the software program, computer platform, or operating system that created them. PDF files use PostScript as a description language, can contain any combination of text, graphics, and images, and can be from one page to thousands of pages long. PDF has become a de facto standard in the industry for sending production files to printers and service bureaus. PDF files are viewed using Adobe Acrobat Reader, which creates the exact look of the finished document independent of devices. Adobe's Acrobat Distiller generates PDF files from text and graphics programs.

PNG   The Portable Network Graphics (PNG) format was formulated to replace the older GIF format specifically for Web use. Released in 1996, PNG is referred to as a "lossless" compression format in that it can compress image files without losing quality.

QuickTime   Apple Computer released the original version of QuickTime (QT) in 1991 as an add-on for the System-7 operating system (OS). QT is the basic system architecture for compressing and displaying motion video on computers, including features for displaying multiple movie tracks and several editing functions. QuickTime version 7, released in late 2005, is MPEG-4 compliant and runs on Apple OS 10.x as well as Windows 2000 and XP. Apple offers free QuickTime media players for the Mac OS and Windows. QuickTime Pro, a feature-rich version of the basic media player that includes editing, compression options, and media creation add-ons, is available at an additional cost.

RIFF   The Resource Interchange File Format was developed by Microsoft and is used by many applications like Windows and Corel Draw.

SECAM   SECAM is the television standard used in France.

TIFF   TIFF stands for Tagged Image File Format and was originally developed by Aldus and Microsoft in 1987, then updated in 1992. The Aldus Corporation was bought by Adobe, which now owns the TIFF copyright. TIFF is a cross-platform specification that can operate equally well in the PC, Mac, and Unix environments and is especially well suited for numerous image processing and pre-press software applications. TIFF was originally designed to become the industry standard for image file exchange and has largely lived up to that expectation. TIFF describes bitmapped data and does not contain text or vector (line) data. The name TIFF implies the use of tags, or keywords, that define the characteristics of the image described by a file. For example, an illustration measuring 640×480 pixels would include a width tag followed by the number 640 and a height tag followed by the number 480.

TWAIN protocol   TWAIN is a software interface standard released in 1992 and used to link image processing software to scanners and digital cameras. The name comes from the literary expression "never the twain shall meet," describing the difficulty experienced in the early 1990s when scanners were first connected to personal computers. Placing the term in capital letters made it sound more professional and technical than the literary designation, although the acronym has unofficially been said to stand for Technology Without An Interesting Name. The TWAIN standard was developed by the Twain Working Group, a not-for-profit association that continues to upgrade the TWAIN standard as new technologies emerge.

Video for Windows   Video for Windows (VFW), the Microsoft version of QuickTime, is a program for storing audio and video files on a Windows PC. VFW files have .avi extensions. VFW files are limited to 30 frames per second at a resolution of 320×240 pixels—far less than what is required for full-screen, full-motion video display. Because VFW files require no special hardware, multimedia applications often generate video files in this format so they can be played successfully on the large installed base of lower-end computers.

VIPP   Variable Data Intelligent PostScript Printware (VIPP) is a data merge application used in variable-data printing, Developed by the Xerox Corporation, the VIPP format was introduced to enable high-speed data merge printing on Xerox VIPP-enabled printers.

WAV   WAV files are the default format for digital audio files running on Windows PCs. Although created by Microsoft for use on the PC platform, WAV files can be used on Macintosh computers as well as those running Linux.

**Suggested Reading:
Appendix II**

PERIODICALS

CMYK Magazine

CMYK features student graphic design, advertising, illustration, and photography. The magazine is an ongoing competition that students from all over the world may enter. (http://www.cmykmag.com)

Communication Arts

Communication Arts is a print publication featuring graphic design, advertising, illustration, and commercial photography from top firms around the world. Its Web site includes competitions, forums, feature articles, a job bank, graphic design resources, and online shopping. (http://www.commarts.com)

Eye, The International Review of Graphic Design

Eye is a British magazine that features current and historical articles about graphic design and typography; this is one of the best-written magazines about graphic design. Its Web site features additional articles and archives. (http://www.eyemagazine.com)

How

How features in-depth articles about graphic designers, design studios, and professional practices. This how-to publication is a good reference for students who want to learn more about the field of graphic design. (http://www.howdesign.com)

I.D. (International Design)

I.D. covers all forms of design—from graphics to architecture to product design. Its annual design review is always worth reading. Its Web site has information about competitions and a job board but is primarily designed to solicit subscriptions. (http://www.idonline.com)

Lürzer's Archive

Lürzer's Archive is an Austrian magazine (in English) covering advertising from around the world but focusing on Europe and Asia. The magazine has large, high-quality photographs of ads and little text except for an interview with an advertising designer or company in each issue. The magazine also sells DVDs of contemporary award-winning television ads, but these are expensive. (http://www.luerzersarchive.us)

Print

America's longest-running graphic design publication, *Print* magazine covers contemporary and historical graphic design and has well-written articles from top authors in the field. Its Regional Design Annual highlights the best of the year's designs from studios across the United States. Each year it holds a student competition to design one of the magazine's covers. Its Web site features competitions, jobs, forums, and news. (http://www.printmag.com)

STEP Inside Design

A cross between *Print*, *I.D.*, and *How* magazines, *STEP* attempts to cover it all. Its extensive Web site includes a wide variety of topics, from professional practices to education, and offers some articles from the magazine along with special Web articles. (http://www.stepinsidedesign.com)

Studio Monthly

Studio Monthly focuses on the current state of digital media, along with predictions of new software and hardware technologies in the pipeline. The magazine is published by Access Intelligence Corporation. (http://www.studiomonthly.com)

Quick Printing

Management and profitability of the quick and small commercial printing industries are the heart of this periodical, which is published by Cygnus Business Media, Inc. (http://www.quickprinting.com)

techdirections

techdirections links technical education to careers in technical and associated areas. It is published by Prakken Publications. (http://www.techdirections.com)

Wide-Format Imaging

This magazine is devoted to the industry of wide-format and grand-format imaging devices and technologies. It is published by Cygnus Business Media, Inc. (http://www.wide-formatimaging.com)

BOOKS

Adams, J. Michael, and Penny Dolin. *Printing Technology.* Thomson Delmar Learning.

Adobe Creative Team, Andrew Faulkner. *The Official Adobe Print Publishing Guide.* Adobe Press.

AIGA. *Graphic Design: A Career Guide and Educational Directory.* AIGA Press.

Baines, Phil, and Andrew Haslam. *Type & Typography,* 2nd edition. Watson-Guptill.

Berger, John. *Ways of Seeing.* Penguin Books.

Bierut, Michael, William Drenttel, Steven Heller, and DK Holland, ed. *Looking Closer: Critical Writings on Graphic Design.* Allworth Press.

Bierut, Michael, William Drenttel, Steven Heller, and DK Holland, ed. *Looking Closer 2: Critical Writings on Graphic Design.* Allworth Press.

Bierut, Michael, Jessica Helfand, Steven Heller, and Rick Poyner, ed. *Looking Closer 3: Classical Writings on Graphic Design.* Allworth Press.

Blackwell, Lewis. *20th Century Type.* Rizzoli.

Bringhurst, Robert. *The Elements of Typographic Style,* 3rd edition. Hartley and Marks Publishers.

Bruno, Michael H. *Pocket Pal: The Handy Little Book of Graphic Arts Production.* International Paper.

Carter, Rob, Philip B. Meggs, and Ben Day. *Typographic Design: Form and Communication,* 3rd edition. John Wiley & Sons.

Clark, Paul, and Julian Freeman. *Design: A Crash Course.* Watson-Guptill.

Dolin, Penny Anne. *Exploring Digital Workflow.* Thomson Delmar Learning.

Dondis, Donis A. *A Primer of Visual Literacy.* MIT Press.

Drew, John T., and Sarah A. Meyer. *Color Management: A Comprehensive Guide for Graphic Designers.* RotoVision Sa.

Ewen, Stuart. *All Consuming Images,* revised edition. Basic Books.

Ewen, Stuart and Elizabeth. *Channels of Desire: Mass Images and the Shaping of American Consciousness.* University of Minnesota Press.

Fletcher, Alan. *The Art of Looking Sideways.* Phaidon Press.

Foote, Cameron. *The Business Side of Creativity: The Complete Guide for Running a Graphic Design or Communications Business.* W. W. Norton.

Friedman, Mildred. *Graphic Design in America: A Visual Language.* Harry N. Abrams.

Gottschall, Edward M. *Typographic Communications Today.* MIT Press.

Graphic Artists Guild. *Handbook of Pricing & Ethical Guidelines.* Graphic Artists Guild.

Hanks, Corrine. *Draw! A Visual Approach to Thinking, Learning, and Communicating.* Crisp Learning.

Heller, Steven, ed. *The Education of a Graphic Designer.* Allworth Press.

Heller, Steven, and Teresa Fernandez. *Becoming a Graphic Designer: A Guide to Careers in Design.* John Wiley & Sons.

Heller, Steven, and Karen Pomeroy. *Design Literacy: Understanding Graphic Design.* Allworth Press.

Hird, Kenneth F. *Offset Lithographic Technology.* Goodheart-Wilcox.

Hollis, Richard. *Graphic Design: A Concise History.* Thames & Hudson, Ltd.

Johnson, Harald. *Digital Printing Start-Up Guide.* Thomson Delmar Learning.

Johnson, Michael. *Problem Solved: A Primer in Design and Communication.* Phaidon Press.

Landa, Robin. *Graphic Design Solutions,* 3rd edition. Thomson Delmar Learning.

Landa, Robin. *Thinking Creatively: New Ways to Unlock Your Visual Imagination.* How Design Books.

Lin, Mike W. *Drawing and Designing with Confidence: A Step-by-Step Guide.* John Wiley & Sons.

Lupton, Ellen. *Thinking with Type: A Critical Guide for Designers, Writers, Editors, & Students.* Princeton Architectural Press.

Lupton, Ellen, and J. Abbott Miller. *Design Writing Research.* Kiosk.

Lyons, Daniel J. *Graphic Communications Dictionary.* Prentice Hall.

McCreight, Tim. *Design Language.* Brynmorgen Press.

Meggs, Philip B., and Alston Purvis. *Megg's History of Graphic Design,* 4th edition. John Wiley & Sons.

Oldach, Mark. *Creativity for Graphic Designers.* North Light Books.

Rand, Paul. *A Designer's Art.* Yale University Press.

Roberts, Lucienne. *Good: An Introduction to Ethics in Graphic Design.* AVA Academia/Theory.

Rogondino, Michael and Pat. *Process Color Manual: 24,000 CMYK Combinations for Design, Prepress, and Printing.* Chronicle Books.

Romano, Frank J. *Pocket Guide to Digital Prepress.* Delmar Publishers.

Roth, Laszlo, and George L. Wybenga. *The Packaging Designer's Book of Patterns.* John Wiley & Sons.

Ryan, William E., and Theodore E. Connover. *Graphic Communications Today,* 4th edition. Thomson Delmar Learning.

Samara, Timothy. *Typography Workbook: A Real-World Guide to Using Type in Graphic Design,* new edition. Rockport Publishers.

Shaughnessy, Adrian. *How to Be a Graphic Designer without Losing Your Soul.* Princeton Architectural Press.

Spencer, Herbert. *Pioneers of Modern Typography,* revised edition. MIT Press.

Spiekermann, Erik, and E. M. Ginger. *Stop Stealing Sheep and Find Out How Type Works.* Adobe Press/Prentice Hall Computer Publishing.

Tambini, Michael. *The Look of the Century: Design Icons of the 20th Century.* DK Publishing.

Torreano, John. *Drawing by Seeing.* Harry N. Abrams.

Wheeler, Susan G. and Gary S. *TypeSense: Making Sense of Type on the Computer,* 2nd edition. Prentice Hall.

**Relevant Web Sites:
Appendix III**

DESIGN JOURNALS AND BLOGS

Advertising from Around the World	http://adsoftheworld.com/
Book Cover Design	http://covers.fwis.com
Computer Love	http://www.cpluv.com
Creativity Online	http://creativity-online.com/
Designboom	http//www.designboom.com/eng
Design Directory	http://www.dexigner.com/directory
The Design Encyclopedia	http://www.thedesignencyclopedia.org
Design Observer	http://www.designobserver.com
Identity Works (logo design)	http://www.identityworks.com
Kaliber 10000	http://www.k10k.net
Logo Design History	http://www.logoorange.com/logodesign-A.php
Logo Lounge (logo design)	http://www.logolounge.com
News Today	http://www.newstoday.com
Package Design	http://dieline.typepad.com/
Pixelcreation Magazine (in French)	http://www.pixelcreation.fr/
Speak Up	http://www.underconsideration.com/speakup
Tokyo Art Beat	http://www.tokyoartbeat.com
Typophile	http://typophile.com/

DESIGN COLLECTIONS

Cooper Hewitt/National Design Museum	http://www.cooperhewitt.org
Cooper Union Herb Lubalin Study Center	http://www.cooper.edu/art/lubalin
Design Archive online at RIT	http://design.rit.edu/
Museum of Modern Art	http://www.moma.org

DESIGN TOOLS

Apple Computer	http://www.apple.com
Adobe Creative Suite	http://www.adobe.com
Canon (copiers and printers)	http://www.usa.canon.com
Epson (scanners and printers)	http://www.epson.com
Fontlab (for type design)	http://www.fontlab.com
Hewlett-Packard (printers)	http://www.hp.com
QuarkXPress	http://www.quark.com
Wacom (drawing tablets)	http://www.wacom.com

STOCK PHOTOGRAPHY AND ILLUSTRATION SOURCES

Comstock	http://www.comstock.com
Corbis Images	http://www.corbisimages.com
CSA Images	http://www.csaimages.com
Getty Images	http://www.gettyimages.com
The Ispot	http://www.theispot.com
Images.com	http://www.images.com
Jupiter Images	http://www.jupiterimages.com

Laughing Stock Illustration	http://www.laughing-stock.com
Magnum Photos	http://www.magnumphotos.com
Photo Japan	http://www.photojapan.com
Phototake (medical and scientific photos)	http://www.phototakeusa.com
Veer	http://www.veer.com

TYPE SUPPLIERS

Adobe Type	http://www.adobe.com/type
Creamundo	http://www.creamundo.com
Font Bureau	http://www.fontbureau.com
Font Factory	http://www.fontfactory.com
Font Shop	http://www.fontshop.com
Hamilton Woodtype Museum	http://www.woodtype.org
Hoeffler & Frere-Jones	http://www.typography.com
House Industries	http://www.houseind.com
International Typeface Corporation	http://www.itcfonts.com
Identifont (typeface identifier)	http://www.identifont.com
Linotype	http://www.linotype.com
Monotype	http://www.fonts.com
MyFonts	http://www.myfonts.com
Porchez Typefonderie	http://www.typofonderie.com
Typotheque	http://www.typotheque.com
You Work for Them	http://www.youworkforthem.com
Veer	http://www.veer.com

JOB SITES

AIGA	http://www.aigadesignjobs.org
Aquent	http://www.aquent.com
Cheryl Roshak	http://www.croshak.com
Coroflot	http://www.coroflot.com
The Creative Group	http://www.creativegroup.com
Creative Hot List	http://www.creativehotlist.com
Flipdog	http://www.flipdog.com
Hot Jobs	http://hotjobs.yahoo.com
Janou Pakter	http://www.pakter.com
Roz Goldfarb	http://www.rgarecruiting.com

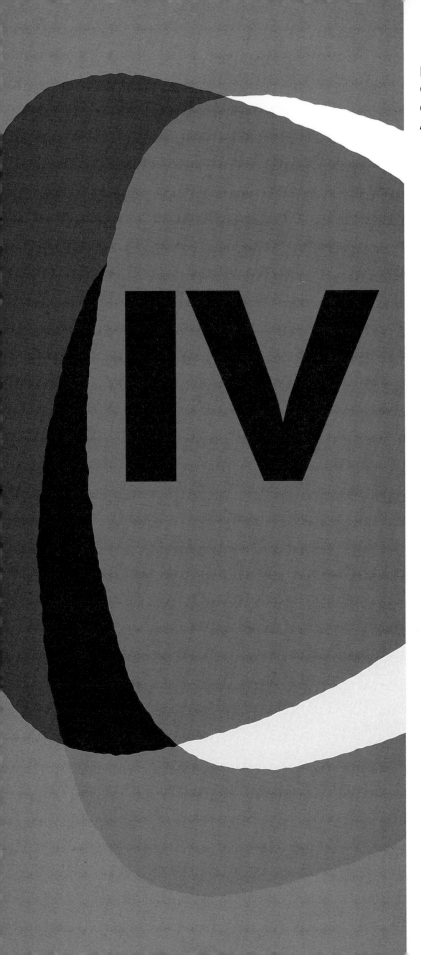

**Professional Design
Organizations
and Associations:
Appendix IV**

AIGA: The Professional Organization for Design
164 5th Avenue
New York, NY 10010
212.807.1990
http://www.aiga.org

Art Directors Club of New York
250 Park Avenue South
New York, NY 10001
212.643.1440
http://www.adcglobal.org

Graphic Artists Guild
11 West 20th Street
New York, NY 10011
212.791.3400
http://www.gag.org

Graphic Artists Information Network
200 Deer Run Road
Sewickley, PA 15143-2600
800.910.4283
http://www.gain.net

Society for Environmental Graphic Design
401 F Street NW, Suite 333
Washington, DC 20001
202.638.5555
http://www.segd.org

Society of Children's Book Writers and Illustrators
8271 Beverly Boulevard
Los Angeles, CA 90048
323.782.1010
http://www.scbwi.org

Society of Illustrators
128 E. 63rd Street
New York, NY 10021-7303
212.838.2560
http://www.societyillustrators.org

Society of Publication Designers
17 East 47th Street, 6th Floor
New York, NY 10017
212.223.3332
http://www.spd.org

Type Directors Club
127 West 25th Street, 8th Floor
New York, NY 10001
212.633.8943
http://www.tdc.org

Glossary of Terms

8 bits   Eight bits of computer information are equivalent to one byte. One thousand bytes equal one kilobyte (KB).

21-step gray scale   A small wedge of photographic paper in which all of the tonal areas, from white to black and intermediate shades of gray, are represented in a series of 21 distinct wedges.

42-line Bible   Named from the number of lines of text on each page, the 42-line Bible was published around 1455 by Johann Gutenberg.

A

abstract logo   A logo that has no representational picture elements, but relies purely on principles of shape and form.

Acrobat   Software developed by Adobe Systems, Inc., for creating editing portable document format (PDF) files.

Adams press   The first steam-powered printing press developed in America by Isaac and Seth Adams in 1830.

additive plates   Plates are classified as additive when, during processing, a lacquer-based material is applied, or added, to the plates over the image areas, fixing the images and giving them long-run characteristics.

Adobe Systems, Inc.   The software publisher of Adobe CS, which contains Illustrator, Photoshop, InDesign, and related tools.

Aldus Manutius   A famous Italian printer, noted for developing the italic typeface.

algorithm   A mathematical formula or plan used as a framework to build a computer software application program. Software interpolation programs used by scanner manufacturers to increase scanner resolution are all based on mathematical algorithms, which enable the software to "fill in the blanks" and increase the resolution of a scanned document.

Alois Senefelder   Perfected the technique of direct lithography; his process was patented around 1818.

Altair 8800   The first personal computer to gain public acceptance, in the mid-1970s based on an Intel Z-80 microprocessor and offered to computer and electronic hobbyists in a do-it-yourself kit.

alteration fees   Fees charged to a client by a designer or design studio for design changes that were not included in the original contract for the job.

analog   A term used to describe the natural world—shades of gray rather than black and white and subtle variations of virtually all phenomena. Analog data are the opposite of digital data.

anchor points   An element of creating shapes within a computer design application. Anchor points connect one line to another to create a shape. In the Bezier process, anchor points work with control points to create a curved line.

Antoni Gaudi   A famous Art Nouveau Spanish architect.

applied styles   Styles of type—bold, italic, outline, underline, and drop shadow—that are not part of the typeface design, but are applied by computer software. These should be avoided in creating professional design work.

Art Deco   Beginning around 1925, Art Deco designs and artwork were characterized by the use of materials such as aluminum, stainless steel, wood and metal inlays, and highly lacquered finishes. Designs featured the use of a zigzag, stepped form and sweeping curves with a strong geometric basis.

Art Nouveau A style of decoration and architecture, characterized by intricate patterns of curved lines based on forms found in nature.

Arts and Crafts movement A British reformist movement around the turn of the twentieth century offering an idealized view of the craftsman, including furniture, interior, and graphic design, led by William Morris.

artwork Term for photographs or illustrations used in a design.

ascender A typographic term for the part of a character that rises above the character's x-height, as in the letters b, f, h, k, l, and t.

ASCII Stands for American Standard Code for Information Interchange. The ASCII code is an eight-bit code, using eight bits, or digits, to represent a letter or punctuation mark.

aseptic brick A type of packaging made from laminated layers of plastic, paper, and aluminum. It is used for packaging liquids.

ATAPI ATAPI (ATA Packet Interface) drives connect directly to an IDE port; however, they require a device driver or software interface.

autoscreen film Orthochromatic film that incorporates a halftone screen built into the emulsion of the film. This film can be used to shoot halftone images without the use of a conventional halftone screen.

B

baseline Typographic term for the line on which all characters in a line of type are positioned, or rest.

Bauhaus The landmark school of architecture and design in Germany from 1919 to 1933. An extension of the Arts and Crafts movement, its philosophical goal was to combine architecture, sculpture, and painting within the framework of the artist as a craftsman, without the traditional class distinctions that existed among these disciplines.

Benjamin Franklin The most famous of all early American printers, Franklin wore many hats, including those of printer, political leader, statesman, inventor, and philosopher. He published the *New England Courant*, established the *Pennsylvania Gazette*, and began printing *Poor Richard's Almanac* in 1732, and helped frame the Declaration of Independence.

Bezier curve A mathematical curve based on anchor points and control points, used within computer design applications. The control points are used to create the articulation of curved lines.

bimetallic plates Bimetallic plates are manufactured from two dissimilar metals that have been bonded together. One of the metallic plate layers acts as a grease-receptive image area. The other layer functions as the water-receptive, nonimage area of the plate.

binary Binary describes a numbering system in which there are only two values for any number: 0 and 1.

binary digit A binary number with eight digits.

binary system A numbering system describing digital data, based on 0s and 1s.

bit A binary number or digit used to describe data for the computer.

bit depth The term used primarily by computer graphic artists to describe the number of bits used to represent color in a single pixel of a bitmapped image.

bitmapped images Bitmapped images are sometimes called *computer raster images*. Pictures in bitmaps are made up of individual dots or pixels and are commonly generated in paint and image editing programs.

Blackletter The oldest classification of typeface design. Blackletter is based on the hand lettering created by monks in Medieval manuscripts.

blanket cylinder The rubber-lined cylinder on an offset printing press on which the image is printed from the plate cylinder. The blanket cylinder then "offsets" its image onto a sheet of paper, giving the printing process its name.

bleed Images that extend beyond the edges of the trimmed sheet, cropped to the very edge of the paper.

blurring (image doubling) Causes of double-printed images may be loose blankets and excessive pressure on the impression cylinders of offset presses.

body size Within any given typeface, the distance measured from the lowest descender to the highest ascender. Also known as point size.

body text The typeface, point size, leading, and paragraph formatting of the written text for a book or article. Also sometimes called *body*.

Book of Psalmes The first book published in North America, in 1640. Also see *Stephen Daye*.

borders Rules used to define the edges of boxes and other shapes.

boxes Shapes used to contain pictures or text.

bubble jet printer Also referred to as *thermal inkjet printing*, the print cartridge contains a series of small heaters. When a small current passes through the heaters, an ink vapor bubble quickly forms and is ejected from the printhead onto the paper.

budget The total expenditures for a graphic design job. The budget is presented to and approved by the client at the time the contract is signed.

bugs A term referring to modern computer problems and software malfunctions. The term originated from the problems that occurred in ENIAC when insects were found stuck between the contacts of switching terminals.

byte Most commonly composed of eight bits to represent digital data. A byte also represents a unit of measurement used to describe memory storage capability in a computer.

C

California Job Case A wooden case with individual boxes to hold all of the letters of a particular font and size of foundry type, including specialty characters, ligatures, and numbers. The arrangement of the letters within the case is referred to as the "lay" of the case.

camera obscura A dark room with a pinhole opening in one outside wall. Light from an object illuminated outside the camera obscura passes through this small pinhole opening and is projected upside down on the opposite wall of the room.

cap height The height of capital (uppercase) letters in a typeface.

capstan image setter A series of transport rollers to keep the film or plate media under tension, moving it from the supply cassette to a take-up cassette as the imaging takes place.

case binding A binding technique of applying a hard cover to a book or pamphlet.

catalog A publication created for the listing and/or advertising of multiple products from a single source.

CD-R Recordable compact disks. CD-Rs are sold as blank disks and then recorded using a compact disk recorder.

CD-ROM The conventional read-only CD. These disks can be written to only once.

No further changes on the disk are possible after the initial writing.

CD-RW Rewritable compact disks. These disks can be recorded, erased, and then recorded again.

chain delivery system The paper delivery system on offset printing presses that uses two chains connected to a series of gripper bars that grab the printed sheet as it leaves the press cylinders and then drop it onto the paper pile.

character A name for a letter, numeral, or other typographic mark within a typeface. Also known as a *glyph* or *letterform*.

character styles In a page layout program, character styles are created to apply consistent formatting to a series of typographic elements. Character styles contain information on typeface, point size, and color.

charge-coupled device (CCD) A CCD is an electronic device used in flatbed scanners. The CCD is housed on a small wafer of silicon and consists of an array of individual light-sensitive elements called *photosites*.

Charles Rennie Mackintosh A famous Scottish designer and architect of the Art Nouveau period.

Chester Carlson The inventor of the process of electrostatic printing.

Christopher Sholes The man who invented the first typewriter around 1868.

classification In typography, the term classification is used as a parent term for all typeface categories. May also be known as *Races* or, incorrectly, as *Styles*.

Claude Garamond A French printer and typographer, Garamond was the first person to approach type design and typecasting as separate undertakings.

client changes Changes that are requested by the client when working on a design project. A certain number of changes are worked into the contract (also see *alteration fees*).

clock speed The speed at which a computer chip processes instructions, measured in millions of cycles per second (MHz).

CMYK An abbreviation for the four colors used in conventional process color printing: cyan, magenta, yellow, and the key color (black).

coating Takes place either during printing or as a postpress operation in which special liquid-based materials, such as varnish, lacquer, or perfume, are applied to the finished printed sheets.

coaxial cable Data transmission cable composed of an inner core of solid cable that carries the actual data signal, surrounded by an outer layer of sheathing serving as the ground.

codec A device or program, sometimes called an *algorithm*, used for encoding, decoding, or compressing data onto a CD or a similar digital storage device.

cold type composition Text prepared from computers or digital typesetting machines in which no foundry type or hot lead type is used.

collating The process of manually or automatically arranging sheets of paper, signatures, and so forth in sequential order.

collect for output A process of placing copies of all the files needed for proper printing of a document created in a page layout program. Collecting for output makes copies of all document, image, text, and typeface files, and places them in a single folder, no matter where they reside on the computer's drives. In Adobe InDesign, the process is called *packaging*.

color   (1) Hue. (2) The relative shade of gray that a paragraph of typeset type creates on the page.

color bars   Used in color separation negatives to give the press operator a visual indication of the colors resulting from the overlay of transparent color separation inks during printing.

color depth   Often used interchangeably with *bit depth* to describe the number of bits used to represent color in a single pixel of a bitmapped image.

color separation   The process of taking a full-color continuous-tone photograph and creating four separate images that will be printed in the four printing colors of cyan, magenta, yellow, and black, and aligned on-press to create a full-color printed image.

color systems   The various ways that artists and designers work with color. These include RYB, RGB, CMYK, Hexachrome, and Pantone (spot color).

column   The width and height of a block of typeset text.

column depth   The placement of a column of text on the page and its relationship to the bottom of the page.

comp (or comprehensive)   A presentation graphic shown to a client or supervisor to obtain feedback on a design before it is approved for further work.

compact disks   Introduced by Philips and Sony around 1982 to store and play back high-quality stereo analog audio data files.

compact image sensors (CIS)   Used in a variety of digital cameras, a CIS records the intensity of light reflected from different parts of an original and digitizes this information.

complementary metal-oxide semi-conductors (CMOS)   A class of integrated circuitry used in a variety of digital circuits and image sensing equipment.

composing stick   A handheld device that holds the individual letters of foundry type while they are being assembled.

computer-to-film (CTF)   Outputting printing files from a computer to an image setter that exposes and processes a film negative of the file, ready for stripping and plate making.

computer-to-plate (CTP)   Outputting printing files from a computer directly to a plate setter. This process bypasses traditional film technology and delivers plates ready for the printing press.

computer-to-press (CTP)   A process in which images are sent directly from a computer to the printing press. CTP eliminates the intermediate photographic, stripping, and plate making steps associated with offset imaging.

constant angular velocity (CAV)   Modern CD drives operate on this principle, in which the angular velocity of the CD is kept constant. In this scheme, the linear velocity of the disk data tracks will be larger when data are read from or written to the outer tracks. Thus the read and write speeds of the drive vary from track to track.

constant linear velocity (CLV)   On drives with a constant linear velocity, the motor speed decreases the spin speed, or rpm, of the disk as the read head moves toward the outer data tracks. This lets the data tracks move past the laser at a constant speed throughout the overall diameter of the disk.

continuous inkjet printer   Continuous inkjet printing differs from piezoelectric and bubble jet printers in that a continuous stream of ink, rather than individual droplets, is delivered through the print nozzles.

continuous-tone copy Continuous-tone copy contains blacks and whites as well as intermediate shades of gray, or a gradation of tonal ranges. Examples of continuous-tone copy include original black-and-white and color photographs, charcoal sketches, and airbrush renderings. Also see *halftone*.

control points Used in a Bezier curve, control points adjust the relationship of a line to the anchor points, and are used in changing the shape of the curved line.

copyright In 1709 the British Parliament passed the Statutes of Anne, which, for the first time in history, extended the right of copyright protection to all citizens. Copyright gives the creator of a work ownership of that work for a specified period of time.

credit line A small line of type placed below or beside a photograph or illustration noting the creator of the artwork. Most often seen in magazine and book design.

crop marks Printed guidelines that show the paper cutter operator where to trim a finished sheet.

cropping Eliminating unwanted areas from photographs, scans, and the like. In a photographic darkroom, cropping is performed on an enlarger during the printing process; on a computer, cropping is accomplished through the use of a cropping tool in an image editing program.

D

Dada An art movement founded in Zurich, Switzerland, during World War I. Dada was opposed to the chaos of war, rejecting traditional ideas of art making. Dada graphic works experimented with new methods of formatting and layout.

daguerreotype A wet-plate photographic process developed by Frenchman Louis Daguerre and patented around 1839.

Daguerreotypes are made with a glass photographic plate that is coated with a light-sensitive chemical emulsion and placed inside a light-tight camera box. After a long exposure, the plate is processed to develop and fix the image.

daylight processors Machines that process (develop) cassette-loaded film in normal room light.

decorative and display classification of typefaces that do not fit easily into other type classifications. Decorative and display typefaces are primarily created for use in logos, headlines, and other instances when type will be printed at sizes above 14 points, and should not be used for paragraphs of text.

deep-etch plates Deep-etch plates feature a photographic emulsion coating on the printing plate that is bonded and etched into the base metal of the plate.

delivery cylinder A cylinder sometimes incorporated on a commercial offset press that routes the printed sheet around the cylinder and to a delivery tray or table.

densitometer A device designed to measure the optical density of either reflection (print) or transmission (negative) materials. Although most densitometers are electronic devices, density can also be measured using optical densitometers to compare various shades of gray in original copy to calibrated patches on the densitometer.

densitometry The process of determining how much light is reflected from, or is transmitted through, a photographic negative or print.

density The ability of a substance (such as the developed silver particles in the emulsion layer of a piece of photographic film) to prevent light from passing through the film. Density is measured with a device called a *densitometer* using a scale numbered from 0.0 to 4.0.

descender   The elements of a character that fall below the baseline, as in the letters g, j, p, q, and y.

descreening   Removing the halftone dots from a printed image during scanning.

design contract   A legal document drawn up by the design studio and signed by the client to agree on the elements and fees associated with any design project.

design fees   The amount of money to be paid to the designer(s) for the creative design of a project.

die cutting   A specialized postpress process in which cutting dies, made from tool steel, are assembled to cut and shape a wide variety of products. For example, the windows in return address envelopes are first die cut; then a piece of transparent cellophane is glued to the inside surface of each envelope to finish creating the address window.

diffusion transfer processing   Diffusion transfer uses special paper and chemistry to transfer an image from an intermediate transfer negative onto a sheet of photographic paper. This process is accomplished through the use of a special processor and chemistry, resulting in prints that are often referred to as *velox* prints.

digital cameras   Cameras that record images in digital format on disks or erasable memory rather than conventional film.

digital color proof   Digital color proofing techniques use high-end inkjet and dye sublimation printers to produce high-quality proof prints.

digital images   Images whose analog information including color, black and white tints, and shading have been converted to the binary information required for interpretation by a computer or digital image processor.

digital printing presses   Presses that utilize digital data files for printing text and graphics on a variety of media, including paper, cardboard, vinyl, and so on.

digital subscriber line (DSL)   Twisted pair copper wires used for transmitting both analog data, such as voice telephone signals, and high-speed digital information over conventional telephone networks.

digital video disks   The name given to DVDs when they were first introduced to the market.

direct dampening system   A direct dampening system on an offset press delivers fountain solution to the printing plate using a roller delivery system that is separate from the ink delivery system.

direct image offset plates   Offset plates usually manufactured from paper and prepared by drawing directly on the plate.

direct imaging press (DI)   A waterless offset press that images silicone-based plates directly on the press.

direct photographic plate processing   A process that uses a special camera system loaded with presensitized plate media. The camera is also equipped with a processing unit to develop the plate material after exposure.

direct-to-plate (DTP)   See *computer-to-plate (CTP)*.

display advertising   Advertisements that run in magazines and newspapers.

distribution   The process of getting the finished design to its audience.

doctor blade   A steel blade found on the ink feed systems of offset printing presses that controls the amount of ink delivered to the ink rollers. This is accomplished by varying the distance between the doctor blade and the ink fountain.

dot gain The tendency of halftone dots on an offset printing plate to become larger when they are printed. This is caused primarily by the pressure exerted by the rubber blanket on the press during printing, as well as the ink and water used in printing.

dot matrix printer Early-generation computer printers that used a series of steel pins to punch through a modified typewriter ribbon to produce both text and rudimentary graphics.

double sheet detector The system on offset presses, collators, and the like used to detect double sheets and, if necessary, halt the paper feed until the double sheet can be eliminated.

drawing programs Computer applications that are vector-based. Adobe Illustrator and AutoCad are examples of drawing programs.

drilling Drilling holes in paper using either single- or multiple-spindle drilling machines.

drum scanner An image scanner that uses a glass drum, or cylinder, onto which the image to be scanned is mounted. The drum spins while a beam of light moves across the copy to digitize it.

drum-type image setters During the imaging process, media are fed from a supply roll onto a drum, where they remain during the exposure sequence. Drum-type image setters are configured as either internal or external systems.

dry offset printing (dryography) A modification of the wet offset process that works without using a dampening solution. Special silicone-based plates separate the image and nonimage areas (see also *letterset printing*).

ductor roller A roller incorporated in the dampening and ink systems of offset presses

that first picks up either ink or dampening solution and then delivers it to the feed rollers.

duotone A printing process of printing a photo in two colors. Using two different exposures of the same photo allows for greater color tonal variation than would be possible with either one color or by printing a solid block of color over the photo.

duplexing Printing on both sides of a sheet, or roll, of paper during one pass through a printing press.

DVD+R/RW Although this format is supported by several manufacturers, the DVD Forum does not support it. DVD+ recorders let users add, overwrite, and divide titles and make changes without any loss of player compatibility. The + format also allows background editing so that the user can start to make changes without waiting to use the disk.

DVD-R Standing for DVD *dash* R (not *minus* R), specifies the DVD disk as record/only.

DVD-RAM Early-generation recordable DVD disks used this DVD recordable format.

DVD-RW A DVD rewritable format.

dye sublimation printer Dye-sub printers use heat to transfer CMYK dyes from the print cartridge to the print paper. In this process, heat turns the dye into a gas, which then diffuses or sublimates onto the paper and solidifies. Dye-sub printers are capable of delivering very high-quality color prints, used primarily for proofing.

E

edition binding The most expensive type of binding procedure, in which the signatures are sewn together, end sheets are applied, and a hard cover is glued onto the book.

Edwin Land An American scientist and inventor who developed the process of instant photography and established the Polaroid Corporation in 1937.

electron beam (EB) printer EB printers (sometimes referred to as *ion deposition printers*) employ four steps to produce an image: generating the image on the drum with electron beams; developing the image; transferring and fusing the image onto paper; and cleaning the drum.

electrophotographic printing Digital imaging, or printing, based on a transfer drum imparted with an electrostatic charge to produce an image from a digital file or scanned image.

electrostatic printing See *electrophotographic printing.*

elliptical dots Halftone dots with an elliptical shape. Elliptical dots are often used where a smooth transition is required from light to dark areas in a print, such as in the facial areas of a portrait.

em A unit of measure in typography equal to the square of the body size of the typeface.

embossing The process of creating raised surfaces in paper by placing the sheet between male and female embossing dies.

emulsion layer The layer in film that holds the light-sensitive silver halide emulsion.

engraving See *intaglio printing.*

ENIAC The Electronic Numerical Integrator and Computer, developed at the Moore School of Engineering at the University of Pennsylvania during World War II.

EPA The Environmental Protection Agency of the U.S. federal government.

Ethernet A networking standard used for transmitting data to linked computers.

external drum image setter Film is cut and held on the outside of the image setter drum during exposure.

F

father disk When a disk is electroplated onto a completed glass master, producing a negative-image disk, this master is referred to as a father disk.

fiber optic cable Data transmission cable manufactured from very fine strands of glass, with a high rate of internal reflection keeping the data moving within the cable at very high speeds.

file servers Computer configurations made up of multiple high-capacity hard drives to store large amounts of information and application programs. File servers often act as a core computer, providing several computers, sometimes referred to as *dumb terminals,* on the network with programs and operability.

film cassette The light-tight container that stores exposed film from an image setter during file output.

film sensitivity The degree to which photographic film reacts to light conditions. The more sensitive the film is to light, the less light is needed to produce a correct exposure. Film sensitivity is expressed in either ASA or ISO numbers; the higher the number, the more sensitive the film is to light.

final comp A final design in a form most like the piece will look when printed. Final comps are presented to the client for final approval of the design.

final production After the design has received final approval from the client, final production involves creation of all of the computer files needed for printing.

final project review A final project review takes place after the design has been created and distributed, and is used to review the entire design process from beginning to end.

finishing Processes that take place after a piece is printed, such as cutting, binding, and assembly.

Firewire Apple Computer's personal computer high-speed serial bus interface, which has largely replaced the old serial and parallel port interfaces. Most computers are now equipped with built-in Firewire ports.

flag The designed name of a magazine, newspaper, or periodical as it appears on the cover. Sometimes referred to as the *banner* and often mistakenly called the *masthead*.

flash memory devices A flash drive consists of a built-in controller with a USB interface and a nonvolatile memory interface connected to one or more nonvolatile memory chips that retain their data when power to the chips is turned off.

flat This is the name given to a goldenrod sheet after all its negatives have been stripped in and it is ready for plate making.

flatbed scanner A device that uses a light source and mirrors to reflect light from original copy through a focusing lens, electronic image sensor, and software for image interpretation.

flexography (flexo) A relief printing process using flexible printing plates made from rubber or plastic to print on cardboard, folding cartons, plastic bags, milk and beverage containers, newspapers, and candy and food wrappers.

floppy disks Widely used devices for storing small files in computers. Floppy disks started out as 8-inch disks used in first-generation typesetters. They then moved to 5¼-inch disks and finally to the 3½-inch format currently available. With the advent of newer, high-capacity drives using flexible media, floppy drives, as standard equipment, are being phased out by most computer manufacturers.

flyer A one-page graphic piece that is distributed to provide information about programs and events, or to give additional information on a subject. They may be distributed flat or folded. Usually small in size, most commonly 8.5 × 11 inches.

folding The process of folding sheets into a variety of configurations on specialized folding machines.

font A generic term used for the smallest unit of packaged type, consisting of a complete assortment of type of one size and family. A traditional font of foundry type consists of three packages: lowercase, uppercase, and figures. Computer fonts are electronically packaged in the same configuration and stored on the computer's hard drive (see also *typeface*).

format The manner in which information is organized to describe the contents of a data file.

foundry type Type cast as individual letters and symbols, made from lead, tin, and antimony.

fountain solution A working solution of water and fountain concentrate used as the wetting agent in conventional offset printing presses.

four-cylinder offset press A press design used in large commercial offset presses, made up of a plate, blanket, and impression and delivery cylinders.

Fourdrinier brothers Built the first commercially successful papermaking machine in England in 1804.

Fourdrinier process The commercial process for making paper based on the technology developed by the Fourdrinier brothers.

FPO "For position only"—a term used to refer to images that will be used for layout but will be replaced with higher-quality images before printing.

Frank Lloyd Wright The landmark American architect of the late nineteenth to middle twentieth centuries. Famous for his designs of "Fallingwater" in Pennsylvania and the Guggenheim Museum in New York.

frequency modulation (FM) screening
Also referred to as *stochastic screening,* FM screening varies the spacing between the dot patterns of same-size dots to reproduce a continuous-tone color or black-and-white printed image.

Futurism   A graphic design movement of the early twentieth century, Futurists attempted to express the meaning of words and sounds in their designs, largely disregarding earlier established principles of graphic design.

G

general-purpose interface board (GPIB)   An add-on computer board that operates a peripheral computer device and is installed in one of the expansion slots on a computer's motherboard.

George Eastman   Developed a process of a gelatin-coated flexible film base and founded the Kodak Corporation.

Giclee print   Custom art prints output on a wide-format inkjet printer, usually on canvas.

gigabyte (GB)   One gigabyte is equivalent to 1,000 megabytes.

glass master   Made from optically ground glass with a very fine (1/10μ) photoresist layer, a glass master is exposed to an imaging laser that burns on pit and land patterns in preparation for duplicating a CD.

Glyphic   Typefaces based on hand-carved letters or classical forms originally created with a pen or brush.

goldenrod   A sheet of specially prepared paper on which all of the negatives that make up a page are positioned. The sheet of paper is known as *goldenrod* because of its yellow color.

graphic arts process cameras   Large-format cameras used to photograph original copy for subsequent plate making and printing.

graphic arts   A combination of trades and professions within the printing and publishing industries.

graphic design   The art of combining type and images to interest, inform, persuade, or sell an idea, event, or product to a specific audience.

graphic design problem-solving model   A system of problem solving used by most graphic designers. The model includes a series of steps, from research and development of an idea via quick sketches through to a finished design.

graphical user interface (GUI)   The graphical user interface, incorporated by most modern computers, that lets a person use the various computer functions without having to navigate the computer's operating system (OS).

gravure   Printing from a recessed surface. The image to be printed is cut into, and below, the surface of the printing plate. Also see *intaglio printing.*

grayscale images   Images that contain black and white as well as intermediate shades of gray.

green cleaning   Employing environmentally friendly, nontoxic detergents and cleaners to reduce or eliminate volatile organic compounds and other hazardous waste products.

grid structure   The underlying structure of a layout, used primarily in magazine, book, and catalog design. The grid consists of rules marking the margins and columns in which text and images will be composed.

gripper margin   The margin or space incorporated into a goldenrod flat that represents the nonprinting area on a sheet of paper created by the gripper fingers on the feed system of an offset printing press. This margin is usually between ¼ and ⅜ inch.

Gutenberg Bible   A milestone achievement in the history of technology, the Gutenberg Bible is also known as the 42-line Bible (based on the number of lines of text on each page) and is attributed to Johann Gutenberg around 1455.

gutter   The space between columns of text. Also, the space from the bound center of a book to the inside edge of the column of text.

H

halftone   A black-and-white or color continuous-tone image reproduced as a series of different-sized dots to visually recreate tonal gradation.

halftone picture process   The process of converting a continuous tone original black-and-white or color picture into a series of dots that can be printed on a digital or conventional offset press to reproduce to tonal range of the original picture.

halftone screens   Sheets of glass or plastic that contain built-in perpendicular rulings at right angles to one another. The screens are placed over a sheet of film in a process camera when photographing continuous-tone originals to break up the picture into halftone dots. The dot structure enables the continuous-tone illustration to be printed on conventional printing presses.

halftone screen rulings   The method used to classify halftone screens, based on the number of dots per inch incorporated into the screen.

hard drive   Named for its hard platter (or platters), coated with a metal oxide and used for data storage in computers.

heading   A word or group of words that functions as a title to a paragraph of text. Headings appear before the paragraph and are formatted to stand out from the text.

Herman Hollerith   Invented a punch card tabulating machine to help analyze the data for the 1890 U.S. Census. Hollerith's company eventually became IBM.

HFS   The hierarchal file system used by Macintosh computers.

hickey   Hickeys are small blemishes or dots that print in either image or nonimage areas and are caused by small pieces of paper or ink that adhere to the plate or blanket cylinder during the press run.

hieroglyphics   Pictures and symbols that represent ideas, objects, and symbols in a formalized writing system.

high-definition DVD   HD-DVD uses a blue–violet laser instead of the red laser used in conventional DVDs to achieve high-definition pictures for television playback.

hot type composition   Composing text from foundry type or from typecasting machines using hot lead for typecasting.

I

IDE controller   Any disk drive in which the controller is built into the drive using the IDE (integrated drive electronics) protocol.

ideogram   A system of ancient writing in which each sign or drawing represents some object or concept that is derived from the graphic.

ideogram logo   A logo design that uses an image to represent an idea, rather than to illustrate what the company makes.

illustrations   Images created by an artist. Illustrations are often used when a photograph cannot express the intended concept. Charts and graphs also fall under the category of illustration.

illustrator   (1) A person who creates images such as drawings or paintings for use in graphic design projects. (2) Software by Adobe Systems, Inc., that is widely used for vector-based drawing.

image   One of the two primary elements of all graphic design. Images may be included in a work of graphic design by the use of photography, illustration, or abstract graphic elements.

image quality   The resolution of an image for its use in graphic design. Image quality must match what is required for the intended use of the image, i.e. 72 dpi for Web use or 300 dpi for print.

image setter   A digital output device that processes data files from the computer and records, or *rasterizes,* that data onto photographic film, paper, or plates.

image-based logo   A logo design that uses an image for its primary means of communication, such as the use of a box for a packaging company.

imposition   The placement of each image on a flat so that it will print in the right order and position on the press-printed page.

impression cylinder   The cylinder of an offset press that creates a solid backing for a sheet or roll of paper during printing.

inclination   In typefaces, the amount of lean that a character has to the left or to the right.

indent   The position to the left or right of a paragraph's left margin that is given to the first line of the paragraph. Indents are generally to the right of the paragraph margin. When they are to the left, they are called *hanging indents.*

InDesign   The page layout program manufactured by Adobe Systems, Inc. InDesign is a standard layout program used in the design and publishing industry.

indirect dampening systems   Indirect dampening systems on offset presses carry both the ink and fountain solutions on the same set of rollers; there is no need for a separate set of dampening rollers like that used in a direct dampening system.

info graphics   Illustrations that combine statistical data in conjunction with images. Used often in newspapers to show data on everything from household incomes to election results.

ink fountain   The ink fountain is a reservoir from which ink is fed to the press. The ink fountain, consisting of a shallow tray and a doctor blade, meters ink to the press rollers evenly during each rotation of the printing press.

inkjet printers   A variety of highly sophisticated printing technologies that rely on liquid-based colored inks.

intaglio printing   Printing an image from a recessed surface.

internal drum image setter   On internal drum image setters, the media must first be cut, then held in place on the inside of the drum during exposure.

International Standards Organization (ISO)   See *ISO Standard 9660.*

international style   A graphic design style primarily from the 1950s and 1960s. The style is characterized by strong use of a grid and significant use of white space, along with sans-serif typography. Also known as the *Swiss Style,* as it had it roots in Switzerland.

interpolated resolution   Interpolated resolution programs rely on sophisticated mathematical formulas, called *algorithms,* that analyze original scans and add pixels to fill in the spaces between the original and final dot density scanning requirements to boost the resolution of a final scanned image.

ion deposition printing Also known as *electron beam printing*, where an electron cartridge transfers electrical charges onto the surface of a rotating dielectric drum made of aluminum oxide.

Ira Rubel Built his first offset printing press around 1904 in his Nutley, New Jersey, print shop.

ISO Standard 9660 The standard for CD-ROMs, formulated by the International Standards Organization to ensure that ordinary CDs can be read on any computer platform, including DOS/Windows, Macintosh, or Unix systems,

italic typeface Using graceful, slanting letters to mimic handwritten characters, italic type was originally created by Venetian type designer Aldus Manutius.

J

jogging Aligning all the paper sheets in a stack by placing them on a rapidly vibrating table, causing the sheets to align perfectly as gravity forces them into place.

Johann Gutenberg A German goldsmith credited with the invention of moveable type and the first commercially viable printing press around 1455.

John Baskerville A type designer and printer, Baskerville also developed newer, rich-toned printing inks and glossy papers. As the official printer to Cambridge University, Baskerville printed a Bible in 1763—a book that is thought of as one of the finest examples of eighteenth-century printing

JPEG JPEG is an acronym for Joint Photographic Experts Group. JPEG images use a codec (for coding/decoding) that removes repeated elements between frames to compress the image file size. JPEG is the common format used for illustrations on the Web.

K

kerning Adjusting the space between two characters of text. Kerning is done in headlines and large type applications to make the letters fit evenly.

kilobytes (KB) One thousand bytes of information. One thousand kilobytes are equivalent to one megabyte (MB) of information.

knockouts Printing a background shape in which type is left to show through as the paper color. When using knockouts, the designer must select a typeface that has enough weight so that it stands out against the printed fill.

L

laminating Adhering clear plastic to one or both sides of a printed sheet of paper or other substrate.

lands The untouched areas between adjacent pits on a CD-ROM.

latent image In photography, exposing film to light causes a chemical change in the film emulsion, producing a latent image. The term *latent image* refers to the fact that the light striking the film has been recorded by the emulsion of the film but requires further chemical processing for the image to become visible. Latent images also exist on electrostatic copiers and image setters after the imaging drum has been sensitized and before the toner has been applied.

leading The space between lines in a paragraph of text.

letterpress printing Printing from the raised image on foundry type, photoengravings, block prints, and the like. Letterpress printing is also a type of relief printing process.

letterset printing See *dry offset*.

ligature Two letters that are designed as a single character to avoid typesetting problems that could happen when two letters that are placed next to one another collide, as with "f" and "i"— fi instead of fi.

light-emitting diode (LED)   A small device, composed of a semiconductor material, that gives off light and operates with very little power.

line copy   An image consisting of line and tonal areas only, with no intermediate shades of gray or color.

line length   The width of a line of type within a paragraph. Too short of a line makes for choppy reading, while too long of a line makes it difficult for readers to find their place from one line to the next.

linen tester   A high-quality magnifying lens, sometimes called a *loupe,* for close inspection of photographic negatives and prints.

linking   In the process of placing images into a page layout or drawing program, linking allows for a connection to the image without adding to the size of the file. When linking is used, the original image files must be included with the application file for the images to print properly.

Linotype machine   See *Ottmar Merganthaler.*

litho stone   A polished piece of cut stone, usually limestone, on which an image is drawn using special grease-based materials for printing in a lithography press.

lithography   See *planography.*

local area network (LAN)   A series of computers wired or linked together via Ethernet cables within a small, localized system.

logo   A designed mark for a company that is used to represent them in their design and advertising.

lowercase   The characters within a typeface that are not capitalized. Also known as *miniscules.*

Ludlow typesetting machine   A machine used to set display type for headlines and large captions. Often used together with the Linotype machine in setting type for newspapers and magazines.

M

magazine   A periodical publication containing articles, images, and advertisements, usually on a particular subject.

magneto optical (MO) disk   MO disks resemble thick floppy diskettes and are available in different capacities and sizes for backing up small to large data files. MO drives are now largely outdated devices.

magnetography   Works by creating magnetic latent images on the surface of a hard metal cylinder.

main exposure   The main exposure captures most of the detail, highlight, and middle tones of the original in the halftone photographic process.

make-ready   Press preparation time, including all the steps needed before an actual press run.

man-on-the-street rule   This rule states that if someone with no graphic design or technical training feels that two images bear a striking resemblance to each other, it is reasonable to assume that a copyright infringement in the use of an image has probably taken place.

margin   The space between a column of text and the edge of the paper.

masking sheet   See *goldenrod.*

master pages   In a page layout program, master pages allow the designer to create a template of elements—such as grids, guides, rules, page numbers, and so forth—that can be applied to any page of the document.

The use of master pages saves time in laying out the publication.

mastering The process of producing multiple copies of a CD-ROM.

masthead The list of people involved in the editing, design, and production of a publication, usually found near the front of a periodical after the table of contents.

matrix A piece of brass with the indented, three-dimensional image of a character of type embossed into it. A matrix is used in the typecasting process to create type for use on a letterpress.

mechanical A mechanical contains all the photo-ready page elements that would be photographed to produce a complete page in a book, pamphlet, brochure, or the like. The mechanical is assembled by hand, and all of its elements are glued or hot-waxed in place.

megabytes (MB) One megabyte (MB) is equivalent to 1,000 kilobytes.

microprocessor Combines thousands of individual electronic circuit components on one small chip; introduced by the Intel Corporation in 1971.

modulation The variation of stroke weight within a letterform.

moiré pattern A pattern, generally objectionable, produced by improper alignment of halftone dots. Moiré patterns occur most frequently in rescreened scans and prints. These patterns can be minimized by selecting the descreening option available in most scanner software programs.

monitor profile Established in a monitor calibration procedure, a step-by-step guide is followed that enables the user to adjust brightness, contrast, ideal black-and-white images, and the color phosphors in the monitor to accurately display both color and black-and-white images.

monks Religious clerics who devoted their lives to copying books by hand using quills and reeds as writing and illustrating instruments.

monospaced A typeface in which each character is given the exact same width when typeset. Manual typewriters used monospaced typefaces as they did not have the ability to set characters with varied horizontal spacing.

mother disk Mother disks are made by electroplating the father disk. Mothers are used to produce additional CDs.

moveable type Individual letters and characters of foundry and wood type that can be moved, rearranged, and reused when setting type.

MP3 compression standard MP3 compression eliminates the sounds at both the top and bottom of the audible tonal spectrum that are not easily discernible to the human ear. Removing these audio sections, while not easily noticeable in reproduced sound quality, significantly reduces the size of the audio file.

MPEG MPEG is an acronym for Motion Pictures Experts Group. MPEG compression uses an algorithm that creates one compressed interframe and then removes repeated elements from succeeding frames and codes only the differences.

multiplatform Computer programs developed on one computer platform or operating system (for example, a Macintosh) that will run on a different platform, like a Windows PC.

N

nameplate Another term for the title of a magazine.

negative-acting plates Negative-acting plates use photographic negative images to create positive images on the printing plate.

newsletter A periodical publication put out by a company or organization to distribute news items to its members. Printed newsletters are generally twelve pages or less and in one or two colors. Many newsletters are now published online as PDFs.

Nicolas Jensen A Venetian printer who was responsible for perfecting the basic form and beauty of the Roman typeface.

Nicolas Robert Developed the mechanized process for making paper, still in use today, around 1798.

node An individual computer station connected into a networking system.

nonimpact printing Digital and electronic printing techniques that rely on electrostatic charges, rather than physical contact, to transfer images to the printed sheet.

noninterlaced monitors Monitors that refresh, or redisplay, all of the lines on the screen during each refresh cycle.

numbering The process of printing sequential numbers on a variety of items. Sometimes items may be numbered separately on a numbering machine as part of postpress processing.

O

object-oriented/vector images Images generated on a computer screen and stored as a series of connected lines and shapes. Vector graphics are the file type generated by CAD and drawing programs.

offset lithography Developed by Ira Rubel in 1904, an image is first printed onto an intermediate rubber-covered roller and then transferred onto paper.

offset printing press A printing press that prints, or offsets, a primary image from a printing plate on to a rubber blanket and then transfers this image from the blanket to a piece of paper or other media to produce the final printed image.

oil and water principle The chemical process on which lithography is based, relying on the fact that oil (ink) and water (fountain solution) don't mix to separate the image and nonimage areas during printing.

on-demand printing Short-run (fewer than 1,000 copies) print jobs. On-demand printing often contains variable data and customized material possible only on digital presses that can deliver short-run jobs at a reduced cost.

on-press imaging See *direct imaging press (DI)*.

opacity Opacity is the same thing as density (the light-stopping ability of an emulsion layer of film). Opacity is measured on a decimal scale from 1 to 100.

opaque proofs Opaque proofs incorporate a heavy paper or plastic support base on top of which sensitized color sheets or toners are added to create progressive proofs of a job. After all the exposures have been made, the finished proof results in a high-quality representation of the finished job.

opaque solution A liquid applied to photographic film with either a brush or special applicator to cover small pinholes and unwanted image areas in the negative.

OpenType A type file format that may contain Postscript or TrueType information. OpenType is compatible with both Macintosh and PCs, and is quickly becoming the industry standard.

optical character recognition (OCR) OCR software lets a computer compare the letters of scanned text to predefined alphabet letters contained within the algorithm of the OCR software.

optical resolution The mechanical resolution of a scanner, utilizing its built-in optical and hardware components, to physically capture image details while scanning original copy.

ornaments   Typefaces made up of graphic elements or pictures that are used as bullets or decorative elements in conjunction with other typefaces. They may also be called *dingbats*.

orphan   A word or line of text appearing alone at the top of a column of text. Orphans should be eliminated by adjusting paragraph tracking or leading.

ortho film   Photographic film sensitive to the blue and green portion of the visible spectrum. Ortho film is red-blind, enabling the use of dim red safelights when handling this film in the darkroom.

Ottmar Merganthaler   Mechanized production of the printed word when he invented the Linotype machine around 1886.

P

package   The designed container for a product.

packaging   Generally referring to the type of materials used in a package design, but may also be used in place of the term *package design*.

page description language (PDL)   A program that contains the commands for a printer to properly place on a printed page the text and graphics generated on a computer.

page layout programs   Computer applications used for the design and layout of multiple-page designs such as magazines, catalogs, and books.

painting programs   Image-editing computer applications that are pixel-based. Adobe Photoshop is a popular painting program.

Paleolithic art   Refers primarily to cave and stone art dating from around 30,000 BC to about 10,000 BC.

panchromatic film   Film sensitive to the entire visible light spectrum.

paper   Substance on which almost all printing is done. Paper is made from fibrous materials spread into thin sheets and dried.

paper drilling   A finishing process whereby holes are drilled into a sheet or stack of papers in preparation for binding them together.

paper sizes   Standard sheet sizes of paper (such as letter, legal, and tabloid) used in design and printing.

papyrus   A reed that grows on the banks of the Nile River from which a paperlike sheet can be made. Most Egyptian hieroglyphic texts were printed on papyrus.

paragraph alignment   The relationship of lines of type within a paragraph. Standard alignments are aligned left, aligned right, centered, and justified.

paragraph articulation   The relationship between one paragraph and the next. Paragraph articulation may be shown by using a first line indent or with space between paragraphs.

paragraph break   Another term for space between paragraphs.

paragraph color   The relative amount of gray that a typeset paragraph creates on a page.

paragraph styles   In a page layout application, paragraph styles define the typeface, type size, and color as well as the paragraph alignment, leading, tracking, and articulation. Paragraph styles are created and applied to text elements to allow for easy design changes.

parchment   Writing material made from dried animal skins.

parking zone   The area on a computer's hard drive to which the drive head moves when the drive is either turned off or is offline.

Paul Rand The American designer who defined the art and spirit of modern graphic design. Perhaps best known as a freelance corporate identity design consultant, he created the famous corporate logos for IBM, Cummins Engine, Westinghouse, and United Parcel Service.

PCMCIA (Personal Computer Memory Card International Association) An international standard for peripheral interface cards for laptop computers.

PDF Stands for Portable Document Format—a file format developed by Adobe Systems, Inc., that embeds typefaces and images into a document that can be read on most computers with the free Acrobat Reader program.

perfect binding A binding process in which all pages of a book are glued together along its spine.

perfect printing Printing on two sides of a sheet or web of paper.

perfecting press A digital or conventional printing press that can print on both sides of a sheet or web of paper during a pass through the press. Some perfecting presses will first print one side of a sheet or web of paper, then mechanically turn the paper over to print the second side.

perforating The process of creating a series of holes so that paper can be torn more easily along a line. Perforating is accomplished by a perforating rule installed on a press during the printing process.

phase-change inkjet (solid inkjet) printers Ink is supplied in solid form, resembling crayon sticks. During the printing process, the ink in the stick is heated and quickly melts while the printhead travels across the paper, spraying ink droplets onto the paper.

Phoenician alphabet The Phoenicians developed the modern system of writing, wherein sounds were first represented with written symbols, around 3,000 BC.

photoelectric effect The effect that takes place in a charge-coupled device (CCD). Electrons are released in response to incoming light energy, called *photons*. Electrons accumulate in proportion to the amount of light striking a photosite of the CCD.

photographic gray scale A gray scale is a small (½ × 3-inch) strip of photographic paper divided into twelve steps. Step 1 is bright white; step 12 is solid black; and the steps in between are the intermediate shades of gray that represent the overall contrast range in a convenient wedge format. A gray scale is used as a quality control device for exposing and developing line and halftone negatives and offset printing plates. Gray scales are also used to ensure the output quality of image setters and plate setters.

photography The process of recording images onto either film or light-sensitive digital circuitry based on capturing reflected light from the original object.

photomechanical proofs Inexpensive photosensitive materials, exposed through the flat and developed, to offer a rendition of what a finished job will look like without the expense of using the actual papers and printing inks.

photomultiplier tube (PMT) An electronic device used in drum scanners to analyze reflected light and convert it to electrical signals that are sent to a computer when an image is scanned.

photoresist layer The layer on a glass master compact disk through which a laser burns pits onto the glass surface below. During manufacture, the photoresist layer prevents etching of the disk in all areas other than those exposed to the laser to produce the data pits on the disk.

photosensitive drum   Based on photocopier technology, a photosensitive drum is coated with a semiconductor material. The surface of this drum changes its electrical resistance in response to light striking it from an imaging laser beam.

Photoshop   The market-dominant photo editing software program produced by Adobe Systems, Inc.

photosite   A light-sensitive element in a charge-coupled device (CCD).

pictogram logo   A logo designed using a pictograph, see *pictograph*.

pictograph   Literally means "writing with pictures." Prehistoric cave paintings are pictographs that are limited to communicating simple messages and representations.

piezoelectric printing   Inkjet printing using a small piezoelectric (PE) crystal to control the flow of ink from a small nozzle onto the printing substrate.

pitch   The track spacing on a conventional CD-ROM.

pits   Small pits, or indentations of varying lengths into the media on the disk, within the spiral data tracks of a CD during encoding of data in a CD burner.

pixel   A shortening of the term *picture element*, which computer monitors use to display images.

planography   A process in which the printing and nonprinting surfaces are on the same plane. This term is often used to describe the process of lithography.

plastic binding   The use of plastic combs, inserted into prepunched holes, to hold a book or pamphlet together.

plate cylinder   The cylinder on an offset printing press that holds the printing plate.

plate maker   A device used to expose printing plates. Plate makers consist of a high-intensity ultraviolet light source coupled to a vacuum frame. Offset flats of stripped goldenrod sheets are placed in contact with the printing plate and exposed in the plate maker.

plate setter   A computer-driven device that images offset printing plates directly from the computer. Plate setters are composed of two parts: the raster image processor (RIP) and the imaging section that exposes, or generates, the image on the printing plate.

plug-ins   Software applications that reside and work within larger software programs. Scanner software and special effects filters for Photoshop, Illustrator, InDesign, and QuarkXPress are examples of plug-in applications.

PMT gray contact screens   Screens used in the diffusion transfer process, or photomechanical transfer (PMT) process, for making screened paper prints from continuous-tone originals. These prints are referred to as *velox* prints.

point system   The system of mathematics used to measure and specify type in the printing and publishing industry. The basic unit of measurement in this system is the "point" which is equivalent to 1/72 inch.

Polaroid camera   The instant picture camera invented by Edwin Land, founder of the Polaroid Corporation, in 1947.

pop art   Coinciding with the youth culture and pop music phenomenon of the 1950s and 1960s, and reflective of the then-new consumer culture. The period is immortalized in images like Andy Warhol's painting of Campbell's soup cans.

positive-acting plates   Positive-acting plates use film positives, rather than film negatives, to expose plates.

poster   A single-sided piece of graphic design, generally printed on a large sheet of paper. Posters are designed to be hung in public places to attract the attention of passers-by.

postpress   Work done to a printed piece to take it to its final form. This may include folding, trimming, die cutting, and binding (see also *finishing*).

Postscript Type 1   A computer type file format that uses two files, a printer file and screen files, to display and print type.

preliminary comps   Designs that are used to explore thumbnail concepts worked up to actual size and in color. They may be used in presentations to clients to get feedback on the progress of the project. Also known as *roughs*.

pre-mastering   Converting original data into the standard ISO 9660 format before mastering a CD.

pre-press   Processes completed before the printing of a piece, including imposition, color separations, scanning, and so on.

prescan   A fast scan performed on a scanner before final scanning to ensure proper positioning, tonal balance, and cropping of both the original and the digitized image.

presensitized additive plates   A special chemical solution that adds a lacquer, or long-run coating, to the image areas of the plate during development.

presensitized subtractive plates   A processing solution that removes all of the plate coating from the nonimage areas of the plate, thus "subtracting" the image coating from the plate during processing.

press proof   The most accurate method of proofing a job before a press run is to use the actual printing plates, inks, and papers specified for the job. Press proofs exactly duplicate conditions of the actual press run to achieve this accuracy.

principles of composition   Basic design principles applied to composition: picture plane, contrast, harmony, scale, proportion, unity, and balance, to mention a few.

print engine   Imaging devices incorporated in laser printers and black-and-white and color electrostatic copiers and digital printing presses.

printer control language (PCL)   Printers have corresponding page description languages known as their *printer control languages* (PCLs). PCLs let printers properly place on the printed page the text and graphics generated on computers.

production   The process of preparing a final design for printing. This includes bringing together all the elements of artwork, copy, and properly prepared computer files needed for printing.

production fees   Charges incurred for the printing and manufacturing of a final designed project.

profit   The monetary or intellectual benefit gained through the graphic design process.

project bid   A proposal made to the client referencing all of the costs involved in a design project.

project brief   A statement describing a project so that others at the studio will be aware of the goals and needs of the project. It may be shared with the client to make sure the design proposal meets the client's goals.

project folder   A virtual or analog file folder in which all of the materials associated with the project are kept.

project schedule   A timeline of a project from beginning to end. The project schedule is used to keep the project moving smoothly towards completion.

proportion scale   Using a proportion scale is the most efficient method of determining the size required for enlargements or reductions of originals. The scale uses a series of dials that, when aligned, read out the percentage of enlargement or reduction based on the dimensions of the original and the reproduced copy.

pull quote   A line or two of text repeated at a larger size than the body text on a page layout. Pull quotes can add visual interest and variety to a design.

Q

QuarkXPress   The page layout program manufactured by Quark, Inc. QuarkXPress is a standard layout program used in the design and publishing industries.

QuickTake camera   The early-generation, single-exposure, point-and-shoot camera released by Apple Computer in the mid-1990s. The QuickTake was the first digital camera to open up the desktop publishing industry.

QWERTY   The modern keyboard configuration found on typewriters and computers, credited to inventor Christopher Sholes.

R

RAID array   (Redundant Array of Independent Disks) File servers containing multiple hard drives arranged either as separate drives or in multiple-drive configurations, or *arrays*, the purposes of which are to increase network and system speed and performance and also automatically back up all data.

raster image processor (RIP)   Interprets digital data from a computer printing file to a printable image that can be output on film, paper, or plate material.

raster images   Images whose original page description has been interpreted and processed into a bit map image that can be output to a typesetter or digital image setter.

Raymond Lowey   The landmark American graphic and industrial designer of the modernist period. When Lowey wasn't designing automobiles, locomotives for the Pennsylvania Railroad, or the interior of NASA's Skylab Space Station, his work as a graphic designer created familiar icons like the Exxon, Shell, and Lucky Strike logos.

read–write   The electronic device in a computer's hard drive that either writes data to the drive disk or retrieves data from the drive platter for interpretation by the computer.

reflectance   Reflectance, or reflection, is the percentage of incident light that reflects off copy (a photographic print, for example) in a particular tonal area of the print.

register pins   Metal pins used to line up multiple flats on a light table during stripping. The use of register pins helps to ensure proper registration of multiple colors and images during printing.

registration marks   Registration marks are placed in pairs at each corner of a printed piece to allow printing and alignment of successive colors in multicolor printing applications.

relief printing   The oldest printing technique, this involves printing an image from a raised surface that is in relief from nonprinting areas.

replica typecasting   Printing type that is cast one letter at a time in a reusable matrix.

rescreening   The process of taking a picture that has already been screened and either scanning or photographing it again to produce a different halftone pattern in the print. During rescreening, care must be taken to prevent moiré patterns in the rescreened print.

research An important step of the graphic design problem-solving model that focuses on finding historic and current materials for inspiration and development of a design project.

RGB The three additive primary colors: red, green, and blue. This color reproduction scheme is used in almost all color television sets and computer monitors.

Roman alphabet The Romans adapted the Greek alphabet to their own language, eventually creating the 26-letter alphabet we continue to use today.

Rosetta Stone The major key to deciphering ancient Egyptian hieroglyphic texts. The stone contains a decree issued in 196 BC and written in three languages: Greek, Egyptian hieroglyphics, and Demotic (a cursive evolution of hieroglyphic text and symbols).

rotogravure The process historically used to print the color sections of Sunday newspapers.

round dots Halftone dots in a circular shape. Round dots are used most often when printing continuous-tone copy because they allow the most surface area in the print to be covered with dots.

rubber blanket The blanket attached to the blanket cylinder of an offset printing press. This blanket accepts the image from the plate cylinder and offsets the image onto a sheet of paper—thus the term *offset lithography*.

ruby masking film Masking film, whose name comes from its color, often used for preparing multicolor printing jobs in which only one flat is used for making multiple exposures on a printing plate. Ruby film is cut by hand to expose window areas on a flat for separate exposures during plate making.

rules A term for straight lines used in graphic design for emphasis or to delineate space. Rules are measured in width by points.

Russian Constructivism Sparked by the Russian Revolution, this movement sought to combine the new technologies of photography and film to create dynamic compositions for posters, books, magazines, buildings, and interior designs.

S

saddle-stitched book A bindery process that staples the pages through the center or spine of the signature(s).

saddle stitching A binding technique accomplished by sewing a book, or a series of signatures, through the spines of the signatures along the centerfolds of the pages.

safelight A low-intensity light source that does not affect, or expose, specific types of photographic films. The color of the safelight varies based on the type of film being handled in the darkroom.

sans serif A classification of typefaces that do not have serifs at the end of their strokes.

scanner/recorders Devices used to produce color separations from original reflections or transparent copy.

scoring The process of placing a fold, or impression, on a sheet of paper, cardboard, or the like during printing or postprocessing to make the sheet easy to fold or tear later.

screen process printing Also known as *stencil duplicating* and *serigraphy*, this process involves printing through a stencil adhered to a silk or nylon screen onto a variety of flat or round objects.

screen size The number of dots per inch in a halftone screen.

screen tint Adding screening or shading effects to a job during plate making.

Commercial tint screens are stripped into a flat for subsequent exposure.

screening   The process of breaking a continuous-tone image into halftone dots for printing.

scribe   A monk who devoted his life to copying books by hand using quills and reeds as writing and illustrating instruments.

script and hand-lettered   A classification of typefaces that are designed to imitate handwriting with a pen or a brush.

scumming   A printing condition in which a printing plate picks up and prints ink in nonimage areas of a print.

search and replace   A feature found in most computer programs that allows the designer to search for a particular word within a document and replace it with another word.

serif   A classification of typefaces for letterforms that have tiny flared elements—serifs at the end of each stroke.

serigraphy   See *screen process printing*.

sheeter   A device used on the output side of web-fed presses to cut the web (roll) of paper into individual sheets.

sheet-fed press   A printing press whose paper feed system relies on stacks of individual sheets of paper—rather than rolls or webs—for printing.

sheetwise layout   Printing both sides of a sheet of paper with two different images, using two separate printing plates.

side stitching   Stapling or sewing a group of signatures or a book through the side of the binding or cover.

signature   A series of pages printed on one sheet of paper and positioned so that when the large printed sheet is folded and trimmed, all of the pages are in their proper sequence.

silver emulsion–based photography   A photographic process that relies on a developer, a stop bath, and a fixer to develop an image in a silver halide photographic film emulsion.

single-knife paper cutter   An electric–hydraulic paper cutter that employs a single blade to make a series of cuts to a finished stack of paper.

soft proofing   The practice of using a computer monitor to provide an accurate preview of how screen images will print on a specific inkjet printer. To ensure the accuracy of soft proofing, a color management system must be in place that enables the designer to first calibrate the computer monitor so that the image on the computer screen is identical to the image produced by a specific printer.

solid ink printing   Used primarily in the packaging and industrial design areas, solid ink printers use sticks of colored wax-based inks that are melted and then sprayed through small stainless steel nozzles in a printhead.

square dots   Halftone dots that are square. Square dots offer starker transition from lights to darks than do their elliptical or round counterparts.

stampers   Stampers are made from a mother disk and are used to reproduce its pit and land structure onto compact disks.

star targets   Printed at diagonal corners of a printed sheet, a star target shows the amount of ink spread; as ink spread increases, the center wedge of the star target begins to fill with ink. In addition to ink spread, the target also shows the amount of ink slur or line doubling on the print.

Statutes of Anne   This law established that intellectual property belongs to its creator. United States copyright laws are based on this statute.

steam-driven lithography press   Early lithographic press using steam to power the printing press.

stencil duplicating   Also referred to as *screen process printing*.

stencil printing   See *screen process printing*.

step and repeat   A process used when the same image is to be printed many times on the same sheet of paper. Often multiple exposures at exact locations on the plate are made, as determined by the technician during the plating process.

Stephen Daye   A locksmith from Cambridge, England, who in 1640 published *The Book of Psalmes*—the first book printed in British North America.

stereotype plates   Printing plates used on early printing presses, which were identical castings made from the original type and photoengraved images, using papier mâché or plaster as the intermediate casting media.

stochastic screening   Stochastic screening uses dots that are all the same size but vary in their spacing to reproduce continuous-tone copy.

stock images   Photographs and illustrations available for purchase from companies that represent photographers and illustrators. Stock images are less expensive than hiring a photographer or illustrator to create an original artwork, but may be purchased by multiple people for multiple uses, and are therefore not unique.

stone lithography printing   Developed around the beginning of the twentieth century, this process involved drawing images in reverse on treated slabs of stone, which were then wetted, inked, and printed.

stop bath   A mild acidic chemical, usually acetic acid, used in developing film to stop the action of the developer at a specified time. The acidic stop bath neutralizes the chemically basic developing solution.

stress   The variation of modulation in a letter from the inside to the outside of its form, and its ability to make the letter appear to incline in one direction.

stripping   (1) Cutting windows into a goldenrod flat to precisely locate and place line and halftone negatives in preparation for plating. (2) Data segments written to successive hard drives in a RAID array.

stroke weight   The thickness of the line used to create a letterform.

style   The personality of a designed work.

style sheets   A generic term for Character Styles and Paragraph Styles as used in a page layout program.

subheading   A minor heading placed before a paragraph of text.

substrate   The clear polycarbonate base of a compact disk.

subtractive plate   In the subtractive process, emulsion is removed, or subtracted from, the unexposed areas of the plate during postexposure plate processing.

surface-coated plate   Surface-coated plates feature a photographic emulsion that is coated, or layered, onto the base metal of the plate.

swatchbooks   Small books of paper samples that are provided to designers by paper companies. The books are used to select and order paper for a print job.

symbol   A picture-based design used to communicate information without the need for words.

T

tabloid   Standard American paper size measuring 11 × 17 inches.

template   A document created for simplifying the design and production of multiple designs that follow the same format. Templates are most often used in book, magazine, and package design, but may be used for any series-based projects.

thermal wax printers   These printers are used for generating high-quality presentation transparencies and for color proofing. The printheads of these units contain heating elements, or contacts, that melt colored wax from belt-driven ribbons onto the paper. Thermal wax printers print only one color at a time, so the paper must be fed through the printer four separate times to produce a full-color print.

thermography   A process used to simulate the raised printing effect achieved through engraving. To achieve this effect artificially, a resinous powder is applied to a printed piece before the printing ink dries; when heated, the powder melts and achieves the raised-type effect.

three-cylinder offset press   The standard configuration used in small offset presses and duplicators, made up of plate, blanket, and impression cylinders.

thumbnail sketch   A small sketch created during the conceptual phase of a design project. Thumbnails are produced to explore many design possibilities and are usually created in large numbers for each project.

tints   Using various sized printed dots of an ink color to create lighter variations of the color. Tints are displayed as a percentage of the solid color.

TOC   A common term for the table of contents in any publication.

toner particles   Delivered in either a dry or liquid form, toner is fed onto a developing cylinder. From there it is deposited onto a charged drum, based on the varying electrical charges imparted by an imaging laser.

Toulouse Lautrec   A French artist of the Art Nouveau period.

tracking   Controlling the amount of space between words and characters in a line of text.

transistor   An electronic device; essentially an electronically controlled switch.

transmittance   The proportion of light striking a photographic negative that penetrates the emulsion layer of the film in any particular area.

TrueType   A file format for type that uses one file to contain both on-screen display and printing information.

Tsai Lun   The Chinese court official credited with the invention of paper in AD 105.

TWAIN   The TWAIN standard was developed by the Twain Working Group, a not-for-profit association, to link image processing software to scanners and digital cameras.

twisted pair cable   Data transmission cable made from twisted pairs of solid copper wires.

type   Term for letters, numbers, and other characters used to format the look of words.

type design   The creation of letterforms for use in graphic design.

type family   A group of typefaces designed to work together. A family of type shares the same surname but has a variety of weights and styles, such as Helvetica, Helvetica Bold, Helvetica Italic, and Helvetica Light.

type hierarchy   The relative importance of each word or letter and their relationship to one another within a typographic composition or as used with images in a design.

type scaling   Stretching type vertically or horizontally within a computer program. Type scaling should be kept to less than 10 percent to avoid distortion of the type.

type slug   A piece of cast metal type.

type speccing   Short for "type specification," type speccing is the selection of typeface, point size, and composition of type for use in a work of graphic design.

type style   Variations of weight—extra light, light, book, medium, demibold, bold, extra bold, and black; inclination—italic and oblique; character width—condensed and expanded; and case—all caps and small caps, found within a family of type.

typecasting   Creating type by casting liquid metal for use in letterpress printing.

typeface   A complete set of characters of a particular type design, weight, and style. Also often called a *font*.

type-high   The standard height of all material printed on a letterpress. Type-high is .918 of an inch.

typesetting   Using hand or computer-based methods to compose type.

typewriter   The mechanical device used to set characters on to a sheet of paper by pressing individual keys, the typewriter was invented by Christopher Sholes in 1868.

typo   The common term for a typographic error found in a designed piece.

typographic logo   A logo design that is created solely with type.

U

Ukiyo-e   A style of Japanese posters from the seventeenth to nineteenth centuries that used flatness of space in their composition. The style was inspirational to Art Nouveau poster artists in Europe and America.

uniform resource locater (URL)   The unique address of each Web resource.

UNIVAC   The Universal Automatic Computer was delivered by the Remington Rand Corporation to the United States Census Bureau in 1951.

universal serial bus (USB)   USB was developed by USB Implements Forum, Inc., and replaces older serial and parallel port connections with one standardized plug and port connection.

unsharp masking (USM)   Creates an invisible outline around an image, giving it a greater sense of detail.

UPC   The "bar code" found on packaging. UPC stands for Universal Product Code.

uppercase   Capital letters.

UV curing inks   These inks contain no volatile solvents and cure under the influence of ultraviolet light.

V

variable-data printing   The process of including customized data on every printed sheet in a press run. Variable-data technology is based on the ability of the digital printing press to re-image the electrostatic drum for each print.

vectors   Representation of an object in a computer program based on lines.

viscosity   A printing ink's resistance to flow. Inks that flow readily are referred to as *low-viscosity inks;* heavy-bodied inks that don't flow readily are referred to as *high-viscosity inks.*

visual hierarchy   The order of importance of visual elements within a design.

volatile organic compounds   Hazardous fumes generated from industrial processing and other sources. In the printing industries, most of these fumes come from evaporating inks and solvents.

W

washed-out copy   Copy that prints with a gray tone, reducing the contrast and quality of the image.

Washington press   Designed by Robert Hoe in 1847, this was the first American version of the rotary cylinder press.

waterless offset printing   In waterless offset printing, a principle known as *differential adhesion* is used to separate the image and nonimage areas during printing. Differential adhesion is achieved by using a silicone surface on the printing plate.

wax thermal printer   See *thermal wax printers.*

web-fed press   A press that prints on paper fed into it from a large roll, or web, rather than on individual sheets.

white space   Areas within a design that contain neither type nor images, used by the designer to give the viewer a visual "rest."

wide-format printers   Primarily inkjet and UV printers capable of printing on media wider than 24 inches.

widow   One or more short words on the last line of a paragraph. Widows create uneven visual spacing between paragraphs and should be corrected via tracking adjustments.

William Caslon   An engraver, Caslon set up the first type foundry in London. He printed a type specimen sheet in 1734 that included typeface designs that still bear his name.

William Caxton   Caxton produced the first book printed in the English language in Bruges, Belgium, around 1477.

William Morris   Led a group of artists and social reformers who sought to reestablish the roles of artists and craftsmen away from mass production, referred to as the *Arts and Crafts movement,* around 1851.

Windows   The operating system produced by Microsoft Corporation and installed on most personal computers (PCs).

wire binding   The use of thin coiled wire, inserted into prepunched holes, to hold a book or pamphlet together.

work and tumble   Work and tumble uses one plate for printing both sides of a sheet. In this format, the paper pile is tumbled so that the opposite end of each sheet serves as its leading edge during the second press run.

work and turn   Here one printing plate is used to print both sides of the same sheet of paper. After the first press run, the pile of paper is turned over and fed into the press using the same leading edges on the sheets during the second press run.

X

X rating   The ability of a CD drive to transfer data from the disk to the computer.

xerography   The generic term used to describe all electrostatic printing, developed by Chester Carlson and sold to the Xerox Corporation in 1938.

x-height   The height of lowercase letters from the baseline to the top of the letterform, based on the height of the lowercase "x" in any given typeface.

Z

zinc line cut   A line or halftone engraving etched onto a zinc plate and mounted on a piece of type-high wood (.918″). Zinc line cuts have largely been replaced by magnesium line cuts and are printed on conventional letterpresses.

zip disk   Classified as super floppy diskettes, these are removable disks that range in capacity from 100 MB to 750 MB. The advent of removable flash storage memory sticks has made the use of zip disks virtually obsolete.

Index